The Basel II Risk Parameters

Bernd Engelmann
Robert Rauhmeier
(Editors)

The Basel II
Risk Parameters

Estimation, Validation,
and Stress Testing

With 7 Figures and 58 Tables

 Springer

Dr. Bernd Engelmann
Quanteam Dr. Bernd Engelmann
und Sören Gerlach GbR
Basaltstraße 28
60487 Frankfurt
bernd.engelmann@quanteam.de

Dr. Robert Rauhmeier
Dresdner Bank AG
Risk Instruments – Methods
Gallusanlage 7
60329 Frankfurt
robert.rauhmeier@dresdner-bank.com

ISBN-10   3-540-33085-2 Springer Berlin Heidelberg New York
ISBN-13   978-3-540-33085-1 Springer Berlin Heidelberg New York

Cataloging-in-Publication Data
Library of Congress Control Number: 2006929673

Springer is a part of Springer Science+Business Media

springeronline.com

© Springer Berlin · Heidelberg 2006
Printed in Germany

Softcover-Design: Design & Production, Heidelberg

SPIN 121883975   43/3180 - 5 4 3   – Printed on acid-free paper

Preface

In the last decade the banking industry has experienced a significant development in the understanding of credit risk. Refined methods were proposed concerning the estimation of key risk parameters like default probabilities. Further, a large volume of literature on the pricing and measurement of credit risk in a portfolio context has evolved. This development was partly reflected by supervisors when they agreed on the new revised capital adequacy framework, Basel II. Under Basel II, the level of regulatory capital depends on the risk characteristics of each credit while a portfolio context is still neglected.

The focus of this book is on the estimation and validation of the three key Basel II risk parameters, probability of default (PD), loss given default (LGD), and exposure at default (EAD). Since the new regulatory framework will become operative in January 2007 (at least in Europe), many banks are in the final stages of implementation. Many questions have arisen during the implementation phase and are discussed by practitioners, supervisors, and academics. A 'best practice' approach has to be formed and will be refined in the future even beyond 2007. With this book we aim to contribute to this process. Although the book is inspired by the new capital framework, we hope that it is valuable in a broader context. The three risk parameters are central inputs to credit portfolio models or credit pricing algorithms and their correct estimation is therefore essential for internal bank controlling and management.

This is not a book about the Basel II framework. There is already a large volume of literature explaining the new regulation at length. Rather, we attend to the current state-of-the-art of quantitative and qualitative approaches. The book is a combination of coordinated stand-alone articles, arranged into fifteen chapters so that each chapter can be read exclusively. The authors are all experts from science, supervisory authorities, and banking practice. The book is divided into three main parts: Estimation techniques for the parameters PD, LGD and EAD, validation of these parameters, and stress testing.

The first part begins with an overview of the popular and established methods for estimating PD. Chapter II focuses on methods for PD estimation for small and medium sized corporations while Chapter III treats the PD estimation for the retail segment. Chapters IV and V deal with those segments with only a few or even no default data, as it is often the case in the large corporate, financial institutions, or sovereign segment. Chapter IV illustrates how PD can be estimated with the shadow rating approach while Chapter V uses techniques from probability theory. Chapter VI describes how PDs and Recovery Rates could be estimated under considerations of systematic and idiosyncratic risk factors simultaneously. This is a perfect changeover to the chapters VII to X dealing with LGD and EAD estimation which is quite new in practice compared to ratings and PD estimation. Chapter VII describes how LGD could be modelled in a point-in-time framework as a function of risk drivers, supported by an empirical study on bond data. Chapter VIII provides a general survey of LGD estimation from a practical point of view. Chapters IX and X are concerned with the modelling of EAD. Chapter IX provides a general overview of EAD estimation techniques while Chapter X focuses on the estimation of EAD for facilities with explicit limits.

The second part of the book consists of four chapters about validation and statistical back-testing of rating systems. Chapter XI deals with the perspective of the supervisory authorities and gives a glance as to what is expected when rating systems will be used under the Basel II framework. Chapter XII has a critical discussion on measuring the discriminatory power of rating systems. Chapter XIII gives an overview of statistical tests for the dimension calibration, i.e. the accuracy of PD estimations. In Chapter XIV these methods are enhanced by techniques of Monte-Carlo-Simulations which allows e.g. for integration of correlation assumptions as is also illustrated within a back-testing study on a real-life rating data sample.

The final part consists of Chapter XV, which is on stress testing. The purpose of stress testing is to detect limitations of models for the risk parameters and to analyse effects of (extreme) worse scenarios in the future on a bank's portfolio. Concepts and implementation strategies of stress test are explained and a simulation study reveals amazing effects of stress scenarios when calculating economic capital with a portfolio model.

All articles set great value on practical applicability and mostly include empirical studies or work with examples. Therefore we regard this book as a valuable contribution towards modern risk management in every financial institution, whereas we steadily keep track on the requirements of Basel II. The book is addressed to risk managers, rating analyst and in general quantitative analysts who work in the credit risk area or on regulatory issues. Furthermore, we target internal auditors and supervisors who have to evaluate the quality of rating systems and risk parameter estimations. We hope that this book will deepen their understanding and will be useful for their daily work. Last but not least we hope this book will also be of interest to academics or students in finance or economics who want to get an overview of the state-of-the-art of a currently important topic in the banking industry.

Finally, we have to thank all the people who made this book possible. Our sincere acknowledgements go to all the contributors of this book for their work, their enthusiasm, their reliability, and their cooperation. We know that most of the writing had to be done in valuable spare time. We are glad that all of them were willing to make such sacrifices for the sake of this book. Special thank goes to Walter Gruber for bringing us on the idea to edit this book.

We are grateful to Martina Bihn from Spinger-Verlag who welcomed our idea for this book and supported our work on it.

We thank Dresdner Bank AG, especially Peter Gassmann and Dirk Thomas, and Quanteam AG for supporting our book. Moreover we are grateful to all our colleagues and friends who agreed to work as referees or discussion partners.

Finally we would like to thank our families for their continued support and understanding.

Frankurt am Main

Bernd Engelmann
Robert Rauhmeier
June 2006

Contents

XI. Validation of Banks' Internal Rating Systems - A Supervisory Perspective

Stefan Blochwitz and Stefan Hohl

XII. Measures of a Rating's Discriminative Power – Applications and Limitations

Bernd Engelmann

XIII. Statistical Approaches to PD Validation

Stefan Blochwitz, Marcus R. W. Martin, and Carsten S. Wehn

I. Statistical Methods to Develop Rating Models

Evelyn Hayden and Daniel Porath

Österreichische Nationalbank[1] and University of Applied Sciences at Mainz

1. Introduction

The Internal Rating Based Approach (IRBA) of the New Basel Capital Accord allows banks to use their own rating models for the estimation of probabilities of default (PD) as long as the systems meet specified minimum requirements. Statistical theory offers a variety of methods for building and estimation rating models. This chapter gives an overview of these methods. The overview is focused on statistical methods and includes parametric models like linear regression analysis, discriminant analysis, binary response analysis, time-discrete panel methods, hazard models and nonparametric models like neural networks and decision trees. We also highlight the benefits and the drawbacks of the various approaches. We conclude by interpreting the models in light of the minimum requirements of the IRBA.

2. Statistical Methods for Risk Classification

In the following we define statistical models as the class of approach which uses econometric methods to classify borrowers according to their risk. Statistical rating systems primarily involve a search for explanatory variables which provide as sound and reliable a forecast of the deterioration of a borrower's situation as possible. In contrast, structural models explain the threats to a borrower based on an economic model and thus use clear causal connections instead of the mere correlation of variables.

The following sections offer an overview of parametric and nonparametric models generally considered for statistical risk assessment. Furthermore, we discuss the advantages and disadvantages of each approach. Many of the methods are described in more detail in standard econometric textbooks, like Greene (2003).

---

[1] The opinions expressed in this chapter are those of the author and do not necessarily reflect views of the Österreichische Nationalbank.

In general, a statistical model may be described as follows: As a starting point, every statistical model uses the borrower's characteristic indicators and (possibly) macroeconomic variables which were collected historically and are available for defaulting (or troubled) and non-defaulting borrowers. Let the borrower's characteristics be defined by a vector of n separate variables (also called covariates) $x = x_1,...,x_n$ observed at time $t - L$. The state of default is indicated by a binary performance variable y observed at time t. The variable y is defined as $y = 1$ for a default and $y = 0$ for a non-default.

The sample of borrowers now includes a number of individuals or firms that defaulted in the past, while (typically) the majority did not default. Depending on the statistical application of this data, a variety of methods can be used to predict the performance. A common feature of the methods is that they estimate the correlation between the borrowers' characteristics and the state of default in the past and use this information to build a forecasting model. The forecasting model is designed to assess the creditworthiness of borrowers with unknown performance. This can be done by inputting the characteristics x into the model. The output of the model is the estimated performance. The time lag L between x and y determines the forecast horizon.

3. Regression Analysis

As a starting point we consider the classical regression model. The regression model establishes a linear relationship between the borrowers' characteristics and the default variable:

$$y_i = \beta' \cdot x_i + u_i \tag{1}$$

Again, y_i indicates whether borrower i has defaulted ($y_i = 1$) or not ($y_i = 0$). In period t, x_i is a column vector of the borrowers' characteristics observed in period $t - L$ and β is a column vector of parameters which capture the impact of a change in the characteristics on the default variable. Finally, u_i is the residual variable which contains the variation not captured by the characteristics x_i.

The standard procedure is to estimate (1) with the ordinary least squares (OLS) estimators of β which in the following are denoted by b. The estimated result is the borrower's score S_i. This can be calculated by

$$S_i = E(y_i \mid x_i) = b' \cdot x_i. \tag{2}$$

Equation (2) shows that a borrower's score represents the expected value of the performance variable when his or her individual characteristics are known. The score can be calculated by inputting the values for the borrower's characteristics into the linear function given in (2).

Note that S_i is continuous (while y_i is a binary variable), hence the output of the model will generally be different from 0 or 1. In addition, the prediction can take on values larger than 1 or smaller than 0. As a consequence, the outcome of the model cannot be interpreted as a probability level. However, the score S_i can be used for the purpose of comparison between different borrowers, where higher values of S_i correlate with a higher default risk.

The benefits and drawbacks from model (1) and (2) are the following:

- OLS estimators are well-known and easily available.
- The forecasting model is a linear model and therefore easy to compute and to understand.
- The random variable u_i is heteroscedastic (i.e. the variance of u_i is not constant for all i) since

$$Var(u_i) = Var(y_i) = E(y_i \mid x_i) \cdot [1 - E(y_i \mid x_i)] = b' \cdot x_i (1 - b' \cdot x_i). \qquad (3)$$

As a consequence, the estimation of β is inefficient and additionally, the standard errors of the estimated coefficients b are biased. An efficient way to estimate β is to apply the Weighted Least Squares (WLS) estimator.

- WLS estimation of β is efficient, but the estimation of the standard errors of b still remains biased. This happens due to the fact that the residuals are not normally distributed as they can only take on the values $b'x_i$ (if the borrower does not default and y therefore equals 0) or $(1 - b'x_i)$ (if the borrower does default and y therefore equals 1). This implies that there is no reliable way to assess the significance of the coefficients b and it remains unknown whether the estimated values represent precise estimations of significant relationships or whether they are just caused by spurious correlations. Inputting characteristics which are not significant into the model can seriously harm the model's stability when used to predict borrowers' risk for new data. A way to cope with this problem is to split the sample into two parts, where one part (the training sample) is used to estimate the model and the other part (the hold-out sample) is used to validate the results. The consistency of the results of both samples is then taken as an indicator for the stability of the model.
- The absolute value of S_i cannot be interpreted.

4. Discriminant Analysis

Discriminant analysis is a classification technique applied to corporate bankruptcies by Altman as early as 1968 (see Altman, 1968). Linear discriminant analysis is based on the estimation of a linear discriminant function with the task of separating individual groups (in this case of defaulting and non-defaulting borrowers) according to specific characteristics. The discriminant function is

$$S_i = \beta' \cdot x_i . \qquad (4)$$

The Score S_i is also called the discriminant variable. The estimation of the discriminant function adheres to the following principle:

Maximization of the spread between the groups (good and bad borrowers) and minimization of the spread within individual groups

Maximization only determines the optimal proportions among the coefficients of the vector β. Usually (but arbitrarily), coefficients are normalized by choosing the pooled within-group variance to take the value 1. As a consequence, the absolute level of S_i is arbitrary as well and cannot be interpreted on a stand-alone basis. As in linear regression analysis, S_i can only be used to compare the prediction for different borrowers ("higher score, higher risk").

Discriminant analysis is similar to the linear regression model given in equations (1) and (2). In fact, the proportions among the coefficients of the regression model are equal to the optimal proportion according to the discriminant analysis. The difference between the two methods is a theoretical one: Whereas in the regression model the characteristics are deterministic and the default state is the realization of a random variable, for discriminant analysis the opposite is true. Here the groups (default or non-default) are deterministic and the characteristics of the discriminant function are realizations from a random variable. For practical use this difference is virtually irrelevant.

Therefore, the benefits and drawbacks of discriminant analysis are similar to those of the regression model:

- Discriminant analysis is a widely known method with estimation algorithms that are easily available.
- Once the coefficients are estimated, the scores can be calculated in a straightforward way with a linear function.
- Since the characteristics x_i are assumed to be realizations of random variables, the statistical tests for the significance of the model and the coefficients rely on the assumption of multivariate normality. This is, however, unrealistic for the variables typically used in rating models as for example financial ratios from the balance-sheet. Hence, the methods for analyzing the stability of the model and the plausibility of the coefficients are limited to a comparison between training and hold-out sample.
- The absolute value of the discriminant function cannot be interpreted in levels.

5. Logit and Probit Models

Logit and probit models are econometric techniques designed for analyzing binary dependent variables. There are two alternative theoretical foundations.

The latent-variable approach assumes an unobservable (latent) variable y^* which is related to the borrower's characteristics in the following way:

$$y_i^* = \boldsymbol{\beta}' \cdot \boldsymbol{x}_i + u_i \tag{5}$$

Here $\boldsymbol{\beta}$, $\boldsymbol{x}_i$ and u_i are defined as above. The variable y_i^* is metrically scaled and triggers the value of the binary default variable y_i:

$$y_i = \begin{cases} 1 & \text{if } y_i^* > 0 \\ 0 & \text{otherwise} \end{cases} \tag{6}$$

This means that the default event sets in when the latent variable exceeds the threshold zero. Therefore, the probability for the occurrence of the default event equals:

$$P(y_i = 1) = P(u_i > -\boldsymbol{\beta}' \cdot \boldsymbol{x}_i) = 1 - F(-\boldsymbol{\beta}' \cdot \boldsymbol{x}_i) = F(\boldsymbol{\beta}' \cdot \boldsymbol{x}_i). \tag{7}$$

Here $F(.)$ denotes the (unknown) distribution function. The last step in (7) assumes that the distribution function has a symmetric density around zero. The choice of the distribution function $F(.)$ depends on the distributional assumptions about the residuals (u_i). If a normal distribution is assumed, we are faced with the probit model:

$$F(\boldsymbol{\beta}' \cdot \boldsymbol{x}_i) = \frac{1}{\sqrt{2\pi}} \int_{-\infty}^{\boldsymbol{\beta}' \cdot \boldsymbol{x}_i} e^{\frac{-t^2}{2}} \, dt \tag{8}$$

If instead the residuals are assumed to follow a logistic distribution, the result is the logit model:

$$F(\boldsymbol{\beta}' \cdot \boldsymbol{x}_i) = \frac{e^{\boldsymbol{\beta}' \cdot \boldsymbol{x}_i}}{1 + e^{\boldsymbol{\beta}' \cdot \boldsymbol{x}_i}} \tag{9}$$

The second way to motivate logit and probit models starts from the aim of estimating default probabilities. For single borrowers, default probabilities cannot be observed as realizations of default probabilities. However, for groups of borrowers the observed default frequencies can be interpreted as default probabilities. As a starting point consider the OLS estimation of the following regression:

$$p_i = \boldsymbol{b}' \cdot \boldsymbol{x}_i + u_i \tag{10}$$

In (10) the index i denotes the group formed by a number of individuals, p_i is the default frequency observed in group i and $\boldsymbol{x}_i$ are the characteristics observed for group i. The model, however, is inadequate. To see this consider that the outcome (which is $E(y_i|x_i) = \boldsymbol{b}' \boldsymbol{x}_i$) is not bounded to values between zero and one and therefore cannot be interpreted as a probability. As it is generally implausible to assume that a probability can be calculated by a linear function, in a second step the linear expression $\boldsymbol{b}' \boldsymbol{x}_i$ is transformed by a nonlinear function (link function) F:

$$p_i = F(\boldsymbol{b'}\cdot\boldsymbol{x}_i).$$ (11)

An appropriate link function transforms the values of $\boldsymbol{b'}\boldsymbol{x}_i$ to a scale within the interval $[0,1]$. This can be achieved by any distribution function. The choice of the link function determines the type of model: with a logistic link function equation (11) becomes a logit model, while with the normal distribution (11) results in the probit model.

However, when estimating (10) with OLS, the coefficients will be heteroscedastic, because $Var(u_i) = Var(p_i) = p(\boldsymbol{x}_i)\cdot(1-p(\boldsymbol{x}_i))$. A possible way to achieve homoscedasticity would be to compute the WLS estimators of $\boldsymbol{b}$ in (10). However, albeit possible, this is not common practice. The reason is that in order to observe default frequencies, the data has to be grouped before estimation. Grouping involves considerable practical problems like defining the size and number of the groups and the treatment of different covariates within the single groups. A better way to estimate logit and probit models, which does not require grouping, is the Maximum-Likelihood (ML) method. For a binary dependent variable the likelihood function looks like:

$$L(\boldsymbol{b}) = \prod_i P(\boldsymbol{b'}\cdot\boldsymbol{x}_i)^{y_i}\left[1 - P(\boldsymbol{b'}\cdot\boldsymbol{x}_i)^{1-y_i}\right].$$ (12)

For the probit model $P(.)$ is the normal density function and for the logit model $P(.)$ is the logistic density function. With equation (12) the estimation of the model is theoretically convincing and also easy to handle. Furthermore, the ML-approach lends itself for a broad set of tests to evaluate the model and its single variables (see Hosmer and Lemeshow (2000) for a comprehensive introduction).

Usually, the choice of the link function is not theoretically driven. Users familiar with the normal distribution will opt for the probit model. Indeed, the differences in the results of both classes of models are often negligible. This is due to the fact that both distribution functions have a similar form except for the tails, which are heavier for the logit model. The logit model is easier to handle, though. First of all, the computation of the estimators is easier. However, today computational complexity is often irrelevant as most users apply statistical software where the estimation algorithms are integrated. What is more important is the fact that the coefficients of the logit model can be more easily interpreted. To see this we transform the logit model given in (9) in the following way:

$$\frac{P_i}{1-P_i} = e^{\beta'\cdot x_i}$$ (13)

The left-hand side of (13) are the odds, i.e. the relation between the default probability and the probability of survival. Now it can be easily seen that a variation of a single variable x_k of one unit has an impact of e^{β_k} on the odds, when β_k denotes the coefficient of the variable x_k. Hence, the transformed coefficients e^{β} are called odds-ratios. They represent the multiplicative impact of a borrower's characteristic on the odds. Therefore, for the logit model, the coefficients can be interpreted in a plausible way, which is not possible for the probit model. Indeed, the most important weakness of binary models is the fact that the interpretation of the coefficients is not straightforward.

The strengths of logit and probit models can be summarized as:

- The methods are theoretically sound
- The results generated can be interpreted directly as default probabilities
- The significance of the model and the individual coefficients can be tested. Therefore, the stability of the model can be assessed more effectively than in the previous cases.

6. Panel Models

The methods discussed so far are all cross-sectional methods because all covariates are related to the same period. However, typically banks dispose of a set of covariates for more than one period for each borrower. In this case it is possible to expand the cross-sectional input data to a panel dataset. The main motivation is to enlarge the number of available observations for the estimation and therefore enhance the stability and the precision of the rating model. Additionally, panel models can integrate macroeconomic variables into the model. Macroeconomic variables can improve the model for several reasons. First, many macroeconomic data sources are more up-to-date than the borrowers' characteristics. For example, financial ratios calculated from balance sheet information are usually updated only once a year and are often up to two years old when used for risk assessment. The oil price, instead, is available on a daily frequency. Secondly, by stressing the macroeconomic input factors, the model can be used for a form of stress-testing credit risk. However, as macroeconomic variables primarily affect the absolute value of the default probability, it is only reasonable to incorporate macroeconomic input factors into those classes of models that estimate default probabilities.

In principle, the structure of, for example, a panel logit or probit model remains the same as given in the equations of the previous section. The only difference is that now the covariates are taken from a panel of data and have to be indexed by an additional time series indicator, i.e. we observe x_{it} instead of x_i. At first glance panel models seem similar to cross-sectional models. In fact, many developers ignore the dynamic pattern of the covariates and simply fit logit or probit models. However, logit and probit models rely on the assumption of independent observations. Generally, cross-sectional data meets this requirement, but panel data does not. The reason is that observations from the same period and observations from the same borrower should be correlated. Introducing this correlation in the estimation procedure is cumbersome. For example, the fixed-effects estimator known from panel analysis for continuous dependent variables is not available for the probit model. Besides, the modified fixed-effects estimator for logit models proposed by Chamberlain (1980) excludes all non-defaulting borrowers from the analysis and therefore seems inappropriate. Finally, the random-effects estimators proposed in the literature are computationally extensive and can only be computed with specialized software. For an econometric discussion of binary panel analysis, refer to Hosmer and Lemeshow (2000).

7. Hazard Models

All methods discussed so far try to assess the riskiness of borrowers by estimating a certain type of score that indicates whether or not a borrower is likely to default within the specified forecast horizon. However, no prediction about the exact default point in time is made. Besides, these approaches do not allow the evaluation of the borrowers' risk for future time periods given they should not default within the reference time horizon.

These disadvantages can be remedied by means of hazard models, which explicitly take the survival function and thus the time at which a borrower's default occurs into account. Within this class of models, the Cox proportional hazard model (cf. Cox, 1972) is the most general regression model, as it is not based on any assumptions concerning the nature or shape of the underlying survival distribution. The model assumes that the underlying hazard rate (rather than survival time) is a function of the independent variables; no assumptions are made about the nature or shape of the hazard function. Thus, the Cox's regression model is a semi-parametric model. The model can be written as:

$$h_i\left(t \mid x_i\right) = h_0\left(t\right) \cdot e^{\beta' \cdot x_i} , \tag{14}$$

where $h_i(t|x_i)$ denotes the resultant hazard, given the covariates for the respective borrower and the respective survival time t. The term $h_0(t)$ is called the baseline hazard; it is the hazard when all independent variable values are equal to zero. If the covariates are measured as deviations from their respective means, $h_0(t)$ can be interpreted as the hazard rate of the average borrower.

While no assumptions are made about the underlying hazard function, the model equation shown above implies important assumptions. First, it specifies a multiplicative relationship between the hazard function and the log-linear function of the explanatory variables, which implies that the ratio of the hazards of two borrowers does not depend on time, i.e. the relative riskiness of the borrowers is constant, hence the name Cox *proportional* hazard model.

Besides, the model assumes that the default point in time is a continuous random variable. However, often the borrowers' financial conditions are not observed continuously but rather at discrete points in time. What's more, the covariates are treated as if they were constant over time, while typical explanatory variables like financial ratios change with time.

Although there are some advanced models to incorporate the above mentioned features, the estimation of these models becomes complex. The strengths and weaknesses of hazard models can be summarized as follows:

- Hazard models allow for the estimation of a survival function for all borrowers from the time structure of historical defaults, which implies that default probabilities can be calculated for different time horizons.
- Estimating these models under realistic assumptions is not straightforward.

8. Neural Networks

In recent years, neural networks have been discussed extensively as an alternative to the (parametric) models discussed above. They offer a more flexible design to represent the connections between independent and dependent variables. Neural networks belong to the class of non-parametrical methods. Unlike the methods discussed so far they do not estimate parameters of a well-specified model. Instead, they are inspired by the way biological nervous systems, such as the brain, process information. They typically consist of many nodes that send a certain output if they receive a specific input from the other nodes to which they are connected. Like parametric models, neural networks are trained by a training sample to classify borrowers correctly. The final network is found by adjusting the connections between the input, output and any potential intermediary nodes.

The strengths and weaknesses of neural networks can be summarized as:

- Neural networks easily model highly complex, nonlinear relationships between the input and the output variables.
- They are free from any distributional assumptions.
- These models can be quickly adapted to new information (depending on the training algorithm).
- There is no formal procedure to determine the optimum network topology for a specific problem, i.e. the number of the layers of nodes connecting the input with the output variables.
- Neural networks are black boxes, hence they are difficult to interpret.
- Calculating default probabilities is possible only to a limited extent and with considerable extra effort.

In summary, neural networks are particularly suitable when there are no expectations (based on experience or theoretical arguments) on the relationship between the input factors and the default event and the economic interpretation of the resulting models is of inferior importance.

9. Decision Trees

A further category of non-parametric methods comprises decision trees, also called classification trees. Trees are models which consist of a set of if-then split conditions for classifying cases into two (or more) different groups. Under these methods, the base sample is subdivided into groups according to the covariates. In the case of binary classification trees, for example, each tree node is assigned by (usually univariate) decision rules, which describe the sample accordingly and subdivide it into two subgroups each. New observations are processed down the tree in accordance with the decision rules' values until the end node is reached, which then represents the classification of this observation. An example is given in Figure 1.

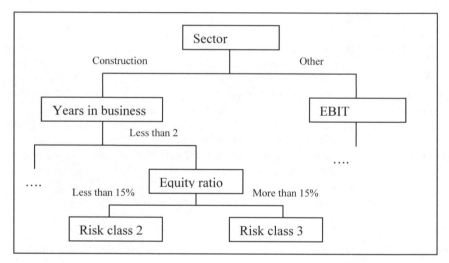

Figure 1. Decision Tree

One of the most striking differences of the parametric models is that all covariates are grouped and treated as categorical variables. Furthermore, whether a specific variable or category becomes relevant depends on the categories of the variables in the upper level. For example, in Figure 1 the variable "years in business" is only relevant for companies which operate in the construction sector. This kind of dependence between variables is called interaction.

The most important algorithms for building decision trees are the Classification and Regression Trees algorithms (C&RT) popularized by Breiman et al. (1984) and the CHAID algorithm (Chi-square Automatic Interaction Detector, see Kass, 1978). Both algorithms use different criteria to identify the best splits in the data and to collapse the categories which are not significantly different in outcome.

The general strengths and weaknesses of trees are:

- Through categorization, nonlinear relationships between the variables and the score can be easily modelled.
- Interactions present in the data can be identified. Parametric methods can model interactions only to a limited extent (by introducing dummy variables).
- As with neural networks, decision trees are free from distributional assumptions.
- The output is easy to understand.
- Probabilities of default have to be calculated in a separate step.
- The output is (a few) risk categories and not a continuous score variable. Consequently, decision trees only calculate default probabilities for the final node in a tree, but not for individual borrowers.
- Compared to other models, trees contain fewer variables and categories. The reason is that in each node the sample is successively partitioned and therefore continuously diminishes.
- The stability of the model cannot be assessed with statistical procedures. The strategy is to work with a training sample and a hold-out sample.

In summary, trees are particularly suited when the data is characterized by a limited number of predictive variables which are known to be interactive.

10. Statistical Models and Basel II

Finally, we ask the question whether the models discussed in this chapter are in line with the IRB Approach of Basel II. Prior to the discussion, it should be mentioned that in the Basel documents, rating systems are defined in a broader sense than in this chapter. Following § 394 of the Revised Framework from June 2004 (cf. BIS, 2004) a rating system "comprises all the methods, processes, controls, and data collection and IT systems that support the assessment of credit risk, the assignment of internal ratings, and the quantification of default and loss estimates". Compared to this definition, these methods provide one component, namely the assignment of internal ratings.

The minimum requirements for internal rating systems are treated in part II, section III, H of the Revised Framework. A few passages of the text concern the assignment of internal ratings, and the requirements are general. They mainly concern the rating structure and the input data, examples being:

- a minimum of 7 rating classes of non-defaulted borrowers (§ 404)
- no undue or excessive concentrations in single rating classes (§§ 403, 406)
- a meaningful differentiation of risk between the classes (§ 410)
- plausible, intuitive and current input data (§§ 410, 411)
- all relevant information must be taken into account (§ 411).

The requirements do not reveal any preference for a certain method. It is indeed one of the central ideas of the IRBA that the banks are free in the choice of the method. Therefore the models discussed here are all possible candidates for the IRB Approach.

The strengths and weaknesses of the single methods concern some of the minimum requirements. For example, hazard rate or logit panel models are especially suited for stress testing (as required by §§ 434, 345) since they contain a time-series dimension. Methods which allow for the statistical testing of the individual input factors (e.g. the logit model) provide a straightforward way to demonstrate the plausibility of the input factors (as required by § 410). When the outcome of the model is a continuous variable, the rating classes can be defined in a more flexible way (§§ 403, 404, 406).

On the other hand, none of the drawbacks of the models considered here excludes a specific method. For example, a bank may have a preference for linear regression analysis. In this case the plausibility of the input factors cannot be verified by statistical tests and as a consequence the bank will have to search for alternative ways to meet the requirements of § 410.

In summary, the minimum requirements are not intended as a guideline for the choice of a specific model. Banks should rather base their choice on their internal aims and restrictions. If necessary, those components that are only needed for the purpose to satisfy the criteria of the IRBA should be added in a second step. All models discussed in this chapter allow for this.

References

Altman EI (1968), Financial Indicators, Discriminant Analysis, and the Prediction of Corporate Bankruptcy, Journal of Finance.

BIS (2004), International Convergence of Capital Measurement and Capital Standards, Basel Committee on Banking Supervision, June 2004.

Breiman L, Friedman JH, Olshen RA, Stone SJ (1984), Classification and Regression Trees, Wadsworth.

Chamberlain G (1980), Analysis of Covariance with Qualitative Data, Review of Economic Studies 47, 225-238.

Cox DR (1972), Regression Models and Life Tables (with Discussion), Journal of Royal Statistical Society, Series B.

Greene W (2003), Econometric Analysis, 5th ed., Prentice-Hall New Jersey.

Hosmer W, Lemeshow S (2000), Applied Logistic Regression, New York, Wiley.

Kass GV (1978), An Exploratory Technique for Investigating Large Quantities of Categorical Data, Applied Statistics 29 (2), pp. 119-127.

II. Estimation of a Rating Model for Corporate Exposures

Evelyn Hayden

Österreichische Nationalbank[1]

1. Introduction

This chapter focuses on the particular difficulties encountered when developing internal rating models for corporate exposures. The main characteristic of these internal rating models is that they mainly rely on financial ratios. Hence, the aim is to demonstrate how financial ratios can be used for statistical risk assessment. The chapter is organised as follows: Section 2 describes some of the issues concerning model selection, while Section 3 presents data from Austrian companies that will illustrate the theoretical concepts. Section 4 discusses data processing, which includes the calculation of financial ratios, their transformation to establish linearity, the identification of outliers and the handling of missing values. Section 5 describes the actual estimation of the rating model, i.e. univariate and multivariate analyses, multicollinearity issues and performance measurement. Finally, Section 6 concludes.

2. Model Selection

Chapter I presents several statistical methods for building and estimating rating models. The most popular of these model types – in the academic literature as well as in practice - is the logit model, mainly for two reasons. Firstly, the output from the logit model can be directly interpreted as default probability, and secondly, the model allows an easy check as to whether the empirical dependence between the potential explanatory variables and default risk is economically meaningful (see Section 4). Hence, a logit model is chosen to demonstrate the estimation of internal rating models for corporate exposures.

Next, the default event must be defined. Historically, rating models were developed using mostly the default criterion bankruptcy, as this information was rela-

---

[1] The opinions expressed in this chapter are those of the author and do not necessarily reflect views of the Österreichische Nationalbank.

tively easily observable. However, banks also incur losses before the event of bankruptcy, for example, when they allow debtors to defer payments without compensation in hopes that later on, the troubled borrowers will be able to repay their debt. Therefore, the Basel Committee on Banking Supervision (2001) defined a reference definition of default that includes all those situations where a bank looses money and declared that banks would have to use this regulatory reference definition of default for estimating internal rating-based models. However, as demonstrated in Hayden (2003), rating models developed by exclusively relying on bankruptcy as the default criterion can be equally powerful in predicting the comprising credit loss events provided in the new Basel capital accord as models estimated on these default criteria. In any case, when developing rating models one has to guarantee that the default event used to estimate the model is comparable to the event the model shall be capable to predict.

Finally, a forecast horizon must be chosen. As illustrated by the Basel Committee on Banking Supervision (1999), even before Basel II for most banks it was common habit to use a modelling horizon of one year, as this time horizon is on the one hand long enough to allow banks to take some action to avert predicted defaults, and on the other hand the time lag is short enough to guarantee the timeliness of the data input into the rating model.

3. The Data Set

The theoretical concepts discussed in this chapter will be illustrated by application to a data set of Austrian companies, which represents a small sample of the credit portfolio of an Austrian bank. The original data, which was supplied by a major commercial Austrian bank for the research project described in Hayden (2002), consisted of about 5,000 firm-year observations of balance sheets and gain and loss accounts from 1,500 individual companies spanning 1994 to 1999. However, due to obvious mistakes in the data, such as assets being different from liabilities or negative sales, the data set had to be reduced to about 4,500 observations. Besides, certain firm types were excluded, i.e. all public firms including large international corporations that do not represent the typical Austrian company and rather small single owner firms with a turnover of less than 5m ATS (about 0.36m EUR), whose credit quality often depends as much on the finances of a key individual as on the firm itself. After eliminating financial statements covering a period of less than twelve months and checking for observations that were included twice or more in the data set, almost 3,900 firm-years were left. Finally, observations were dropped where the default information (bankruptcy) was missing or dubious.

Table 1 shows the total number of observed companies per year and splits the sample into defaulting and non-defaulting firms. However, the data for 1994 is not depicted, as we are going to calculate dynamic financial ratios (which compare current to past levels of certain balance sheet items) later on, and these ratios cannot be calculated for 1994 as the first period in the sample.

Table 1. Number of observations and defaults per year

Year	Non-Defaulting Firms	Defaulting Firms	Total
1995	1,185	54	1,239
1996	616	68	684
1997	261	46	307
1998	27	2	29
1999	23	1	24
Total	2,112	171	2,283

4. Data Processing

Section 4 discusses the major preparatory operations necessary before the model estimation can be conducted. They include the cleaning of the data, the calculation of financial ratios, and their transformation to establish linearity.

4.1. Data Cleaning

Some of the important issues with respect to data cleaning were mentioned in Section 3 when the Austrian data set was presented. As described, it was guaranteed that:

- the sample data was free of (obvious) mistakes,
- the data set comprised only homogeneous observations, where the relationship between the financial ratios and the default event could be expected to be comparable, and
- the default information was available (and reliable) for all borrowers.

In addition, missing information with respect to the financial input data must be properly managed. Typically, at least for some borrowers, part of the financial information is missing. If the number of the observations concerned is rather low, the easiest way to handle the problem is to eliminate the respective observations completely from the data set (as implemented for the Austrian data). If, however, this would result in too many observations being lost, it is preferable to exclude all variables with high numbers of missing values from the analysis. Once the model has been developed and is in use, the missing information needed to calculate the model output can be handled by substituting the missing financial ratios with the corresponding mean or median values over all observations for the respective time period (i.e. practically "neutral" values) in order to create as undistorted an assessment as possible using the remaining input factors.

4.2. Calculation of Financial Ratios

Once the quality of the basic financial data is guaranteed, potential explanatory variables have to be selected. Typically, ratios are formed to standardise the available information. For example, the ratio "Earnings per Total Assets" enables a comparison of the profitability of firms of different size. In addition to considering ratios that reflect different financial aspects of the borrowers, dynamic ratios that compare current to past levels of certain balance sheet items can be very useful for predicting default events. Overall, the selected input ratios should represent the most important credit risk factors, i.e. leverage, liquidity, productivity, turnover, activity, profitability, firm size, growth rates and leverage development.

Table2. Selected input ratios

	Financial Ratio	Risk Factor	Mean	Stand. Dev.	Min.	Max.	Hypo.
1	Total Liabilities / Total Assets	Leverage	0.89	0.18	0.02	1.00	+
2	Equity / Total Assets	Leverage	- 0.04	0.34	- 0.92	0.98	-
3	Bank Debt / T. Assets	Leverage	0.39	0.26	0.00	0.97	+
4	Short Term Debt / Total Assets	Liquidity	0.73	0.25	0.02	1.00	+
5	Current Assets / Current Liabilities	Liquidity	0.08	0.15	0.00	0.72	-
6	Accounts Receivable / Net Sales	Activity	0.13	0.12	0.00	0.41	+
7	Accounts Payable / Net Sales	Activity	0.12	0.12	0.00	0.44	+
8	(Net Sales – Material Costs) / Person. Costs	Productivity	2.56	1.85	1.03	8.55	-
9	Net Sales / Total Assets	Turnover	1.71	1.08	0.01	4.43	-
10	EBIT / Total Assets	Profitability	0.06	0.13	- 0.18	0.39	-
11	Ordinary Business Income / Total Assets	Profitability	0.02	0.13	- 0.19	0.33	-
12	Total Assets (in 1 Mio. EUR)	Size	35.30	72.98	0.22	453.80	-
13	Net Sales / Net Sales Last Year	Growth	1.06	0.34	0.02	2.03	-/+
14	Total Liabilities / Liabilities Last Year	Leverage Growth	1.00	1.03	0.07	1.23	+

After the calculation of the financial input ratios, it is necessary to identify and eliminate potential outliers, because they can and do severely distort the estimated model parameters. Outliers in the ratios might exist even if the underlying financial data is absolutely clean, for example, when the denominator of a ratio is allowed to take on values close to zero. To avoid the need to eliminate the affected observations a typical procedure is to replace the extreme data points by the 1% respectively the 99% percentile of the according ratio.

Table 2 portrays the explanatory variables selected for use for the Austrian data and presents some descriptive statistics. The indicators chosen comprise a small set of typical business ratios. A broader overview over potential input ratios as well as a detailed discussion can be found in Hayden (2002).

The last column in Table 2 depicts the expected dependence between the accounting ratio and the default probability, where + symbolises that an increase in the ratio leads to an increase in the default probability and - symbolises a decrease in the default probability given an increase in the explanatory variable. Whenever a certain ratio is selected as a potential input variable for a rating model, it should be assured that a clear hypothesis can be formulated about this dependence to guarantee that the resulting model is economically plausible. Note, however, that the hypothesis chosen can also be rather complex; for example, for the indicator sales growth, the hypothesis formulated is "-/+". This takes into account that the relationship between the rate at which companies grow and the rate at which they default is not as simple as that between other ratios and default. While it is generally better for a firm to grow than to shrink, companies that grow very quickly often find themselves unable to meet the management challenges presented by such growth - especially within smaller firms. Furthermore, this quick growth is unlikely to be financed out of profits, resulting in a possible build up of debt and the associated risks. Therefore, one should expect that the relationship between sales growth and default is non-monotone, what will be examined in detail in the next section.

4.3. Test of Linearity Assumption

After having selected the candidate input ratios, the next step is to check whether the underlying assumptions of the logit model apply to the data. As explained in Chapter I, the logit model can be written as

$$P_i = P(y_i = 1) = F(\boldsymbol{\beta'} \cdot \boldsymbol{x}_i) = \frac{e^{\boldsymbol{\beta'} \cdot \boldsymbol{x}_i}}{1 + e^{\boldsymbol{\beta'} \cdot \boldsymbol{x}_i}}, \tag{1}$$

which implies a linear relationship between the log odd and the input variables:

$$\text{Log odd} = \ln\left(\frac{P_i}{1 - P_i}\right) = \boldsymbol{\beta'} \cdot \boldsymbol{x}_i \tag{2}$$

This linearity assumption can be easily tested by dividing the indicators into groups that all contain the same number of observations, calculating the historical default rate respectively the empirical log odd within each group, and estimating a linear regression of the log odds on the mean values of the ratio intervals.

When applied to the Austrian data (by forming 50 groups), this procedure permits the conclusion that for most accounting ratios, the linearity assumption is indeed valid. As an example the relationship between the variable "EBIT / Total Assets" and the empirical log odd as well as the estimated linear regression is depicted in Figure 1. The regression fit is as high as 78.02%.

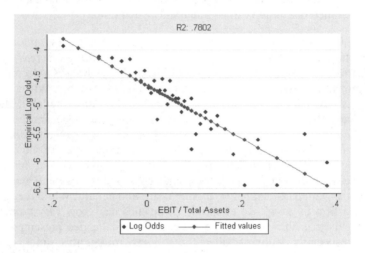

Figure 1. Relationship between "EBIT / Total Assets" and log odd

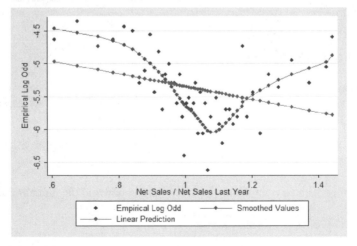

Figure 2. Relationship between "Sales Growth" and log odd

However, one explanatory variable, namely sales growth, shows a non-linear and even non-monotone behaviour, just as was expected. Hence, as portrayed in Figure 2, due to the linearity assumption inherent in the logit model, the relationship between the original ratio sales growth and the default event cannot be correctly captured by such a model.

Therefore, to enable the inclusion of the indicator sales growth into the rating model, the ratio has to be linearised before logit regressions can be estimated. This can be done in the following way: the points obtained from dividing the variable sales growth into groups and plotting them against the respective empirical log odds are smoothed by a filter, for example the one proposed in Hodrick and Prescott (1997), to reduce noise. Then the original values of sales growth are transformed to log odds according to this smoothed relationship, and in any further analysis the transformed log odd values replace the original ratio as input variable.

This test for the appropriateness of the linearity assumption also allows for a first check as to whether the univariate dependence between the considered explanatory variables and the default probability is as expected. For the Austrian data the univariate relationships between the investigated indicators and the default event coincide with the hypotheses postulated in Table 2, i.e. all ratios behave in an economically meaningful way.

5. Model Building

5.1. Pre-selection of Input Ratios

After verifying that the underlying assumptions of a logistic regression are valid, the model building process can be started. However, although typically a huge number of potential input ratios are available when developing a rating model, from a statistical point of view it is not advisable to enter all these variables into the logit regression. If, for example, some highly correlated indicators are included in the model, the estimated coefficients will be significantly and systematically biased. Hence, it is preferable to pre-select the most promising explanatory variables by means of the univariate power of and the correlation between the individual input ratios.

To do so, given the data set at hand is large enough to allow for it, the available data should be divided into one development and one validation sample by randomly splitting the whole data into two sub-samples. The first one, which typically contains the bulk of all observations, is used to estimate rating models, while the remaining data is left for an out-of-sample evaluation. When splitting the data, it should be ensured that all observations of one firm belong exclusively to one of the two sub-samples and that the ratio of defaulting to non-defaulting firms is similar in both data sets. For the Austrian data, about 70% of all observations are chosen for the training sample as depicted in Table 3.

Table 3. Division of the data into in- and out-of-sample subsets

Year	Training Sample		Validation Sample	
	Non-Defaulting	Defaulting	Non-Defaulting	Defaulting
1995	828	43	357	11
1996	429	44	187	24
1997	187	25	74	21
1998	20	2	7	0
1999	17	1	6	0

Table 4. Pairwise correlation of all potential input ratios

Ratio	AR in %	1	2	3	4	5	6	7	8	9	10	11	12	13	14
1	32.0	1	-.81	+.49	+.50	-.48	+.05	+.25	-.05	-.05	-.25	-.36	-.17	+.08	+.38
2	34.6		1	-.42	-.40	+.39	+.10	-.21	+.10	+.13	+.28	+.38	+.22	-.12	-.25
3	20.7			1	-.03	-.33	+.02	+.01	+.06	-.30	-.10	-.24	-.07	+.06	+.14
4	26.5				1	-.32	+.13	+.20	-.09	+.20	-.16	-.18	-.15	+.07	+.24
5	17.2					1	-.12	-.17	+.09	+.14	+.14	+.20	+.04	-.01	-.14
6	16.0						1	+.29	+.02	-.21	-.03	-.02	-.01	+.10	+.03
7	25.4							1	+.11	-.32	-.24	-.24	+.02	+.18	+.10
8	25.5								1	-.05	+.28	+.25	-.01	+.02	-.11
9	2.1									1	+.25	+.25	-.19	-.12	-.05
10	19.7										1	+.96	-.08	-.18	-.25
11	24.1											1	-.02	-.18	-.28
12	6.3												1	-.06	+.00
13	14.2													1	-.01
14	1.4														1

The concrete pre-selection process now looks as follows: At first, univariate logit models are estimated in-sample for all potential input ratios, whose power to identify defaults in the development sample is evaluated via the criterion of the accuracy ratio (AR), a concept discussed in detail in Chapter XII. Afterwards, the pairwise correlation between all explanatory variables is computed to identify subgroups of highly correlated indicators, where by rule of thumb ratios with absolute correlation values of above 50% are pooled into one group. Finally, from each correlation sub-group (that usually contains only ratios from one specific credit risk category) that explanatory variable is selected for the multivariate model building process that has got the highest and hence best accuracy ratio in the uni-variate analysis.

Table 4 displays the accuracy ratios of and the correlation between the financial ratios calculated for the Austrian data set. As can be seen, explanatory variable 1 is highly correlated with indicator 2 (both measuring leverage) and ratio 10 with variable 11 (both reflecting profitability). Besides, the input ratios 2 and 11 have got better (higher) accuracy ratios than the indicators 1 respectively 10, hence, the latter ones are dropped from the list of explanatory variables for the multivariate analysis.

5.2. Derivation of the Final Default Prediction Model

Those ratios pre-selected in the previous step are now used to derive the final multivariate logit model. Usually, however, the number of potential explanatory variables is still too high to specify a logit model that contains all of them, because the optimal model should contain only a few, highly significant input ratios to avoid overfitting. Thus, even in our small example with only 12 indicators being left, we would have to construct and compare $2^{12} = 4,096$ models in order to de-termine the "best" econometric model and to entirely resolve model uncertainty. This is, of course, a tough task, which becomes infeasible for typical short lists of about 30 to 60 pre-selected input ratios. Therefore, the standard procedure is to use forward/backward selection to identify the final model (see Hosmer and Lemenshow, 2000).

For the Austrian data set backward elimination, one possible method of these sta-tistical stepwise variable selection procedures that is implemented in most statisti-cal software packages, was applied to derive the final logit model. This method starts by estimating the full model (with all potential input ratios) and continues by eliminating the worst covariates one by one until the significance level of all re-maining explanatory variables is below the chosen critical level, usually set at 90% or 95%.

Table 5 describes two logit models derived by backward elimination for the Aus-trian data. It depicts the constants of the logit models and the estimated coeffi-cients for all those financial ratios that enter into the respective model. The stars represent the significance level of the estimated coefficients and indicate that the true parameters are different from zero with a probability of 90% (*), 95% (**) or 99% (***).

Table 5. Estimates of multivariate logit models

	Financial Ratio	Risk Factor	Model 1	Model 2 (Final M.)	Hypo.
2	Equity / Total Assets	Leverage	-0.98 **	-0.85 **	-
3	Bank Debt / Total Assets	Leverage	1.55 ***	1.21 ***	+
4	Short Term Debt / Total Assets	Liquidity	1.30 **	1.56 ***	+
6	Accounts Receivable / Net Sales	Activity	1.71 *		+
7	Accounts Payable / Net Sales	Activity	2.31 **	1.53 *	+
8	(Net Sales - Material Costs) / Personnel Costs	Productivity	-0.23 ***	-0.23 ***	-
9	Net Sales / Total Assets	Turnover	0.26 **		-
	Constant		-1.18	-0.95	

Model 1 arises if all 12 pre-selected variables are entered into the backward elimination process. Detailed analysis of this model shows that most signs of the estimated coefficients correspond to the postulated hypotheses, however, the model specifies a positive relationship between the ratio number 9 "Net Sales / Total Assets", while most empirical studies find that larger firms default less frequently. What's more, even for our data sample a negative coefficient was estimated in the univariate analysis. For this reason, a closer inspection of input ratio 9 seems appropriate.

Although the variable "Net Sales / Total Assets" does not exhibit a pairwise correlation of more than 50%, it shows absolute correlation levels of about 30% with several other covariates. This indicates that this particular ratio is too highly correlated (on a multivariate basis) with the other explanatory variables and has to be removed from the list of variables entering the backward elimination process.

Model 2 in Table 5 depicts the resulting logit model. Here all coefficients are of comparable magnitude to those of model 1, except that the ratio "Accounts Receivable / Net Sales" becomes highly insignificant and is therefore excluded from the model. As a consequence, all estimated coefficients are now economically plausible, and we accept model 2 as our (preliminary) final model version.

5.3. Model Validation

Finally, the derived logit model has to be validated. In a first step, some statistical tests should be conducted in order to verify the model's robustness and goodness of fit in-sample, and in a second step the estimated model should be applied to the validation sample to produce out-of-sample forecasts, whose quality can be evaluated with the concept of the accuracy ratio and other methods depicted in Chapter XII.

The goodness-of-fit of a logit model can be assessed in two ways: first, on the basis of some test statistics that use various approaches to measure the distance between the estimated probabilities and the actual defaults, and second, by analysing individual observations which can each have a certain strong impact on the estimated coefficients (for details see Hosmer and Lemenshow, 2000).

One very popular goodness-of-fit test statistic is the Hosmer-Lemenshow test statistic that measures how well a logit model represents the actual probability of default for groups of firms of differently perceived riskiness. Here, the observations are grouped based on percentiles of the estimated default probabilities. For the Austrian data 10% intervals were used i.e. 10 groups were formed. Now for every group the average estimated default probability is calculated and used to derive the expected number of defaults per group. Next, this number is compared with the amount of realised defaults in the respective group. The Hosmer-Lemenshow test statistic then summarises this information for all groups. In our case of 10 groups the test statistic for the estimation sample is chi-square distributed with 8 degrees of freedom, and the corresponding p-value for the rating model can then be calculated as 79.91%, which indicates that the model fits quite well.

However, the Hosmer-Lemenshow goodness-of-fit test can also be regarded from another point of view for the application at hand. Until now we only dealt with the development of a model that assigns each corporation a certain default probability or credit score, which leads towards a ranking between the contemplated firms. However, in practice banks usually want to use this ranking to map the companies to an internal rating scheme that typically is divided into about ten to twenty rating grades. The easiest way to do so would be to use the percentiles of the predicted default probabilities to build groups. If for example 10 rating classes shall be formed, then from all observations the 10% with the smallest default probabilities would be assigned the best rating grade, the next 10% the second and so on till the last 10% with the highest estimated default probabilities would enter into the worst rating class. The Hosmer-Lemenshow test now tells us that, given one would apply the concept described above to form rating categories, overall the average expected default probability per rating grade would fit with the observed default experience per rating class.

Table 6. Validation results of the final logit model

Final Model (Model 2)	Accuracy Ratio	$\sigma_{\hat{A}R}$	95% Conf. Interval	Hosmer-Lemenshow Test Statistic p-Value
In-Sample	0.4418	0.0444	[0.3574, 0.5288]	79.91%
Out-of-Sample	0.4089	0.0688	[0.2741, 0.5438]	68.59%

What's more, as depicted in Table 6, the in-sample accuracy ratio is about 44%, which is a reasonable number. Usually the rating models for corporate exposures presented in the literature have an accuracy ratio between 40% and 70%. As discussed in Chapter XII in detail, AR can only be compared reliably for models that are applied to the same data set, because differences in the data set such as varying relative amounts of defaulters or non-equal data reliability drives this measure heavily, hence, an AR of about 44% seems satisfactory.

Finally, the out-of-sample accuracy ratio amounts to about 41%, which is almost as high as the in-sample AR. This implies that the derived rating model is stable and powerful also in the sense that it produces accurate default predictions for new data that was not used to develop the model. Therefore, we can now eventually accept the derived logit model as our final rating tool.

6. Conclusions

This chapter focused on the special difficulties that are encountered when developing internal rating models for corporate exposures. Although the whole process with data collection and processing, model building and validation usually takes quite some time and effort, the job is not yet completed with the implementation of the derived rating model. The predictive power of all statistical models depends heavily on the assumption that the historical relationship between the model's covariates and the default event will remain unchanged in the future. Given the wide range of possible events such as changes in firms' accounting policies or structural disruptions in certain industries, this assumption is not guaranteed over longer periods of time. Hence, it is necessary to revalidate and eventually recalibrate the model regularly in order to ensure that its predictive power does not diminish.

References

Basel Committee on Banking Supervision (1999), Credit Risk Modelling: Current Practices and Applications, Bank for International Settlements.

Basel Committee on Banking Supervision (2001), The Internal Ratings-Based Approach, Bank for International Settlements.

Hayden E (2002), Modelling an Accounting-Based Rating Model for Austrian Firms, unpublished PhD dissertation, University of Vienna.

Hayden E (2003), Are Credit Scoring Models Sensitive to Alternative Default Definitions? Evidence from the Austrian Market, Working Paper, University of Vienna.

Hodrick R, Prescott C (1997), Post-War U.S. Business Cycles: An Empirical Investigation, Journal of Money, Credit and Banking 29, pp. 1-16.

Hosmer W, Lemenshow S (2000), Applied Logistic Regression, John Wiley & Sons, New York.

III. Scoring Models for Retail Exposures

Daniel Porath

University of Applied Sciences at Mainz

1. Introduction

Rating models for retail portfolios deserve a more detailed examination because they differ from other bank portfolios. The differences can mainly be attributed to the specific data structure encountered when analyzing retail exposures. One implication is that different statistical tools have to be used when creating the model. Most of these statistical tools do not belong to the banker's standard toolbox. At the same time – and strictly speaking for the same reason – the banks' risk management standards for retail exposures are not comparable to those of other portfolios.

Banks often use scoring models for managing the risk of their retail portfolios. Scoring models are statistical risk assessment tools especially designed for retail exposures. They were initially introduced to standardize the decision and monitoring process. With respect to scoring, the industry had established rating standards for retail exposures long before the discussion about the IRBA emerged. The Basel Committee acknowledged these standards and has modified the minimum requirements for the internal rating models of retail exposures. The aim of this chapter is to discuss scoring models in the light of the minimum requirements and to introduce the non-standard statistical modelling techniques which are usually used for building scoring tables.

The discussion starts with an introduction to scoring models comprising a general description of scoring, a distinction of different kinds of scoring models and an exposure of the theoretical differences compared to other parametric rating models. In Section 3, we extract the most important minimum requirements for retail portfolios from the New Basel Capital Framework and consider their relevance for scoring models. Section 4 is dedicated to modelling techniques. Here, special focus is placed on the preliminary univariate analysis because it is completely different from other portfolios. We conclude with a short summary.

2. The Concept of Scoring

2.1. What is Scoring?

Like any rating tool, a scoring model assesses a borrower's creditworthiness. The outcome of the model is expressed in terms of a number called "score". Increasing scores usually indicate declining risk, so that a borrower with a score of 210 is more risky than a borrower with a score of 350. A comprehensive overview about scoring can be found in Thomas et al. (2002).

The model which calculates the score is often referred to as a scoring table, because it can be easily displayed in a table. Table 1 shows an extract of two variables from a scoring model (usually scoring models consist of about 7 up to 15 variables):

Table 1. Extract from a scoring table

Variable	Score of the variables' attributes
Marital status of borrower	
unmarried	20
married or widowed	24
divorced or separated	16
no answer	16
neutral	19
Age of borrower	
$18 \leq 24$	14
$24 \leq 32$	16
$32 \leq 38$	25
$38 \leq 50$	28
$50 \leq 65$	30
65 or older	32
neutral	24

The total customer score can be calculated by adding the scores of the borrower's several characteristics. Each variable contains the category "neutral". The score of this category represents the portfolio mean of the scores for a variable and therewith constitutes a benchmark when evaluating the risk of a specific category. Categories with higher scores than "neutral" are below the average portfolio risk and categories with lower scores are more risky than the average. For example,

divorced borrowers display increased risk compared to the whole portfolio, because for the variable "marital status" the score of a divorced borrower (16) is
lower than the score for the category "neutral" (19).

Scoring models usually are estimated with historical data and statistical methods.
The historical data involves information about the performance of a loan ("good"
or "bad") and about the characteristics of the loan some time before. The time
span between the measurement of the characteristic on the one hand and the performance on the other hand determines the forecast horizon of the model.

Estimation procedures for scoring models are logistic regression, discriminant
analysis or similar methods. The estimation results are the scores of the single
characteristics. Usually the scores are rescaled after estimation in order to obtain
round numbers as in the example shown in Table 1. More details regarding estimation of the scores are shown in Section 4.

2.2. Classing and Recoding

Scoring is a parametric rating model. This means that modelling involves the estimation of the parameters $\beta_0, ..., \beta_N$ in a general model

$$S_i = \beta_0 + \beta_1 x_{i1} + \beta_2 x_{i2} + ... + \beta_N x_{iN}. \tag{1}$$

Here S_i denotes the Score of the loan $i = 1,...,I$ and $x_1, ...,x_N$ are the input parameters or variables for the loan i. The parameters β_n $(n = 0,...,N)$ reflect the impact of
a variation of the input factors on the score.

Scoring differs from other parametric rating models in the treatment of the input
variables. As can be seen from Table 1, the variable "marital status" is a qualitative variable, therefore it enters the model categorically. Some values of the variable have been grouped into the same category, like for example "married" and
"widowed" in order to increase the number of borrowers within each class. The
grouping of the values of a variable is a separate preliminary step before estimation and is called "classing".

The general approach in (1) cannot manage categorical variables and therefore has
to be modified. To this end, the (categorical) variable x_n has to be recoded. An
adequate recoding procedure for scoring is to add the category "neutral" to the existing number of C categories and replace x_n by a set of dummy variables $d_{xn(c)}$,
$c = 1,...,C$ which are defined in the following way:

$$d_{xn(c)} = \begin{cases} 1 & \text{for } x_n = c \\ -1 & \text{for } x_n = \text{"neutral"} \\ 0 & \text{else.} \end{cases} \tag{2}$$

The recoding given in (2) is called effect coding and differs from the standard dummy variable approach where the dummies only take the values 0 and 1. The benefit from using (2) is that it allows for the estimation of a variable-specific mean which is the score of the category "neutral". As can be seen from (2), the value of the category "neutral" is implicitly given by the vector of dummy values (-1,...,-1). The coefficients of the other categories then represent the deviation from the variable-specific mean.

This can be illustrated by recoding and replacing the first variable x_{i1} in (1). Model (1) then becomes

$$S_i = \beta_0 + \left(\beta_{01} + \beta_{11}d_{x_{11,i}} + \beta_{12}d_{x_{12,i}} + ... + \beta_{1C}d_{x_{1C,i}}\right) + \beta_2 x_{i2} + ... + \beta_N x_{iN} \qquad (3)$$

Here $(\beta_{10} - \beta_{11} - \beta_{12} - ... - \beta_{1C})$ is the variable-specific average ("neutral") and the coefficients $\beta_{11},...,\beta_{1C}$ represent the deviation of the individual categories from the average. The scores of the single categories (see Table 1) are given by the sums $\beta_0 + \beta_{11}$, $\beta_0 + \beta_{12}$, ..., $\beta_0 + \beta_{1C}$.

Apart from the special recoding function (2), the procedure discussed so far is the standard procedure for handling categorical variables. The major characteristic of scoring is that the same procedure is conducted for the quantitative variables. This means that all variables are classed and recoded prior to estimation and therefore are treated as categorical variables. As a consequence, the overall mean β_0 in (3) disappears and the model can be rewritten as:

$$S_i = \left(\beta_{10} + \beta_{11}d_{x_{11,i}} + ... + \beta_{1C}d_{x_{1C,i}}\right) + ... + \left(\beta_{N0} + \beta_{N1}d_{x_{N1,i}} + ... + \beta_{NC}d_{x_{NC,i}}\right) \qquad (4)$$

With an increasing number of variables and categories, equation (4) soon becomes unmanageable. This is why scoring models are usually displayed in tables.

The effect of classing and recoding is twofold: On the one hand, the information about the interclass variation of the quantitative variable disappears. As can be seen from Figure 1, an increasing age reduces risk. The model, however, does not indicate any difference between the age of 39 and 49, because the same score is attributed to both ages. If the variable age entered the model as a quantitative variable with the estimated coefficient β_{age}, any difference in age (Δage) would be captured by the model (its effect on risk, i.e. the score, ceteris paribus, being $\beta_{age} \cdot \Delta age$). On the other hand, categorization allows for flexible risk patterns. Referring again to the example of age, the impact on risk may be strong for the lower age categories while diminishing for increasing ages. Such a nonlinear impact on the score S_i can be modelled by selecting narrow classes for lower ages and broad classes for higher ages. The quantitative model, on the contrary, attributes the same impact of β_{age} to a one-year change in age starting from any level. Thus, classing and recoding is an easy way to introduce nonlinearities in the model.

The theoretical merits from classing and recoding, however, were not pivotal for the wide use of scoring models. The more important reason for classing and recoding is that most of the risk-relevant input variables for retail customers are qualitative. These are demographic characteristics of the borrower (like marital status, gender, or home ownership), the type of profession, information about the loan (type of loan, intended use) and information about the payment behaviour in the past (due payment or not). The reason for transforming the remaining quantitative variables (like age or income) into categorical variables is to obtain a uniform model.

2.3. Different Scoring Models

Banks use different scoring models according to the type of loan. The reason is that the data which is available for risk assessment is loan-specific. For example, the scoring of a mortgage loan can make use of all the information about the real estate whereas there is no comparable information for the scoring model of a current account. On the other hand, models for current accounts involve much information about the past payments observed on the account (income, drawings, balance) which are not available for mortgage loans. For mortgage loans, payment information generally is restricted to whether the monthly instalment has been paid or not. As a consequence, there are different models for different products and when the same person has two different loans at the same bank, he or she generally will have two different scores. This is a crucial difference to the general rating principles of Basel II.

Scoring models which are primarily based on payment information are called behavioural scoring. The prerequisite for using a behavioural score is that the bank observes information about the payment behaviour on a monthly basis, so that the score changes monthly. Furthermore, in order to obtain meaningful results, at least several monthly payment transactions should be observed for each customer. Since the behavioural score is dynamic, it can be used for risk monitoring. Additionally, banks use the score for risk segmentation when defining strategies for retail customers, like for example cross-selling strategies or the organization of the dunning process ("different risk, different treatment").

When payment information is sporadic, it is usually not implemented in the scoring model. The score then involves static information which has been queried in the application form. This score is called an application score. In contrast to the behavioural score, the application score is static, i.e. once calculated it remains constant over time. It is normally calculated when a borrower applies for a loan and helps the bank to decide whether it should accept or refuse the application. Additionally, by combining the score with dynamic information it can be used as a part of a monitoring process.

3. Scoring and the IRBA Minimum Requirements

Internal Rating systems for retail customers were in use long before Basel II. The reason is that statistical models for risk assessment are especially advantageous for the retail sector: on the one hand, the high granularity of a retail portfolio allows banks to realize economies of scale by standardization of the decision and monitoring processes. On the other hand, the database generally consists of a broad number of homogenous data. Homogeneity is owed to standardized forms for application and monitoring. As a consequence, the database is particularly suited for modelling. In fact, statistical procedures for risk forecasting of retail loans have a history of several decades (cf. Hand, 2001), starting with the first attempts in the 1960s and coming into wide use in the 1980s. Today, scoring is the industrial standard for the rating of retail customers. Since these standards have developed independently from the New Basel Capital Approach, there are some differences to the IRBA minimum requirements. The Capital Accord has acknowledged these differences and consequently modified the rules for retail portfolios. Hence most banks will meet the minimum requirements, possibly after some slight modifications of their existing scoring systems. In the following subsections we discuss the meaning of some selected minimum requirements for scoring and therewith give some suggestions about possible modifications. The discussion is restricted to the minimum requirements, which according to our view, are the most relevant for scoring. We refer to the Revised Framework of the Basel Committee on Banking Supervision from June 2004 (cf. BIS, 2004) which for convenience in the following is called Capital Framework.

3.1. Rating System Design

Following § 394 of the Capital Framework, a rating system comprises the assignment of a rating to credit risk and the quantification of default and loss estimates. However, scoring models only provide the first component, which is the score S_i. The default and loss estimates (which in the Capital Framework are PD, LGD, and EAD) usually are not determined by the scoring model. When a bank intends to use a scoring model for the IRBA, these components have to be assessed separately.

3.2. Rating Dimensions

Generally, the IRBA requires a rating system to be separated by a borrower-specific component and a transaction-specific component (see § 396 of the Capital Framework). However, in the previous section we have seen that scoring models typically mix variables about the borrower and the type of loan. In order to render scoring models eligible to the IRBA, the Basel Committee has modified the general approach on the rating dimensions for retail portfolios. According to § 401 of the Capital Framework both components should be present in the scoring model, but need not be separated. Consequently, when referring to the risk classification of retail portfolios, the Capital Framework uses the term pool instead of rating grade.

With § 401, banks have greater flexibility when defining pools, as long as the pooling is based on all risk-relevant information. Pools can be customer-specific or loan-specific (like in a scoring model) or a mixture of both. A further consequence of § 401 is that one the same borrower is allowed to have two different scores.

3.3. Risk Drivers

Paragraph 402 of the Capital Framework specifies the risk drivers banks should use in a scoring model. These cover borrower characteristics, transaction characteristics and delinquency. As seen in the previous section, borrower and transaction characteristics are integral parts of a scoring table. Delinquency, on the other hand, is not usually integrated in a scoring model. The rationale is that scoring aims at predicting delinquency and that therefore no forecast is needed for a delinquent account. However, a correct implementation of a scoring model implies that delinquent accounts are separated (and therefore identified), so that the calculation of the score can be suppressed. Hence, when using a scoring model, normally all risk drivers mentioned in § 402 of the Capital Framework are integrated.

3.4. Risk Quantification

Risk quantification in terms of Basel II is the assessment of expected loss as the product from PD, LGD and EAD. Since the expected loss of a loan determines the risk weight for the capital requirement, the regulatory capital framework contains precise definitions for the quantification of these components. This means that the underlying time horizon is fixed to one year and that the underlying default event is explicitly defined.

Scoring models generally do not follow these definitions since their primary aim is not to fulfil the supervisory requirements but to provide internal decision support. The application score, for example, tells whether an application for a loan should be accepted or refused and for this decision it would not suffice to know whether the loan will default in the following year only. Instead, the bank is interested to know whether the loan will default in the long run, and therefore scoring models generally provide long-run predictions. Additionally, the default event sets as soon as the loan becomes no longer profitable for the bank and this is usually not the case when the loan defaults according the Basel definition. It depends, instead, on the bank's internal calculation.

To sum up, scoring models used for internal decision support generally will not comply with the requirements about risk quantification. A strategy to conserve the power of an internal decision tool and at the same time achieve compliance with the minimum requirements is:

- Develop the scoring model with the internal time-horizons and definitions of default
- Define the pools according to § 401 of the Capital Framework
- Estimate the pool-specific PD, LGD and EAD following the Basel definitions in a separate step.

Finally, it should be noted that the time horizon for assigning scores is not specified in the Basel Accord. In paragraph 414 of the Capital Framework it is stated that the horizon should be generally longer than one year. The long-term horizon normally used by scoring systems therefore is conforming to the minimum requirements.

3.5. Special Requirements for Scoring Models

In § 417 the Capital Framework explicitly refers to scoring models (and other statistical models) and specifies some additional requirements. The rationale is that the implementation of a scoring model leads to highly standardized decision and monitoring processes where failures may be overlooked or detected too late. Therefore, the requirements given in § 417 refer to special qualitative features of the model and special control mechanisms.

These requirements will generally be met when banks follow the industrial standards for the development and implementation of scoring models. The most important standards which have to be mentioned in this context are:

- the use of a representative database for the development of the model
- documentation about the development including univariate analysis
- preparation of a user's guide
- implementation of a monitoring process

4. Methods for Estimating Scoring Models

The statistical methods which are suitable for estimating scoring models comprise the techniques introduced in Chapter I, e.g. logit analysis, or discriminant analysis, with the special feature that all input variables enter the model as categorical variables. This requires an extensive preliminary data analysis which is referred to as "univariate analysis". Univariate analysis generally is interesting for rating analysis because it serves to detect problems concerning the data and helps to identify the most important risk-drivers. However, for retail portfolios, univariate analysis is more complex and more important than in the general case. There are several reasons for this:

- Univariate analysis determines the classes on which the recoding is based (see Section 2) and hereby becomes an integral part of the model-building process.
- In retail portfolios, qualitative information is predominant (e.g. a person's profession, marital status).
- In retail portfolios, many qualitative variables are hard factors and do not involve human judgement. Examples include a person's profession, marital status and gender. Note that qualitative information encountered in rating systems for corporate loans, often require personal judgement on part of the analyst (e.g. a company's management, the position in the market or the future development of the sector where the company operates).
- For retail portfolios, a priori, it is often unknown whether a variable is relevant for the risk assessment. For example, there is no theory which tells whether a borrower's profession, gender or domicile helps in predicting default. This is different for the corporate sector where the main information consists of financial ratios taken from the balance sheet. For example, EBIT ratios measure the profitability of a firm and since profitability is linked to the firm's financial health, it can be classified as a potential risk factor prior to the analysis. For retail portfolios, univariate analysis replaces a priori knowledge and therefore helps to identify variables with a high discriminatory power.
- Often, the risk distribution of a variable is unknown a priori. This means that before analyzing a variable, it is not clear which outcomes correlate with high risks and which outcomes correlate with low risks. This is completely different from the corporate sector, where for many financial ratios, the risk patterns are well-known. For example, it is a priori known that ceteris paribus, high profitability leads to low risk and vice versa. For retail portfolios, the risk distribution has to be determined with the help of univariate analysis.

The consequences are two-fold: On one hand, univariate analysis is particularly important for replacing a priori knowledge. On the other hand, the statistical methods applied in the univariate analysis should be designed to handle qualitative hard factors.

The basic technique for creating a scoring model is crosstabulation. Crosstabs display the data in a two-dimensional frequency table, where the rows $c = 1, ..., C$ are the categories of the variable and the columns are the performance of the loan. The cells contain the absolute number of loans included in the analysis. Crosstabulation is flexible because it works with qualitative data as well as quantitative data - quantitative information simply has to be grouped beforehand. A simple example for the variable "marital status" is displayed in Table 2:

Table 2. Crosstab for the variable "Marital status"

	No. of good loans	No. of bad loans
Marital status of borrower		
unmarried	700	500
married or widowed	850	350
divorced or separated	450	650

The crosstab is used to assess the discriminative power. The discriminative power of a variable or characteristic can be described as its power to discriminate between good and bad loans. However, it is difficult to compare the absolute figures in the table. In Table 2, the bank has drawn a sample of the good loans. This is a common procedure, because often it is difficult to retrieve historical data. As a consequence, in the crosstab, the number of good loans cannot be compared to the number of bad loans of the same category. It is therefore reasonable to replace the absolute values by the column percentages for the good loans $P(c|Good)$ and for the bad loans $P(c|Bad)$, see Table 3:

Table 3. Column percentages, WoE and IV

	$P(c|Good)$	$P(c|Bad)$	WoE
Marital status of borrower			
Unmarried	0.3500	0.3333	0.0488
married or widowed	0.4250	0.2333	0.5996
divorced or separated	0.2250	0.4333	-0.6554
		IV	0.2523

The discriminative power can be assessed by regarding the risk distribution of the variable which is shown by the Weight of Evidence WoE_c (see Good, 1950). The Weight of Evidence can be calculated from the column percentages with the following formula:

$$WoE = \ln(P(c \mid Good)) - \ln(P(c \mid Bad)) \tag{5}$$

The interpretation of WoE is straightforward: Increasing values of the Weight of Evidence indicate decreasing risk. A value of $WoE_c > 0$ ($WoE_c < 0$) means that in category c good (bad) loans are over-represented. In the above example, the Weight of Evidence shows that loans granted to married or widowed customers have defaulted with a lower frequency than those granted to divorced or separated customers. The value of WoE close to 0 for unmarried customers displays that the risk of this group is similar to the average portfolio risk.

The Weight of Evidence can also be interpreted in terms of the Bayes theorem. The Bayes theorem expressed in log odds is

$$\ln\frac{P(Good|c)}{P(Bad|c)} = \ln\frac{P(c|Good)}{P(c|Bad)} + \ln\frac{P(Good)}{P(Bad)}. \tag{6}$$

Since the first term on the right hand of Equation 6 is the Weight of Evidence, it represents the difference between the a posteriori log odds and the a priori log odds. The value of WoE_c therefore measures the improvement of the forecast through the information of category c. Hence it is a performance measure for category c.

A comprehensive performance measure for all categories of an individual variable can be calculated as a weighted average of the Weights of Evidence for all categories $c = 1,...,C$. The result is called Information Value, IV (cf. Kullback, 1959) and can be calculated by:

$$IV = \sum_{c=1}^{C} Woe_c \left(P(c|Good) - P(c|Bad) \right) \tag{7}$$

A high value of IV indicates a high discriminatory power of a specific variable. The Information Value has a lower bound of zero but no upper bound. In the example of Figure 3, the Information Value is 0.2523. Since there is no upper bound, from the absolute value we cannot tell whether the discriminatory power is satisfactory or not. In fact, the Information Value is primarily calculated for the purpose of comparison to other variables or alternative classings of the same variable and the same portfolio.

The Information Value has the great advantage of being independent from the order of the categories of the variable. This is an extremely important feature when analyzing data with unknown risk distribution. It should be noted that most of the better-known performance measures like the Gini coefficient or the power curve do not share this feature and therefore are of limited relevance only for the univariate analysis of retail portfolios.

Crosstabulation is a means to generate classings which are needed for the recoding and estimation procedures. There are three requirements for a good classing. First, each class should contain a minimum number of good and bad loans, otherwise the estimation of the coefficients β in (4) tend to be imprecise. Following a rule of thumb there should be at least 50 good loans and 50 bad loans in each class. Probably this is why in the above example there is no separate category "widowed". Second, the categories grouped in each class should display a similar risk profile. Therefore, it is feasible to combine the categories "separated" and "divorced" to one single class. Third, the resulting classing should reveal a plausible risk pattern (as indicated by the Weight of Evidence) and a high performance (as indicated by a high Information Value).

Fixing a classing is complex, because there is a trade-off between the requirements. On one hand, the Information Value tends to increase with an increasing number of classes, on the other hand, estimation of the coefficients β tends to improve when the number of classes decreases.

In order to fix the final classing analysts produce a series of different crosstabs and calculate the corresponding Weights of Evidence and Information Values. Finally, the best classing is selected according to the criteria above. The final classing therefore is the result of a heuristic process which is strongly determined by the analyst's know-how and experience.

5. Summary

In this section, we briefly summarise the ideas discussed here. We have started from the observation that for retail portfolios, the methods for developing rating models are different from those applied to other portfolios. This is mainly due to the different type of data typically encountered when dealing with retail loans: First, there is a predominance of hard qualitative information which allows the integration of a high portion of qualitative data in the model. Second, there is little theoretical knowledge about the risk relevance and risk distribution of the input variables. Therefore, analyzing the data requires special tools. Finally, there is a high amount of comparably homogenous data. As a consequence, statistical risk assessment tools were developed long before rating models for other banks' portfolios have boosted and the standards have been settled independently from Basel II. The standard models for the rating of retail portfolios are scoring models. Generally, scoring models comply with the IRBA minimum requirements as long as they fulfill the industrial standards. However, usually they only constitute risk classification systems in terms of the IRBA and it will be necessary to add a component which estimates PD, EAD and LGD.

The estimation of a scoring model requires the classing of all individual variables. This is done in a preliminary step called univariate analysis. The classings can be defined by comparing the performance of different alternatives. Since risk distribution of the variables is often completely unknown, the univariate analysis should rely on performance measures which are independent from the ordering of the single classes, like for example the Weight of Evidence and the Information Value. Once the classing is settled the variables have to be recoded in order to build the model. Finally, the model can be estimated with standard techniques like logit analysis or discriminant analysis.

References

BIS (2004), International Convergence of Capital Measurement and Capital Standards, Basel Committee on Banking Supervision, June 2004.

Good IJ (1950); Probability and the Weighing of Evidences, Charles Griffin, London.

Hand DJ (2001), Modelling consumer credit risk, IMA Journal of Management Mathematics 12, pp. 139-155.

Kullback S (1959), Information Theory and Statistics, Wiley, New York.

Thomas, LC, Crook J, Edelman D (2002), Credit Scoring and its applications, Siam Monographs on Mathematical Modeling and Computation

IV. The Shadow Rating Approach – Experience from Banking Practice

Ulrich Erlenmaier

KfW Bankengruppe[1]

1. Introduction

In this article we will report on some aspects of the development of shadow rating systems found to be important when re-devising the rating system for large corporations of KfW Bankengruppe (KfW banking group). The article focuses on general methodological issues and does not necessarily describe how these issues are dealt with by KfW Bankengruppe. Moreover, due to confidentiality we do not report estimation results that have been derived. In this introductory section we want to describe briefly the basic idea of the shadow rating approach (SRA), then summarise the typical steps of SRA rating development and finally set out the scope of this article.

The shadow rating approach is typically employed when default data are rare and external ratings from the three major rating agencies (Standard & Poor's, Moody's or Fitch) are available for a significant and representative part of the portfolio. As with other approaches to the development of rating systems, the first modelling step is to identify *risk factors* – such as balance sheet ratios or qualitative information about a company – that are supposed to be good predictors of future defaults. The SRA's objective is to choose and weight the risk factors in such a way as to mimic external ratings as closely as possible when there is insufficient data to build an explicit default prediction model (the latter type of model is e.g. described in Chapter I. To make the resulting rating function usable for the bank's internal risk management as well as for regulatory capital calculation, the external rating grades (AAA, AA, etc.) have to be calibrated, i.e. a probability of default (PD) has to be attached to them. With these PDs, the external grades can then be mapped to the bank's internal rating scale.

The following modular architecture is typical for SRA but also for other types of rating systems:

---

[1] The opinions expressed in this article are those of the author and do not reflect views of KfW Bankengruppe (or models applied by the bank).

1. Statistical model
2. Expert-guided adjustments
3. Corporate group influences / Sovereign Support
4. Override

The statistical model constitutes the basis of the rating system and will most likely include balance sheet ratios, macroeconomic variables (such as country ratings or business cycle indicators) and qualitative information about the company (such as quality of management or the company's competitive position). The statistical model will be estimated from empirical data that bring together companies' risk factors on the one hand and their external ratings on the other hand. The model is set up to predict external ratings – more precisely, external PDs – as efficiently as possible from the selected risk factors.

The second modelling layer of the rating system, that we have termed "Expert-guided adjustments" will typically include risk factors for which either no historical information is available or for which the influence on external ratings is difficult to estimate empirically.[2] Consequently, these risk factors will enter the model in the form of adjustments that are not estimated empirically but that are determined by credit experts.

The third modelling layer will take into account the corporate group to which the company belongs or probably some kind of government support.[3] This is typically done by rating both the obligor on a standalone basis and the entity that is supposed to influence the obligor's rating. Both ratings are then aggregated into the obligor's overall rating where the aggregation mechanism will depend on the degree of influence that the corporate group / sovereign support are assessed to have.

Finally, the rating analyst will have the ability to override the results as derived by steps 1 to 3 if she thinks that – due to very specific circumstances – the rating system does not produce appropriate results for a particular obligor.

This article will focus on the development of the rating system's first module, the statistical model.[4] The major steps in the development of the statistical model are:

1. Deployment of software tools for all stages of the rating development process
2. Preparation and validation of the data needed for rating development (typically external as well as internal data sets)[5]

---

[2] This occurs e.g. when a new risk factor has been introduced or when a risk factor is relevant only for a small sub-sample of obligors.

[3] There also might be other types of corporate relationships that can induce the support of one company for another one. For example, a company might try to bail out an important supplier which is in financial distress. However, since this issue is only a minor aspect of this article we will concentrate on the most common supporter-relationship in rating practice, i.e. corporate groups and sovereign support.

[4] We will, however, also include a short proposal for the empirical estimation of corporate group influences / sovereign support (step 3).

3. Calibration of external ratings
4. Sample construction for the internal rating model
5. Single (univariate) factor analysis
6. Multi factor analysis and validation
7. Impact analysis
8. Documentation

This article deals with steps 3 to 6, each of which will be presented in one separate section. Nevertheless, we want to provide comments on the other steps and emphasise their relative importance both in qualitative as in quantitative terms for the success of a rating development project:

- Initial project costs (i.e. internal resources and time spent for the initial development project) will be very high and mainly driven by steps 1 to 3 (but also 8) with step 1 being the single biggest contributor. In contrast, follow-up costs (future refinement projects related to the same rating system) can be expected to be much lower and more equally distributed across all steps with step 2 most likely being the single biggest contributor.
- The importance of step 2 for the statistical analyses that build on it must be stressed. Moreover, this step will be even more important when external data sets are employed. In this case, it will also be necessary to establish compatibility with the internal data set.
- Step 7: Once a new rating system has been developed and validated, it will be important to assess the impact of a change to the new system on key internal and regulatory portfolio risk measures, including for example, expected loss or regulatory and economic capital.
- Regarding step 8 we found it very helpful and time saving to transfer a number of the results from statistical analyses to appendices that are automatically generated by software tools.

Finally, we want to conclude the introduction with some comments on step 1, the deployment of software tools. The objective should be to automate the complex rating development process as completely as possible through all the necessary steps, in order to reduce the manpower and a-priori know how required to conduct a development project. Therefore, different, inter-connected tools are needed, including:

---

[5] In this article, the term "external data sets" or "external data" will always refer to a situation where – additional to internally rated companies – a typically much larger sample of not internally-rated companies is employed for rating development. This external data set will often come from an external data provider such as e.g. Bureau van Dijk but can also be the master sample of a data-pooling initiative. In such a situation, usually only quantitative risk factors will be available for both, the internal and the external data set while qualitative risk factors tend to be confined to the internal data set. In this situation, a number of specific problems arise that have to be taken into account. The problems we found most relevant will be dealt with in this article.

- *Datamarts:* Standardised reports from the bank's operating systems or data warehouse covering all information relevant for rating development / validation on a historical basis
- *Data set management:* to make external data compatible with internal data, for sample construction, etc.
- *Statistical analysis tools:* tailor made for rating development and validation purposes. These tools produce documents that can be used for the rating system's documentation (step 8). These documents comprise all major analyses as well as all relevant parameters for the new rating algorithm.
- *Generic rating algorithm tool:* Allows the application of new rating algorithms to the relevant samples. It should be possible to customise the tool with the results from the statistical analyses and to build completely new types of rating algorithms.

2. Calibration of External Ratings

2.1. Introduction

The first step in building an SRA model is to calibrate the external agencies' rating grades, i.e. to attach a PD to them. The following list summarises the issues we found important in this context:

- *External rating types:* which types of ratings should be employed?
  - Probability of default (PD) / Expected loss (EL) ratings,
  - Long- / Short-term ratings,
  - Foreign / Local currency ratings
- *External rating agencies:* pros and cons of the different agencies' ratings with respect to the shadow rating approach
- *Default definition / Default rates:* differences between external and internal definitions of the default event and of default rates will be discussed
- S*amples for external PD estimation:* which time period should be included, are there certain obligor types that should be excluded?
- *PD estimation technique:* discussion of the pros and cons of the two major approaches, the cohort and the duration-based approach
- *Adjustments of PD estimates:* if PD estimates do not have the desired properties (e.g. monotonicity in rating grades), some adjustments are required
- *Point-in-time adjustment:* external rating agencies tend to follow a through-the-cycle-rating philosophy. If a bank's internal rating philosophy is point-in-time then either
  - the external through-the-cycle ratings must be adjusted to make them sensitive to changes in macroeconomic conditions or,

- the effects of developing on a through-the-cycle benchmark must be taken into account

The above mentioned issues will be addressed in the following sections.

2.2. External Rating Agencies and Rating Types

For SRA ratings systems, typically the ratings of the three major ratings agencies – Standard & Poors (S&P), Moody's and Fitch – are employed. Two questions arise:

1. For each rating agency, which type of rating most closely matches the bank's internal rating definition?
2. Which rating agencies are particularly well suited for the purpose of SRA development?

Regarding question 1 *issuer credit ratings* for S&P and Fitch and *issuer ratings* for Moody's were found to be most suitable since these ratings assess the obligor and not an obligor's individual security. Moreover, it will usually make sense to choose the *long-term, local currency versions* for all rating agencies and rating types.[6]

Regarding question 2 the major pro and cons were found to be the following:

- Length of rating history and track record: S&P and Moody's dominate Fitch. See e.g. Standard & Poor's (2005), Moody's (2005), and Fitch (2005).
- Rating scope: while both S&P and Fitch rate an obligor with respect to its probability of default (PD), which is consistent with banks' internal ratings as required by Basel II, Moody's assesses its expected loss (EL).This conclusion draws on the rating agencies' rating definitions (cf. Standard and Poor's (2002), Moody's (2004), and Fitch, 2006), discussions with rating agency representatives and the academic literature (cf. Güttler, 2004).
- Are differences between local and foreign currency ratings (LC and FC) always identifiable? While S&P attaches a local and foreign currency rating to almost every issuer rating, this is not always the case for Moody's and Fitch.

Based on an assessment of these pros and cons it has to be decided whether one agency will be preferred when more than one external rating is available for one obligor.

---

[6] Long-term ratings because of the Basel II requirements that banks are expected to use a time horizon longer than one year in assigning ratings (BCBS (2004), § 414) and because almost all analyses of external ratings are conducted with long-term ratings. Local currency ratings are needed when a bank measures transfer risk separately from an obligor's credit rating.

The following sections will deal with PD estimations for external rating grades. In this context we will – for the sake of simplicity – focus on the agencies S&P and Moody's.

2.3. Definitions of the Default Event and Default Rates

For the PD estimates from external rating data to be consistent with internal PD estimates, a) the definition of the default event and b) the resulting definition of default rates (default counts in relation to obligor counts) must be similar. While there might be some minor differences regarding the calculation of default rates[7], the most important differences in our opinion stem from different definitions of the default event. Here are the most important deviations:[8]

- Different types of defaults (bank defaults vs. bond market defaults): a company that has problems meeting its obligations might e.g. first try to negotiate with its bank before exposing it to a potential default in the bond market.
- Differences in qualitative default criteria: according to Basel II, a company is to be classified as default when a bank considers that the obligor is unlikely to pay its credit obligations in full. This could easily apply to companies that are in the lowest external non-default rating grades.[9]
- Number of days of delayed payment that will lead to default
  - Basel II: 90 days
  - S&P: default when payments are not made within grace period which typically ranges from 10 to 30 days
  - Moody's: 1 day
- Materiality: While external agencies will measure defaults without respect to the size of the amount due, under Basel II, payment delays that are small with respect to the company's overall exposure will not be counted as defaults.

In order to assess the effects of these and other differences in default definition on estimated PDs, the default measurement of S&P and Moody's has to be compared with the bank's internal default measurement. In a first step S&P and Moody's could be compared with each other (a). If the differences between the two external agencies are not significant, internal defaults can be compared with the pooled ex-

---

[7] Examples: a) While the external agencies count the number of obligors only at the beginning of the *year* and then the resulting defaults from these obligors over the year, a bank might count on a finer basis (e.g. monthly) in order to track as many obligors as possible; b) defaults that occur because of foreign currency controls and not because the individual obligor is not able to meet its obligations should not be counted as default for the purpose of PD-estimation if a bank quantifies transfer risk separately.

[8] The Basel II default definition is given in (BCBS (2004), § 452). The rating agencies' default definitions are described in their respective default reports (cf. Standard & Poor's (2005), Moody's (2005), and Fitch, 2005).

[9] This assessment draws on external agencies' verbal definitions of those rating grades (cf. Standard and Poor's (2002), Moody's (2004), and Fitch, 2006).

ternal defaults of S&P and Moody's (b). The following technique might be useful for steps a) and b):

1. Estimation of the ratio of Moody's defaults for each S&P default and the ratio of external defaults for each internal default respectively.
2. This ratio can be interpreted as an adjustment factor with which a) PDs derived for Moody's have to be scaled in order to arrive at PDs compatible with S&P and b) with which external PDs have to be adjusted in order to be comparable with internally derived PDs.
3. Calculation of confidence intervals for the resulting estimators using a multinomial model and a Chi-square-type test statistic[10]

Depending on the estimation results it has to be decided whether an adjustment factor should be applied. If estimators prove to be very volatile, additional default data (e.g. form data pooling initiatives) might be needed to arrive at more confident estimates.

2.4. Sample for PD Estimation

For the estimation of external PDs the obligor samples of S&P and Moody's as used by these agencies to derive default rates in their annual default reports can be employed.[11] The following two dimensions of sample construction should in our opinion be closely analysed:

1. Obligor sector and country: should all obligor types be included irrespective of industry sector and country?
2. Length of time series

With respect to 1) one can start with the hypotheses that – as ratings agencies claim – external ratings are comparable across industry sectors and countries.[12] Consequently, for those rating types (S&P and Fitch) that aim to measure an obligor's PD, PD estimates would only have to be conditional on an obligor's rating grade, not its industry sector or country. Where ratings measure an obligor's EL for senior unsecured obligations (Moody's), however, PD estimates would also have to be conditional on all obligor characteristics that affect the LGD on these obligations, as could – for example – be the case for a company's industry sector

---

[10] For example, for the comparison of external and internal defaults, the multinomial random variable would for each defaulted company indicate one of three potential outcomes: 1) External and internal default, 2) External default but no internal default, 3) Internal default but no external default. Moreover, due to the typically small amount of data, no large-sample approximation but the exact Chi-square distribution should be employed. Confidence limits can be estimated by applying the test statistic on a sufficiently fine grid for the parameters of the multinomial distribution.

[11] See Standard and Poor's (2005) and Moody's (2005).

[12] See agencies' rating definitions: Standard and Poor's (2002) and Moody's (2004) respectively.

or home country. But if LGD differences across obligors are small compared to PD differences between rating grades, estimates based only on the rating grade might be tolerable for pragmatic reasons.

To address the first issues (comparability of ratings across countries/sectors), the literature on differences between external default rates across industry sectors and countries should be reviewed. We found only three papers on the default rate issue.[13] None identified country specific differences while they were inconclusive with respect to sector specific differences.[14]

Regarding the second issue (relative size of the LGD effect), the bank's internal LGD methodology should be analysed with respect to differences between senior unsecured LGDs across industries and countries.[15] Based on the assessment of both issues it should be decided as to whether country or industry sector specific estimates are needed.

We now turn to the second dimension of sample construction, i.e. the length of the time series. On the one hand, a long time series will reduce statistical uncertainty and include different states of the business cycle. On the other hand, there is the problem that because of structural changes, data collected earlier, might not reflect current and future business conditions. A sensible starting point will be the time horizon that is most often used by both the rating agencies and the academic literature (starting with the years 1981 and 1983 respectively). One can then analyse changes in rating grade default rates over time and assess whether structural changes in the default rate behaviour can be identified or whether most of the variability can be explained by business cycle fluctuations.

2.5. PD Estimation Techniques

Once the sample for PD estimation has been derived, the estimation technique must be specified. Typically, the so called *cohort method (CM)* is applied where the number of obligors at the beginning of each year in each rating grade and the number of obligors that have defaulted in this year are counted respectively. Both figures are then summed over all years within the time horizon. The resulting PD estimate is arrived at by dividing the overall number of defaults by the overall number of obligors.[16]

---

[13] See Ammer and Packer (2000), Cantor and Falkenstein (2001), and Cantor (2004)

[14] Ammer and Packer (2000) found default-rate differences between banks and non-banks. However, they pointed out that these differences are most likely attributable to a specific historic event, the US Savings and Loans crisis, and should therefore not be extrapolated to future default rates. Cantor and Falkenstein (2001), in contrast, found no differences in the default rates of banks and non-banks once one controls for macroeconomic effects.

[15] For a discussion of LGD-estimation methods we refer to Chapter VIII of this book.

[16] This method can be improved on by counting on a monthly or even finer base.

The *duration-based (DB) approach* aims to improve on the cohort-method by including information on rating migration in the estimation process. The underlying idea is to interpret default events as the result of a migration process. In the simplest setting where the migration process can be assumed to follow a stationary Markov process, a T-year migration matrix M_T can be derived by applying the one year migration matrix M_T T times:

$$M_T = M_1{}^T \tag{1}$$

The continuous time analogue of (1) is

$$M_t = \text{Exp}(m \cdot t), \tag{2}$$

where m is the marginal migration matrix, t the time index and Exp(.) the matrix exponential.[17] Hence, M_1 (including in particular 1-year default probabilities) can be derived by first estimating m from transition counts and then applying the matrix exponential to the estimated marginal transition matrix. A detailed description of the duration-based approach (DB) and the cohort method (CM) can be found in Schuermann and Hanson (2004). They also state the major differences between CM and DB estimates, in particular, that the latter produce PDs that spread more widely across the rating scale, i.e. PDs for good rating grades will be much lower and PDs for bad ratings will be much higher under DB than under CM.

Both estimation techniques have their pros and cons:
- DB makes more use of the available information by also taking into account rating migrations. For this reason, the DB method can also produce positive PD estimates for the best rating grades where no default observations are available.
- CM is more transparent and does not rely on as many modelling assumptions as the DB method.

As long as there is no clear-cut empirical evidence on the relative performance of both methods, it seems therefore sensible to apply both techniques and compare the resulting estimates. However, it is likely that in the future such comparisons will become available and therefore it will be helpful to keep an eye on the corresponding regulatory and academic discussion.

2.6. Adjustments

Because the PD estimates resulting from the application of the estimation methods as described in the previous section will not always be monotonic (i.e. not always will PD estimates for better rating grades be lower than for worse rating grades), the estimates have to be adapted in these non-monotonic areas. One option is to

---

[17] The matrix exponential applies the exponential series to matrices: $exp\ (m) = I + m^1/1! + m^2/2! + \dots$, where I is the identity matrix.

regress the logarithm of the PD estimates on the rating grades and to check whether the interpolations that result for the non-monotonic areas are within confidence limits. Here are some comments on the underlying techniques:

- Regression
  - In order to perform the regression, a metric interpretation has to be given to the ordinal rating grades. Plots of PD estimates against rating grades on a logarithmic scale suggest that this approach is sensible from a pragmatic point of view (cf. Altman and Rijken, 2004).
  - It may make sense to weight the regression by the number of observations available for each rating grade since the precision of PD estimates is dependent on it.
- Confidence intervals (CI)
  - For the cohort approach, confidence intervals can be derived from the binomial distribution by assuming independent observations.[18]
  - It is usually assumed that default observations are correlated because of macroeconomic default drivers that affect the default behaviour of different obligors. Hence, binomial confidence intervals will be a conservative estimate (they are tighter then they would be under correlated defaults). CIs derived from a Merton style simulation model (cf. Chapter XIV of this book) could be the logical next step.
  - In the context of the duration-based method, CIs are typically derived via Bootstrap methods (cf. Schuermann and Hansen, 2004). These tend to be even tighter. The topic of correlated defaults/migrations has to our knowledge not yet been addressed in this context.

2.7. Point-in-Time Adaptation

In the context of Basel II, a bank's rating system is supposed to measure an obligor's probability of default (PD) over a specific time horizon (the next T years). In practice, the objective of rating systems differs, particularly with respect to:

1. The time horizon chosen by a bank
2. Whether PDs are conditional on the state of the business cycle (through-the-cycle philosophy, TTC) or not (point-in-time philosophy, PIT)

While the first point can be taken into account by correspondingly adjusting the time horizon for default rate estimation, a bank that follows a PIT approach will have to apply PIT-adjustments to the PD estimates derived for external rating grades since external rating agencies tend to follow a TTC-approach.[19]

---

[18] For an efficient derivation and implementation of exact confidence limits for the binomial distribution see Daly (1992).

[19] The TTC-property of external ratings has been observed in the academic literature (cf. Löffler, 2004) and has also been proved to be significant by our own empirical investiga-

In the remainder of this section we will a) analyse the effects resulting from the development of ratings systems on TTC-PDs and b) outline a technique for PIT adjustments of external rating grades. To address both points, we first summarise the most important properties of PIT and TTC rating systems in Table 1. These properties follow straightforwardly from the above definitions. A detailed discussion can be found in Heitfield (2004).

Table 1. Comparison of point-in-time and through-the-cycle rating systems

Issue	Point-in-Time (PIT)	Through-the-cycle (TTC)
What does the rating system measure?	Unconditional PD	PD conditional on the state of the business cycle. The PD estimate might be either conditional on a worst case ("bottom of the cycle scenario")[20] or on an average business cycle scenario
Stability of an obligor's rating grade over the cycle	Pro-cyclical: Rating improves during expansions and deteriorates in recessions	Stable: Rating grades tend to be unaffected by changes in the business cycle
Stability of a rating grade's unconditional PD	Stable: Unconditional PDs of ratings grades do not change. Obligor's higher unconditional PDs during recession are accounted for by migrations to lower rating grades and vice versa	Pro-cyclical: PDs improve during expansions and deteriorate during recessions

Turning to the first point of investigation, we now list the most important consequences when developing a rating system on a TTC-PD benchmark:

- Pure macroeconomic risk factors that focus on business cycle information will explain only the (typically quite small) PIT-part of external ratings and will therefore tend to receive very low weights in statistical models.
- This effect should be less pronounced for "mixed factors" that contain both business cycle information and non-business cycle elements, for example balance sheet ratios or country ratings.

A bank that follows a PIT rating approach but has not yet finalised a fully-fledged PIT-adaptation of external ratings might therefore manually adjust regression results in order to attach higher weights to pure business-cycle risk factors. For

---

tions. It must, however, be stressed that in practice rating systems will neither be completely TTC or PIT but somewhere in between.

[20] This has for example been suggested by a survey of bank rating practices by the Basel Committee's Model Task Force (cf. BCBS, 2000).

banks that already want to implement a statistically founded PIT-adaptation of external ratings, the following approach could be considered:

- Estimation of a classic default prediction model, for example via logistic regression (see Chapter I), with external PDs and business cycle factors (on a regional, country or industry level) as risk factors
- The dependent variable is the company's default indicator as measured by the external ratings agencies' default definition (or, where available, the bank's own default definition). Accordingly, data from external rating agencies will be needed on a single obligor level while for TTC-PD estimation, aggregate obligor and default counts are sufficient.

When estimating such a model, the following challenges are pertinent:

- Different countries have different macroeconomic indicators that might not be comparable.
- Because estimating separate models for separate countries will not be feasible due to data restrictions, it will be important to use indicators that are approximately comparable across countries.
- To get a picture of the related effects, it might be sensible to start by building a model for the US (where data availability is high) and see how parameter estimates change when other countries are added. Probably separate regional models can help.

An alternative approach would be to use external point-in-time rating systems for the PIT-adaptation of through-the-cycle agency ratings. An example of a point-in-time external rating is Moody's KMV's EDF credit risk measure that builds on a Merton style causal default prediction model.[21] Analysis is then required as to whether it would not be better to skip the through-the-cycle agency ratings altogether and replace them with the external point-in-time ratings. In deciding on which approach to take, a bank must trade off the associated costs with the availability of the respective benchmarks.[22]

3. Sample Construction for the SRA Model

3.1. Introduction

Once external PDs have been calibrated, and all internal and external data required for the development of the SRA model have been compiled, it is necessary to construct samples from this data. As we will see, different samples will be needed for

---

[21] See http://www.moodyskmv.com/.
[22] For example, market-based measures such as Moody's KMV's EDF are only available for public companies.

different types of statistical analysis. In this section we mention these analysis techniques in order to map them to the corresponding samples. The techniques will be described in Section 4 and Section 5. In this section, the following issues will be dealt with:

- Which *types of samples* are needed?
- How can these samples be *constructed*?
- *Weighted observations:* If the information content of different observations differs significantly, it might be necessary to allow for this by attaching different weights to each observation.
- *Correlated observations:* We discuss the correlation structure that may result from the described sample construction technique and discuss the consequences.

It should be noted that some parts of the sample construction approach described in this section might be too time consuming for an initial development project. Nevertheless, it can serve as a benchmark for simpler methods of sample construction and could be gradually implemented during future refinements of the initial model.

3.2. Sample Types

The samples relevant for the development of SRA rating systems can be classified by the following dimensions:

- Samples for single (univariate) factor analysis (e.g. univariate discriminatory power, transformation of risk factors) vs. multi factor analysis samples (e.g. regression analysis, validation)
- Samples that include only externally rated obligor vs. samples that include externally and only internally rated obligors
- External data vs. internal data[23]
- Development vs. validation sample

We will start with the first dimension. Univariate analysis investigates the properties of each single risk factor separately. Therefore, for this type of analysis each change of the *one* analysed factor will generate a new observation in the data set; for the multi factor analysis, each change of *any* risk factor will produce a new observation. This can be taken into account by the following approach to sample construction:

1. Risk factors are divided in different categories. All factors for which changes are triggered by the same event are summarised into the same risk factor category.[24]

---

[23] External data are often employed for the development of SRA rating systems in order to increase the number of obligors and the number of points in time available for each obligor. See section 1 for more details.

2. The samples for the univariate risk factor analysis are constructed separately for each category. A complete series of time intervals is build that indicates which risk factor combination is valid for the category in each time interval or whether no observation was available in the interval. The time intervals are determined by the points in time where the risk factors of the category under consideration change. This is done separately for each obligor.
3. All single category samples from step 2 are merged into a new series of time intervals. Each interval in the series is defined as the largest interval for which the risk factors in each category remain constant. This is done separately for each obligor.

In the following table we give an example comprising two risk factor categories (balance sheet data and qualitative factors) and hence two different samples for univariate factor analysis. The table displays the observations for one single obligor:

Table 2. Stylised example for different samples and observations involved in rating development.

Sample	Trigger	ID	Valid from	Valid until
Balance sheet data	Accounts	1	Jan 03	Dec 03
		2	Jan 04	Dec 04
Qualitative factors	Internal rating	1	May 03	March 04
		2	April 04	Dec 04
Multi factor (merged)	Accounts	1	Jan 03	April 03
	Internal rating	2	May 03	Dec 03
	Accounts	3	Jan 04	March 04
	Internal rating	4	April 04	Dec 04

For each of the sample types described above, two sub-types will be needed, one that includes only externally rated obligors and one that contains all obligors. The first sub-type will be needed e.g. for discriminatory power analysis, the second e.g. for risk factor transformation or validation.

A third dimension is added when external as well as internal data are employed. Typically, for SRA models, external data will be used to estimate the quantitative model (comprising balance sheet factors as well as macroeconomic indicators) while the complete model, consisting of both, quantitative and qualitative risk factors will be calculated on the internal data set because qualitative risk factors are not available for the external data set.

---

[24] One category might for example include all balance sheet factors (triggered by the release of a company's accounts). Another category will be qualitative factors as assessed by the bank's loan manger. They are triggered by the internal rating event. A third category might be macroeconomic indicators.

A fourth dimension comes with the need to distinguish between development and validation samples. Moreover, validation should not only rely on the external PD but should also include default indicator information, i.e. the information whether a company has or has not defaulted within a specific period of time after its rating has been compiled.

When validating with respect to the default indicator, the need for the separation of development and validation samples is not so pressing since the benchmarks employed for development and validation are different. Due to the typical scarcity of internal default data (the rationale for the SRA approach), it is sensible to perform this type of validation on the complete internal data set.

However, when validating with respect to external PDs, a separation between development and validation sample is desirable. If the quantitative model has been developed on external data, the internal data set should typically be an appropriate validation sample.[25] For the validation of the complete model, – depending on the number of observations available relative to the number of risk factors, the following options can be considered:

- Constructing two completely different samples (preferably out-of-time[26])
- Developing on the complete internal sample and validating on a subset of this sample, e.g. the most recent observations for each obligor or some randomly drawn sub-sample
- Application of bootstrap methods[27]

Summarising the issues raised in this section, the following table gives a simple example of the different samples involved in SRA rating development and the types of statistical analysis performed on these samples. For simplicity, our example comprises only two input categories of which only one (balance sheet data) is available for the external and the internal data set and the other (qualitative factors) is only available for the internal data set:

---

[25] Note that the external sample will typically also include some or almost all internal obligors. To construct two completely different sets, internal obligors would have to be excluded from the external data. However, if the external data set is much larger than the internal data set, such exclusion might not be judged necessary.

[26] "Out-of-time" means that development and validation are based on disjoint time intervals.

[27] For an application of bootstrap methods in the context of rating validation see Appasamy et al. (2004). A good introduction to and overview over bootstrap methods can be found in Davison and Hinkley (1997).

Table 3. Stylised example for the different samples and corresponding types of analysis that are needed for the development of SRA type rating systems

ID[28]	Input catego-ries	Sample type[29]			Type of analysis
E1	Balance sheet data	SC	EX	DEV	Representativeness, Fillers for missing values, Univariate discriminatory power, Estimation of the quantitative multi factor model[30]
I1a	Balance sheet data	SC	ALL	DEV	Representativeness, Truncation and standardisation of risk factors, Fillers for missing values
I1b			EX	VAL-E / DEV	Univariate discriminatory power, Validation of the quantitative multi factor model developed on sample E1
I2a	Qualitative factors	SC	ALL	DEV	Standardisation of risk factors, Fillers for missing values
I2b			EX		Score calculation, Univariate discriminatory power
I3a	Balance sheet data and qualitative	M	EX		Risk factor correlations / multicollinearity, Estimation of the complete multi factor model (quantitative and qualitative)
I3b	factors		ALL	DEV / VAL-D	Risk factor correlations / multicollinearity, default indicator validation of the complete multi factor model developed on sample I3a
I4			EX	VAL-E	Separate validation sample, for example most recent observations for all obligors from sample I3a or a randomly drawn sub-sample

3.3. External PDs and Default Indicator

For those samples consisting only of externally rated obligors (EX) and for those samples that are employed for validation on the default indicator (VAL-D), an external PD or the default indicator have to be attached to each line of input vari-

---

[28] E denotes external and I denotes internal data.

[29] We write SC for single-category samples and M for merged samples. ALL and EX are standing for "all obligors" and "only externally rated obligors" respectively. DEV denotes development sample, VAL-E and VAL-D denote validation samples where validation is performed on external PDs and on the default indicator respectively.

[30] Note that in this case it is not necessary to merge different single-factor samples in order to perform the multi-factor analysis, because only one input-category exists. Moreover, a separate validation sample for the external data is not necessary since validation is performed on the internal data set.

ables respectively. At least two different approaches to achieve this can be considered:

1. External PDs / the default indicator are treated as yet another risk factor category, i.e. a series of time intervals is constructed for each external rating agency / for the default indicator indicating the time spans for which a specific external rating / default indicator realisation had been valid. These intervals are then merged with the relevant single factor or merged factor samples in the same way as single factor samples are merged with each other.[31] If there are competing PDs from different external agencies at the same time, an aggregation rule will be applied. We will discuss this rule in the second part of this section.
2. For each risk factor time interval, a weighted average is determined for each external agency PD and for the default indicator respectively. The weights are chosen proportionally to the length of the time interval for which the external rating / the default indicator has been valid. As under 1), an aggregation rule is applied to translate the PDs of different external agencies into one single external PD.

For the default indicator the first approach seems to be more adequate, since with the second approach the 0/1 indicator variable would be transformed into a continuous variable on the interval [0,1] and many important analytical tools (e.g. the ROC curve) would not be directly applicable.

This argument, obviously does not apply to the external PDs since they are already measured on the interval [0,1]. Moreover, external PDs tend to change more frequently than the default indicator and hence the number of observations would increase markedly compared to the corresponding risk factor samples. Additionally, the PDs of not only one but three different rating agencies would have to be merged, further increasing the number of observations. Since the information content of different observations belonging to the same risk factor combination will tend to differ only slightly, such a procedure will produce many highly correlated observations which is not desirable (see Section 3.5). Consequently the second approach appears to be more adequate for external PDs.

As mentioned above, an aggregation rule has to be devised for cases where more than one external rating is valid at some point in time. The most straightforward choice will be weighted averages of the different external PDs with a preferential treatment of those rating agencies that are assessed to be most suitable for SRA development (see Section 2.2).

---

[31] Note that the time intervals of input factors and default indicator are shifted against each other by the length of the time horizon for which the rating system is developed. For example, if the horizon is one year and the default indicator is equal to zero from Jan 2003 to Dec 2004 then this value will be mapped to the risk-factor interval from Jan 2002 to Dec 2003.

3.4. Weighting Observations

The information content of a single observation in the different samples depends on the length of the time interval it is associated with. If, for example, a particular balance sheet B is valid from Jan 04 to Dec 04 and we observe two corresponding sets of qualitative factors, Q1 (valid until Feb 04) followed by Q2 (valid from Feb 04 until Dec 04) we would obviously like to put a much higher weight on the observation (B, Q2) than on (B, Q1).

The most straightforward way is to choose weights that are proportional to the length of the time interval associated with a specific observation. In this context, the following issues are of particular interest:

- *Stochastic interpretation of weighted observations:* The weight attached is a measure for the size of the error term associated with each observation, i.e. its standard deviation: the lower the weight, the higher the standard deviation.
- *Practical implementation:* Most statistics software packages include options to perform statistical computations with weighted observations. This usually applies for all techniques mentioned in this article.

3.5. Correlated Observations

Correlated observations (or, more precisely, correlated error terms) are a general problem in single and multi factor analysis. Basic techniques assume independence. Using these techniques with correlated observations will affect the validity of statistical tests and confidence intervals, probably also reducing the efficiency of estimators. To resolve this problem, information about the structure of the correlations is necessary. In this article, the correlation issue will be dealt with in two steps:

1. In this section we will address the specific correlations structure that may arise from the method of sample construction described above
2. In Section 5.3 we will analyse the statistical techniques that can be used to address this or other correlation structures in the context of multi factor analysis.

When constructing samples according to the method described above, the degree of correlation in the data will rise when the time intervals associated with each observation become smaller. It will also depend on the frequency and intensity of changes in the risk factor and the external rating information employed. It is worth noting that the resulting type of correlation structure can be best described within a *panel data* setting where the correlations within the time series observations for each single obligor will be different to the cross-sectional correlation between two obligors. Cross-sectional correlations in SRA development may result from country or industry sector dependencies. Time series correlations will typically be due to the fact that there are structural similarities in the relationship between a single company's risk factors and its external rating over time. Since models for cross-sectional correlations are widely applied in credit portfolio models[32], we will focus on time series correlations in this article.

In what follows we propose some options for dealing with correlations in the time series parts. The options are listed in order of rising complexity:

- For simplicity, basic statistical techniques are employed that do not account for correlated error terms. With this option, as much correlation as possible can be eliminated by dropping observations with small weights. If all observations have approximately the same weight, a sub-sample can be drawn. Here, the appropriate balance has to be found between losing too much information in the sample and retaining a degree of correlation that still appears to be compatible with not modelling these correlations explicitly. In any case, the remaining correlation in the data should be measured and the modeller should be aware of the resulting consequences, in particular with respect to confidence intervals (they will tend to be too narrow) and with respect to statistical tests (they will tend to be too conservative, rejecting the null too often).
- Simple models of autocorrelation in the time series data are employed, the most obvious being a first order autoregressive process (AR1) for the time series error terms. Of course, higher order AR processes or more complex correlation models might also be considered appropriate.[33]
- A continuous time model for the relation between risk factors and external ratings is built (e.g. Brownian motion or Poison process type models) and the resulting correlation structure of the discrete observations' error terms is derived from this model. This of course is the most complex option and will most probably be seen as too time consuming to be applied by most practitioners. It might, however, be a road for academic researchers that in turn could make the method available for practitioners in the future.

4. Univariate Risk Factor Analysis

4.1. Introduction

Before building a multi factor model, each risk factor has to be analysed separately in order to determine whether and in which form it should enter the multi factor model. This type of analysis is referred to as univariate risk factor analysis. The following issues should be dealt with in this context:

- Measurement of a risk factor's *univariate discriminatory power*

---

[32] See Erlenmaier (2001).

[33] For an introduction to such models and further references see Greene (2003).

- *Transformation of risk factors* to a) improve their linear correlation – as assumed by the multi factor regression model – with the log external PD[34] or b) to make different risk factors comparable with each other
- Checking whether the samples on which the rating system is developed are *representative* for the samples to which the rating system will be applied (development vs. "target" sample)
- Treatment of *missing values*

Each of these issues will be dealt with separately in the following sections.

4.2. Discriminatory Power

A rating system is defined as having a high discriminatory power if good rating grades have a comparatively low share of obligors that will default later on and vice versa. Accordingly, its discriminatory power will deteriorate with an increase in the relative share of later on defaulted obligors in good rating grades. There are several statistical measures for this important attribute of a rating system, the Gini coefficient being the most popular.[35]

Due to the lack of a sufficient number of default observations in SRA models, these types of discriminatory power measurement will usually only be applied as an additional validation measure. In the development stage, discriminatory power will be defined in terms of the usefulness of the rating system or – in the context of univariate factor analysis – a single risk factor in predicting an obligor's external PD: The better a rating system or a risk factor can be used to predict an obligor's external PD, the higher its discriminator power for the SRA approach.[36]

The following techniques can be helpful to measure a risk factor's discriminatory power for the SRA approach:

- Linear and rank-order correlations of the risk factors with the log external PD[37]
- Bucket plots

---

[34] See Section 5.2. Throughout this article we will use the term "log external PD" to denote the natural logarithm of the PD of an obligor's external rating grade. How PDs are derived for each external rating grade has been described in Section 2.

[35] For an overview on measures of discriminatory power see Deutsche Bundesbank (2003) or Chapter XII

[36] A good discriminatory power of the internal rating system in terms of predicting external ratings and a good discriminatory power of the external ratings in terms of predicting future defaults will then establish a good discriminatory power of the internal rating system in terms of predicting future defaults.

[37] Linear correlations are typically termed Pearson correlations while rank-order correlations are associated with Spearman. Linear correlations are important since they measure the degree of linear relationship which corresponds with the linear model employed for the multi-factor analysis. Rank-order correlations can be compared with linear correlations in order to identify potential scope for risk factor transformation.

While the correlation measures are straightforward, the bucket plots require further comment. The underlying rationale for applying bucket plots is to visualise the complete functional form of the relationship between the risk factor and the external PD – in contrast to the correlation measures that aggregate this information into a single number. This is done to make sure that the risk factors indeed display an approximately linear relationship with external PDs as is required by the multi factor model. Bucket plots for continuous risk factors can for example be constructed in the following way:

- Each risk factor range was divided into *n* separate *buckets*, where we chose the 0, 1/*n*, 2/*n*, ..., (*n*-1)/*n*, 1 quantiles of each risk factor's distribution as interval boarders.
- For each bucket we calculated the average associated external PD. By constructing the bucket boarders using quantiles it can be made sure that each interval contains the same number of observations.
- The number *n* of intervals has to be chosen with regard to the overall number of PD observations available for each risk factor: with increasing *n* it will be possible to observe the functional form of the relationship on an ever finer scale. However, the precision of the associated PD estimates for each bucket will decrease and their volatility will increase.
- In order to quantify the degree of uncertainty, confidence intervals for the PD estimates of each bucket can be calculated.
- The resulting PD estimates and confidence intervals are then plotted against the mean risk factor value of each bucket. If a logarithmic scale is used for the PD axis, an approximately linear relationship should result when the risk factor has been appropriately transformed. Figure 1 shows an example of a bucket plot for a continuous risk factor.

Bucket plots for discrete risk factors can be devised according to the same method as described above with only one difference: for discrete factors, each realisation should represent one bucket irrespective of the number of observations available.

4.3. Transformation

The following types of transformation typical for the development of rating models will be considered in this section:

- Truncation
- Other non-linear transformations of continuous risk factors (e.g. taking a risk factor's logarithm)
- Attaching a score to discrete risk factors
- Standardisation, i.e. a linear transformation in order to achieve the same mean and standard deviation for each risk factor

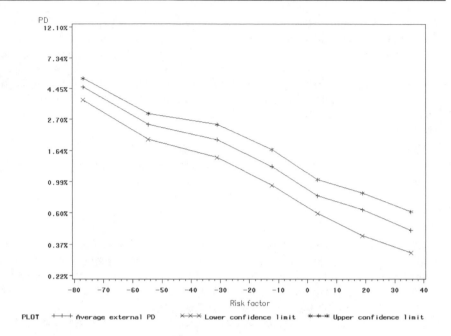

Fig. 1. Example of a bucket plot. It illustrates the functional relationship between a risk factor and corresponding external PDs where the latter are measured on a logarithmic scale. The relationship on this scale should be approximately linear.

We will discuss each of these types of transformations in turn. Truncation means that continuous risk factors will be cut off at some point on the left and right, more precisely,

$$x_{trunc} = \min\{x_u, \max\{x_l, x\}\}$$

where x_u is the upper and x_l the lower border at which the risk factor x is truncated. Note that the truncation function described above can be smoothed by applying a logit-type transformation instead. Truncation is done mainly for the following reasons:

- To reduce the impact of outliers and to concentrate the analysis on a risk factor's typical range[38]
- To reduce a risk factor to the range on which it has discriminatory power

Other types of non-linear transformations are typically applied to continuous risk factors to achieve an approximately linear relationship with the log external PD.

---

[38] This is often necessary for sensible visualization of the risk factor's distribution.

An overview of methods to achieve linearity can be found in Chapter II. These methods will therefore not be discussed here.

In contrast to continuous risk factors, discrete factors (such as qualitative information about the obligor, e.g. its quality of management or competitive position) do not have an a priori metric interpretation. Therefore, a score has to be attached to each of the discrete risk factor's potential realisations (e.g., excellent, good, medium or poor quality management). As with the non-linear transformation for the continuous risk factors, the scores have to be chosen in such a way as to achieve the linear relationship of risk factors with log PDs. This can typically be achieved by calculating the mean external PD for each risk factor realisation and then applying the logarithm to arrive at the final score.

However, the resulting scores will not always be monotonic in the underlying risk factor (i.e. the average PD may not always decrease when the assessment with respect to this risk factor improves). In such cases it has to be decided whether the effect is within statistical confidence levels or indeed indicates a problem with the underlying risk factor. If the first holds true (typically for risk factor realisations where only very few observations are available), interpolation techniques can be applied augmented by expert judgements. In the second case, depending on the severity of the effects identified, it may be necessary a) to analyse the reasons for this effect, or b) to merge different realisations of the risk factor to a single score, or c) to eliminate the risk factor from subsequent analysis.

All transformations that have been described up to now have been performed in order to improve the risk factor's linear correlation with log external PDs. The remaining transformation (*standardisation*) has a linear functional form and will therefore not alter linear correlations. It is performed in order to unify the different risk factor's scales and, accordingly, improve their comparability, primarily in the following two respects:
- How good or bad is a risk factor realisation compared with the portfolio average?
- Interpretability of the coefficients resulting from the linear regression as weights for the influence of one particular risk factor on the rating result

Typically, the risk factors are standardised to the same mean and standard deviation. This transformation only makes sure that the risk factors are comparable with respect to the *first and second moment* of the distribution. Perfect comparability will only be achieved when *all moments* of the standardised risk factor's distribution will be roughly the same, i.e. if they follow a similar probability distribution. This will typically not be the case, in particular since there are risk factors with continuous and discrete distributions respectively. However, some degree of overall distributional similarity should be achieved by the need to establish an approximately linear relationship between each risk factor and the log external PD. Moreover, we will comment on the rationale of and the potential problems with the interpretation of regression estimates as weights of influence in Section 5.4 where we deal with multi factor analysis.

4.4. Representativeness

Representativeness, while important for other types of rating systems, should be treated with particular care when developing SRA rating systems.[39] The following two types of comparisons are of specific interest:

- Comparison of the internal samples types IE (including *only externally rated obligors*) and IA (comprising *all internal obligors*) with each other. This comparison is necessary since SRA rating systems are developed on samples that include only externally rated obligors but are also applied to obligors without external ratings.
- Comparison of the external data set (E) with the internal data set IA. This comparison arises from the need to increase the available number of observations for rating development by including external data.

Representativeness can be analysed by comparing the distribution of the risk factors and some other key factors (such as countries/regions, industry sectors, company type, obligor size, etc.) on each sample. In this context frequency plots (for continuous factors, see Figure 2) and tables ordered by the frequency of each realisation (for discrete factors) can be particularly useful.

These tools can be supplemented with basic descriptive statistics (e.g. difference of the medians of both samples relative to their standard deviation or the ratio of the standard deviations on both samples). Formal statistical tests on the identity of distributions across samples were not found to be useful since the question is not whether distributions are identical (typically they are not) but whether they are sufficiently similar for the extrapolation of results and estimates derived on one sample to the other sample.

---

[39] An SRA-rating system will always face the problem that – due to the relative rareness of default data – it is difficult to validate it for obligors that are not externally rated. While some validation techniques are available (see Section 5.8), showing that the data for externally rated obligors is comparable with that of non-externally rated obligors will be one of the major steps to make sure that the derived rating system will not only perform well for the former but also for the latter.

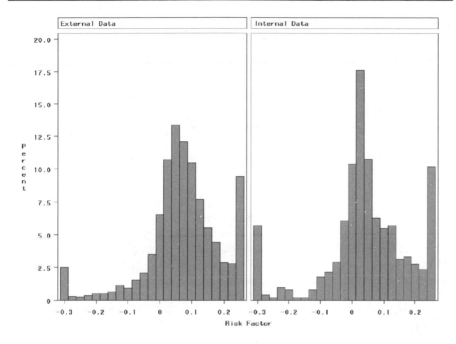

Fig. 2. Example for a frequency plot that compares a risk factor's distribution on the external data set with its distribution on the internal data set.

What can be done when data is found to be unrepresentative?

- First, it has to be ascertained whether the problem occurs only for a few risk factors / key figures or for the majority.
- In the first case, the reasons for the differences have to be analysed and the development samples adjusted accordingly. One reason, for example, might be that the distribution of obligors across regions or industry sectors is extremely different. The development sample can then be adjusted by reducing the amount of obligors in those regions / industry sectors that are over-represented in the development sample.
- In the second case, a variety of approaches can be considered, depending on the specific situation. Examples include:
  - The range of the risk factors can be reduced so that it only includes areas that are observable on both the development and the target sample.
  - The weight of a risk factor found to be insufficiently representative can be reduced manually or it can be excluded from the analysis.

4.5. Missing Values

A missing value analysis typically includes the following steps:

- Decision as to whether a risk factor will be classified as missing for a particular observation
- Calculation of fillers for missing values / exclusion of observations with missing values

While for some risk factors such as qualitative assessments (e.g. management quality), the first issue can be decided immediately, it is not always that clear-cut for quantitative risk factors such as balance sheet ratios that may be calculated from a number of different single positions. Typical examples are balance sheet ratios that include a company's cashflow that in turn is the sum of various single balance sheet items.

The problem – typically arising on the external data set – is that for a large proportion of observations at least one of these items will be missing. Hence, in a first step the relative sizes of the balance sheet items have to be compared with each other and based on this comparison, rules must be devised as to which combination of missing values will trigger the overall position to be classified as missing: if components with a large absolute size are missing, the risk factors should be set to missing; if not, the aggregate position can be calculated by either omitting the missing items or using fillers which, however, should be chosen *conditional* on the size of the largest components.

We now come back to the second issue raised at the beginning of this section, i.e. the calculation of fillers for missing values on the risk factor level. It is, of course, related to the issue of calculating fillers on the component level. However, the need to employ conditional estimates is not so severe. Typically, there will be quite a lot of risk factors that are correlated with each other. Hence, making estimates for missing values of one risk factor conditional on *other* risk factors should produce more accurate fillers. However, it will also be time consuming. Therefore, in practice, only some very simple bits of information will typically be used for conditioning, e.g. the portfolio to which an obligor belongs (external or internal data set).

Moreover, different quantiles of the distribution might be employed for the calculation of fillers on the external and internal data set respectively. For the external sample, a missing value may not constitute a significant negative signal in itself. For the internal sample, on the other hand, missing values usually are negative signals, since a company could be expected to provide to the bank the information it needs to complete its internal rating assessment. Therefore, missing values on the internal sample will typically be substituted by more conservative quantiles than missing values on the external data set.

Finally, depending on the relative frequency of missing values in the sample, it might be necessary to exclude some observations with missing values to avoid biases in statistical estimates.

4.6. Summary

Concluding this section we want to summarise the techniques that we have presented for univariate risk factor analysis and map them to the samples on which they should be performed. Since we have already dealt with the sample issue in Section 3, here we will focus on those two sample dimensions that we think are most important for univariate factor analysis, i.e. externally rated obligors vs. all obligors and external vs. internal data set. As in Section 4.4 we use the following shortcuts for these sample types:

- E: External data set, only externally rated obligors,
- IE: Internal data set, only externally rated obligors.
- IA: Internal data set, all obligors,

The univariate analysis techniques and corresponding sample types are summarised in Table 4.

Table 4. Univariate analysis techniques and corresponding sample types

Type of univariate analysis	Sample type	Description
Factor transformation	IE,IA[40]	a) Truncation b) other non-linear transformations of continuous risk factors (e.g. taking a risk factor's logarithm) c) calculating scores for discrete risk factors d) standardisation: linear transformation in order to achieve the same median (mean) and standard deviation for all risk factors
Discriminatory power	E,IE	a) Correlation (rank order and linear) with external PD b) Bucket plots
Representativeness	IE,IA E,IA	a) Comparison of internal samples with each other (IE and IA) b) Comparison of external sample (E) with internal sample (IA)
Missing values	E,IA	Fillers for missing values in the external and internal samples respectively

---

[40] IE is only needed to derive the scores for the qualitative risk factors. All other types of analysis are performed on IA.

5. Multi-factor Model and Validation

5.1. Introduction

Once the univariate analysis described in Section 4 has been completed, the multi-factor model has to be estimated and the estimation results communicated, adjusted (if necessary), and validated. These issues will be dealt with in Section 5 in this order:

- *Model selection:* which type of model is chosen and which risk factors will enter the model?
- *Model assumptions:* Statistical models typically come with quite a few modelling assumptions that guarantee that estimation results are efficient and valid. Therefore, it has to be analysed whether the most important assumptions of the selected model are valid for the data and if not, how any violations of modelling assumptions can be dealt with.
- *Measuring the influence of risk factors:* We will discuss how the relative influence of single risk factors on the rating result can be expressed in terms of weights to facilitate the interpretation of the estimated model. In a second step, we comment on the problems associated with the calculation and interpretation of these weights.
- *Manual adjustments and calibration:* We discuss the rationale and the most important issues that must be dealt with when model estimates are adjusted manually and describe how the resulting model can be calibrated.
- *Two-step regression:* It is briefly noted that with external data the regression model will typically have to be estimated in two steps.
- *Corporate groups and government support:* We propose a simple method to produce an empirical estimate for the optimal absolute influence of supporters on an obligor's rating.
- *Validation:* We briefly itemise the validation measures that we found most useful for a short-cut validation in the context of rating development.

5.2. Model Selection

The issue of model selection primarily has two dimensions. First, the model type has to be chosen and then it has to be decided which risk factors will be included in the model. Regarding the first question the most simple and most frequently used model in multi factor analysis is *linear regression*. A typical linear regression models for SRA type rating systems will have the following form:[41]

---

[41] Throughout this article Log denotes the natural logarithm with base e.

$$\text{Log}(PD_i) = b_0 + b_1 x_{i1} + \ldots + b_m x_{im} + \varepsilon_i \quad (i = 1, \ldots, n), \tag{3}$$

where PD_i denotes the external PD, x_{ij} the value of risk factor j, ε_i the regression model's error term for observation i, and $b_0, \ldots, b_m$ are the regression coefficients that must be estimated from the data. Note that each observation i describes a specific firm over a specific time span.

Risk factors are regressed on log PDs because on the one hand, this scale is typically most compatible with the linear relationship assumed by the regression model and on the other hand, because internal master scales that translate PDs into rating grades, are often logarithmic in PDs.

We now turn to the second issue in this section, the selection of those risk factors that will constitute the final regression model employed for the rating system. The following types of analysis are useful for risk factor selection:

- Univariate discriminatory power (on internal and external data set)
- Representativeness
- Correlations / multicollinearity between risk factors
- Formal model selection tools

We have already dealt with the issues of discriminatory power and representativeness in Section 4. For correlations between risk factors and multicollinearity we refer the reader to Chapter II. In this section we will add some comments on typical formal model selection tools in the context of linear regression:

- Formal model selection tools are no substitute for a careful single factor and correlation analysis.
- There are quite a variety of formal model selection methods.[42] We found the R^2 maximisation method that finds the model with the best R^2 for each given number of risk factors particularly useful for the following reasons:
  - It allows to trade off the reduction in multicollinearity against the associated loss in the model's R^2 on the development sample.
  - The R^2 measure is consistent with the linear correlation measure employed in the single factor analysis.[43]

5.3. Model Assumptions

Three crucial stochastic assumptions about the error terms ε constitute the basis of linear regression models:[44]

---

[42] For reviews on formal model-selection methods see Hocking (1976) or Judge et al. (1980).

[43] R^2 is the square of the linear correlation between the dependent variable (the log external PD) and the model prediction for this variable.

[44] For a comprehensive overview on applied linear regression see Greene (2003).

- Normal distribution (of error terms)
- Independence (of all error terms from each other)
- Homoscedasticity (all error terms have the same standard deviation)

For all three issues there are a variety of statistical tests (e.g. Greene, 2003). If these tests reject the above hypotheses, it is up to the modeller to decide on the severity of these effects, i.e. whether they can be accepted from a practical point of view or not.

As for normality, looking at distribution plots of the residuals[45] we found that they often came very close to a normal distribution even in cases where statistical tests reject this hypothesis. Moreover, even under the violation of the normality assumption, estimators are still efficient (or, more precisely, BLUE).[46] Only the related statistical tests and confidence intervals are no longer valid. But even here convergence is achieved for large sample size.

Violations of the two other assumptions (independence and homoscedasticity) tend to be more severe. They can be summarised as deviations from the regression model's error term covariance matrix which is assumed to have identical values for each entry of the diagonal (homoscedasticity) and zeros for each entry that is not on the diagonal (independence).

If statistical tests reject the hypotheses of independence / homoscedasticity, this problem can be dealt with when a) plausible assumptions about the structure of the covariance matrix can be made and b) when this structure can be described with a sufficiently small set of parameters. If this is the case these parameters and hence the covariance matrix can be estimated from the data (or, more precisely, from the residuals). The least square method employed for parameter estimation in the regression model can then be adjusted in such a way that the original desirable properties of the ordinary least square estimators (OLS) can be restored. In the literature (e.g. Greene 2003) this method is referred to as generalised least square (GLS).

In order to proceed, hypotheses on the structure of the covariance matrix have to be derived. In Section 3 dealing with sample construction, we have already described one possible source of heteroscedasticity[47] and correlation in the data respectively.

---

[45] Residuals (e) are the typical estimators for the (unobservable) theoretical error terms (ε). They are defined as the difference between the dependent variable and the model predictions of this variable.

[46] BLUE stands for best linear unbiased estimator.

[47] The term heteroscedasticity refers to cases where standard deviations of error terms are different as opposed to the assumption of identical standard deviations (homoscedasticity).

We argued that the size (i.e. the standard deviation) of the error term might sensibly be assumed to be proportional to the length of the time interval to which the observation is attached. Hence, we proposed to weight each observation with the length of the corresponding time interval. In the context of regression analysis, weighting observations exactly means to assume a specific type of heteroscedastic covariance matrix and application of the corresponding GLS estimation.

We also concluded that autocorrelation in the time series part of the data might well increase when time intervals become smaller and smaller. One of the simplest and most commonly employed structures for correlated error terms assumes an AR(1) correlation structure between subsequent error terms:

$$\varepsilon_t = \rho\varepsilon_{t-1} + u_t \quad (t = 1,\ldots,T), \tag{4}$$

where the variables u_t are independent of each other. Hence, the issue could be dealt with by estimating the parameter ρ from the data, deriving the correlation matrix and applying GLS.[48] There is, however, one crucial problem with this procedure: it is not logical to assume this correlation structure for the complete data set as would be done in a standard time series regression setting. Rather, the rating development data set at hand will typically have a *panel data* structure where the correlation structure of the cross section's error terms (different obligors) will most likely be different from the correlation structure of the time series part (different points in time for the same obligor). Applying a panel data model with an AR(1) structure in the time series part could be a sensible first approximation. Corresponding error term models offered by statistics software packages are often of the type

$$\varepsilon_{it} = \rho_i\varepsilon_{i,t-1} + u_{it} \quad (t = 1,\ldots,T; i = 1,\ldots,n). \tag{5}$$

Note that the AR parameter ρ is estimated separately for each cross section (i.e. firm): $\rho = \rho_i$. Therefore, quite a few time series observations are required for each single obligor to make confident estimates, which often will not be feasible for rating development data. A more practicable model would estimate an average AR parameter ρ for all obligors:

$$\varepsilon_{it} = \rho\varepsilon_{i,t-1} + u_{it} \quad (t = 1,\ldots,T; i = 1,\ldots,n). \tag{6}$$

There might be other sources of correlation or heteroscedasticity in the data requiring a different structure for the covariance matrix than the one described above. If no specific reasons can be thought of from a theoretical point of view, one will usually look at residual plots to identify some patterns. Typically, residuals will be plotted a) against the independent variable (log PD in our case), b)

---

[48] Indeed, a standard procedure for dealing with autocorrelated error terms in the way described above is implemented in most statistical software packages.

against those dependent variables (risk factors) with the highest weights or c) against some other structural variable, such as the length of the time interval associated with each observation. If effects can be identified, first a parametrical model has to be devised and then the associated parameters can be estimated from the residuals. That will give a rough picture of the severity of the effects and can hence provide the basis for the decision as to whether to assess the deviations from the model assumptions as acceptable or whether to incorporate these effects into the model – either by weighting observation (in the case of heteroscedasticity) or by devising a specific correlation model (in the case of deviations from independence).

5.4. Measuring Influence

Once a specific regression model has been chosen and estimated, one of the most important aspects of the model for practitioners will be each risk factor's influence on an obligor's rating. Hence, a measure of influence has to be chosen that can also be used for potential manual adjustments of the derived model.

To our knowledge, the most widely applied method is to adjust for the typically different scales on which the risk factors are measured by multiplying the estimator for the risk factor's coefficient in the regression model by the risk factor's standard deviation and then deriving weights by mapping these adjusted coefficients to the interval [0,1] so that the absolute values of all coefficients add up to 1.[49]

What is the interpretation of this approach to the calculation of weights? It defines the weight of a risk factor x_j by the degree to which the log PD predicted by the regression model will fluctuate when all other risk factors $(x_k)_{k \neq j}$ are kept constant: the more log PD fluctuates, the higher the risk factor's influence. As a measure for the degree of fluctuation, the predictor's standard deviation is used. Hence, the weight w_j of a risk factor x_j with coefficient b_j can be calculated as

$$w_j = \frac{w_j^*}{\left|w_1^*\right| + \ldots + \left|w_m^*\right|},$$

(7)

where

$$w_j^* = \text{STD}\left\{\text{Log}(PD) \big| (x_k)_{k \neq j}\right\} = \text{STD}(b_j \, x_j) = b_j \, \text{STD}(x_j),$$

(8)

---

[49] Note that this method is also suggested by standard regression outputs. The associated estimates are typically termed "standardized coefficients". Moreover, if the risk factors have already been standardized to a common standard deviation – as described in section 4 – they already have the same scale and coefficients only have to be mapped to [0,1] in order to add up to 1.

and STD denotes the standard deviation operator.

However, when using this type of influence measure, the following aspects have to be taken into account:

- The standard deviation should be calculated on the internal data set containing all obligors, not only the externally rated obligors.
- The master rating scale will typically be logarithmic in PDs. Therefore, measuring the risk factor's influence on predicted log PDs is approximately equivalent to measuring its influence on the obligor's rating. This should usually be what practitioners are interested in. However, if the influence on an obligor's predicted PD is to be measured, the above logic will not apply anymore since predicted PDs are an exponential function of the risk factor and hence their standard deviation cannot be factored in the same fashion as described above. Moreover, the standard deviation of the external PD will depend on the realisations of the other risk factors $(x_k)_{k \neq j}$ that are kept constant.
- The problems described in the previous point also arise for the log-PD influence when risk factors are transformed in a non-linear fashion, e.g. when a risk factor's logarithm is taken. In this case, the above interpretation of influence can only be applied to the transformed risk factors which usually have no sensible economic interpretation.
- Also, the above mentioned interpretation does not take into account the risk factor's correlation structure. The correlation between risk factors is usually not negligible. In this case the conditional distribution (in particular, the conditional standard deviation) of the log-PD predictor, given that the other risk factors are constant, will depend on the particular values at which the other risk factors are kept constant.
- Making the risk factor's distributions comparable only by adjusting for their standard deviation might be a crude measure if their distributional forms differ a lot (e.g. continuous vs. discrete risk factors).[50]
- The weights described above measure a risk factor's average influence over the sample. While this may be suitable in the model development stage when deciding, e.g., about whether the resulting weights are appropriate, it may not be appropriate for practitioners interested in the influence that the risk factors have for a specific obligor. Other tools can be applied here, e.g. plotting how a change in one risk factor over a specified range will affect an obligor's rating.

Despite the above cited theoretical problems standard deviation based measures of influence have proved to work quite well in practice. However, there appears to be some scope for further research on alternative measures of influence. Moreover, it should be noted that, when correlations between risk factors are non-negligible, a risk factor's correlation with predicted log PDs can be quite high, even if the

---

[50] Additionally, the standard deviation tends to be a very unstable statistical measure that can be very sensitive to changes in the risk factor's distribution. However, this problem should be reduced significantly by the truncation of the risk factors which reduces the influence of outliers.

weight as defined above is not. We therefore found it important for the interpretation of the derived regression model, to evaluate these correlations for all risk factors and report them together with the weights.

5.5. Manual Adjustments and Calibration

There may be quite a variety of rationales for manually adjusting the estimation results derived from the statistical model, for instance, expert judgements that deviate significantly from those estimations, insufficient empirical basis for specific portfolio segments, insufficient representativeness of the development sample, or excessively high weights of qualitative as opposed to quantitative risk factors.[51] When manual adjustments are made, the following subsequent analyses are important:

1. Ensuring that the ratings system's discriminatory power is not reduced too much
2. Re-establishing the calibration that statistical models provide automatically in the SRA context

Regarding the first issue, the standard validation measures – as briefly described in Section 5.8 – will be applied. The second issue can be addressed by regressing the score resulting from the manually adjusted weights $\omega_1,..,\omega_n$ against log PDs:

$$\text{Log}(PD_i) = c_0 + c_1[\omega_1 x_{i1} + ... + \omega_m x_{im}] + \varepsilon_t \quad (i = 1,...n). \qquad (9)$$

Note that c_0 and c_1 are the coefficients that must be estimated in this second regression. The parameter c_0 is related to the average PD in the portfolio while c_1 controls the rating system's implicit discriminatory power, i.e. the degree to which predicted PDs vary across the obligors in the portfolio.[52]

The estimates for c_0 and c_1 will give additional evidence for the degree to which the manual adjustments have changed the rating system's overall properties: If changes are not too big, then c_0 should not differ much from b_0 and c_1 should be close to $b_\Sigma = [| b_1 | + ... + | b_m |]$ if all risk factors have been standardised to the same standard deviation.[53]

---

[51] With the SRA approach to rating development, there is the problem that the loan manager may use qualitative risk factors in order to make internal and external ratings match. If that is the case, the relative weight of qualitative factors as estimated by the statistical model will typically be too high compared to the weights of quantitative risk factors. The validation measures that are not linked to external ratings (see Section 5.8) and also expert judgement may then help to readjust those weights appropriately.

[52] More formally, the implicit discriminatory power is defined as the expected value of the (explicit) discriminatory power – as measured by the Gini coefficient (cf. Chapter XII).

[53] This can be derived from equations (7) and (8).

Finally, for each observation i, a PD estimate can be derived from the above regression results by the following formulas:

$$E[PD_i \mid X_i] = \exp(\mu_i + \sigma_i^2 / 2) \quad (i = 1,...,n), \text{ where} \tag{10a}$$

$$\mu_i = E[\log(PD_i) \mid X_i] = c_0 + c_1[\omega_1 x_{i1} + ... + \omega_m x_{im}] \quad \text{and} \tag{10b}$$

$$\sigma_i^2 = \text{Var}(\varepsilon_i). \tag{10c}$$

Note that X_i denotes the vector of all risk factor realisations for observation i and $E[.]$ is the expectation operator. The result is derived from the formula for the mean of log-normally distributed random variables.[54] For the formula to be valid, the error terms ε_i have to be approximately normally distributed which we found typically to be the case (see Section 5.3). Moreover, the most straightforward way to estimate σ_i from the residuals would be to assume homoscedasticity, i.e. $\sigma_i = \sigma$ $(i=1,...,n)$. If homoscedasticity cannot be achieved, the estimates for σ_i will have to be conditional on the structural variables that describe the sources of heteroscedasticity.

5.6. Two-step Regression

In this section we note that – when external data are employed – it will typically be necessary to estimate *two* models and, therefore, go through the process described in the previous sections twice. If, for example, only balance sheet ratios and macroeconomic risk factors are available for the external data set, then a first quantitative model will have to be estimated on the external data set. As a result, a quantitative score and corresponding PD can be calculated from this model that in turn can be used as an input factor for the final model. The final model will then include the quantitative score as one aggregated independent variable and the qualitative risk factors (not available for the external data set) as the other independent variables.

5.7. Corporate Groups and Sovereign Support

When rating a company, it is very important to take into account the corporate group to which the company belongs or probably some kind of government support (be it on the federal, state or local government level). This is typically done by rating both the obligor on a standalone basis (= standalone rating) and the en-

---

[54] If X is normally distributed with mean μ and standard deviation σ, then $E[\exp(X)] = \exp(\mu + \sigma^2/2)$, where E is the expectation operator (Limpert, 2001).

tity that is supposed to influence the obligor's rating (=supporter rating).[55] The obligor's rating is then usually derived by some type of weighted average of the associated PDs. The weight will depend on the degree of influence as assessed by the loan manager according to the rating system's guidelines.

Due to the huge variety and often idiosyncratic nature of corporate group or sovereign support cases, it will be very difficult to statistically derive the correct *individual* weight of each supporter, the *average* weight, however, could well be validated by estimates from the data. More precisely, consider that for the development sample we have $i = 1,...,n$ obligors with PDs PD_i, corresponding supporters with PDs PD_i^S and associated supporter weights $w_i > 0$ as derived by the rating analyst's assessment.[56] Then, a regression model with $[(1-w_i) \cdot PD_i]$ and $[w_i \cdot PD_i^S]$ as independent variables and PD_i^{ex} (the obligor's external PD) as dependent variable can be estimated to determine as to whether the average size of the supporter weights w_i is appropriate or whether it should be increased or decreased.

5.8. Validation

The validation of rating systems is discussed at length in Chapter XI, Chapter XII, and Chapter XIV. Specific validation techniques that are valuable in a low default context (of which SRA portfolios are a typical example) are discussed in BCBS (2005) and in Chapter V. During rating development it will typically not be possible to run through a fully-fledged validation process. Rather, it will be necessary to concentrate on the most important measures. We will therefore briefly itemise those issues that we found important for a short-cut validation of SRA rating systems in the context of rating development:

- Validation on external ratings / external PDs
  - Correlations of internal and external PDs (for all modules of the rating system[57])
  - Case-wise analysis of those companies with the largest differences between internal and external ratings
  - Comparison of average external and internal PDs across the entire portfolio and across sub-portfolios (such as regions, rating grades, etc.)
- Validation on default indicators
  - Gini coefficient (for all modules of the rating system)

---

[55] Note that for the sake of simplicity, the expression "supporter" is used for all entities that influence an obligor's rating, be it in a positive or negative way.

[56] The standalone and supporter PDs have of course been derived from the regression model of the previous sections, probably, after manual adjustments.

[57] The typical modules of a SRA-rating system (statistical model, expert-guided adjustments, corporate-group influence / government support, override) have been discussed in Section 1.

- Comparison of default rates and corresponding confidence intervals with average internal PDs. This is done separately for all rating grades and also across all rating grades
- Formal statistical tests of the rating system's calibration (such as e.g. Spiegelhalter, see Chapter XIV)
- Comparison of the new rating system with its predecessor (if available)
  - Comparison of both rating system's validation results on external ratings and the default indicator
  - Case-wise analysis of those companies with the largest differences between old and new rating system

There are also some other validation techniques not yet discussed but that could enter a short-cut validation process in the rating development context, in particular addressing the relative rareness of default data in SRA portfolios (see BCBS 2005):

- Using the lowest non-default rating grades as default proxies
- Comparison of SRA obligors with the obligors from other rating segments that have the same rating
- Estimation of internal PDs with the duration-based approach, i.e. including information on rating migration into the internal PD estimation process
- Data pooling

6. Conclusions

In this article we have reported on some aspects of the development of shadow rating (SRA) systems found to be important for practitioners. The article focused on the statistical model that typically forms the basis of such rating systems. In this section we want to summarise the major issues that we have dealt with:

- We have stressed the importance both, in terms of the quality of the resulting rating system and in terms of initial development costs of
  - the deployment of sophisticated *software tools* that automate the development process as much as possible and
  - the careful *preparation and validation of the data* that are employed.
- *External PDs* form the basis of SRA type models. We have outlined some major issues that we found to be important in this context:
  - Which external rating types / agencies should be used?
  - Comparison between bank internal and external default definitions and consequences for resulting PD estimates
  - Sample construction for the estimation of external PDs (which time period, which obligor types?)
  - PD estimation techniques (cohort method vs. duration-based approach)
  - Point-in-time adjustment of external through-the-cycle ratings

- In Section 3 we pointed out that different *samples* will be needed for different types of analysis and made a proposal for the construction of such samples. In this context we also dealt with the issues of weighted and correlated observations.
- *Univariate risk factor analysis* is the next development step. In Section 4 we have described the typical types of analysis required – measurement of a risk factor's discriminatory power, transformation of risk factors, representativeness, fillers for missing values – and have mapped them to the samples on which they should be performed.
- In Section 5 we dealt with *multi factor modelling*, in particular with
  - model selection
  - the violation of model assumptions (non-normality, heteroscedasticity, error term correlations)
  - the measurement of risk factor influence (weights)
  - manual adjustments of empirical estimates and calibration
  - a method to empirically validate the average influence of corporate groups or sovereign supporters on an obligor's rating
- Finally, in the same section, we gave a brief overview over the *validation measures* that we found most useful for a short-cut validation in the context of SRA rating development.

While for most modelling steps one can observe the emergence of best practice tools, we think that in particular in the following areas further research is desirable to sharpen the instruments available for SRA rating development:

- Data pooling in order to arrive at more confident estimates for adjustment factors of external PDs that account for the differences between bank internal and external default measurement
- Empirical comparisons of the relative performance of cohort-based vs. duration-based PD estimates and related confidence intervals
- Point-in-time adjustments of external through-the-cycle ratings
- Panel type correlation models for SRA samples and software implementations of these models
- Measurement of risk factor influence (weights)

References

Altman E, Rijken H (2004), How Rating Agencies achieve Rating Stability, Journal of Banking & Finance, 2004, vol. 28, issue 11, pp. 2679-2714.

Ammer J, Packer F (2000), How Consistent Are Credit Ratings? A Geographic and Sectoral Analysis of Default Risk, FRB International Finance Discussion Paper No. 668.

Appasamy B, Hengstmann S, Stapper G, Schark E (2004), Validation of Rating Models, Wilmott magazine, May 2004, pp. 70-74

Basel Committee on Banking Supervision (BCBS) (2005), Validation of low-default portfolios in the Basel II Framework, Basel Committee Newsletter No. 6.

Basel Committee on Banking Supervision (BCBS) (2004), International Convergence of Capital Measurement and Capital Standards, Bank for International Settlements, Basel.

Basel Committee on Banking Supervision (BCBS) (2000), Range of Practice in Banks' Internal Ratings Systems, Bank for International Settlements, Basel.

Cantor R, Falkenstein E (2001), Testing for Rating Consistency in Annual Default Rates, Moody's Investors Service, New York.

Cantor R (2004), Measuring the Quality and Consistency of Corporate Ratings across Regions, Moody's Investors Service, New York.

Daly L (1992), Simple SAS macros for the calculation of exact binomial and Poisson confidence limits, Computers in biology and medicine 22(5), pp. 351-361.

Davison A, Hinkley D (1997), Bootstrap Methods and their Application, Cambridge University Press, Cambridge.

Deutsche Bundesbank (2003), Validierungsansätze für interne Ratingsysteme, Monatsbericht September 2003, pp. 61-74.

Erlenmaier U (2001), Models of Joint Defaults in Credit Risk Management: An Assessment, University of Heidelberg Working Paper No. 358.

Fitch (2005), Fitch Ratings Global Corporate Finance 2004 Transition and Default Study. Fitch Ratings Credit Market Research.

Fitch (2006), Fitch Ratings Definitions.
http://www.fitchratings.com/corporate/fitchResources.cfm?detail=1 [as at 18/02/06]

Greene W (2003), Econometric Analysis, Pearson Education, Inc., New Jersey.

Güttler A (2004), Using a Bootstrap Approach to Rate the Raters, Financial Markets and Portfolio Management 19, pp. 277-295.

Heitfield E (2004), Rating System Dynamics and Bank-Reported Default Probabilities under the New Basel Capital Accord, Working Paper, Board of Governors of the Federal Reserve System, Washington.

Hocking R (1976), The Analysis and Selection of Variables in Linear Regression, Biometrics, 32, pp. 1-50.

Judge G, Griffiths W, Hill R, Lee T (1980), The Theory and Practice of Econometrics, John Wiley & Sons, Inc., New York.

Limpert E, Stahl W, Abbt M (2001), Lognormal distributions across the sciences: keys and clues, BioScience, 51(5), pp. 341-352.

Löffler G (2004), An Anatomy of Rating Through the Cycle, Journal of Banking and Finance 28 (3), pp. 695–720.

Moody's (2004), Moody's Rating Symbols & Definitions. Moody's Investors Service, New York.

Moody's (2005), Default and Recovery Rates of Corporate Bond Issuers, 1920-2004, Special Comment, New York.

Schuermann T, Hanson S (2004), Estimating Probabilities of Default, FRB of New York Staff Report No. 190.

Standard & Poor's (2002), S&P Long-Term Issuer Credit Ratings Definitions.
http://www2.standardandpoors.com/servlet/Satellite?pagename=sp/Page/FixedIncome
RatingsCriteriaPg&r=1&l=EN&b=2&s=21&ig=1&ft=26 [as at 18/02/06]

Standard & Poor's (2005), Annual Global Corporate Default Study: Corporate Defaults Poised to Rise in 2005, Global Fixed Income Research, New York.

V. Estimating Probabilities of Default for Low Default Portfolios

Katja Pluto and Dirk Tasche

Deutsche Bundesbank[1]

1. Introduction

A core input to modern credit risk modelling and managing techniques is probabilities of default (PD) per borrower. As such, the accuracy of the PD estimations will determine the quality of the results of credit risk models.

One of the obstacles connected with PD estimations can be the low number of defaults, especially in the higher rating grades. These good rating grades might enjoy many years without any defaults. Even if some defaults occur in a given year, the observed default rates might exhibit a high degree of volatility due to the relatively low number of borrowers in that grade. Even entire portfolios with low or zero defaults are not uncommon. Examples include portfolios with an overall good quality of borrowers (e.g. sovereign or bank portfolios) as well as high-volume low-number portfolios (e.g. specialized lending).

Usual banking practices for deriving PD values in such exposures often focus on qualitative mapping mechanisms to bank-wide master scales or external ratings. These practices, while widespread in the industry, do not entirely satisfy the desire for a statistical foundation of the assumed PD values. One might "believe" that the PDs per rating grade appear correct, as well as thinking that the ordinal ranking and the relative spread between the PDs of two grades is right, but find that there is insufficient information about the absolute PD figures. Lastly, it could be questioned whether these rather qualitative methods of PD calibration fulfil the minimum requirements set out in BCBS (2004a).

This issue, amongst others, has recently been raised in BBA (2004). In that paper, applications of causal default models and of exogenous distribution assumptions on the PDs across the grades have been proposed as solutions. Schuermann and Hanson (2004) present the "duration method" of estimating PDs by means of migration matrices (see also Jafry and Schuermann, 2004). This way, nonzero PDs

---

[1] The opinions expressed in this chapter are those of the authors and do not necessarily reflect views of the Deutsche Bundesbank.

for high-quality rating grades can be estimated more precisely by both counting the borrower migrations through the lower grades to eventual default and using Markov chain properties.

This paper focuses on a different issue of PD estimations in low default portfolios. We present a methodology to estimate PDs for portfolios without any defaults, or a very low number of defaults in the overall portfolio. The proposal by Schuermann and Hanson (2004) does not provide a solution for such cases, because the duration method requires a certain number of defaults in at least some (usually the low-quality) rating grades.

For estimating PDs, we use all available quantitative information of the rating system and its grades. Moreover, we assume that the ordinal borrower ranking is correct. We do not use any additional assumptions or information. Every additional input would be on the assumption side, as the low default property of these portfolios does not provide us with more reliable quantitative information.

Our methodology delivers confidence intervals for the PDs of each rating grade. The PD range can be adjusted by the choice of an appropriate confidence level. Moreover, by the *most prudent estimation principle* our methodology yields monotone PD estimates. We look both at the cases of uncorrelated and correlated default events, in the latter case under assumptions consistent with the Basel risk weight model.

Moreover, we extend the *most prudent estimation* by two application variants: First we scale our results to overall portfolio central tendencies. Second, we apply our methodology to multi-period data and extend our model by time dependencies of the Basel systematic factor. Both variants should help to align our principle to realistic data sets and to a range of assumptions that can be set according to the specific issues in question when applying our methodology.

The paper is structured as follows: The two main concepts underlying the methodology – estimating PDs as upper confidence bounds and guaranteeing their monotony by the *most prudent estimation principle* – are introduced by two examples that assume independence of the default events. The first example deals with a portfolio without any observed defaults. For the second example, we modify the first example by assuming that a few defaults have been observed.

In a further section, we show how the methodology can be modified in order to take into account non-zero correlation of default events. This is followed by two sections discussing potential extensions of our methodology, in particular the scaling to the overall portfolio central tendency and an extension of our model to the multi-period case. The last two sections are devoted to discussions of the potential scope of application and of open questions. We conclude with a summary of our proposal. In Appendix A, we provide information on the numerics that is needed to implement the estimation approach we suggest. Appendix B provides additional numerical results to Section 5.

2. Example: No Defaults, Assumption of Independence

The obligors are distributed to rating grades A, B, and C, with frequencies n_A, n_B, and n_C. The grade with the highest credit-worthiness is denoted by A, the grade with the lowest credit-worthiness is denoted by C. No defaults occurred in A, B or C during the last observation period.

We assume that the – still to be estimated – PDs p_A of grade A, p_B of grade B, and p_C of grade C reflect the decreasing credit-worthiness of the grades, in the sense of the following inequality:

$$p_A \leq p_B \leq p_C \tag{1}$$

The inequality implies that we assume the ordinal borrower ranking to be correct. According to (1), the PD p_A of grade A cannot be greater than the PD p_C of grade C. As a consequence, the *most prudent estimate* of the value p_A is obtained under the assumption that the probabilities p_A and p_C are equal. Then, from (1) even follows $p_A = p_B = p_C$. Assuming this relation, we now proceed in determining a confidence region for p_A at confidence level γ. This confidence region[2] can be described as the set of all admissible values of p_A with the property that the probability of not observing any default during the observation period is not less than $1-\gamma$ (for instance for $\gamma = 90\%$).

If we have got $p_A = p_B = p_C$, then the three rating grades A, B, and C do not differ in their respective riskiness. Hence we have to deal with a homogeneous sample of size $n_A + n_B + n_C$ without any default during the observation period. Assuming unconditional independence of the default events, the probability of observing no defaults turns out to be $(1-p_A)^{n_A+n_B+n_C}$. Consequently, we have to solve the inequality

$$1 - \gamma \leq \left(1 - p_A\right)^{n_A+n_B+n_C} \tag{2}$$

for p_A in order to obtain the confidence region at level γ for p_A as the set of all the values of p_A such that

$$p_A \leq 1 - (1-\gamma)^{1/(n_A+n_B+n_C)} \tag{3}$$

If we choose for the sake of illustration

$$n_A = 100, \quad n_B = 400, \quad n_C = 300, \tag{4}$$

Table 1 exhibits some values of confidence levels γ with the corresponding maximum values (upper confidence bounds) $\hat{p}_A$ of p_A such that (2) is still satisfied.

---

[2] For any value of p_A not belonging to this region, the hypothesis that the true PD takes on this value would have to be rejected at a type I error level of $1-\gamma$.

Table 1. Upper confidence bound $\hat{p}_A$ of p_A as a function of the confidence level γ. No defaults observed, frequencies of obligors in grades given in (4).

γ	50%	75%	90%	95%	99%	99.9%
$\hat{p}_A$	0.09%	0.17%	0.29%	0.37%	0.57%	0.86%

According to Table 1, there is a strong dependence of the upper confidence bound $\hat{p}_A$ on the confidence level γ. Intuitively, values of γ smaller than 95% seem more appropriate for estimating the PD by $\hat{p}_A$.

By inequality (1), the PD p_B of grade B cannot be greater than the PD p_C of grade C either. Consequently, the *most prudent estimate* of p_B is obtained by assuming $p_B = p_C$. Assuming additional equality with the PD p_A of the best grade A would violate the *most prudent estimation principle*, because p_A is a lower bound of p_B. If we have got $p_B = p_C$, then B and C do not differ in their respective riskiness and may be considered a homogeneous sample of size $n_B + n_C$. Therefore, the confidence region at level γ for p_B is obtained from the inequality

$$1 - \gamma \leq \left(1 - p_C\right)^{n_B + n_C} \tag{5}$$

(5) implies that the confidence region for p_B consists of all the values of p_B that satisfy

$$p_B \leq 1 - \left(1 - \gamma\right)^{1/(n_B + n_C)} \tag{6}$$

If we again take up the example described by (4), Table 2 exhibits some values of confidence levels γ with the corresponding maximum values (upper confidence bounds) $\hat{p}_B$ of p_B such that (6) is still fulfilled.

Table 2. Upper confidence bound $\hat{p}_B$ of p_B as a function of the confidence level γ. No defaults observed, frequencies of obligors in grades given in (4).

γ	50%	75%	90%	95%	99%	99.9%
$\hat{p}_B$	0.10%	0.20%	0.33%	0.43%	0.66%	0.98%

For determining the confidence region at level γ for p_C we only make use of the observations in grade C because by (1) there is no obvious upper bound for p_C. Hence the confidence region at level γ for p_C consists of those values of p_C that satisfy the inequality

$$1 - \gamma \leq \left(1 - p_C\right)^{n_C} \tag{7}$$

Equivalently, the confidence region for p_C can be described by

$$p_C \le 1 - (1-\gamma)^{1/n_C} \tag{8}$$

Coming back to our example (4), Table 3 lists some values of confidence levels γ with the corresponding maximum values (upper confidence bounds) $\hat{p}_C$ of p_C such that (8) is still fulfilled.

Table 3. Upper confidence bound $\hat{p}_C$ of p_C as a function of the confidence level γ. No defaults observed, frequencies of obligors in grades given in (4).

γ	50%	75%	90%	95%	99%	99.9%
$\hat{p}_C$	0.23%	0.46%	0.76%	0.99%	1.52%	2.28%

Comparison of Tables 1, 2 and 3 shows that – besides the confidence level γ – the applicable sample size is a main driver of the upper confidence bound. The smaller the sample size, the greater will be the upper confidence bound. This is not an undesirable effect, because intuitively the credit-worthiness ought to be the better, the greater the number of obligors in a portfolio without any default observation.

As the results presented so far seem plausible, we suggest using upper confidence bounds as described by (3), (6) and (8) as estimates for the PDs in portfolios without observed defaults. The case of three rating grades we have considered in this section can readily be generalized to an arbitrary number of grades. We do not present the details here.

However, the larger the number of obligors in the entire portfolio, the more often some defaults will occur in some grades at least, even if the general quality of the portfolio is very high. This case is not covered by (3), (6) and (8). In the following section, we will show – still keeping the assumption of independence of the default events – how the *most prudent estimation* methodology can be adapted to the case of a non-zero but still low number of defaults.

3. Example: Few Defaults, Assumption of Independence

We consider again the portfolio from Section 2 with the frequencies n_A, n_B, and n_C. In contrast to Section 2, this time we assume that during the last period no default was observed in grade A, two defaults were observed in grade B, and one default was observed in grade C.

As in Section 2, we determine a *most prudent confidence region* for the PD p_A of A. Again, we do so by assuming that the PDs of the three grades are equal. This allows us to treat the entire portfolio as a homogeneous sample of size $n_A + n_B + n_C$. Then the probability of observing not more than three defaults is given by the expression

$$\sum_{i=0}^{3} \binom{n_A + n_B + n_C}{i} p_A^i (1 - p_A)^{n_A + n_B + n_C - i} \tag{9}$$

Expression (9) follows from the fact that the number of defaults in the portfolio is binomially distributed as long as the default events are independent. As a consequence of (9), the confidence region[3] at level γ for p_A is given as the set of all the values of p_A that satisfy the inequality

$$1 - \gamma \le \sum_{i=0}^{3} \binom{n_A + n_B + n_C}{i} p_A^i (1 - p_A)^{n_A + n_B + n_C - i} \tag{10}$$

The tail distribution of a binomial distribution can be expressed in terms of an appropriate beta distribution function. Thus, inequality (10) can be solved analytically[4] for p_A. For details, see Appendix A. If we assume again that the obligors' numbers per grade are as in (4), Table 4 shows maximum solutions $\hat{p}_A$ of (10) for different confidence levels γ.

Table 4. Upper confidence bound $\hat{p}_A$ of p_A as a function of the confidence level γ. No default observed in grade A, two defaults observed in grade B, one default observed in grade C, frequencies of obligors in grades given in (4).

γ	50%	75%	90%	95%	99%	99.9%
$\hat{p}_A$	0.46%	0.65%	0.83%	0.97%	1.25%	1.62%

Although in grade A no defaults were observed, the three defaults that occurred during the observation period enter the calculation. They affect the upper confidence bounds, which are much higher than those in Table 1. This is a consequence of the precautionary assumption $p_A = p_B = p_C$. However, if we alternatively considered grade A alone (by re-evaluating (8) with $n_A = 100$ instead of n_C), we would obtain an upper confidence bound of 1.38% at level $\gamma = 75\%$. This value is still much higher than the one that has been calculated under the precautionary assumption $p_A = p_B = p_C$ – a consequence of the low frequency of obligors in grade A in this example. Nevertheless, we see that the methodology described by (10) yields fairly reasonable results.

In order to determine the confidence region at level γ for p_B, as in Section 2, we assume that p_B takes its greatest possible value according to (1), i.e. that we have $p_B = p_C$. In this situation, we have a homogeneous portfolio with $n_B + n_C$ obligors, PD p_B, and three observed defaults. Analogous to (9), the probability of observing no more than three defaults in one period then can be written as:

---

[3] We calculate the simple and intuitive exact Clopper-Pearson interval. For an overview of this approach, as well as potential alternatives, see Brown et al. (2001).

[4] Alternatively, solving directly (10) for p_A by means of numerical tools is not too difficult either (see Appendix A, Proposition A.1, for additional information).

$$\sum_{i=0}^{3}\binom{n_B+n_C}{i}p_B^i(1-p_B)^{n_B+n_C-i} \tag{11}$$

Hence, the confidence region at level γ for p_B turns out to be the set of all the admissible values of p_B which satisfy the inequality

$$1-\gamma \le \sum_{i=0}^{3}\binom{n_B+n_C}{i}p_B^i(1-p_B)^{n_B+n_C-i} \tag{12}$$

By analytically or numerically solving (12) for p_B – with frequencies of obligors in the grades as in (4) – we obtain Table 5 with some maximum solutions $\hat{p}_B$ of (12) for different confidence levels γ.

Table 5. Upper confidence bound $\hat{p}_B$ of p_B as a function of the confidence level γ. No default observed in grade A, two defaults observed in grade B, one default observed in grade C, frequencies of obligors in grades given in (4).

γ	50%	75%	90%	95%	99%	99.9%
$\hat{p}_B$	0.52%	0.73%	0.95%	1.10%	1.43%	1.85%

From the given numbers of defaults in the different grades, it becomes clear that a stand-alone treatment of grade B would yield still much higher values[5] for the upper confidence bounds. The upper confidence bound 0.52% of the confidence region at level 50% is almost identical with the naïve frequency based PD estimate $2/400 = 0.5\%$ that could alternatively have been calculated for grade B in this example.

For determining the confidence region at level γ for the PD p_C, by the same rationale as in Section 2, the grade C must be considered a stand-alone portfolio. According to the assumption made in the beginning of this section, one default occurred among the n_C obligors in C. Hence we see that the confidence region for p_C is the set of all admissible values of p_C that satisfy the inequality

$$1-\gamma \le \sum_{i=0}^{1}\binom{n_C}{i}p_C^i(1-p_C)^{n_C-i}=(1-p_C)^{n_C}+n_C\,p_C(1-p_C)^{n_C-1} \tag{13}$$

For obligor frequencies as assumed in example (4), Table 6 exhibits some maximum solutions[6] $\hat{p}_C$ of (13) for different confidence levels γ.

---

[5] At level 99.9%, e.g., 2.78% would be the value of the upper confidence bound.

[6] If we had assumed that two defaults occurred in grade B but no default was observed in grade C, then we would have obtained smaller upper bounds for p_C than for p_B. As this is not a desirable effect, a possible - conservative - work-around could be to increment the number of defaults in grade C up to the point where p_C would take on a greater value

Table 6. Upper confidence bound $\hat{p}_C$ of p_C as a function of the confidence level γ. No default observed in grade A, two defaults observed in grade B, one default observed in grade C, frequencies of obligors in grades given in (4).

γ	50%	75%	90%	95%	99%	99.9%
$\hat{p}_C$	0.56%	0.90%	1.29%	1.57%	2.19%	3.04%

So far, we have described how to generalize the methodology from Section 2 to the case where non-zero default frequencies have been recorded. In the following section we investigate the impact of non-zero default correlation on the PD estimates that are effected by applying the *most prudent estimation* methodology.

4. Example: Correlated Default Events

In this section, we describe the dependence of the default events with the one-factor probit model[7] that was the starting point for developing the risk weight functions given in BCBS (2004a)[8]. First, we use the example from Section 2 and assume that no default at all was observed in the whole portfolio during the last period. In order to illustrate the effects of correlation, we apply the minimum value of the asset correlation that appears in the Basel II corporate risk weight function. This minimum value is 12% (see BCBS, 2004a, § 272). Our model, however, works with any other correlation assumption as well. Likewise, the *most prudent estimation principle* could potentially be applied to other models than the Basel II type credit risk model as long as the inequalities can be solved for p_A, p_B and p_C, respectively.

Under the assumptions of this section, the confidence region at level γ for p_A is represented as the set of all admissible values of p_A that satisfy the inequality (cf. Bluhm et al., 2003, Sections 2.1.2 and 2.5.1 for the derivation)

$$1 - \gamma \le \int_{-\infty}^{\infty} \varphi(y) \left(1 - \Phi\left(\frac{\Phi^{-1}(p_A) - \sqrt{\rho}\, y}{\sqrt{1 - \rho}}\right)\right)^{n_A + n_B + n_C} dy, \tag{14}$$

where φ and Φ stand for the standard normal density and standard normal distribution function, respectively. Φ^{-1} denotes the inverse function of Φ and ρ is the *asset correlation* (here ρ is chosen as $\rho = 12\%$). Similarly to (2), the right-hand side

---

than p_B. Nevertheless, in this case one would have to make sure that the applied rating system yields indeed a correct ranking of the obligors.

[7] According to De Finetti's theorem (see, e.g., Durrett (1996), Theorem 6.8), assuming one systematic factor only is not very restrictive.

[8] See Gordy (2003) and BCBS (2004b) for the background of the risk weight functions. In the case of non-zero realized default rates Balthazar (2004) uses the one-factor model for deriving confidence intervals of the PDs.

of inequality (14) tells us the one-period probability of not observing any default among $n_A + n_A + n_A$ obligors with average PD p_A.

Solving[9] Equation (14) numerically[10] for the frequencies as given in (4) leads to Table 7 with maximum solutions $\hat{p}_A$ of (14) for different confidence levels γ.

Table 7. Upper confidence bounds $\hat{p}_A$ of p_A, $\hat{p}_B$ of p_B and $\hat{p}_C$ of p_C as a function of the confidence level γ. No defaults observed, frequencies of obligors in grades given in (4). Correlated default events.

γ	50%	75%	90%	95%	99%	99.9%
$\hat{p}_A$	0.15%	0.40%	0.86%	1.31%	2.65%	5.29%
$\hat{p}_B$	0.17%	0.45%	0.96%	1.45%	2.92%	5.77%
$\hat{p}_C$	0.37%	0.92%	1.89%	2.78%	5.30%	9.84%

Comparing the values from the first line of Table 7 with Table 1 shows that the impact of taking care of correlations is moderate for the low confidence levels 50% and 75%. The impact is much higher for the levels higher than 90% (for the confidence level 99.9% the bound is even six times larger). This observation reflects the general fact that introducing unidirectional stochastic dependence in a sum of random variables entails a redistribution of probability mass from the centre of the distribution towards its lower and upper limits.

The formulae for the estimations of upper confidence bounds for p_B and p_C can be derived analogously to (14) (in combination with (5) and (7)). This yields the inequalities

$$1 - \gamma \leq \int_{-\infty}^{\infty} \varphi(y) \left(1 - \Phi\left(\frac{\Phi^{-1}(p_B) - \sqrt{\rho}\, y}{\sqrt{1-\rho}} \right) \right)^{n_B + n_C} dy \qquad (15)$$

and

$$1 - \gamma \leq \int_{-\infty}^{\infty} \varphi(y) \left(1 - \Phi\left(\frac{\Phi^{-1}(p_C) - \sqrt{\rho}\, y}{\sqrt{1-\rho}} \right) \right)^{n_C} dy, \qquad (16)$$

---

[9] See Appendix A, Proposition A.2, for additional information. Taking into account correlations entails an increase in numerical complexity. Therefore, it might seem to be more efficient to deal with the correlation problem by choosing an appropriately enlarged confidence level in the independent default events approach as described in Sections 2 and 3. However, it remains open how a confidence level for the uncorrelated case, that "appropriately" adjustments for the correlations, can be derived.

[10] The more intricate calculations for this paper were conducted by means of the software package R (cf. R Development Core Team, 2003).

to be solved for p_B and p_C respectively. The numerical calculations with (15) and (16) do not deliver additional qualitative insights. For the sake of completeness, however, the maximum solutions $\hat{p}_B$ of (15) and $\hat{p}_C$ of (16) for different confidence levels γ are listed in lines 2 and 3 of Table 7, respectively.

Secondly, we apply our correlated model to the example from Section 3 and assume that three defaults were observed during the last period. Analogous to Equations (9), (10) and (14), the confidence region at level γ for p_A is represented as the set of all values of p_A that satisfy the inequality

$$1-\gamma \le \int_{-\infty}^{\infty} \varphi(y)z(y)dy,$$

$$z(y) = \sum_{i=0}^{3} \binom{n_A+n_B+n_C}{i} G(p_A,\rho,y)^i (1-G(p_A,\rho,y))^{n_A+n_B+n_C-i},$$

(17)

where the function G is defined by

$$G(p,\rho,y) = \Phi\left(\frac{\Phi^{-1}(p)-\sqrt{\rho}\,y}{\sqrt{1-\rho}}\right).$$

(18)

Solving (17) for $\hat{p}_A$ with obligor frequencies as given in (4), and the respective modified equations for $\hat{p}_B$ and $\hat{p}_C$ yields the results presented in Table 8.

Table 8. Upper confidence bounds $\hat{p}_A$ of p_A, $\hat{p}_B$ of p_B and $\hat{p}_C$ of p_C as a function of the confidence level γ. No default observed in grade A, two defaults observed in grade B, one default observed in grade C, frequencies of obligors in grades given in (4). Correlated default events.

γ	50%	75%	90%	95%	99%	99.9%
$\hat{p}_A$	0.72%	1.42%	2.50%	3.42%	5.88%	10.08%
$\hat{p}_B$	0.81%	1.59%	2.77%	3.77%	6.43%	10.92%
$\hat{p}_C$	0.84%	1.76%	3.19%	4.41%	7.68%	13.14%

Not surprisingly, as shown in Table 8 the maximum solutions for $\hat{p}_A$, $\hat{p}_B$ and $\hat{p}_C$ increase if we introduce defaults in our example. Other than that, the results do not deliver essential additional insights.

5. Potential Extension: Calibration by Scaling Factors

One of the drawbacks of the *most prudent estimation principle* is that in the case of few defaults, the upper confidence bound PD estimates for all grades are higher than the average default rate of the overall portfolio. This phenomenon is not surprising, given that we include all defaults of the overall portfolio in the upper confidence bound estimation even for the highest rating grade. However, these estimates might be regarded as too conservative by some practitioners.

A potential remedy would be a scaling[11] of all of our estimates towards the central tendency (the average portfolio default rate). We introduce a scaling factor K to our estimates such that the overall portfolio default rate is exactly met, i.e.

$$\frac{\hat{p}_A n_A + \hat{p}_B n_B + \hat{p}_C n_C}{n_A + n_B + n_C} K = PD_{\text{Portfolio}}. \tag{19}$$

The new, scaled PD estimates will then be

$$\hat{p}_{X,\text{scaled}} = K \hat{p}_X, \quad X = A, B, C. \tag{20}$$

The results of the application of such a scaling factor to our "few defaults" examples of Sections 3 and 4 are shown in Tables 9 and 10, respectively.

Table 9. Upper confidence bound $\hat{p}_{A,\text{scaled}}$ of p_A, $\hat{p}_{B,\text{scaled}}$ of p_B and $\hat{p}_{C,\text{scaled}}$ of p_C as a function of the confidence level γ after scaling to the central tendency. No default observed in grade A, two defaults observed in grade B, one default observed in grade C, frequencies of obligors in grades given in (4). Uncorrelated default events.

γ	50%	75%	90%	95%	99%	99.9%
Central Tendency	0.375%	0.375%	0.375%	0.375%	0.375%	0.375%
K	0.71	0.48	0.35	0.30	0.22	0.17
$\hat{p}_A$	0.33%	0.31%	0.29%	0.29%	0.28%	0.27%
$\hat{p}_B$	0.37%	0.35%	0.34%	0.33%	0.32%	0.31%
$\hat{p}_C$	0.40%	0.43%	0.46%	0.47%	0.49%	0.50%

The average estimated portfolio PD will now fit exactly the overall portfolio central tendency. Thus, we remove all conservatism from our estimations. Given the poor default data base in typical applications of our methodology, this might be seen as a disadvantage rather than an advantage. By using the *most prudent estimation principle* to derive "relative" PDs before scaling them down to the final re-

---

[11] A similar scaling procedure has recently been suggested by Cathcart and Benjamin (2005).

sults, we preserve the sole dependence of the PD estimates upon the borrower frequencies in the respective rating grades, as well as the monotony of the PDs.

Table 10. Upper confidence bound $\hat{p}_{A,\text{scaled}}$ of p_A, $\hat{p}_{B,\text{scaled}}$ of p_B and $\hat{p}_{C,\text{scaled}}$ of p_C as a
function of the confidence level γ after scaling to the central tendency. No default observed
in grade A, two defaults observed in grade B, one default observed in grade C, frequencies
of obligors in grades given in (4). Correlated default events.

γ	50%	75%	90%	95%	99%	99.9%
Central Tendency	0.375%	0.375%	0.375%	0.375%	0.375%	0.375%
K	0.46	0.23	0.13	0.09	0.05	0.03
$\hat{p}_A$	0.33%	0.33%	0.32%	0.32%	0.32%	0.32%
$\hat{p}_B$	0.38%	0.37%	0.36%	0.36%	0.35%	0.35%
$\hat{p}_C$	0.39%	0.40%	0.41%	0.42%	0.42%	0.42%

The question of the appropriate confidence level for the above calculations remains. Although the average estimated portfolio PD now always fits the overall
portfolio default rate, the confidence level determines the "distribution" of that
rate over the rating grades. In the above example, though, the differences in distribution appear small, especially in the correlated case, such that we would not explore this issue further. The confidence level could, in practice, be used to control
the spread of PD estimates over the rating grades – the higher the confidence
level, the higher the spread.

Table 11. Upper confidence bound $\hat{p}_{A,\text{scaled}}$ of p_A, $\hat{p}_{B,\text{scaled}}$ of p_B and $\hat{p}_{C,\text{scaled}}$ of p_C as a
function of the confidence level γ after scaling to the upper confidence bound of the overall
portfolio PD. No default observed in grade A, two defaults observed in grade B, one default
observed in grade C, frequencies of obligors in grades given in (4). Uncorrelated default
events.

γ	50%	75%	90%	95%	99%	99.9%
Upper bound for portfolio PD	0.46%	0.65%	0.83%	0.97%	1.25%	1.62%
K	0.87	0.83	0.78	0.77	0.74	0.71
$\hat{p}_A$	0.40%	0.54%	0.65%	0.74%	0.92%	1.16%
$\hat{p}_B$	0.45%	0.61%	0.74%	0.84%	1.06%	1.32%
$\hat{p}_C$	0.49%	0.75%	1.01%	1.22%	1.62%	2.17%

However, the above scaling works only if there is a nonzero number of defaults in
the overall portfolio. Zero default portfolios would indeed be treated more severely if we continue to apply our original proposal to them, compared to using
scaled PDs for low default portfolios.

A variant of the above scaling proposal that takes care of both issues is the use of an upper confidence bound for the overall portfolio PD in lieu of the actual default rate. This upper confidence bound for the overall portfolio PD, incidentally, equals the *most prudent estimate* for the highest rating grade. Then, the same scaling methodology as described above can be applied. The results of its application to the few defaults examples as in Tables 9 and 10 are presented in Tables 11 and 12.

Table 12. Upper confidence bound $\hat{p}_{A,\text{scaled}}$ of p_A, $\hat{p}_{B,\text{scaled}}$ of p_B and $\hat{p}_{C,\text{scaled}}$ of p_C as a function of the confidence level γ after scaling to the upper confidence bound of the overall portfolio PD. No default observed in grade A, two defaults observed in grade B, one default observed in grade C, frequencies of obligors in grades given in (4). Correlated default events.

γ	50%	75%	90%	95%	99%	99.9%
Upper bound for portfolio PD	0.71%	1.42%	2.50%	3.42%	5.88%	10.08%
K	0.89	0.87	0.86	0.86	0.86	0.87
$\hat{p}_A$	0.64%	1.24%	2.16%	2.95%	5.06%	8.72%
$\hat{p}_B$	0.72%	1.38%	2.39%	3.25%	5.54%	9.54%
$\hat{p}_C$	0.75%	1.53%	2.76%	3.80%	6.61%	11.37%

In contrast to the situation of Tables 9 and 10, in Tables 11 and 12 the overall default rate in the portfolio depends on the confidence level, and we observe scaled PD estimates for the grades that increase with growing levels. Nevertheless, the scaled PD estimates for the better grades are still considerably lower than the corresponding unscaled estimates from Sections 3 and 4, respectively. For the sake of comparison, we provide in Appendix B the analogous numerical results for the no default case.

The advantage of this latter variant of the scaling approach is that the degree of conservatism is actively manageable by the appropriate choice of the confidence level for the estimation of the upper confidence bound of the overall portfolio PD. Moreover, it works in the case of zero defaults and few defaults, and thus does not produce a structural break between both scenarios. Lastly, the results are less conservative than those of our original methodology.

Consequently, we propose to use the *most prudent estimation principle* to derive "relative" PDs over the rating grades, and subsequently scale them down according to the upper bound of the overall portfolio PD, which is once more determined by the *most prudent estimation principle* with an appropriate confidence level.

6. Potential Extension: The Multi-period case

So far, we have only considered the situation where estimations are carried out on a one year (or one observation period) data sample. In case of a time series with data from several years, the PDs (per rating grade) for the single years could be estimated and could then be used for calculating weighted averages of the PDs in order to make more efficient use of the data. By doing so, however, the interpretation of the estimates as upper confidence bounds at some pre-defined level would be lost.

Alternatively, the data of all years could be pooled and tackled as in the one-year case. When assuming cross-sectional and inter-temporal independence of the default events, the methodology as presented in Sections 2 and 3 can be applied to the data pool by replacing the one-year frequency of a grade with the sum of the frequencies of this grade over the years (analogous for the numbers of defaulted obligors). This way, the interpretation of the results as upper confidence bounds as well as the frequency-dependent degree of conservatism of the estimates will be preserved.

However, when turning to the case of default events which are cross-sectionally and inter-temporally correlated, pooling does not allow for an adequate modelling. An example would be a portfolio of long-term loans, where in the inter-temporal pool every obligor would appear several times. As a consequence, the dependence structure of the pool would have to be specified very carefully, as the structure of correlation over time and of cross-sectional correlation are likely to differ.

In this section, we present a multi-period extension of the cross-sectional one-factor correlation model that has been introduced in Section 4. We will take the perspective of an observer of a cohort of obligors over a fixed interval of time. The advantage of such a view arises from the conceptual separation of time and cross-section effects. Again, we do not present the methodology in full generality but rather introduce it by way of an example.

As in Section 4, we assume that, at the beginning of the observation period, we have got n_A obligors in grade A, n_B obligors in grade B, and n_C obligors in grade C. In contrast to Section 4, the length of the observation period this time is $T > 1$. We consider only the obligors that were present at the beginning of the observation period. Any obligors entering the portfolio afterwards are neglected for the purpose of our estimation exercise. Nevertheless, the number of observed obligors may vary from year to year as soon as any defaults occur.

As in the previous sections, we first consider the estimation of the PD p_A for grade A. PD in this section denotes a long-term average one-year probability of default. Working again with the *most prudent estimation principle*, we assume that the PDs p_A, p_B, and p_C are equal, i.e. $p_A = p_B = p_C = p$. We assume, similar to Gordy (2003), that a default of obligor $i = 1, \ldots, N = n_A + n_B + n_C$ in year $t = 1, \ldots, T$ is triggered if the change in value of their assets results in a value lower than some default threshold c as described below (Equation 22). Specifically, if $V_{i,t}$ denotes the change in value of obligor i's assets, $V_{i,t}$ is given by

$$V_{i,t} = \sqrt{\rho}\, S_t + \sqrt{1-\rho}\, \xi_{i,t}, \tag{21}$$

where ρ stands for the *asset correlation* as introduced in Section 4, S_t is the realisation of the *systematic factor* in year t, and $\xi_{i,t}$ denotes the *idiosyncratic* component of the change in value. The cross-sectional dependence of the default events stems from the presence of the systematic factor S_t in all the obligors' change in value variables. Obligor i's default occurs in year t if

$$V_{i,1} > c, \ldots, V_{i,t-1} > c, V_{i,t} \leq c. \tag{22}$$

The probability

$$P[V_{i,t} \leq c] = p_{i,t} = p \tag{23}$$

is the parameter we are interested to estimate: It describes the long-term average one-year probability of default among the obligors that have not defaulted before. The indices i and t at $p_{i,t}$ can be dropped because by the assumptions we are going to specify below $p_{i,t}$ will neither depend on i nor on t. To some extent, therefore, p may be considered a *through-the-cycle* PD.

For the sake of computational feasibility, and in order to keep as close as possible to the Basel II risk weight model, we specify the factor variables S_t, $t = 1,\ldots,T$, and $\xi_{i,t}$, $i = 1,\ldots,N$, $t = 1,\ldots,T$ as standard normally distributed (cf. Bluhm et al., 2003). Moreover, we assume that the random vector $(S_1,\ldots,S_T)$ and the random variables $\xi_{i,t}$, $i = 1,\ldots,N$, $t = 1,\ldots,T$ are independent. As a consequence, from (21) it follows that the change in value variables $V_{i,t}$ are all standard-normally distributed. Therefore, (23) implies that the default threshold[12] c is determined by

$$c = \Phi^{-1}(p), \tag{24}$$

with Φ denoting the standard normal distribution function.

While the single components S_t of the vector of systematic factors, generate the cross-sectional correlation of the default events at time t, their inter-temporal correlation is affected by the dependence structure of the factors $S_1,\ldots,S_T$. We further

---

[12] At first sight, the fact that in our model the default threshold is constant over time seems to imply that the model does not reflect the possibility of rating migrations. However, by construction of the model, the *conditional* default threshold at time t given the value $V_{i,t-1}$ will in general differ from c. As we make use of the joint distribution of the $V_{i,t}$, therefore rating migrations are implicitly taken into account.

assume that not only the components but also the vector as a whole is normally distributed. Since the components of the vector are standardized, its joint distribution is completely determined by the correlation matrix

$$
\begin{pmatrix}
1 & r_{1,2} & r_{1,3} & \cdots & r_{1,T} \\
r_{2,1} & 1 & r_{2,3} & \cdots & r_{2,T} \\
\vdots & & \ddots & & \vdots \\
r_{T,1} & & & r_{T,T-1} & 1
\end{pmatrix}.
\tag{25}
$$

Whereas the cross-sectional correlation within one year is constant for any pair of obligors, empirical observation indicates that the effect of inter-temporal correlation becomes weaker with increasing distance in time. We express this distance-dependent behaviour[13] of correlations by setting in (25)

$$
r_{s,t} = \vartheta^{|s-t|}, \quad s,t = 1,\cdots,T, \; s \neq t,
\tag{26}
$$

for some appropriate $0 < \vartheta < 1$ to be specified below.

Let us assume that within the T years observation period k_A defaults were observed among the obligors that were initially graded A, k_B defaults among the initially graded B obligors and k_C defaults among the initially graded C obligors. For the estimation of p_A according to the most prudent estimation principle, therefore we have to take into account $k = k_A + k_B + k_C$ defaults among N obligors over T years. For any given confidence level γ, we have to determine the maximum value $\hat{p}$ of all the parameters p such that the inequality

$$
1 - \gamma \leq \mathrm{P}\big[\text{No more than } k \text{ defaults observed}\big]
\tag{27}
$$

is satisfied – note that the right-hand side of (27) depends on the one-period probability of default p. In order to derive a formulation that is accessible to numerical calculation, we have to rewrite the right-hand side of (27).

The first step is to develop an expression for obligor i's conditional probability to default during the observation period, given a realization of the systematic factors $S_1,\ldots,S_T$. From (21), (22), (24) and by using the conditional independence of the $V_{i,1},\ldots,V_{i,T}$ given the systematic factors, we obtain

---

[13] Blochwitz et al. (2004) proposed the specification of the inter-temporal dependence structure according to (26) for the purpose of default probability estimation.

$$P[\text{Obligor } i \text{ defaults} \mid S_1, \cdots, S_T] =$$

$$P\left[\min_{t=1,\dots,T} V_{i,t} \le \Phi^{-1}(p) \mid S_1, \dots, S_T\right] =$$

$$1 - P[\xi_{i,1} > G(p, \rho, S_1), \dots, \xi_{i,T} > G(p, \rho, S_T) \mid S_1, \dots, S_T] = \tag{28}$$

$$1 - \prod_{t=1}^{T}(1 - G(p, \rho, S_t)),$$

where the function G is defined as in (18). By construction, in the model all the probabilities $P[\text{Obligor } i \text{ defaults} \mid S_1, \dots, S_T]$ are equal, so that, for any of the is, we can define

$$\pi(S_1, \dots, S_T) = P[\text{Obligor } i \text{ defaults} \mid S_1, \dots, S_T]$$

$$= 1 - \prod_{t-1}^{T}(1 - G(p, \rho, S_t)) \tag{29}$$

Using this abbreviation, we can write the right-hand side of (27) as

$$P[\text{No more than } k \text{ defaults observed}] =$$

$$\sum_{l=0}^{k} E[P[\text{Exactly } l \text{ obligors default} \mid S_1, \dots, S_T]] = \tag{30}$$

$$\sum_{l=0}^{k} \binom{N}{l} E[\pi(S_1, \dots, S_T)^l (1 - \pi(S_1, \dots, S_T))^{N-l}].$$

The expectations in (30) are expectations with respect to the random vector $(S_1, \dots, S_T)$ and have to be calculated as T-dimensional integrals involving the density of the T-variate standard normal distribution with correlation matrix given by (25) and (26). When solving (27) for $\hat{p}$, we calculated the values of these T-dimensional integrals by means of Monte-Carlo simulation, taking advantage of the fact that the term

$$\sum_{l=0}^{k} \binom{N}{l} E[\pi(S_1, \dots, S_T)^l (1 - \pi(S_1, \dots, S_T))^{N-l}] \tag{31}$$

can be efficiently evaluated by making use of (32) of Appendix A.

In order to present some numerical results for an illustration of how the model works, we have to fix a time horizon T and values for the cross-sectional correlation ρ and the inter-temporal correlation parameter ϑ. We choose $T = 5$ as BCBS (2004a) requires the credit institutions to base their PD estimates on a time series with minimum length five years. For ρ, we chose $\rho = 0.12$ as in Section 4, i.e.

again a value suggested by BCBS (2004a). Our feeling is that default events with a five years time distance can be regarded as being nearly independent. Statistically, this statement might be interpreted as something like "the correlation of S_1 and S_5 is less than 1%". Setting $\vartheta = 0.3$, we obtain $\mathrm{corr}[S_1,\ldots,S_T] = \vartheta^4 = 0.81\%$. Thus, the choice $\vartheta = 0.3$ seems reasonable. Note that our choices of the parameters are purely exemplary, as to some extent choosing the values of the parameters is rather a matter of taste or judgement or of decisions depending on the available data or the purpose of the estimations.

Table 13 shows the results of the calculations for the case where no defaults were observed during five years in the whole portfolio. The results for all the three grades are summarized in one table. To arrive at these results, (27) was first evaluated with $N = n_A + n_B + n_C$, then with $N = n_B + n_C$, and finally with $N = n_C$. In all three cases we set $k = 0$ in (30) in order to express that no defaults were observed. Not surprisingly, the calculated confidence bounds are much lower than those presented as in Table 7, thus demonstrating the potentially dramatic effect of exploiting longer observation periods.

Table 13. Upper confidence bounds $\hat{p}_A$ of p_A, $\hat{p}_B$ of p_B and $\hat{p}_C$ of p_C as a function of the confidence level γ. No defaults during 5 years observed, frequencies of obligors in grades given in (4). Cross-sectionally and inter-temporally correlated default events.

γ	50%	75%	90%	95%	99%	99.9%
$\hat{p}_A$	0.03%	0.06%	0.11%	0.16%	0.30%	0.55%
$\hat{p}_B$	0.03%	0.07%	0.13%	0.18%	0.33%	0.62%
$\hat{p}_C$	0.07%	0.14%	0.26%	0.37%	0.67%	1.23%

For Table 14 we conducted essentially the same computations as for Table 13, the difference being that we assumed that over five years $k_A = 0$, defaults were observed in grade A, $k_B = 2$ defaults were observed in grade B, and $k_C = 1$ defaults were observed in grade C (as in Sections 3 and 4 during one year). Consequently, we set $k = 3$ in (30) for calculating the upper confidence bounds for p_A and p_B, as well as $k = 1$ for the upper confidence bounds of p_C. Compared with the results presented in Table 8, we observe again the very strong effect of taking into account a longer time series.

Table 14. Upper confidence bounds $\hat{p}_A$ of p_A, $\hat{p}_B$ of p_B and $\hat{p}_C$ of p_C as a function of the confidence level γ. During 5 years, no default observed in grade A, two defaults observed in grade B, one default observed in grade C, frequencies of obligors in grades given in (4). Cross-sectionally and inter-temporally correlated default events.

γ	50%	75%	90%	95%	99%	99.9%
$\hat{p}_A$	0.12%	0.21%	0.33%	0.43%	0.70%	1.17%
$\hat{p}_B$	0.14%	0.24%	0.38%	0.49%	0.77%	1.29%
$\hat{p}_C$	0.15%	0.27%	0.46%	0.61%	1.01%	1.70%

7. Potential Applications

The *most prudent estimation* methodology described in the previous sections can be used for a range of applications, both within a bank and in a Basel II context. In the latter case, it might be specifically useful for portfolios where neither internal nor external default data are sufficient to meet the Basel requirements. A good example might be Specialized Lending. In these high-volume, low-number and low-default portfolios, internal data is often insufficient for PD estimations per rating category, and might indeed even be insufficient for central tendency estimations for the entire portfolio (across all rating grades). Moreover, mapping to external ratings – although explicitly allowed in the Basel context and widely used in bank internal applications – might be impossible due to the low number of externally rated exposures.

The (conservative) principle of the *most prudent estimation* could serve as an alternative to the Basel slotting approach, subject to supervisory approval. In this context, the proposed methodology might be interpreted as a specific form of the Basel requirement of conservative estimations if data is scarce.

In a wider context, within the bank, the methodology might be used for all sorts of low default portfolios. In particular, it could complement other estimation methods, whether this be mapping to external ratings, the proposals by Schuermann and Hanson (2004) or others. As such, we see our proposed methodology as an additional source for PD calibrations. This should neither invalidate nor prejudge a bank's internal choice of calibration methodologies.

However, we tend to believe that our proposed methodology should only be applied to whole rating systems and portfolios. One might think of calibrating PDs of individual low default rating grades within an otherwise rich data structure. Doing so almost unavoidably leads to a structural break between average PDs (data rich rating grades) and upper PD bounds (low default rating grades) which makes the procedure appear infeasible. Similarly, we believe that the application of the methodology for backtesting or similar validation tools would not add much additional information. For instance, purely expert-based average PDs per rating grade would normally be well below our proposed quantitative upper bounds.

8. Open Issues

For potential applications, a number of important issues need to be addressed:

- Which confidence levels are appropriate? The proposed most prudent estimate could serve as a conservative proxy for average PDs. In determining the confidence level, the impact of a potential underestimation of these average PDs should be taken into account. One might think that the transformation of average PDs into some kind of "stress" PDs, as done in the Basel II and many other credit risk models, could justify rather low confidence levels for the PD estimation in the first place (i.e. using the models as providers of additional buffers against uncertainty). However, this conclusion would be misleading, as it mixes two different types of "stresses": the Basel II model "stress" of the single systematic factor over time, and the estimation uncertainty "stress" of the PD estimations.

Indeed, we would argue for moderate confidence levels when applying the *most prudent estimation* principle, but for other reasons. The most common alternative to our methodology, namely deriving PDs from averages of historical default rates per rating grade, yields a comparable probability that the true PD will be underestimated. Therefore, high confidence levels in our methodology would be hard to justify.

- At which number of defaults should users deviate from our methodology and use "normal" average PD estimation methods, at least for the overall portfolio central tendency? Can this critical number be analytically determined?
- If the relative number of defaults in one of the better ratings grades is significantly higher than those in lower rating grades (and within low default portfolios, this might happen with only one or two additional defaults), then our PD estimates may turn out to be non-monotone. In which cases should this be taken as an indication of an incorrect ordinal ranking? Certainly, monotony or non-monotony of our upper PD bounds does not immediately imply that the average PDs are monotone or non-monotone. Under which conditions would there be statistical evidence of a violation of the monotony requirement for the PDs?

Currently, we do not have definite solutions to above issues. We believe, though, that some of them will involve a certain amount of expert judgment rather than analytical solutions. In particular, that might be the case with the first item. If our proposed approach would be used in a supervisory – say Basel II – context, supervisors might want to think about suitable confidence levels that should be consistently applied.

9. Conclusions

In this article, we have introduced a methodology for estimating probabilities of default in low or no default portfolios. The methodology is based on upper confidence intervals by use of the *most prudent estimation*. Our methodology uses all available quantitative information. In the extreme case of no defaults in the entire portfolio, this information consists solely of the absolute numbers of counterparties per rating grade.

The lack of defaults in the entire portfolio prevents *reliable* quantitative statements on both the absolute level of *average* PDs per rating grade as well as on the relative risk increase from rating grade to rating grade. Within the *most prudent estimation* methodology, we do not use such information. The only additional assumption used is the *ordinal* ranking of the borrowers, which is assumed to be correct.

Our PD estimates might seem rather high at first sight. However, given the amount of information that is actually available, the results do not appear out of range. We believe that the choice of moderate confidence levels is appropriate within most applications. The results can be scaled to any appropriate central tendency. Additionally, the multi-year context as described in Section 6 might provide further insight.

References

Balthazar L (2004), PD Estimates for Basel II, Risk, April, 84-85.

Basel Committee on Banking Supervision (BCBS) (2004a), Basel II: International Convergence of Capital Measurement and Capital Standards: a Revised Framework. http://www.bis.org/publ/bcbs107.htm

Basel Committee on Banking Supervision (BCBS) (2004b), An Explanatory Note on the Basel II IRB Risk Weight Functions. http://www.bis.org

Basel Committee on Banking Supervision (BCBS) (2004c), Studies on the Validation of Internal Rating Systems, Working Paper No. 14.

British Bankers' Association (BBA), London Investment Banking Association (LIBA) and International Swaps and Derivatives Association (ISDA) (2004), The IRB Approach for Low Default Portfolios (LDPs) – Recommendations of the Joint BBA, LIBA, ISDA Industry Working Group, Discussion Paper. http://www.isda.org/speeches/pdf/ISDA-LIBA-BBA-LowDefaulPortfolioPaper080904-paper.pdf

Blochwitz S, Hohl S, Tasche D, Wehn C (2004), Validating Default Probabilities on Short Time Series. Capital & Market Risk Insights, Federal Reserve Bank of Chicago, December 2004. http://www.chicagofed.org/banking_information/capital_and_market_risk_insights.cfm

Bluhm C, Overbeck L, Wagner C (2003), An Introduction to Credit Risk Modeling, Chapman & Hall / CRC, Boca Raton.

Brown L, Cai T, Dasgupta A (2001), Interval Estimation for a Binomial Proportion. Statistical Science, **16**, (2), 101-133.

Cathcart A, Benjamin N (2005), Low Default Portfolios: A Proposal for conservative PD estimation. Discussion Paper, Financial Services Authority.

Durrett R (1996), Probability: Theory and Examples, Second Edition, Wadsworth, Belmont.

Gordy M (2003), A Risk-Factor Model Foundation for Ratings-Based Bank Capital Rules. Journal of Financial Intermediation **12** (3), 199-232.

Hinderer K (1980), Grundbegriffe der Wahrscheinlichkeitstheorie. Zweiter korrigierter Nachdruck der ersten Auflage, Springer, Berlin.

Jafry Y and Schuermann T (2004), Measurement, estimation, and comparison of credit migration matrices, Journal of Banking & Finance **28**, 2603-2639.

R Development Core Team (2003), R: A Language and Environment for Statistical Computing, R Foundation for Statistical Computing, Vienna. http://www.R-project.org

Schuermann T and Hanson S (2004), Estimating Probabilities of Default, Staff Report no.190, Federal Reserve Bank of New York.
Vasicek O (1997), The Loan Loss Distribution. Working Paper, KMV Corporation.

Appendix A

This appendix provides additional information on the analytical and numerical solutions of Equations (10) and (14).

Analytical solution of Equation (10). If X is a binomially distributed random variable with size parameter n and success probability p, then for any integer $0 \leq k \leq n$, we have

$$\sum_{i=0}^{k} \binom{n}{i} p^i (1-p)^{n-i} = P[X \leq k] = 1 - P[Y \leq p] = \frac{\int_p^1 t^k (1-t)^{n-k-1} dt}{\int_0^1 t^k (1-t)^{n-k-1} dt} \tag{32}$$

with Y denoting a beta distributed random variable with parameters $\alpha = k+1$ and $\beta = n-k$ (see, e.g., Hinderer (1980), Lemma 11.2). The beta distribution function and its inverse function are available in standard numerical tools, e.g. in Excel.

Direct numerical solution of Equation (10). The following proposition shows the existence and uniqueness of the solution of (10), and, at the same time, provides initial values for the numerical root-finding (see (35)).

Proposition A.1. *Let $0 \leq k < n$ be integers, and define the function* $f_{n,k} : (0,1) \to \mathbb{R}$ *by*

$$f_{n,k}(p) = \sum_{i=0}^{k} \binom{n}{i} p^i (1-p)^{n-i}, \quad p \in (0,1) \tag{33}$$

Fix some $0 < v < 1$. Then the equation

$$f_{n,k}(p) = v \tag{34}$$

has exactly one solution $0 < p = p(v) < 1$. Moreover, this solution $p(v)$ satisfies the inequalities

$$1 - \sqrt[n]{v} \leq p(v) \leq \sqrt[n]{1-v} \tag{35}$$

Proof. A straight-forward calculation yields

$$\frac{df_{n,k}(p)}{dp} = -(n-k)\binom{n}{k}p^k(1-p)^{n-k-1}.\tag{36}$$

Hence $f_{n,k}$ is strictly decreasing. This implies uniqueness of the solution of (34). The inequalities

$$f_{n,0}(p) \le f_{n,k}(p) \le f_{n,n-1}(p)\tag{37}$$

imply the existence of a solution of (34) and the inequalities (35).□

Numerical solution of Equation (14). For (14) we can derive a result similar to Proposition A.1. However, there is no obvious upper bound to the solution $p(v)$ of (39) as in (35).

Proposition A.2. *For any probability $0 < p < 1$, any correlation $0 < \rho < 1$ and any real number y define*

$$F_\rho(p,y) = \Phi\left(\frac{\Phi^{-1}(p)+\sqrt{\rho}y}{\sqrt{1-\rho}}\right),\tag{38}$$

where we make use of the same notations as for Equation (14). Fix a value $0 < v < 1$ and a positive integer n. Then the equation

$$v = \int_{-\infty}^{\infty} \varphi(y)(1 - F_\rho(p,y))^n\, dy,\tag{39}$$

with φ denoting the standard normal density, has exactly one solution $0 < p = p(v) < 1$. This solution $p(v)$ satisfies the inequality

$$p(v) \ge 1 - \sqrt[n]{v}.\tag{40}$$

Proof of Proposition (A.2) Note that – for fixed ρ and y – the function $F_\rho(p, y)$ is strictly increasing and continuous in p. Moreover, we have

$$0 = \lim_{p \to 0} F_\rho(p,y) \quad \text{and} \quad 1 = \lim_{p \to 1} F_\rho(p,y)\tag{41}$$

Equation (41) implies existence and uniqueness of the solution of (39).

Define the random variable Z by

$$Z = F_\rho(p,Y),\tag{42}$$

where Y denotes a standard normally distributed random variable. Then Z has the well-known *Vasicek distribution* (cf. Vasicek, 1997), and in particular we have

$$E[Z] = p. \tag{43}$$

Using (42), Equation (39) can be rewritten as

$$v = E[(1-Z)^n]. \tag{44}$$

Since $y \to (1-y)^n$ is convex for $0 < y < 1$, by (43) Jensen's inequality implies

$$v = E[(1-Z)^n] \geq (1-p)^n. \tag{45}$$

As the right-hand side of (39) is decreasing in p, (40) now follows from (45).□

Appendix B

This appendix provides additional numerical results for the "scaling" extension of the *most prudent estimation* principle according to Section 5 in the case of no default portfolios. In the examples presented in Tables 15 and 16, the confidence level for deriving the upper confidence bound for the overall portfolio PD, and the confidence levels for the *most prudent estimates* of PDs per rating grade have always been set equal. Moreover, our methodology always provides equality between the upper bound of the overall portfolio PD and the *most prudent estimate* for p_A according to the respective examples of Sections 2 and 4.

Table 15. Upper confidence bound $\hat{p}_{A,\text{scaled}}$ of p_A, $\hat{p}_{B,\text{scaled}}$ of p_B and $\hat{p}_{C,\text{scaled}}$ of p_C as a function of the confidence level γ after scaling to the upper confidence bound of the overall portfolio PD. No default observed, frequencies of obligors in grades given in (4). Uncorrelated default events.

γ	50%	75%	90%	95%	99%	99.9%
Central Tendency	0.09%	0.17%	0.29%	0.37%	0.57%	0.86%
K	0.61	0.66	0.60	0.58	0.59	0.59
$\hat{p}_A$	0.05%	0.11%	0.17%	0.22%	0.33%	0.51%
$\hat{p}_B$	0.06%	0.13%	0.20%	0.25%	0.39%	0.58%
$\hat{p}_C$	0.14%	0.24%	0.45%	0.58%	0.89%	1.35%

Table 16. Upper confidence bound $\hat{p}_{A,\text{scaled}}$ of p_A, $\hat{p}_{B,\text{scaled}}$ of p_B and $\hat{p}_{C,\text{scaled}}$ of p_C as a function of the confidence level γ after scaling to the upper confidence bound of the overall portfolio PD. No default observed, frequencies of obligors in grades given in (4). Correlated default events.

γ	50%	75%	90%	95%	99%	99.9%
Central Tendency	0.15%	0.40%	0.86%	1.31%	2.65%	5.29%
K	0.62	0.65	0.66	0.68	0.70	0.73
$\hat{p}_A$	0.09%	0.26%	0.57%	0.89%	1.86%	3.87%
$\hat{p}_B$	0.11%	0.29%	0.64%	0.98%	2.05%	4.22%
$\hat{p}_C$	0.23%	0.59%	1.25%	1.89%	3.72%	7.19%

VI. A Multi-Factor Approach for Systematic Default and Recovery Risk[1]

Daniel Rösch and Harald Scheule

University of Regensburg and University of Melbourne

1. Modelling Default and Recovery Risk

Banks face the challenge of forecasting losses and loss distributions in relation to their credit risk exposures. Most banks choose a modular approach in line with the current proposals of the Basel Committee on Banking Supervision (2004), where selected risk parameters such as default probabilities, exposures at default and recoveries given default are modelled independently. However, the assumption of independence is questionable. Previous studies have shown that default probabilities and recovery rates given default are negatively correlated (Carey (1998), Hu and Perraudin (2002), Frye (2003), Altman et al. (2003), or Cantor and Varma, 2005). A failure to take these dependencies into account will lead to incorrect forecasts of the loss distribution and the derived capital allocation.

This paper extends a model introduced by Frye (2000). Modifications of the approach can be found in Pykhtin (2003) and Düllmann and Trapp (2004). Our contribution is original with regard to the following three aspects. First, we develop a theoretical model for the default probabilities and recovery rates and show how to combine observable information with random risk factors. In comparison to the above mentioned models, our approach explains the default and the recovery rate by risk factors which can be observed at the time of the risk assessment. According to the current Basel proposal, banks can opt to provide their own recovery rate forecasts for the regulatory capital calculation. Thus, there is an immediate industry need for modelling.

Second, we show a framework for estimating the joint processes of all variables in the model. Particularly, the simultaneous model allows the measurement of the correlation between the defaults and recoveries given the information. In this model, statistical tests for the variables and correlations can easily be conducted. An empirical study reveals additional evidence on the correlations between risk

---

[1] This article originally appeared in the September 2005 issue of The Journal of Fixed Income and is reprinted with permission from Institutional Investor, Inc. For more information please visit www.iijournals.com.

drivers of default and recovery. Cantor and Varma (2003) analyze the same data-set and identify seniority and security as the main risk factors explaining recovery rates. This paper extends their approach by developing a framework for modelling correlations between factor-based models for default and recovery rates.

Third, the implications of our results on economic and regulatory capital are shown. Note that according to the current proposals of the Basel Committee, only the forecast default probabilities and recovery rates but no correlation estimates, enter the calculation of the latter. We demonstrate the effects of spuriously neglecting correlations in practical applications.

The rest of the paper is organized as follows. The theoretical framework is introduced in the second section ('Model and Estimation') for a model using historic averages as forecasts and a model taking time-varying risk factors into account. The third section ('Data and Results') includes an empirical analysis based on default and recovery rates published by Moody's rating agency and macroeconomic indices from the Conference Board. Section four ('Implications for Economic and Regulatory Capital') shows the implications of the different models on the economic capital derived from the loss distribution and the regulatory capital proposed by the Basel Committee. Section five ('Discussion') concludes with a summary and discussion of the findings.

2. Model and Estimation

2.1. The Model for the Default Process

Our basic framework follows the approach taken by Frye (2000). We assume that n_t firms of one risk segment are observed during the time periods t ($t=1,\ldots,T$). For simplicity, these firms are assumed to be homogenous with regard to the relevant parameters and a latent variable describes each obligor i's ($i=1,\ldots,n_t$) credit quality

$$S_{it} = w \cdot F_t + \sqrt{1-w^2} \cdot U_{it} \qquad (1)$$

($w \in [0,1]$). $F_t \sim N(0,1)$ and $U_t \sim N(0,1)$ are independent systematic and idiosyncratic standard normally distributed risk factors. The Gaussian random variable S_{it} may be interpreted as the return on a firm's assets and therefore w^2 is often called 'asset correlation'.

A default event occurs if the latent variable crosses a threshold c

$$S_{it} < c \qquad (2)$$

which happens with probability $\pi = \Phi(c)$ where $\Phi(.)$ is the standard normal cumulative density function. If an obligor is in default, the indicator variable D_{it} equals one and zero otherwise:

$$D_{it} = \begin{cases} 1 & \text{obligor } i \text{ defaults in period } t \\ 0 & \text{else} \end{cases} \tag{3}$$

Conditional on the realization f_t of the systematic risk factor, default events are assumed to be independent between obligors, i.e., each firm defaults with the conditional default probability

$$\pi(f_t) = P(D_{it} = 1 | F_t = f_t) = \Phi\left(\frac{c - w \cdot f_t}{\sqrt{1 - w^2}}\right). \tag{4}$$

2.2. The Model for the Recovery

In modelling the recovery rate R_{it} of a defaulted obligor, we follow Schönbucher (2003) and Düllmann and Trapp (2004) and use a logistic normal process:

$$R_{it} = \frac{\exp(\widetilde{Y}_{it})}{1 + \exp(\widetilde{Y}_{it})} \tag{5}$$

with the transformed recovery rate

$$\widetilde{Y}_{it} = \mu + b \cdot X_t + Z_{it} \tag{6}$$

where $X_t \sim N(0,1)$, $Z_{it} \sim N(0,\delta^2)$ are independent systematic and idiosyncratic factors and μ and b are parameters. These idiosyncratic factors are independent from the idiosyncratic factors which drive the latent default variable. Compared to the normal distribution assumption for recovery rates Frye (2000), the chosen transformation has the advantage that recovery rates are bounded between 0% and 100%. Note that any other cumulative density function could be used. As a matter of fact, we estimated models using a standard normal transformation and received similar results.

If we observe a homogenous segment of borrowers, the transformed recovery rate is given by

$$\widetilde{Y}_t = \frac{1}{n_t} \sum_{i=1}^{n_t} \widetilde{Y}_{it} = \mu + b \cdot X_t + \frac{1}{n_t} \sum_{i=1}^{n_t} Z_{it} \tag{7}$$

with $Z_t = \dfrac{1}{n_t}\displaystyle\sum_{i=1}^{n_t} Z_{it}$ which is normally distributed with mean zero and variance

δ^2/n_t^2 . The variance converges for large n_t to zero:

$$\lim_{n_t \to \infty} \operatorname{Var}\left(\frac{1}{n_t} \sum_{i=1}^{n_t} Z_{it} \right) = 0 \tag{8}$$

Therefore, we approximate the average transformed recovery rate by

$$\tilde{Y}_t \approx Y_t = \mu + b \cdot X_t, \tag{9}$$

which is driven only by a systematic risk factor and normally distributed $Y_t \sim N(\mu, b^2)$. The link between the recovery and default process is introduced by modelling the dependence of the two systematic risk factors. Since both F_t and X_t are marginally normal distributed, we model their dependence by assuming that they have a bivariate normal distribution with correlation parameter ρ. Alternative, a copula which is different from the Gaussian could have been assumed. It then follows that the average transformed recovery rate and latent default triggering variable have a correlation

$$\operatorname{Corr}(S_{it}, Y_t) = w \cdot \rho \tag{10}$$

The correlation equals one in the special case that a single systematic factor drives both the default events as well as the recoveries given these events.

2.3. A Multi-Factor Model Extension

So far, we presented a model for systematic risk in defaults and recoveries where systematic risk is driven by common factors which are not directly observable. These unobservable factors induce uncertainties into the forecasts of loss distributions. The higher their impact, ceteris paribus, the more skewed the resulting distributions are and the higher key risk measures such as the Value-at-Risk or the Conditional Value-at-Risk will be. Since the true parameters of the models are unknown, the severity of the impact must be estimated from observable data.

As an alternative to the models above, we analyze a model, which has already been used in the context of default modelling. Examples are Rösch and Scheule (2004) and Hamerle et al. (2003). These models show that part of the cyclical fluctuations in default rates can be attributed to observable systematic risk factors. Once these factors are identified and incorporated into the model, a large part of uncertainty from unobservable factors can be explained. These types of models are also exhibited in Heitfield (2005) and are related to a concept broadly known as a point-in-time approach because losses are forecast based on information on the prevailing point of the business cycle.

In our extension, it is assumed that the default threshold for the factor model of the default process fluctuates over time. Alternatively, we could introduce a factor model with time-varying mean. This variation with time is introduced by K observable macroeconomic risk factors, such as GDP growth or interest rates. We assume that these state variables are observed in prior time periods and denote them by $z_{t-1}^D = \left(z_{t-1,1}^D, \ldots, z_{t-1,K}^D\right)$. As a result, the conditional default probability for each borrower within the risk segment is modified (compare Rösch (2003) and Heitfield (2005) who additionally condition default probabilities on firm-specific factors):

$$\pi*\left(z_{t-1}^D, f_t\right) = P\left(D_{it} = 1 \mid z_{t-1}^D, f_t\right) = \Phi\left(\frac{\gamma_0 + \gamma'\cdot z_{t-1}^D - w*\cdot f_t}{\sqrt{1 - w*^2}}\right) \tag{11}$$

where $\gamma = (\gamma_1, \ldots, \gamma_K)'$ denotes a vector of exposures to the common observable factors and γ_0 is a constant. The mean of this conditional default probability with respect to the unobservable standard normally distributed factor f_t is given by

$$\pi*\left(z_{t-1}^D\right) = \int_{-\infty}^{\infty} \pi*\left(z_{t-1}^D, f_t\right) d\Phi(f_t) = \Phi\left(c* + \gamma'\cdot z_{t-1}^D\right) \tag{12}$$

In a similar way, we assume that the mean of the log-transformed systematic recovery rate depends on common macroeconomic factors $z_{t-1}^R = \left(z_{t-1,1}^R, \ldots, z_{t-1,L}^R\right)$. This vector may or may not contain factors which also describe the default process:

$$Y_t^* = \beta_0 + \beta'\cdot z_{t-1}^R + b*\cdot X_t \tag{13}$$

where $\beta = (\beta_1, \ldots, \beta_L)$ denotes a vector of exposures and β_0 the constant.

If models (12) and (13) hold, i.e., defaults and recoveries are driven by observable lagged systematic risk factors, it can be shown that their means are fluctuating with the change of the economy. Moreover, if these models hold, then model (4) and (9) with constant mean are misspecifications. Consequently, fitting model (4) and (9) to observable data will have the effect that all time variation is captured in the estimates of the exposures to the unobservable random factors F_t and X_t. On the other hand, attributing time variation to observable factors will lead to lower parameter estimates for the influences of the unobservable factors, thereby reducing uncertainty with regard to the forecasts of the loss distributions. We will demonstrate these effects on the economic and regulatory capital below.

2.4. Model Estimation

Once the models are specified, an algorithm for estimating the parameters from observable data is needed. Following work by Frye (2000) we choose the Maximum-Likelihood method. Extending these studies, we suggest an ML-procedure which allows the joint estimation of all coefficients, including those of models (11) and (13) with observable factors.

Let us consider a realization f_t of the unobservable random factor F_t. Given this realization the default events are independent and the number of defaults $D_t = \sum_{i=1}^{n_t} D_{it}$ is conditionally binomial distributed with probability distribution

$$P(D_t = d_t \mid f_t) = \begin{cases} \binom{d_t}{n_t} \pi(f_t)^{d_t} \cdot [1 - \pi(f_t)]^{n_t - d_t}, & d_t = 0,1,\dots,n_t \\ 0, & else \end{cases} \tag{14}$$

with $\pi(f_t)$ as in (4). Note that the transformed recovery rate can also be modelled given a realization f_t. It holds that the random vector $(F_t, Y_t)'$ is normally distributed with

$$\binom{F_t}{Y_t} \sim N\left[\binom{0}{\mu}, \binom{1 \quad b\rho}{b\rho \quad b^2}\right].$$

From the law of conditional expectation it follows that Y_t has conditional mean

$$\mu(f_t) = E(Y_t \mid f_t) = \mu + b \cdot \rho \cdot f_t \tag{15}$$

and conditional standard deviation

$$\sigma(f_t) = +\sqrt{\mathrm{Var}(Y_t \mid f_t)} = b \cdot \sqrt{1 - \rho^2} \tag{16}$$

Hence, the joint density $g(.)$ of d_t defaults and a transformed recovery rate y_t given f_t is simply the product of the density of y_t and the probability of d_t, i.e.,

$$g(d_t, y_t \mid f_t)$$

$$= \frac{1}{\sigma(f_t) \cdot \sqrt{2 \cdot \pi}} \cdot \exp\left\{-\frac{[y_t - \mu(f_t)]^2}{2 \cdot [\sigma(f_t)]^2}\right\} \cdot \binom{d_t}{n_t} \cdot \pi(f_t)^{d_t} \cdot [1 - \pi(f_t)]^{n_t - d_t} \tag{17}$$

Note, $g(.)$ depends on the unknown parameters of the default and the recovery process. Since the common factor is not observable we establish the unconditional density

$$g(d_t, y_t)$$

$$= \int_{-\infty}^{\infty} \frac{1}{\sigma(f_t) \cdot \sqrt{2 \cdot \pi}} \cdot \exp\left\{-\frac{[y_t - \mu(f_t)]^2}{2 \cdot [\sigma(f_t)]^2}\right\} \cdot \binom{d_t}{n_t} \cdot \pi(f_t)^{d_t} \cdot [1 - \pi(f_t)]^{n_t - d_t} \, d\Phi(f_t) \qquad (18)$$

Observing a time series with T periods leads to the final unconditional log-likelihood function

$$l(\mu, b, c, w, \rho) = \sum_{t=1}^{T} \ln(g(d_t, y_t)) \qquad (19)$$

This function is optimized with respect to the unknown parameters. In the appendix we demonstrate the performance of the approach by Monte-Carlo simulations.

For the second type of models which include macroeconomic risk factors, we replace $\pi(f_t)$ from (4) by $\pi*(z_{t-1}^D, f_t)$ from (11) and $\mu(f_t)$ from (15) by $\beta_0 + \beta' \cdot z_{t-1}^R + b \cdot \rho \cdot f_t$ and obtain the log-likelihood $l(\beta_0, \beta, b, \gamma_0, \gamma, w, \rho)$.

3. Data and Results

3.1. The Data

The empirical analysis is based on the global corporate issuer default rates and issue recovery rates (cf. Moody's, 2005). In this data set, default rates are calculated as the ratio of defaulted and total number of rated issuers for a given period. According to Moody's (2005), a default is recorded if

- Interest and/or principal payments are missed or delayed,
- Chapter 11 or Chapter 7 bankruptcy is filed, or
- Distressed exchange such as a reduction of the financial obligation occurs.

Most defaults are related to publicly traded debt issues. Therefore, Moody's defines a recovery rate as the ratio of the price of defaulted debt obligations after 30 days of the occurrence of a default event and the par value. The recovery rates are published for different levels of seniority such as total (Total), senior secured (S_Sec), senior unsecured (S_Un), senior subordinated (S_Sub), subordinated (Sub) and junior subordinated debt. We excluded the debt category junior subordinated from the analysis due to a high number of missing values.

In addition, the composite indices published by The Conference Board (www.tcb-indicators.org) were chosen as macroeconomic systematic risk drivers, i.e., the

- Index of 4 coincident indicators (COINC) which measures the health of the U.S. economy. The index includes the number of employees on non-agricultural payrolls, personal income less transfer payments, index of industrial production and manufacturing as well as trade sales.
- Index of 10 leading indicators (LEAD) which measures the future health of the U.S. economy. The index includes average weekly hours in manufacturing, average weekly initial claims for unemployment insurance, manufacturers' new orders of consumer goods and materials, vendor performance, manufacturers' new orders of non-defence capital goods, building permits for new private housing units, stock price index, money supply, interest rate spread of 10-year treasury bonds less federal funds and consumer expectations.

The indices are recognized as indicators for the U.S. business cycle. Note that for the analysis, growth rates of the indices were calculated and lagged by three months.

Due to a limited number of defaults in previous years, the compiled data set was restricted to the period 1985 to 2004 and split into an estimation sample (1985 to 2003) and a forecast sample (2004). Table 1 and Table 2 include descriptive statistics and Bravais-Pearson correlations for default rates, recovery rates and time lagged macroeconomic indicators of the data set. Note that default rates are negatively correlated with the recovery rates of different seniority classes and macroeconomic variables.

Table 1. Descriptive statistics of the variables

Variable	Mean	Median	Max.	Min.	Std. Dev.	Skew.	Kurt.
Default Rate	0.0176	0.0144	0.0382	0.0052	0.0103	0.6849	2.2971
Recovery Rate (Total)	0.4208	0.4300	0.6170	0.2570	0.0902	0.2883	3.0464
Recovery Rate (S_Sec)	0.5794	0.5725	0.8360	0.3570	0.1379	0.2631	2.0440
Recovery Rate (S_Un)	0.4481	0.4450	0.6280	0.2310	0.1158	-0.1816	2.2725
Recovery Rate (S_Sub)	0.3703	0.3695	0.5190	0.2030	0.0984	-0.1868	1.7668
Recovery Rate (Sub)	0.2987	0.3245	0.4620	0.1230	0.1117	-0.2227	1.7387
COINC	0.0215	0.0245	0.0409	-0.0165	0.0160	-0.9365	3.0335
LEAD	0.0130	0.0154	0.0336	-0.0126	0.0151	-0.4568	1.9154

Table 2. Bravais-Pearson correlations of variables

Variable	Default Rate	Total	S_Sec	S_Un	S_Sub	Sub	COINC	LEAD
Default Rate	1.00	-0.67	-0.72	-0.72	-0.53	-0.34	-0.75	-0.47
Recovery Rate (Total)		1.00	0.78	0.68	0.72	0.29	0.32	0.54
Recovery Rate (S_Sec)			1.00	0.66	0.48	0.37	0.33	0.55
Recovery Rate (S_Un)				1.00	0.56	0.42	0.49	0.48
Recovery Rate (S_Sub)					1.00	0.24	0.20	0.40
Recovery Rate (Sub)						1.00	0.41	0.17
COINC							1.00	0.28
LEAD								1.00

Figure 1 shows that both, the default and recovery rate fluctuate over time in opposite directions. This signals that default and recovery rates show a considerable share of systematic risk which can be explained by time varying variables.

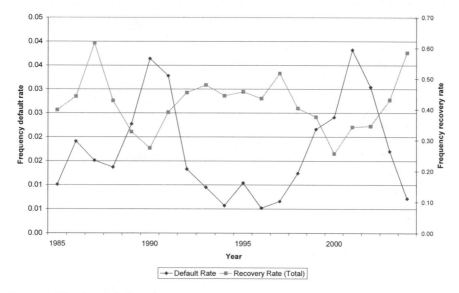

Figure 1. Moody's default rate vs. recovery rate

Figure 2 contains similar graphs for the recovery rates of the different seniority classes. Note that the recovery rates increase with the seniority of a debt issue and show similar patterns over time. This indicates that they may be driven by the same or similar systematic risk factors.

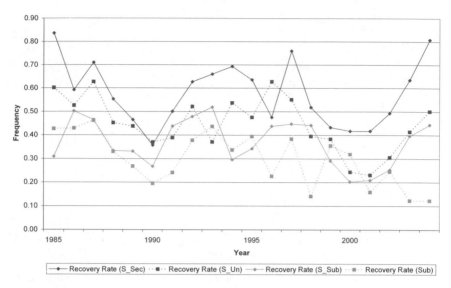

Figure 2. Moody's recovery rates by seniority class

Next to the business cycle and the seniority, it is plausible to presume that recovery rates depend on the industry, the collateral type, the legal environment, default criteria as well as the credit quality associated with an obligor. Tables 3 and 4 show the recovery rates for different industries and issuer credit ratings (cf. Moody's, 2004, 2005). Refer to these documents for a more detailed analysis of the properties of recovery rates.

3.2. Estimation Results

Based on the described data set, two models were estimated:

- Model without macroeconomic risk factors (equations (4) and (9)): we refer to this model as a through-the-cycle model because the forecast default and recovery rate equal the historic average from 1985 to 2003;
- Model with macroeconomic risk factors (equations (11) and (13)): we refer to this model as a point-in-time model because the forecast default and recovery rates fluctuate over time.

Within the credit risk community, a discussion on the correct definition of a through-the-cycle and point-in-time model exists, in which the present article does not intend to participate. We use these expressions as stylized denominations, being aware that other interpretations of these rating philosophies may exist (cf. Heitfield, 2005).

Table 3. Recovery rates for selected industries (Moody's, 2004)

Industry	Recovery Rate (1982-2003)
Utility-Gas	0.515
Oil	0.445
Hospitality	0.425
Utility-Electric	0.414
Transport-Ocean	0.388
Media, Broadcasting and Cable	0.382
Transport-Surface	0.366
Finance and Banking	0.363
Industrial	0.354
Retail	0.344
Transport-Air	0.343
Automotive	0.334
Healthcare	0.327
Consumer Goods	0.325
Construction	0.319
Technology	0.295
Real Estate	0.288
Steel	0.274
Telecommunications	0.232
Miscellaneous	0.395

Table 4. Recovery rates for selected issuer credit rating categories (Moody's, 2005)

Issuer Credit Rating	Recovery Rate (1982-2004)
Aa	0.954
A	0.498
Baa	0.433
Ba	0.407
B	0.384
Caa-Ca	0.364

Due to the limitations of publicly available data, we use Moody's global default rates, total recoveries, and recoveries by seniority class. Table 5 shows the estimation results for the through-the-cycle model (4) and (9) and Table 6 for the point-in-time model (11) and (13) using the variables COINC and LEAD as explanatory variables. In the latter model we choose both variables due to their statistical significance.

Table 5. Parameter estimation results for the through-the-cycle model; Annual default and recovery data from 1985 to 2003 is used for estimation; standard errors are in parentheses; *** significant at 1% level, ** significant at 5% level, * significant at 10% level

Parameter	Total	S_Sec	S_Un	S_Sub	Sub
c	-2.0942***	-2.0951***	-2.0966***	-2.0942***	-2.0940***
	(0.0545)	(0.0550)	(0.0546)	(0.0544)	(0.0549)
w	0.2194***	0.2212***	0.2197***	0.2191***	0.2210***
	(0.0366)	(0.0369)	(0.0367)	(0.0366)	(0.0369)
μ	-0.3650***	0.2976**	-0.2347*	-0.5739***	-0.8679***
	(0.0794)	(0.1284)	(0.1123)	(0.0998	(0.1235)
b	0.3462***	0.5598***	0.4898***	0.4351***	0.5384***
	(0.0562)	(0.0908)	(0.0795)	(0.0706)	(0.0873)
ρ	0.6539***	0.7049***	0.7520***	0.5081**	0.3979*
	(0.1413)	(0.1286)	(0.1091)	(0.1799)	(0.2013)

Table 6. Parameter estimation results for the point-in-time model; Annual default and recovery data from 1985 to 2003 is used for estimation; standard errors are in parentheses; *** significant at 1% level, ** significant at 5% level, * significant at 10% level.

Parameter	Total	S_Sec	S_Un	S_Sub	Sub
γ_0	-1.9403***	-1.9484***	-1.9089***	-1.9232***	-1.9040***
	(0.0524)	(0.05210)	(0.0603)	(0.05660)	(0.0609)
γ_1	-8.5211***	-8.1786***	-10.078***	-9.2828***	-10.134***
	(1.8571)	(1.7964)	(2.2618)	(2.0736)	(2.2884)
	COINC	COINC	COINC	COINC	COINC
w	0.1473***	0.1522***	0.1485***	0.1483***	0.1508***
	(0.0278)	(0.0286)	(0.0276)	(0.0277)	(0.0279)
β_0	0.4557***	0.1607	-0.5576***	-0.6621***	-1.1883***
	(0.0867)	(0.1382)	(0.1635)	(0.1194)	(0.1845)
β_1	7.4191*	11.1867*	15.0807**	7.2136	14.9625**
	(4.1423)	(6.4208)	(6.1142)	(6.0595)	(6.8940)
	LEAD	LEAD	COINC	LEAD	COINC
b	0.3063***	0.4960***	0.4260***	0.4071***	0.4820***
	(0.0513)	(0.0838)	(0.0691)	(0.0673)	(0.0279)
ρ	0.6642***	0.7346***	0.6675***	0.4903**	0.1033
	(0.1715)	(0.1520)	(0.1481)	(0.2088)	(0.2454)

First, consider the through-the-cycle model. Since we use the same default rates in each model, the estimates for the default process are similar across models, and consistent to the ones found in other studies (compare Gordy (2000) or Rösch, 2005). The parameter estimates for the (transformed) recovery process reflect estimates for the mean (transformed) recoveries and their fluctuations over time. Most important are the estimates for the correlation of the two processes which are positive and similar in size to the correlations between default rates and recovery rates found in previous studies. Note that this is the correlation between the systematic factor driving the latent default triggering variable 'asset return' S_{it} and the systematic factor driving the recovery process. Therefore, higher 'asset returns' (lower conditional default probabilities) tend to come along with higher recovery. A positive value of the correlation indicates negative association between defaults and recoveries. The default rate decreases while the recovery rate increases in boom years and vice versa in depression years.

Next, consider the point-in-time model. The default and the recovery process are driven by one macroeconomic variable in each model. The parameters of all macroeconomic variables show a plausible sign. The negative sign of the COINC index in the default process signals that a positive change of the index comes along with subsequent lower number of defaults. The positive signs of the variables in the recovery process indicate that higher recoveries follow a positive change in the variable. In addition, most variables are significant at the 10% level. The only exception is the parameter of the macroeconomic index LEAD for the senior subordinated recovery rate, which indicates only a limited exposure to systematic risk drivers. Note that the influence of the systematic random factor is reduced in each process by the inclusion of the macroeconomic variable. While we do not mean to interpret these indices as risk drivers themselves, but rather as proxies for the future state of the economy, these variables are able to explain part of the previously unobservable systematic risk. The remaining systematic risk is reflected by the size of w and b and is still correlated but cannot be explained by our proxies.

Once the point estimates for the parameters are given, we forecast separately the defaults and recoveries for year 2004. Table 7 shows that the point-in-time model leads to forecasts for the default and recovery rates that are closer to the realized values than the ones derived from the through-the-cycle model.

Table 7. Forecasts and realizations for year 2004 (through-the-cycle versus point-in-time)

Parameter	Total	S_Sec	S_Un	S_Sub	Sub
Default Rate					
Forecast TTC	0.0181	0.0181	0.0180	0.0181	0.0181
Forecast PIT	0.0162	0.0162	0.0160	0.0162	0.0162
Realization	0.0072	0.0072	0.0072	0.0072	0.0072
Recovery Rate					
Forecast TTC	0.4097	0.5739	0.4416	0.3603	0.2957
Forecast PIT	0.4381	0.6159	0.4484	0.3867	0.3014
Realization	0.5850	0.8080	0.5010	0.4440	0.1230

4. Implications for Economic and Regulatory Capital

Since the main contribution of our approach lies in the joint modelling of defaults and recoveries, we now apply the forecast default rates, recovery rates for the year 2004 as well as their estimated correlation to a portfolio of 1,000 obligors. To simplify the process, we take the senior secured class as an example and assume a credit exposure of one monetary unit for each obligor.

Figure 3 and Table 8 compare two forecast loss distributions of the through-the-cycle model. To demonstrate the influence of correlation between the processes we compare the distribution which assumes independence to the distribution which is based on the estimated correlation between the default and recovery rate transformations of 0.7049. Economic capital or the credit portfolio risk is usually measured by higher percentiles of the simulated loss variable such as the 95-, 99-, 99.5- or 99.9- percentile (95%-, 99%-, 99.5%- or 99.9%-Value-at-Risk). It can be seen that these percentiles are considerably higher if correlations between default and recovery rates are taken into account. If we take the 99.9%-Value-at-Risk as an example, the percentile under dependence exceeds the percentile under independence by approximately 50 percent. In other words, if dependencies are not taken into account, which is a common feature in many of today's credit risk models, the credit portfolio risk is likely to be seriously underestimated.

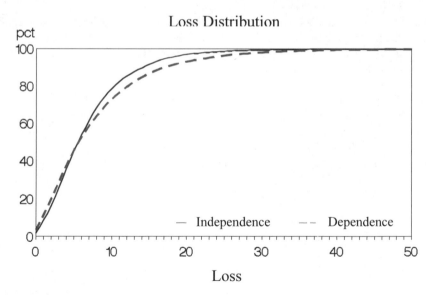

Figure 3. Loss distributions for the through-the-cycle model (S_Sec)

Table 8. Descriptive statistics of loss distributions for the through-the-cycle model; Portfolios contain 1,000 obligors with an exposure of one monetary unit each, 10,000 random samples were drawn for each distribution with and without correlation between systematic factors

	Mean	Std. dev.	Med	95	99	99.5	99.9	Basel II Capital (Standardized)	Basel II Capital (Foundation IRB)	Basel II Capital (Advanced IRB)
Ind. Factors	7.82	5.59	6.53	18.55	27.35	31.92	39.02	80.00	74.01	70.08
Corr. Factors	8.73	7.59	6.62	23.81	36.04	42.43	58.75	80.00	74.01	70.08

Forecast default and recovery rates can be used to calculate the regulatory capital for the hypothetical portfolio. For corporate credit exposures, the Basel Committee on Banking Supervision (2004) allows banks to choose one of the following options:

- Standardized approach: regulatory capital is calculated based on the corporate issuer credit rating and results in a regulatory capital between 1.6% and 12% of the credit exposure. The regulatory capital equals 8% of the credit exposure if firms are unrated;
- Foundation Internal Ratings Based (IRB) approach: regulatory capital is calculated based on the forecast default probabilities and a proposed loss given default for senior secured claims of 45% (i.e. a recovery rate of 55%) and for subordinated claims of 75% (i.e. a recovery rate of 25%).
- Advanced IRB approach: regulatory capital is calculated based on the forecast default probabilities and forecast recovery rates.

For the through-the-cycle model, the Standardized approach and the Foundation IRB approach result in a relatively close regulatory capital requirement (80.00 vs. 74.01). The reason for this is that the forecast default rate (0.0181) is close to the historic average which was used by the Basel Committee when calibrating regulatory capital to the current level of 8%. The Advanced IRB approach leads to a lower regulatory capital (70.08 vs. 74.01) due to a forecast recovery rate which is higher than the assumption in the Foundation IRB approach (57.39% vs. 55%). Note that Foundation IRB's recovery rate of 55% is comparable to the average recovery rate of the senior secured seniority class but is proposed to be applied to both the senior secured (unless admitted collateral is available) as well as the senior unsecured claims. This could indicate an incentive for banks to favour the Foundation approach over the Advanced IRB approach especially for senior unsecured credit exposures. Similar conclusions can be drawn for the Foundation IRB's recovery rate of 25% which will be applied for both senior subordinated as well as subordinated claims.

Figure 4 and Table 9 compare the respective loss distributions with and without correlations using the point-in-time model.

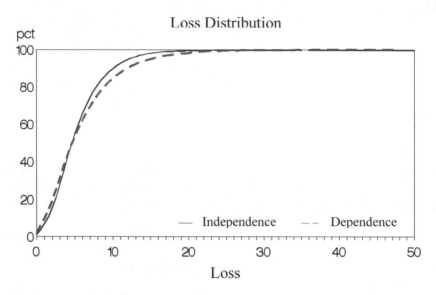

Figure 4. Loss distributions for the point-in-time model (S_Sec)

Table 9. Descriptive statistics of loss distributions for the point-in-time model. Portfolios contain 1,000 obligors with an exposure of one monetary unit each, 10,000 random samples were drawn for each distribution with and without correlation between systematic factors

	Mean	Std. dev.	Med	95	99	99.5	99.9	Basel II Capital (Standardized)	Basel II Capital (Foundation IRB)	Basel II Capital (Advanced IRB)
Ind. Factors	6.33	3.61	5.64	13.10	18.01	20.43	25.77	80.00	71.16	60.74
Corr. Factors	6.78	4.71	5.64	16.03	22.78	25.60	31.77	80.00	71.16	60.74

It can be observed that the economic capital, expressed as Value-at-Risk, is considerably lower for the point-in-time model than for the through-the-cycle model. The reasons are twofold. First, the inclusion of macroeconomic variables leads to a lower forecast of the default rate (1.62%), a higher forecast of the recovery rate (61.59%) for 2004 and therefore to lower expected losses. Second, the exposure to unknown random systematic risk sources is reduced by the inclusion of the observable factors. This leads to less uncertainty in the loss forecasts and therefore to lower variability (measured, e.g., by the standard deviation) of the forecast distribution. Moreover, the regulatory capital is the lowest for the Advanced IRB approach which takes both the forecast default and recovery rate into account.

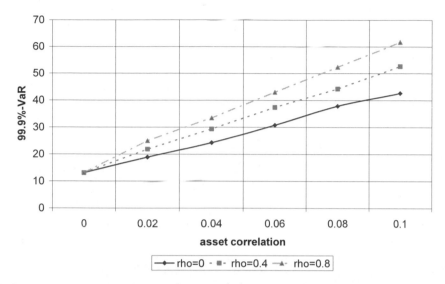

Figure 5. Economic capital gains from decrease in implied asset correlation for correlated risk factors; Figure shows 99.9 percentiles of loss distributions for the senior secured seniority class depending on asset correlation and correlation of systematic risk factors. Portfolio contains 1,000 obligors each with default probability of 1%, exposure of one monetary unit, and expected recovery of 50%.

We also notice another important effect. The economic capital, measured by the higher percentiles of the credit portfolio loss, increases if the estimated correlation between the default and recovery rates is taken into account. This increase is not as dramatic as in the through-the-cycle model, although the correlation between risk factors of defaults and recoveries has slightly increased. The inclusion of macroeconomic factors renders the systematic unobservable factors less important and diminishes the impact of correlations between both factors. To the extent that recoveries and defaults are not exposed at all to unobservable random factors, the correlations between these factors are negligible for loss distribution modelling. Figure 5 shows this effect. We assumed constant exposure of $b = 0.5$ to the recovery factor and varied the exposure to the systematic factor for the defaults (asset correlation) for given correlation between the systematic factors. The benchmark case is a correlation of zero between the factors. Here, we notice a reduction of economic capital from 44 (i.e., 4.4% of total exposure) for an asset correlation of 0.1 to 13 (1.3%) when the asset correlation is zero. In the case of a correlation between the factors of 0.8, the Value-at-Risk is reduced from 61 (6.1%) to 13 (1.3%). Thus, the higher the correlation of the risk factors, the higher the economic capital gains are from lowering the implied asset correlation by the explanation with observable factors.

5. Discussion

The empirical analysis resulted in the following insights:

1. Default events and recovery rates are correlated. Based on an empirical data set, we found a positive correlation between the default events and a negative correlation between the default events and recovery rates.
2. The incorporation of the correlation between the default events and recovery rates increases the economic capital. As a result, most banks underestimate their economic capital when they fail to account for this correlation.
3. Correlations between defaults decrease when systematic risk drivers, such as macroeconomic indices are taken into account. In addition, the impact of correlation between defaults and recoveries decreases.
4. As a result, the uncertainty of forecast losses and the economic capital measured by the percentiles decreases when systematic risk drivers are taken into account.

Most empirical studies on recovery rates (including this article) are based on publicly available data provided by the rating agencies Moody's or Standard and Poor's and naturally lead to similar results. The data sets of the rating agencies are biased in the sense that only certain exposures are taken into account. Typically, large U.S. corporate obligors in capital intensive industries with one or more public debt issues and high credit quality are included. Thus, the findings can not automatically be transferred to other exposure classes (e.g., residential mortgage or credit card exposures), countries, industries or products.

Moreover, the data is limited with regard to the number of exposures and periods observed. Note that our assumption in (8) of a large number of firms is crucial since it leads to the focus on the mean recovery. If idiosyncratic risk can not be fully diversified the impact of systematic risk in our estimation may be overstated. Due to the data limitations, we cannot draw any conclusions about the cross-sectional distribution of recoveries which is often stated to be U-shaped (see, e.g., Schuermann, 2003). In this sense, our results call for more detailed analyses, particularly with borrower-specific data which possibly includes financial ratios or other obligor characteristics and to extend our methodology to a panel of individual data. As a result, we would like to call upon the industry, i.e., companies, banks and regulators for feedback and a sharing of their experience.

In spite of these limitations, this paper provides a robust framework, which allows creditors to model default probabilities and recovery rates based on certain risk drivers and simultaneously estimates interdependences between defaults and recoveries. It can be applied to different exposure types and associated information levels. Contrary to competing modeis, the presence of market prices such as bond or stock prices is not required.

References

Altman E, Brady B, Resti A, Sironi A (2003), The Link between Default and Recovery Rates: Theory, Empirical Evidence and Implications, forthcoming Journal of Business.

Basel Committee on Banking Supervision (2004), International Convergence of Capital Measurement and Capital Standards - A Revised Framework, Consultative Document, Bank for International Settlements, June.

Cantor R, Varma P (2005), Determinants of Recovery Rates on Defaulted Bonds and Loans for North American Corporate Issuers: 1983-2003, Journal of Fixed Income 14(4), pp. 29-44.

Carey M (1998), Credit Risk in Private Debt Portfolios, Journal of Finance 53, pp. 1363-1387.

Düllmann K, Trapp M (2004), Systematic Risk in Recovery Rates- An Empirical Analysis of U.S. Corporate Credit Exposures, Discussion Paper, Series 2: Banking and Financial Supervision, No 02/2004.

Frye J (2000), Depressing Recoveries, Risk 3(11), pp. 106-111.

Frye J (2003), A False Sense of security, Risk 16(8), pp. 63-67.

Gordy M (2003), A Risk-Factor Model Foundation for Ratings-Based Bank Capital Rules, Journal of Financial Intermediation 12, pp. 199-232.

Gordy M (2000), A Comparative Anatomy of Credit Risk Models, Journal of Banking and Finance 24, pp. 119-149.

Hamerle A, Liebig T, Rösch D (2003), Benchmarking Asset Correlations, Risk 16, pp. 77-81.

Heitfield A (2005), Dynamics of Rating Systems, in: Basel Committee on Banking Supervision: Studies on the Validation of Internal Rating Systems, Working Paper No. 14, February, pp. 10-27.

Hu T, Perraudin W (2002), The Dependence of Recovery Rates and Defaults, Working Paper, Birkbeck College.

Moody's (2004), Default and Recovery Rates of Corporate Bond Issuers 1920-2003.

Moody's (2005), Default and Recovery Rates of Corporate Bond Issuers 1920-2004.

Pykhtin M (2003), Unexpected Recovery Risk, Risk, 16(8), pp. 74-78.

Rösch D (2005), An Empirical Comparison of Default Risk Forecasts from Alternative Credit Rating Philosophies, International Journal of Forecasting 21, pp. 37-51.

Rösch D (2003), Correlations and Business Cycles of Credit Risk: Evidence from Bankruptcies in Germany, Financial Markets and Portfolio Management 17, pp. 309-331.

Rösch D, Scheule H (2004), Forecasting Retail Portfolio Credit Risk, Journal of Risk Finance 5 (2), pp. 16-32.

Schönbucher J (2003), Credit Derivatives Pricing Models: Models, Pricing and Implementation, Jon Wiley and Sons, New York.

Schuermann T (2003), What Do We Know About Loss-Given-Default?, Working Paper, Federal Reserve Bank of New York.

Appendix: Results of Monte-Carlo Simulations

In order to prove the reliability of our estimation method, a Monte-Carlo simulation was set up which comprises four steps:

- Step 1: Specify model (1) and model (9) with a given set of population parameters w, c, b, μ, and ρ.
- Step 2: Draw a random time series of length T for the defaults and the recoveries of a portfolio with size N from the true model.
- Step 3: Estimate the model parameters given the drawn data by the Maximum-Likelihood method.
- Step 4: Repeat Steps 2 and 3 for several iterations.

We used 1,000 iterations for different parameter constellations and obtained 1,000 parameter estimates which are compared to the true parameters. The portfolio consists of 10,000 obligors. The length of the time series T is set to $T = 20$ years. We fix the parameters at $w = 0.2$, $\mu = 0.5$, and $b = 0.5$ and set the correlations between the systematic factors to 0.8, 0.1, and -0.5. In addition, we analyze three rating grades A, B, and C where the default probabilities and thresholds c in the grades are:

- A: $\pi = 0.005$, i.e., $c = -2.5758$
- B: $\pi = 0.01$, i.e., $c = -2.3263$
- C: $\pi = 0.02$, i.e., $c = -2.0537$

Table 10 contains the results from the simulations. The numbers without brackets contain the average of the parameter estimates from 1,000 simulations. The numbers in round (.)-brackets represent the sample standard deviation of the estimates (which serve as an approximation for the unknown standard deviation). The numbers in square [.]-brackets give the average of the estimated standard deviations for each estimate derived by Maximum-Likelihood theory. It can be seen in each constellation that our ML–approach for the joint estimation of the default and recovery process works considerably well: the averages of the estimates are close to the originally specified parameters. Moreover, the estimated standard deviations reflect the limited deviation for individual iterations. The small downward bias results from the asymptotic nature of the ML-estimates and should be tolerable for practical applications.

Table 10. Results from Monte-Carlo simulations

Grade	ρ	c	w	μ	b	ρ
A		-2.5778	0.1909	0.4991	0.4784	0.7896
	0.8	(0.0495)	(0.0338)	(0.1112)	(0.0776)	(0.1085)
		[0.0468]	[0.0317]	[0.1070]	[0.0756]	[0.0912]
		-2.5789	0.1936	0.4970	0.4824	0.1139
	0.1	(0.0484)	(0.0336)	(0.1154)	(0.0788)	(0.2269)
		[0.0475]	[0.0322]	[0.1079]	[0.0763]	[0.2185]
		-2.5764	0.1927	0.5048	0.4826	-0.4956
	-0.5	(0.0492)	(0.0318)	(0.1116)	(0.0798)	(0.1923)
		[0.0472]	[0.0320]	[0.1078]	[0.0763]	[0.1697]
B		-2.3287	0.1927	0.4999	0.4852	0.7951
	0.8	(0.0480)	(0.0327)	(0.1104)	(0.0774)	(0.0920)
		[0.0460]	[0.0306]	[0.1084]	[0.0765]	[0.0856]
		-2.3291	0.1906	0.4927	0.4831	0.0861
	0.1	(0.0472)	(0.0306)	(0.1105)	(0.0778)	(0.2330)
		[0.0456]	[0.0305]	[0.1080]	[0.0764]	[0.2152)]
		-2.3305	0.1900	0.4988	0.4805	-0.4764
	-0.5	(0.0479)	(0.0324)	(0.1115)	(0.0806)	(0.1891)
		[0.0453]	[0.0303]	[0.1074]	[0.0759]	[0.1703]
C		-2.0536	0.1935	0.4972	0.4855	0.7915
	0.8	(0.0489)	(0.0315)	(0.1104)	(0.0804)	(0.0956)
		[0.0448]	[0.0297]	[0.1080]	[0.0763]	[0.0843]
		-2.0542	0.1943	0.5030	0.4851	0.1067
	0.1	(0.0580)	(0.0382)	(0.1168)	(0.0782)	(0.2374)
		[0.0448]	[0.0298]	[0.1085]	[0.0770]	[0.2128]
		-2.0554	0.1923	0.4998	0.4833	-0.4898
	-0.5	(0.0510)	(0.0359)	(0.1085)	(0.0852)	(0.1815)
		[0.0443]	[0.0295]	[0.1076]	[0.0766]	[0.1656]

VII. Modelling Loss Given Default: A "Point in Time"-Approach

Alfred Hamerle, Michael Knapp, Nicole Wildenauer

University of Regensburg

1. Introduction

In recent years the quantification of credit risk has become an important topic in research and in finance and banking. This has been accelerated by the reorganisation of the Capital Adequacy Framework (Basel II).[1] Previously, researchers and practitioners mainly focused on the individual creditworthiness and thus the determination of the probability of default (PD) and default correlations. The risk parameter LGD (loss rate given default) received less attention. Historical averages of LGD are often used for practical implementation in portfolio models. This approach neglects the empirical observation that in times of a recession, not only the creditworthiness of borrowers deteriorates and probabilities of default increase, but LGD also increases. Similar results are confirmed in the empirical studies by Altman et al. (2003), Frye (2000a), and Hu and Perraudin (2002). If LGD is only integrated in portfolio models with its historical average, the risk tends to be underestimated. Hence, adequate modelling and quantification of LGD will become an important research area. This has also been advocated by Altman and Kishore (1996), Hamilton and Carty (1999), Gupton et al. (2000), Frye (2000b), and Schuermann (2004).

The definitions of the recovery rate and the LGD have to be considered when comparing different studies of the LGD, since different definitions also cause different results and conclusions. Several studies distinguish between market LGD, implied market LGD and workout LGD.[2] This paper uses recovery rates from Moody's defined as market recovery rates.

In addition to studies which focus only on data of the bond market or data of bonds and loans,[3] there are studies which focus on loans only.[4] Loans generally

---

[1] Basel Committee on Banking Supervision (2004)

[2] For a definition of these values of LGD see Schuermann (2004) and Basel Committee on Banking Supervision (2005)

[3] Schuermann (2004)

[4] Asarnow and Edwards (1995), Carty and Lieberman (1996), and Carty et al. (1998)

have higher recovery rates and therefore lower values of LGD than bonds.[5] This result relies especially on the fact that loans are more senior and in many cases also have more collectible collaterals than bonds.

Studies show different results concerning the factors potentially determining the LGD which are presented briefly below. The literature gives inconsistent answers to the question if the borrower's sector has an impact on LGD. Surveys such as Altman and Kishore (1996) confirm the impact of the sector. Gupton et al. (2000) conclude that the sector does not have an influence on LGD. They trace this finding back to the fact that their study only examines loans and not bonds.

The impact of the business cycle is approved by many authors, e.g., Altman et al. (2003). In contrast, Asarnow and Edwards (1995) conclude that there is no cyclical variation in LGD. Comparing these studies one has to consider that different data sources have been used, and the latter only focused on loans.

Several studies support the influence of the borrower's creditworthiness or the seniority on LGD.[6] Nearly all studies analysing LGD using empirical data calculate the mean of the LGD per seniority, per sector, per rating class or per year. Sometimes the means of the LGD per rating class and per seniority are calculated. We refer to the latter prices as "matrix prices" sometimes enabling a more accurate determination of LGD than the use of simple historical averages.[7] The authors agree that the variance within the classes is high and there is a need for more sophisticated models. Altman et al. (2003) suggest a first extension of the model by using a regression model with several variables as the average default rate per year or the GDP growth to estimate the average recovery rate.

The present paper makes several contributions. A dynamic approach for LGD is developed which allows for individual and time dependent LGDs. The model provides "point in time" predictions for the next period. The unobservable part of systematic risk is modelled by a time specific random effect which is responsible for dependencies between the LGDs within a risk segment in a fixed time period. Furthermore, the relationship between issuer specific rating developments and LGD can be modelled adequately over time.

The rest of this chapter is organised as follows: Section two states the statistical modelling of the LGD. Section three describes the dataset and the model estimations. Section four concludes and discusses possible fields for further research.

---

[5] Gupton et al. (2000)
[6] Carty and Lieberman (1996), Carty et al. (1998), and Gupton et al. (2000)
[7] Araten et al. (2004), Gupton et al. (2000), and Schuermann (2004)

2. Statistical Modelling

The dataset used in this chapter mainly uses bond data. Recovery rates will be calculated as market value of the bonds one month after default. The connection between LGD and recovery rate can be shown as:

$$LGD_{t(i)} = 1 - R_{t(i)}.$$

Here, $LGD_{t(i)}$ and $R_{t(i)}$ denote the LGD and recovery rate of bond i that defaults in year t, $i=1,...,n_t$. The number of defaulted bonds in year t, $t=1,...,T$ is denoted with n_t.

The resulting recovery rates and loss rates normally range between 0 and 1, although there are exceptions.[8] Firstly, the LGDs will be transformed. The transformation used in this chapter is

$$y_{t(i)} = \log \frac{LGD_{t(i)}}{1 - LGD_{t(i)}}.$$

Written in terms of the recovery rate, the following relation is obtained:

$$y_{t(i)} = \log \frac{1 - R_{t(i)}}{R_{t(i)}} = -\log \frac{R_{t(i)}}{1 - R_{t(i)}}.$$

This logit transformation of the recovery rate is also proposed by Schönbucher (2003) and Düllmann and Trapp (2004).[9] The LGD can be written as:

$$LGD_{t(i)} = \frac{\exp(y_{t(i)})}{1 + \exp(y_{t(i)})}.$$

Analogous, to the model used in Basel II, the following approach for the transformed values $y_{t(i)}$ is specified (cf. Düllmann and Trapp, 2004):

$$y_{t(i)} = \mu + \sigma \sqrt{\omega} \, f_t + \sigma \sqrt{1 - \omega} \, \varepsilon_{t(i)} \qquad (1)$$

The random variables f_t and $\varepsilon_{t(i)}$ are standard normally distributed. All random variables are assumed to be independent. The parameter σ is non-negative and values of ω are restricted to the interval $[0;1]$.

---

[8] Recovery rates greater than one are unusual. In these cases the bond is traded above par after the issuer defaults. These values are excluded from the dataset in the empirical research, see section 3.1.

[9] This transformation ensures a range between 0 and 1 of the estimated and predicted LGD.

Other specifications are also discussed. Frye (2000a) suggests an approach according to (1) for the recovery rate itself. Pykthin (2003) assumes log-normally distributed recovery rates and chooses a specification like (1) for $\log(R_{t(i)})$.

In the next step, model (1) is extended including firm and time specific observable risk factors. The dependence upon the observable risk factors is specified by the following linear approach:

$$\mu_{t(i)} = \beta_0 + \beta' x_{t-1(i)} + \gamma' z_{t-1},$$ (2)

where $i=1,...,n_t$, $t=1,...,T$. Here $x_{t-1(i)}$ characterises a vector of issuer and bond specific factors observed in previous periods. Examples for these issuer and bond specific variables are the issuer rating of the previous year or the seniority. By z_{t-1} we denote a vector of macroeconomic variables representing potential systematic sources of risk. The macroeconomic variables are included in the model with a time lag. Generally it can be assumed that regression equation (2) holds for a pre-defined risk segment, e.g. a sector.

Regarding (1) and (2) it can be seen that the logit transformed values of LGD are normally distributed with mean $\mu_{t(i)}$ and variance σ^2. The random time effects f_t cause a correlation of the transformed values of LGD $y_{t(i)}$ of different bonds defaulting in year t. This correlation shows the influence of systematic sources of risk which are not explicitly included in the model or which affect LGD contemporarily. If fundamental factors are having an impact on the LGD of all defaulted bonds – at least in one sector – a correlation of LGD is obtained as a result (as long as these systematic risk factors are not included in the model). It can be seen that the factors have different effects in different segments, e.g. different time lags or sensitivities in different sectors. If in contrast, the relevant systematic risk factors are included in the vector z_{t-1} and if no other risk factors influence LGD contemporarily, the impact of time effects should be reduced significantly.

The unknown parameters in (1) and (2) are estimated by maximum likelihood considering (1) - extended by (2) - as a panel regression model with random effects, (cf. Baltagi (1995), Chapter 3). Note that a bond specific random effect does not enter the model, since defaulted bonds in different periods t and s ($t \neq s$) are different. Parameter estimates are obtained using PROC MIXED in SAS.[10]

For the covariance and correlation of the transformed values of LGD in year t, the following relationships hold:

$$\text{Cov}(y_{t(i)}, y_{t(j)}) = \sigma^2 \omega$$
$$\text{Corr}(y_{t(i)}, y_{t(j)}) = \omega \quad, i \neq j.$$

---

[10] Wolfinger et al. (1994)

3. Empirical Analysis

3.1. The Data

A dataset from Moody's Default Risk Service is used for empirical analyses. It contains data from about 2,000 defaulted debt obligations, i.e. bonds, loans and preferred stock from 1983 to 2003. More than 1,700 debt obligations are from American companies.

The dataset includes information about the recovery rates of defaulted bonds. The LGD and the transformed LGD used in this analysis can be calculated from the recovery rate as described in section two. When a borrower defaulted for the first time, this event was recorded and all default events after the first one are not considered in this study.[11]

About 90% of these debt obligations are bonds. To ensure a homogenous dataset, only bonds are used in this study. For the same reason, only data from companies in the sector "industry"[12] are used in the final analysis. In this sector there are 84% of the bonds. In the sectors "financial service providers" and "sovereign/public utility" there are fewer defaulted borrowers and therefore fewer defaulted bonds. After restricting the data to American bonds in the (aggregated) sector "industry", there are 1,286 bonds in the dataset. Additionally, the dataset is limited to bonds with a debt rating of "Ba3" or worse. The reason for this constraint was that the rating categories "A3" to "Ba2" have sparse observations in several years of the period 1983 to 2003. In addition, several defaulted issuers hold five or more bonds. Some of these bonds have the same LGD at the time of default although they have distinct debt ratings or distinct seniorities. Other bonds have a different LGD although they dispose of the same issuer and debt rating and the same seniority. These differences cannot be explained with the data at hand. Probably they

---

[11] This constraint naturally only affects borrowers who defaulted several times. Furthermore, observations with LGD equal to zero and negative LGD are excluded from the analysis, because the transformed LGD $y_{t(i)}$ cannot be calculated. If the recovery rate is greater than 1, i.e. if the market value of a bond one month after default is greater than the nominal value of the bond, the LGD becomes negative. In the dataset this was the case in 0.5% of all observations.

[12] The (aggregated) sector "industry" contains the sectors "industrial", "transportation" and "other non-bank" of Moody's sectoral classification (with twelve sectors) in Moody's Default Risk Service (DRS) database. For reason of completeness one has to know that there are two other aggregated sectors. On the one hand there is the (aggregated) sector "financial service providers" containing the sectors "banking", "finance", "insurance", "real estate finance", "securities", "structured finance" and "thrifts" and on the other hand the (aggregated) sector "sovereign/public utility" containing the sectors "public utility" und "sovereign". This aggregation was made as several sectors did not have enough observations.

can be traced back to issuer's attributes not available in the dataset. For this reason, only issuers with four or fewer bonds remain in the dataset.[13] Additionally, bonds of companies with obvious cases of fraud like Enron or Worldcom were eliminated from the dataset to ensure a homogenous pool.

Subsequently, the dataset is adjusted marginally. On the one hand, there is only one bond with a rating "B2" defaulting in 1996. This bond has a very small LGD and is removed from the dataset because it could cause a biased estimation of random effects. On the other hand, four bonds having a bond rating of "Ca" and "C" in the years 1991, 1992 and 1995 are eliminated from the dataset because they also have only one or two observations per year. Consequently, there are 952 bonds from 660 issuers remaining in the dataset.

The random effect f_t and the error term $\varepsilon_{t(i)}$ are assumed to be independent, with a standard normal distribution as described in section two. The transformed LGD $y_{t(i)}$ is tested for an approximately normally distribution. As a result, a normal distribution of the data can be assumed. This distribution can also be confirmed when the distribution of $y_{t(i)}$ by year is tested.

In the analysis, the influence of issuer- and bond-specific variables $x_{t-1(i)}$ is examined as mentioned in section two. In the analyses the following variables are tested:

- Issuer rating: Moody's estimated senior rating has 21 grades between "Aaa" (highest creditworthiness) and "C" (low creditworthiness).[14] An aggregation of the rating categories is tested as well. A possible classification would be the distinction between investment grade ratings (rating "Aaa" to "Baa3") and speculative grade ratings (rating "Ba1" to "C"). Besides this relatively rough classification the ratings are classified into the categories "Aaa" to "A3", "Baa1" to "Baa3", "Ba1" to "Ba3", "B1" to "B3", "Caa"[15], "Ca" and "C". The issuer rating has a time lag of one year in the analyses.
- Debt rating: Its classification is analogous to the issuer rating and has a time lag of one year. In addition to the classifications mentioned above, the ratings are classified into the categories "Ba3" to "B3" and "Caa" to "C".
- Difference between issuer and debt rating: the fact that the issuer rating is one, two, three or more than three notches better than the debt rating is tested on its

---

[13] In principle, only issuers with one bond could be left in the dataset if the effect of several bonds per issuer should be eliminated. As this restriction would lead to relatively few observations, only issuers with five or more bonds are excluded. Hence the dataset is only diminished by 4%.

[14] For withdrawn ratings, Moody's uses a class "WR". Because of the lagged consideration of rating there are no bonds in the dataset with rating "WR" one year before default.

[15] Moody's used to name this rating class with "Caa" until 1997. Since 1998, this class has been separated into the three rating classes "Caa1", "Caa2" and "Caa3". To use the data after 1998, the latter three ratings have been aggregated in one rating class which is named "Caa" in the following.

impact on the transformed LGD. Additionally, the impact of the fact that the issuer rating is better or worse than the debt rating is tested. The rating classification of an issuer and a bond can differ if the bond finances a certain project which has a different risk and solvency appraisal compared to the issuer.

- Seniority: Starting with Moody's classification, the classes "senior secured", "senior unsecured", "senior subordinated", "subordinated" and "junior subordinated" are distinguished.[16] To distinct these seniority classes from the relative seniority, they are sometimes referred to as absolute seniority.
- Relative seniority: According to Gupton and Stein (2005) the relative importance of the seniority is surveyed. This variable can be best explained by an example: If issuer 1 has two bonds –one is secured "subordinated" and the other "junior subordinated"– and issuer 2 has three bonds –one with seniority "senior secured", another with "senior subordinated" and the third bond with seniority "subordinated"– then the "subordinated" bond from issuer 1 is going to be served first and possibly has a lower LGD than the bond with seniority "subordinated" from issuer 2 which is served after the two other bonds from issuer 2.
- Additional backing by a third party: If the bond is secured additionally by a third party beside the protection by the issuer emitting the bond, then this information is also used in the analyses.
- Maturity (in years): The maturity of the bond is calculated as the difference of the maturity date and the default date. It indicates the remaining time to maturity if the bond would not have defaulted.
- Volume of defaulted bond (in million dollars): The number of outstanding defaulted bonds times the nominal of this defaulted bond denotes the volume of the defaulted bond. It quantifies the influence of the volume of one defaulted bond, not the influence of the volume of defaulted bonds in the market altogether. Certain companies like insurances are not allowed to hold defaulted bonds. On the other hand, there are speculative investors who are interested in buying defaulted bonds. The higher the volume of the defaulted bond, the higher the supply of defaulted bonds on the market. Therefore it can be more difficult for the defaulted issuers to find enough buyers or to claim high prices for the defaulted bond.
- Issuer domicile: The country of the issuer is implicitly considered by the limitation on American data. This limitation can be important because different countries may be in different stages of the economic cycle in the same year. If the data is not limited to a certain country, the macroeconomic condition of all countries included in the dataset should be considered. Additionally, different legal insolvency procedures exist in different countries, so that a country's legal procedure can influence the level of recovery rates and LGD.

In Figure 1 the average (realised) LGD for bonds in the (aggregated) sector "industry" per year in the period 1983 to 2003 are depicted:

---

[16] For a consideration of the hierarchy of seniority classes see Schuermann (2004, p. 10).

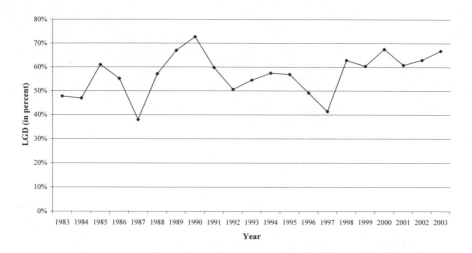

Figure 1. Average LGD per year for bonds in the (aggregated) sector "industry"

As can be seen from Figure 1, the LGD is obviously underlying cyclical variability. This is why the cyclical variations of LGD are explained with the help of macroeconomic variables in the vector z_{t-1}. Therefore, a database with more than 60 potential macroeconomic variables is established. It contains interest rates, labour market data, business indicators like gross domestic product, consumer price index or consumer sentiment index, inflation data, stock indices, the Leading Index etc.[17] In addition, the average default rate per year of the bond market is taken into account. All variables are included contemporarily and with a time lag of at least one year. The consideration of these variables should enable a "point in time" model.

3.2. Results

Two different model specifications for the (aggregated) sector "industry" are examined.[18] In contrast to model (1), another (but equivalent) parameterisation is used. The models can be instantaneously estimated with the procedure MIXED in the statistical program SAS. In the next step, the parameter estimates for σ and ω can be determined from the estimates for b_1 and b_2. Table 1 summarises the results.

---

[17] A list of potential macroeconomic factors can be found in the appendix.
[18] Additionally, models for all sectors are estimated containing dummy variables for the different sectors in addition to the variables mentioned below. The use of a single sector leads to more homogenous data.

Model I: $\qquad y_{t(i)} = \beta_0 + \boldsymbol{\beta}' \boldsymbol{x}_{t-1(i)} + b_1 f_t + b_2 \varepsilon_{t(i)}$.

Model II: $\qquad y_{t(i)} = \beta_0 + \boldsymbol{\beta}' \boldsymbol{x}_{t-1(i)} + \boldsymbol{\gamma}' \boldsymbol{z}_{t-1} + b_1 f_t + b_2 \varepsilon_{t(i)}$.

Table 1. Parameter estimates and p-values (in parentheses) for models I and II (only bonds of the (aggregated) sector "industry")

	Model I	Model II
AIC	3,224.3	3,222.8
b_2^2	1.7336 (<0.0001)	1.7327 (<0.0001)
b_1^2	0.3421 (0.0052)	0.2859 (0.0064)
Constant	-0.3868 (0.1146)	-0.8697 (0.0164)
Debt rating "Ba3" to "B3" (t-1)	-0.1938 (0.0463)	-0.1783 (0.0672)
Seniority "senior unsecured"	0.6194 (0.0004)	0.6064 (0.0005)
Seniority "senior subordinated"	0.7061 (0.0002)	0.6909 (0.0002)
Seniority "subordinated" and "junior subordinated"	1.0487 (<0.0001)	1.0443 (<0.0001)
Relative Seniority "2" and "3"	0.5041 (0.0001)	0.5084 (<0.0001)
Additional backing by a third party	-0.2717 (0.0325)	-0.2697 (0.0338)
Bond maturity (in years)	0.03407 (0.0020)	0.03546 (0.0013)
Volume of defaulted bonds (in million dollars)	0.001118 (0.0001)	0.001087 (0.0002)
Average default rate (in percent) (t-1)		0.2186 (0.0358)

The results of models I and II can be interpreted as follows:[19] If a bond is rated "Ba3", "B1", "B2" or "B3" one year before default, it has a significantly smaller LGD than a bond with rating "Caa", "Ca" or "C". In addition to the debt rating, the seniority also affects LGD. Bonds with seniority "senior unsecured" as well as bonds secured "senior subordinated", "subordinated" or "junior subordinated"

---

[19] In general, all interpretations according to the quoted model refer to the transformed LGD $y_{t(i)}$. As $y_{t(i)}$ is the result of a strictly monotonic transformation of LGD all interpretations hold as well for LGD.

have a significantly higher LGD than "senior secured" bonds. When the seniority classes are compared, it can be stated that "senior unsecured" bonds have a smaller LGD than "senior subordinated" bonds. Bonds secured "subordinated" or "junior subordinated" have the highest LGD. Using well secured bonds a creditor can exploit better securities than a creditor secured with lower ranked bonds resulting in lower losses. Generally, this result sustains the results published by Moody's.[20]

However, not only the (absolute) seniority, but also the relative seniority affects LGD. If a bond is ranked second or third in terms of collateralisation, the LGD of this bond is significantly higher than the LGD of a bond secured at first rank. If the company is going to be commercialised, the latter are served before the bonds ranking second or third and therefore have to bear fewer losses.

Regarding the coherence between absolute and relative seniority and LGD, it must be recognised that besides the creditworthiness of the bond, the seniority also plays a role for the determination of LGD. The fact that in addition to the absolute seniority, relative seniority also influences LGD is an interesting result. This coherence is also detected in the models of Gupton and Stein (2002, 2005).

If in addition to the collateralisation by the direct issuer, the bond is protected by a third party, these bonds have a significantly lower LGD than bonds without this additional backing. These additional providers of collateral could fill in for the defaulted company if the latter does not have a substantial value. Therefore, it can reduce the loss of these bond creditors.

Another impact on LGD is given by the maturity of the bond. A longer maturity leads to higher LGDs. This result can possibly be explained by the fact that future payments are insecure. The recovery rate and LGD are calculated as the market price one month after default. If maturity is longer, higher cash flows are achieved in the future which are generally more insecure. This is reflected in lower recovery rates and higher LGDs. Gupton and Stein (2005) negate the influence of maturity on LGD in their recent paper. In their opinion the maturity does not play a role for defaulted bonds. Only the risk horizon matters, which is one year in their analysis. However, Gupton and Stein (2005) neglect the uncertainty of future cash flows.

Additionally, the volume of the defaulted bonds influences LGD as a factor of the supply side. As mentioned above, a higher volume of defaulted bonds leads to a higher supply and to lower prices for these bonds, i.e. to lower recovery rates and higher LGDs.[21]

The incorporation of macroeconomic factors in model II tries to explain the cyclical variations of LGD. These factors can be interpreted as follows: The average

---

[20] Hamilton and Carty (1999)

[21] Altman et al. (2003) also detected a relationship between the average LGD per year and the volume of defaulted bonds.

default rate of the bond market (in percent) with a time lag of one year is taken into account in the model as a possible proxy for the cyclical influence. An increasing lagged average default rate leads to significantly higher LGDs. This result is supported by Altman et al. (2003) who detected a positive relationship between the default rate and the (average) LGD as well.

The cyclical variation in LGD (see Figure 1) can be explained by the fact that more borrowers and therefore more bonds are defaulting during a recession. More companies and collaterals have to be commercialised leading on the one hand to a greater supply of collateral and therefore lower collateral prices. On the other hand, the demand for these commercialised collaterals declines because the non-defaulted companies are not able to invest the same amount of money during a recession as during an expansion. Macroeconomic variables like the lagged default rate try to explain these cyclical variations.

Apart from the models described above, several other models were tested: A potential variable is the difference between issuer and debt rating in the year before default.[22] If the issuer rating is better than the debt rating, the LGD of this bond is expected to be smaller than the LGD of bonds with an issuer rating equal to or worse than the debt rating. Because issuers with an issuer rating better than the debt rating dispose of a higher borrower's creditworthiness, we can expect that there is an additional protection of the bond by the issuer. However, this variable did not influence LGD significantly.

Alongside, the interactions between absolute and relative seniority were tested. As they are only partially significant they are not included in the model. The interactions between issuer rating and absolute and relative seniority were included as well but do not show a significant influence on LGD.

Additionally, a finer sectoral classification is tested to distinguish the impact of several sectors. This finer classification does not have sufficient observations for all sectors so a model with this fine classification cannot be estimated.

Moreover, other macroeconomic factors are integrated in the model. They comprise the GDP (gross domestic product) growth and the "index of leading indicators" which are included in the models contemporarily and with a time lag of one or two years. Furthermore, several macroeconomic variables such as the unemployment rate, the consumer sentiment index, the yield of the consumer sentiment index and different interest rates are tested with several lags. The average LGD per year is included with a time lag of one year in the model. These variables do not affect LGD significantly when the default rate one year before default is also included in the models. Altman et al. (2001, 2003) receive similar results. They conclude that fundamental macroeconomic variables do not have a significant influence on the average LGD in a multivariate context if the model contains the default rate.

---

[22] For example the issuer rating could be "Aaa" and the debt rating "A".

The variance of the error term b_2^2 is 1.9266 if a model without explanatory variables is used. Only the constant term reflecting the average level of the transformed value of LGD is taken into account in this model. In models I and II the variance of the error term declines slightly to about 1.7336 and 1.7327, respectively. This can be attributed to the improved estimation of LGD including issuer specific and macroeconomic variables and thus to a decreasing prediction risk.

In model II, the variance of the random time effect b_1^2 decreases because appropriate macroeconomic factors have been integrated compared to model I. This result indicates that the integration of the default rate leads to a decrease in the variance of the random effect.

Taking equation (1) into account, the variance of the transformed LGD σ^2 and the correlation ω for two different borrowers in the same year are examined. A standard deviation $\hat{\sigma}$ of 1.4883 for a model without explanatory variables, 1.4407 for model I and 1.4208 for model II is obtained.[23] The correlation $\hat{\omega}$ between the predicted LGDs for next year is 16.48 percent in model I. It declines to 14.16 percent in model II because of the effect of systematic economic risk factors.[24]

Finally, it should be mentioned that the variance estimates $\hat{\sigma}^2$ for models I and II are still high. This result indicates that there may be further important issuer specific variables which explain the variation of LGD. Examples are balance sheet variables not available in Moody's dataset.

4. Conclusions

In most empirical analyses concerning LGD, the distribution of LGD is implied to be constant and LGD is generally estimated using historical averages. Therefore, the individual values of LGD of issuers within a certain time period as well as the values of LGD over time should deviate only randomly from a certain mean. Such an assumption seems to be unrealistic given the fact that in times of a recession, not only the creditworthiness of the borrowers declines and PDs rise, but that also LGD is systematically higher.

In this chapter a dynamic approach which generalises other approaches is presented. LGD is modelled depending on issuer and bond specific as well as macroecomic factors. As the variables are lagged, the LGDs for the next year can be predicted on the basis of values that are known at the time the prediction is made.

---

[23] $\sigma^2 = b_1^2 + b_2^2$.

[24] $\omega = b_1^2 / \sigma^2$.

Reduced uncertainty in the prediction of LGD is important for the determination of LGD, not only for Basel II but also for internal risk management using credit portfolio models. At a given state of the economy, more precise predictions about the economic capital can be made than using historical averages. Furthermore, in a credit portfolio model, the prediction uncertainty can be taken into account at the simulation of the predicted loss distribution, e.g. resulting from the estimation of the parameters $\hat{\beta}$ and $\hat{\gamma}$.

In a next step, further bond specific performance figures that could not be reproduced in the dataset at hand will be analysed. This could lead to a further reduction of prediction uncertainty, which is relatively high in comparison to PD predictions. If banks have a database which is large enough to estimate individual LGDs, the model presented in this chapter can be used. Although there may be other factors influencing LGD in a bank, e.g. type of collateral (financial collaterals, real estate etc.), the LGD can be estimated individually using an econometric approach. The "point in time" predictions of LGD can also be used to predict downturn LGDs demanded by Basel II can be predicted using downturn states of the macroeconomic variables. At present there are relatively few studies for the determination of recovery rates and LGD on the basis of individual data. Moreover, the availability of data is restricted. Therefore, further research is necessary in this area.

References

Altman E, Brady B, Resti A, Sironi A (2003), The Link between Default and Recovery Rates: Theory, Empirical Evidence and Implications, March.
http://pages.stern.nyu.edu/~ealtman/Link_between_Default_and_Recovery_Rates.pdf

Altman E, Kishore V (1996), Almost Everything You Wanted to Know About Recoveries on Defaulted Bonds, Financial Analysts Journal, November/December, pp. 57-64.

Altman E, Resti A, Sironi A (2001), Analyzing and Explaining Default Recovery Rates. A Report Submitted to The International Swaps & Derivatives Association, December.

Araten M, Jacobs M, Varshney P (2004), Measuring LGD on Commercial Loans: An 18-Year Internal Study, The RMA Journal, May, pp. 28-35.

Asarnow F, Edwards D (1995), Measuring loss on defaulted bank loans: A 24-year study, The Journal of Commercial Lending, March, pp. 11-23.

Baltagi B (1995), Econometric Analysis of Panel Data, Chichester et al., Wiley.

Basel Committee on Banking Supervision (2004), International Convergence of Capital Measurement and Capital Standards: A Revised Framework, June.

Basel Committee on Banking Supervision (2005), Studies on the Validation of Internal Rating Systems - Revised version, Working Paper No. 14, May.

Carty L, Hamilton D, Keenan S, Moss A, Mulvaney M, Marshella T, Subhas M (1998), Bankrupt Bank Loan Recoveries, Moody's Special Comment, June.

Carty L, Lieberman D (1996), Defaulted Bank Loan Recoveries, Moody's Special Report, November.

Düllmann K, Trapp M (2004), Systematic Risk in Recovery Rates - An Empirical Analysis of US Corporate Credit Exposures, Deutsche Bundesbank Discussion Paper, 02/2004.

Frye J (2000a), Depressing Recoveries, Risk, November, pp. 108-111.

Frye J (2000b), Depressing Recoveries, Policy Studies, Federal Reserve Bank of Chicago.

Gupton G, Gates D, Carty L (2000), Bank Loan Loss Given Default, Moody's Special Comment, November.

Gupton G, Stein R (2002), LossCalcTM: Model for Predicting Loss Given Default (LGD), Moody's Rating Methodology, February.

Gupton G, Stein R (2005), LossCalc V2: Dynamic Prediction of LGD, Moody's Rating Methodology, January 2005.

Hamilton D, Carty L (1999), Debt Recoveries for Corporate Bankruptcies, Moody's Special Comment, June.

Hu Y, Perraudin W (2002), The Dependence of Recovery Rates and Defaults, Working Paper, Birkbeck College, February.

Pykthin M (2003), Unexpected Recovery Risk, Risk, April, pp. 74-78.

Schönbucher P (2003), Credit Derivatives Pricing Models: Models, Pricing and Implementation, Chichester, Wiley.

Schuermann T (2004), What Do We Know About Loss-Given-Default? London, UK, Risk Books.

Wolfinger R, Tobias R, Sall J (1994), Computing Gaussian Likelihoods and their Derivatives for General Linear Mixed Models, SIAM Journal of Scientific and Statistic Computing, Vol. 15, No. 6, November, pp. 1294-1310.

Appendix: Macroeconomic variables

Interest Rate Fed Fund – monthly
Interest Rate Treasuries, constant maturity 6 months, nominal, monthly
Interest Rate Treasuries, constant maturity 1 year, nominal, monthly
Interest Rate Treasuries, constant maturity 5 years, nominal, monthly
Interest Rate Treasuries, constant maturity 7 years, nominal, monthly
Interest Rate Treasuries, constant maturity 10 years, nominal, monthly
Interest Rate Conventional mortgages, fixed rate – monthly
Commercial bank interest rates, 48-month new car, quarterly
Commercial bank interest rates, 24 months personal, quarterly
Commercial bank interest rates, all credit card accounts, quarterly
Commercial bank interest rates, Credit card accounts, assessed interest
Interest Rate, new car loans at auto finance companies, monthly
Interest Rate, bank prime loan, monthly

Civilian Labour Force Level
Employment Level
Unemployment Level
Unemployment rate
Initial Claims for Unemployment Insurance
Challenger Report, Announced Layoffs
Mass Layoffs
Manufacturing Data:
Shipments Total Manufacturing
New Orders Total Manufacturing
Unfilled Orders Total Manufacturing
Inventory Total Manufacturing
Inventory to shipments Total Manufacturing
Capacity Utilization total
Business Bankruptcy Filings
Non-business Bankruptcy Filings
Total Bankruptcy Filings
Dow Jones Industrial Index
S&P500
NASDAQ100
Price Indices:
GDP Implicit Price Deflator (2000=100)
Consumer Price Index, All Urban Consumers; U.S. city average, all items
Producer Price Index; U.S. city average, Finished Goods
Gross Domestic Product
Gross Private Domestic Investment
Percent Change From Preceding Period in Real Gross Domestic Product
Public Debt
Tax Revenues
Uni Michigan Consumer Sentiment Index

PMI (Purchase Manager Index, Institute for Supply Management)
Retail Sales total (excl. Food Services)
Revised Estimated Monthly Sales of Merchant Wholesalers
Business Cycle Indicator: Index of Leading Indicators (The Conference Board)
Average crude oil import costs (US$/barrel)
Average default rate of issuers at the bond market

VIII. Estimating Loss Given Default – Experiences from Banking Practice

Christian Peter

KfW Bankengruppe[1]

1. Introduction

Modern credit risk measurement and management systems depend to a great extend on three key risk parameters: probability of default (PD), exposure at default (EAD), and loss given default (LGD). PD describes the probability that the lending institution will face the default of some obligor or transaction. EAD gives an estimate of the exposure outstanding at the time of default, also indicating the maximum loss on the respective facility. Finally, LGD measures the percentage of a defaulted exposure that the lending bank expects not to recover. In other words, despite default it still expects to recover 1- LGD percent of the defaulted exposure.

In its advanced internal rating based approach (IRBA), the New Basel Accord (Basel II) underpins the importance of these key parameters by allowing financial institutions to apply their own estimates for PD, EAD, and LGD in the computation of regulatory capital. As for EAD, the formula for computing risk-weighted assets is linear in the value of the loss quota. The bank's ability to appropriately estimate LGDs for its portfolios will therefore directly affect the amount of regulatory capital required under Basel II.

LGD numbers will, however, not only play a significant role in internal credit risk management and future regulatory reporting, but may also be used in accounting. For example, a bank may want to apply modified LGDs in its fair value as well as impairment computations required for IAS/ IFRS.[2] Despite all these fields of application, LGD estimation has only recently started to gain more attention in the literature.[3]

---

[1] The material and opinions presented and expressed in this article are those of the author and do not necessarily reflect views of KfW Bankengruppe or models applied by the bank. I would like to thank all colleagues working with me on the LGD topic for the many fruitful discussions during the last years.

[2] International Accounting Standard/ International Financial Reporting Standard

[3] See for example Altman el al. (2005) or the articles available at www.defaultrisk.com

This article approaches LGD estimation from a perspective gained in banking practice, intending to address not only the estimation problem itself but also to touch on some aspects of the development process as well as the later application of these numbers. It is organized as follows: The first section discusses the requirements arising from different domains of application for LGD estimates. Economic loss and LGD are introduced next. The following section presents a short survey of different approaches for LGD estimation. A model for workout LGD as well as the design of an LGD model for performing and defaulted exposures is discussed in the next three sections. Finally, the article closes with some concluding remarks.

2. LGD Estimates in Risk Management

A bank may apply LGD estimates for different domains of application and tools, which often impose different requirements on LGD estimates. Regulatory requirements as defined in BCSB (2004) are surveyed in Section 2.1. Afterwards, additional requirements from internal risk management processes and accounting are outlined in Section 2.2.

2.1. Basel II Requirements on LGD Estimates – a Short Survey

BCBS (2004) defines several requirements on LGD estimates eligible for determining regulatory capital. The following provides a short survey:[4]

- *Scope*: Application of foundation IRB approach requires LGD estimates for retail exposures only (§ 331). The advanced IRB approach also allows banks to use their own estimates for corporate, sovereign, and bank exposures (§§ 297 and 298).[5]
- *Default definition* (§§ 452 – 457): The reference definition of default given in BCBS (2004) provides the basis for LGD estimation. When using internal or external loss data inconsistent with this definition, appropriate adjustments have to be made.
- *Loss definition* (§ 460): LGD is based on economic loss; see Section 3 for details.
- *LGD estimates* (§§ 468 – 471): "*A bank must estimate an LGD for each facility that aims to reflect economic downturn conditions where necessary to capture the relevant risks*" (downturn LGD). The "*long-time, default-weighted average of loss rate given default calculated based on the average economic loss of all observed defaults [...] for that type of facility*" provides a lower limit for LGD

---

[4] See BCBS (2004) for the full text as well as additional rules not mentioned here (for example, concerning documentation, stress tests, overrides, etc.). The reader should also take the respective regulations of national supervisors into account.

[5] For purchased receivables, see §§ 364 and 367.

estimates. If existent, cyclical variation has to be taken into account. Dependencies between the risk of the borrower and the collateral or its provider as well as the effect of currency mismatches must be considered in a conservative manner. *"LGD estimates must be grounded in historical recoveries and, where applicable, must not solely be based on the collateral's estimated market value."* An institute must fulfil certain requirements on its collateral management processes for all collaterals that are recognized in the bank's LGD estimates.

For defaulted exposures, banks have to determine a best estimate LGD, which is based *"[...] on the current economic circumstances and facility status"*, as well as a conservative estimate reflecting *"[...] the possibility that the bank would have to recognize additional, unexpected losses during the recovery period"*.

- *Data requirements* (§§ 472 – 473): The data basis should ideally cover at least one economic cycle, but must be no shorter than 7 years for sovereign, bank, and corporate exposures or 5 years for retail exposures, respectively.

- *Assessing the effect of guarantees and credit derivatives* (§§ 480 – 489): Banks are allowed to reflect the effect of guarantees through adjustment of either PD or LGD estimates. The respective adjustment criteria must be clearly specified, plausible, and appropriate. The bank must adopt the chosen technique in a consistent way (both over time and across different types of guarantees). Furthermore, it must assign a rating to each guarantor, fulfilling all minimum requirements defined for borrower ratings. Except for certain types of obligors, guarantors, and instruments, the adjustment of PD or LGD is restricted in a way such that the risk weight of the guaranteed exposure need not be lower than the risk weight of a comparable direct exposure to the guarantor (no recognition of double-default effects). There are no restrictions on eligible guarantors. Guarantees must fulfil certain standards (for example, evidenced in writing, non-cancellable on the part of the guarantor, etc.) to be eligible.

- *Validation* (§§ 500 – 505): *"Banks must have a robust system in place to validate the accuracy and consistency of rating systems, processes and all relevant risk components."* Comparisons between realized and estimated LGDs must be performed regularly (at least annually) to demonstrate that realized LGDs are within the expected range. *"Banks must also use other quantitative validation tools and comparisons with relevant external data sources."* They must demonstrate that methods do not vary systematically with the economic cycle. Furthermore, the bank must define reaction standards for the case that deviations between realized and estimated LGDs turn to be significant enough to question the validity of the estimates.

2.2. LGD in Internal Risk Management and Other Applications

While Basel II provides the focus of this book, banks generally use LGD numbers in many applications apart from regulatory reporting. Figure 1 depicts some of these applications as well as the various connections between them. A bank's internal credit risk reporting and management processes require LGD estimates for different purposes: Internal reporting (risk bearing ability, performance measurement, etc.), transaction pricing, the bank's credit approval authority regulations, and limit management are some of these applications.

Accounting can become another field of application for LGD estimates or derivatives of them. When considering IAS/ IFRS, LGD figures may enter fair value computations and impairment tests. IAS asks banks to disclose fair values for financial assets and liabilities at least in the notes of the annual statement.[6] These numbers can, for example, be computed applying a discounted cash flow model, with LGD numbers used to adjust cash flows for credit risk.[7]

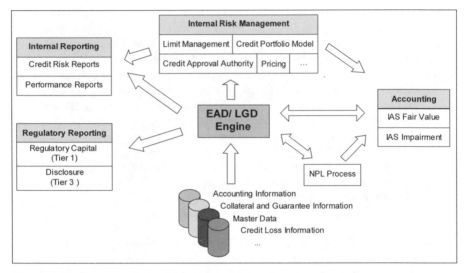

Figure 1. LGD computation – data sources and domains of application[8]

Impairment tests provide further possibilities for connecting accounting and credit risk management processes. General provisions can be computed using a modified[9] LGD number based on the finding that the concepts of incurred loss – as defined by IAS/ IFRS – and expected loss – as used for credit risk measurement – are quite similar.[10] Furthermore, best estimate LGDs as required for regulatory purpose and specific provisions computed following the rules of IAS/ IFRS are

---

[6] See IAS 39.8, IASB (2005), for a definition of fair value.

[7] As an alternative to cash flow adjustment, one may apply a discount rate adjustment approach. In this case, one may refer under certain circumstances to similar risk-adjusted discount rates as used for LGD estimation; see Section 6.2.4.

[8] NPL is used as an abbreviation for non-performing loan.

[9] Some of the necessary modifications are addressed below.

[10] Due to restricted data availability, differences might be greater in theory than in banking practice.

both based on expectations about future cash flows from a defaulted facility, its collaterals, and guarantees. Therefore, one may derive both specific provisions and best estimate LGDs from the same information base. This will be discussed in more detail in Section 7.

A great part of the functionality required for these three domains of application, i.e. regulatory reporting, internal risk reporting and management, as well as accounting, is identical. However, there are differences due to diverging intentions – stability of the bank in case of Basel II and objective reporting of the bank's assets in case of IAS/ IFRS. This may concern definitions of EAD as well as LGD. For example, impairment considers book value as EAD. Fair value computations may not take future drawings into account, while these are part of Basel II compliant exposure at default. Internal risk management, on the other hand, may recognize future redemption to a larger extent than regulatory requirements allow.

In addition to the impact of different EAD definitions, the loss definition underlying LGD can slightly vary with the domain of application. The level of conservatism underlying the estimates will be different due to diverging intentions. Definition of loss components can differ; for example, internal costs may not be part of IAS numbers, while Basel II and internal applications will recognize them. Furthermore, one may decide to consider separate LGDs for different credit events, for example, political risks in internal models.[11] In addition to the one-year horizon considered in Basel II, a bank will generally be interested in a dynamic, multi-period projection of risk numbers for all domains of application (including future regulatory capital). Another potential field of deviations is the assessment of risk mitigation effects.

Dealing with different definitions of EAD and LGD can cause some confusion in internal communication – despite their different domains of application – and therefore requires bridging one EAD or LGD number into the other in order to explain the differences. Furthermore, the complexity of an LGD engine, which takes all these different requirements into account, can be high, also resulting in increased costs of development and maintenance. Before stating bank specific additional requirements, one should therefore carefully check whether the expected gain in explanatory power rectifies effort and costs.

3. Definition of Economic Loss and LGD

Basel II requires measuring economic loss as a basis for LGD estimation. *"[...] When measuring economic loss, all relevant factors should be taken into account. This must include material discount effects and material direct and indirect costs associated with collecting on the exposure. [...]"* (see BCBS (2004), § 460). The

---

[11] This will be necessary if a bank defines its PD ratings as local currency ratings.

directive only mentions basic components while leaving the exact definition of economic loss to the banks.

One may think of economic loss as the change in a facility's value the bank faces due to default,[12] i.e.

$$EcoLoss_j(t_{DF}) = V_j(t_{DF}, p) - V_j(t_{DF}, np)$$ (1)

with $V(t_{DF}, (n)p)$ describing the value of a (non)performing facility j in t_{DF}, the time of default. Following the current discussion, the value of the performing facility, $V_j(t_{DF}, p)$, is generally approximated by the amount outstanding at default plus eventual further drawings after default, i.e. by EAD.[13] [14] The residual value of the defaulted facility, $V_j(t_{DF}, np)$, can be expressed as the net present value of all recoveries from the exposure diminished by all direct and indirect costs arising from default. The LGD of a facility j then follows as the ratio of economic loss to exposure at default, i.e.

$$LGD_j(t_{DF}) = \frac{EAD_j(t_{DF}) - NPV(Rec_j(t), t \geq t_{DF}) + NPV(Costs_j(t), t \geq t_{DF})}{EAD_j(t_{DF})}$$ (2)

with $NPV(.)$ the net present value, $Rec_j(t)$ and $Costs_j(t)$ all recoveries and costs observed at t, respectively. Negative economic loss or LGD indicate gains. While negative LGDs are sometimes observed in practice, LGD estimates are generally required to be greater than or equal to zero. This article will refer to realisations of LGD as ex-post LGDs, while estimates of loss quotas will also be named ex-ante LGDs.

Recoveries after default result from facility or collateral sale, guarantees, bankrupt's assets, as well as restructured or cured exposures. Further unexpected sources of recoveries may sometimes also be observed. While ex-post LGDs may include all types of recoveries received for a defaulted exposure, the reference dataset (RDS) for model development should not reflect extraordinary recoveries, for example stemming from non-eligible collateral or guarantees, in order to avoid distortion.

Material direct and indirect costs arising from the handling of a defaulted exposure are, for example, external and internal labour costs, legal costs, costs for forced administration, insurance fees, costs for storage, maintenance, repairs of assets, etc. Furthermore, one should include ongoing costs, for example, corporate overhead. Refinancing costs resulting from incongruence of cash flows due to default

---

[12] Note that differences in default definition will therefore affect economic loss.

[13] As an alternative, one might define $V(t, p)$ as the net present value of all future recoveries and costs of the facility in case of no default in t. While theoretically appealing, such a definition can be difficult to implement in practice. Furthermore, it would also require a respective definition of EAD as might be done in internal models only.

[14] See for example Chapter IX and Chapter X for more details on EAD estimation.

may also be considered if material.[15] On the other hand, losses of future gains are generally not considered as part of economic loss. With respect to Eq. (1), one may recognize only additional costs, i.e. the difference between costs arising from the performing and the defaulted exposure, respectively. As mentioned above, economic loss and LGD used for IAS purpose should not include internal costs.

In order to recognize discount effects, all recoveries and costs have to be discounted. Since workout processes can be time demanding, the chosen discount rate may significantly affect the resulting economic loss and LGD; see Section 6.2.4.

4. A Short Survey of Different LGD Estimation Methods

The following provides a short survey of main approaches for LGD estimation currently discussed among academia and practitioners. When classifying different LGD approaches, a first distinction can be made between subjective and objective methods. A bank may have insufficient data to rely solely on quantitative methods. This can occur for low default portfolios, new products, or during the introduction of LGD methodology. In these situations, the bank may think of subjective methods primarily based on expert judgment as a valuable source of information. While there seems to be no special literature on subjective methods in LGD estimation, techniques known from other fields of application can easily be adopted. Interviews with experts from different units of the institute, comparisons with similar portfolios, or scenario techniques may help to develop an idea of the loss quotas one should expect to observe. As far as possible, the bank should incorporate all kinds of available loss (related) information into subjective methods. Subjective methods may also prove valuable for a validation of the results obtained from applying one of the objective methods described next.

Objective methods can be further classified as being either explicit or implicit, depending on the characteristics of the data sources on which they are based. Datasets analysed in explicit methods allow for a direct computation of LGDs. The so-called market LGD approach, a first explicit method, is applied by comparing market prices of bonds or marketable loans shortly after default with their par values. To compute workout LGDs, it is necessary to discount all recoveries and costs observed after default to determine the value of the defaulted facility, which is then compared with the defaulted exposure.

Different from explicit approaches, implicit methods rely on data sources which do not allow for a direct LGD computation but implicitly contain LGD relevant information. This information has to be extracted applying appropriate procedures.

---

[15] Incongruence can lead to losses or gains depending on the level of interest rates at the time of credit granting and default. It is therefore sometimes argued that gains will offset losses due to the mean reversion property of the interest rate.

The two approaches currently discussed in banking practice and in the literature are implied market LGD and implied historical LGD method, respectively.

The basis of the implied market LGD technique is to derive LGD estimates from market prices of non-defaulted loans, bonds, or credit default instruments. The spreads observed for these instruments at the market express among other things the loss expectation of the market, which may be broken down into PD and LGD. Implied market LGDs can be especially useful for low default portfolios (banks, sovereigns, and large corporates). However, if default experience is rare for all market participants, one should not expect implied market LGDs to provide more than an expert judgment of the market.

The computation of implied historical LGDs is described in the Basel II framework as one approach to determine LGDs for retail portfolios (see BCBS (2004), § 465). This approach involves deriving LGDs from realized losses and an estimate of default probabilities.

Except for implied market LGDs, which may sometimes deliver directly (or with minor modifications) estimates for non-performing facilities, all other concepts considered before at first hand deliver ex-post LGDs. The rest of this section will consider different approaches for estimating ex-ante LGDs. The main interest of a bank is generally to derive estimates for workout LGDs, since these best reflect its losses. Ex-post observations of market LGDs may also be used in model development; however, doing so may require appropriate adjustments since market LGDs include components as risk premiums for unexpected losses, which may not be considered in workout LGDs. Furthermore, required components like the institute's specific workout costs are not part of these loss quotas.

As an initial simple approach, one may consider an ex-ante LGD estimation procedure where LGDs are assigned top-down to exposures based on facility grades or pool identities. Such a procedure requires a segmentation of the considered portfolio into a small number of, in terms of their loss quota, relatively homogeneous groups of facilities. Statistical analysis as well as expert judgment provides the basis to identify these segments and to develop the necessary assignment rules. Since individual characteristics of facilities can only be recognized to a limited extent in such a two-stage approach[16], one will expect reasonable performance especially for standardized loan programs or retail portfolios.

For portfolios of less standardized transactions, one may presuppose better performance from direct or bottom-up estimation approaches. Higher individual credit volumes and smaller portfolio sizes will often be other arguments rectifying the development and application of more sophisticated estimation procedures. The basic idea of direct estimation techniques is to estimate LGDs based on a model, which takes individual characteristics of each facility, its collateralization, as well

---

[16] See CEBS (2005), § 234.

as other important risk factors explicitly into account. As for PD prediction, empirical statistical or simulation-based models may be applied.

Simulation approaches are often used for specialized lending transactions where the ability of the borrower to fulfil his obligations primarily depends on the cash flows generated by the financed object. An individual model of the transaction that describes the free cash flows generated by the financed object – and therefore the ability to pay interest rates and redemption – as a function of important risk factors provides the basis for the simulation. By simulating different scenarios of the transaction's progress, an institute will be able to derive estimates for PD, EAD, and LGD. While such approaches provide great flexibility, costs for modelling a specific transaction and performing the simulation can be high, depending on the structure of the simulation tool.

LGD estimates based on empirical statistical models can be generated by applying a single equation or a component-based approach. While the first approach intends to describe LGD by a single (for example regression) model, the latter one consists of a set of models each describing a certain component of LGD, e.g. the recovery rate for a certain collateral type or costs of certain workout activities. LGD estimates are then generated by appropriately aggregating the results of these component estimates. Statistical models for LGD or single LGD components can also be used in simulations.

Banks will often apply different techniques depending on the characteristics of the respective portfolio segment, its importance with respect to the whole portfolio, and the availability of loss data. This allows on the one hand measuring LGDs for different products with customized estimation procedures. On the other hand, however, it can make a consistent measurement of credit risk over the whole portfolio more difficult.

5. A Model for Workout LGD

Consider the situation that a bank faces after a borrower's default. While default itself marks a unique reference point for loss measurement, the performance of a facility after default as well as the resulting loss can vary substantially. However, one will probably observe a certain pattern of typical developments, called after-default scenarios in this paper. Table 1 provides a reasonable set of such scenarios. Depending on the banks portfolio as well as its workout strategy, the number and definition of after-default scenarios can slightly differ.

Table 1. A set of possible after-default scenarios

Scenario sc_i	Definition and explanation [a]
Cure	The defaulted address cures after a short time and continues to fulfil its contractual obligations. No significant losses; no changes in the structure or conditions of the facilities.
Restructuring	The defaulted address recovers after a restructuring of its facilities. Usage of collateral may sometimes be part of the restructuring. Loss amount may vary; customer relationship maintained.
Liquidation	All facilities of the defaulted address are liquidated, i.e. sale of loans, usage of collateral, etc. Loss amount generally higher than observed for restructuring; end of customer relationship.

[a] Scenarios will generally be defined on the address level (i.e. for borrower or guarantors) and may therefore not always correspond with what is observed for a single facility.

While the loss observed within a certain scenario may be similar for different (comparable) facilities, it will generally be impossible to know the after-default scenario in advance. One may therefore consider the loss quota of a facility j, LGD_j, as a random variable following a mixture distribution. With SC_j a discrete-valued random variable describing the occurrence of after-default scenarios and $LGD_j(sc_i)$ a second, continuous-valued random variable describing the loss of a facility depending on the scenario sc_i and $\delta(.)$ the indicator function[17], LGD_j can be defined as[18]

$$LGD_j = \sum_i \delta_{sc_i}\left(SC_j\right) \cdot LGD_j\left(sc_i\right) \qquad (3)$$

Collaterals and guarantees will generally have a strong impact on the loss quota realized for a defaulted facility. Consider a facility, which is secured by $n \geq 1$ risk mitigation instruments.[19] Each of these instruments k collateralizes sq_k percent of the exposure. One can now break down the exposure into $m \leq n$ parts, each collateralized by at least one instrument and an additional part, sq_0, which remains unsecured. The percentage of loss realized on each exposure part sq_l, $0 \leq l \leq m$, may depend on the respective risk mitigation instrument as well as the after-default scenario currently under consideration. The total loss quota in scenario sc_i is therefore given by

---

[17] I.e. $\delta_{sc}(SC) = 1$ for $SC = sc$ and $\delta_{sc}(SC) = 0$ otherwise.

[18] To simplify the presentation, time references are left out in Eq. (3) as well as in most of the formulas following. It is generally assumed in this article that one intends to predict the loss quota for a default occurring within a time interval $T = [t_a, t_e)$ given the information up to t_0 (the time where the computation takes place), i.e. $LGD_j = LGD_j(T|t_0)$.

[19] This article uses the expression "risk mitigation instrument" (rmi) as a general notion for collaterals and guarantees.

$$LGD_j(sc_i) = \sum_{0 \le l \le m} sq_{j,l} \cdot LGD_{j,l}(sc_i) \qquad (4)$$

where $LGD_{j,l}(sc_i)$ describes the percentage of loss observed on an (un)secured exposure part of size $sq_{j,l}$. Since the breakdown in Eq. (4) is equivalently performed for each of the after-default scenarios, one may alternatively write

$$LGD_j = \sum_{0 \le l \le m} sq_{j,l} \cdot LGD_{j,l} \qquad (5)$$

with

$$LGD_{j,l} = \sum_i \delta_{sc_i}(SC_j) \cdot LGD_{j,l}(sc_i) \qquad (6)$$

With respect to Eq. (2), $LGD_{j,l}(sc_l)$ can be expressed as

$$LGD_{j,l}(sc_i) = \max\{0; 1 - RR_{j,l}(sc_i) + Costs_{j,l}(sc_i)\}, \qquad (7)$$

with $RR_{j,l}(sc_i)$ and $Costs_{j,l}(sc_i)$ the percentage of recovery and costs on exposure sq_l of facility j in scenario sc_i.

Eq. (5) follows the structure of the formula provided in BCBS (2004) for risk mitigation. The extension of considering after-default scenarios may prove helpful as a theoretical model as well as for analysing the characteristics of observed economic loss or model development. The relatively simple structure of the model, which demonstrates the main idea while hiding most of the complexity of the underlying statistical models, will also be easy to communicate within the bank. This can increase acceptance of the estimation procedures, which may appear as a black box for credit analysts. Ex-ante estimates, however, are often generated based on a reduced form of the model presented here.

6. Direct Estimation Approaches for LGD

The following considers direct estimation approaches for LGD. Setting up such a procedure requires a description of the components of economic loss, i.e. recoveries on secured and unsecured exposures as well as costs, in terms of appropriate explanatory variables with respect to the requirements imposed by different domains of application, i.e. Basel II, IAS, or internal risk management, respectively. The development process for an LGD estimation procedure can generally be structured along the following steps:

1. Data collection, pre-processing & analysis
2. Model design and estimation
3. Model validation

During the development, some steps may have to be repeated several times before a satisfactory solution is found. Figure 2 depicts a series of projects a bank may require to set up an LGD engine. The implementation of a credit loss database is often the first step. It creates the basis for a systematic collection of loss data required for model development. The respective project generally incorporates (or is followed by) activities to transfer (a part of) the bank's loss history from paper files to the database. The LGD estimation model as well as the required validation procedures and processes are developed afterwards.

Following the initial project phase, the LGD engine will be subject to regular development and maintenance activities. Trigger events can be additional requirements (e.g., new products) as well as the results of the annual validation.

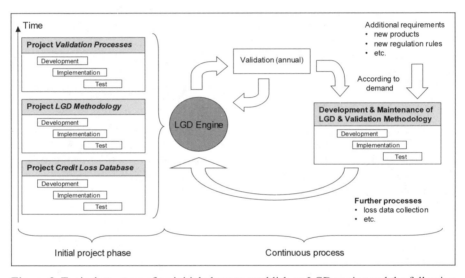

Figure 2. Typical structure of an initial phase to establish an LGD engine and the following annual validation process

The following concentrates on the first two steps of the development process for an LGD engine. The presentation starts with a short discussion of some aspects of data collection, mainly through a description of typical elements of a credit loss database. Afterwards, different aspects of model development are discussed.

6.1. Collecting Loss Data – the Credit Loss Database

One may expect that the most valuable information for LGD model development will come from the bank's own loss history, since it directly reflects the characteristics of the institute's workout processes. Loss data is therefore generally collected in a credit loss database (CLDB). For LGD model development, the complete history of the loss case (i.e. the time after default) as well as information about the time before default and supplemental information is required. The history of a loss case consists of

- possible further drawings after default,
- all recoveries related to the defaulted address, its facilities, and risk mitigation instruments,
- all costs arising from the workout process, and
- additional information about the workout process (for example, events and remarks as well as identifiers of restructured facilities and repossessed assets, which later allows to identify these objects within the bank's IT-systems).

Further information collected within the CLDB includes cash flows before default (or exposure at the time of default), master data, rating history, collateral values, etc. The later model development and estimation process generally requires additional information, for example, time series of macroeconomic variables or version numbers of the tools used in risk measurement (ratings tools, collateral valuation tools, etc.), which may also be incorporated in the database.

It will often take a time to realize all cash flows from cured or restructured facilities as well as from repossessed assets. Since workout usually ends much earlier and facilities or assets are then transferred from the workout unit to another unit of the bank or an external service provider, loss files will often be closed by the end of the respective workout activities. Cured or restructured facilities as well as repossessed assets are valued by that time and the result stored as non-cash recovery in the loss file.[20]

Since the number of loss observations is often small and loss data coming from the latest defaults also contains the most up-to-date information about current loss quotas, it appears attractive to include incomplete loss files as early as possible in the reference dataset (RDS) for model development. The decision as to whether an incomplete loss file should be incorporated in the reference dataset will generally be made on a case-by-case basis and can also depend on the application. A reasonable decision criterion may be defined based on the uncertainty still inherent in the value of economic loss due to the incompleteness of the loss case. Often, the end of the workout process is a reasonable time to include a loss file into the RDS. A component-based estimation approach may provide possibilities for earlier use, for example by considering incomplete loss files in the RDS of some LGD components only. While the use of incomplete loss files will make loss data available more quickly, this data, still incorporating estimates, can only be used to a limited extent, which may limit the benefit.

---

[20] However, as mentioned above one should include references into the loss file in order to allow for a later replacement of non-cash recoveries by the corresponding cash recoveries. Note that non-cash recoveries are generally estimates of future, uncertain cash flows.

A number of other aspects must be considered during data collection and pre-processing; the following outlines a few of them:

- Most of the requisite data can generally be found in existing IT-systems, allowing for the automatic collection of loss data. However, additional manual inputs are probably necessary during the workout process. These will include most additional information about the workout process, i.e. events, remarks, etc. While remarks allow entering information in an unstructured way, events provide the possibility of marking specified states and decisions, milestones, or turning points in order to structure the workout process for later analysis.[21] The extent to which such data must be added should be specified carefully in order to get informative loss files without causing too much extra work and costs.

- Since estimation procedures will improve over time, it will be beneficial to collect a superset of the loss data currently required for model estimation. The degree of detail may be different depending on the business line or facility type. This may, for example, result in more detailed loss data collection for large corporate than for retail exposures.

- Assuring the quality of loss data can be more time-consuming than expected at first glance. Simple automatic consistency checks might help to detect irregularities in the data; however, a larger part requires a deeper understanding of the workout processes as well as the loss cases and therefore has to be done in collaboration with experts from restructuring and workout units.

6.2. Model Design and Estimation

The general structure of an LGD estimation procedure normally consists of the following three steps:

1. *Data collection*: Identification and collection of all data required to generate an LGD estimate.
2. *Pre-processing*: Transformation of raw data into a form suitable for the estimation of LGD or LGD-related numbers. This may already include estimates for single LGD components.
3. *Generating estimates*: Generation of LGD estimates by appropriately assembling the results of pre-processing. In particular, this includes recognizing the risk mitigation effect of guarantees and collaterals. As a by-product, the procedure may also provide other information, for example, that required for an analysis of concentration in risk mitigation instruments, etc.

Figure 3 shows the basic structure of an LGD engine as it might be implemented within a bank's IT-systems. Depending on the IT-infrastructure, institutes may run various engines for different applications or portfolio segments or refer to a central engine as depicted here. In the later case, a controller will organize the computation of LGD estimates for different applications.

---

[21] An example of how this information may be used in LGD estimation is given in Section 6.2.3.

The LGD estimate is generated in the last two steps. Regression-type models are generally preferred as a flexible approach for modelling LGD or its components. Such approaches have been considered in several publications on LGD estimation; see for example Altman el al. (2003) or Chapter VII.

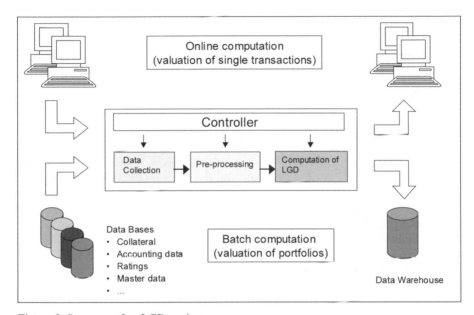

Figure 3. Structure of an LGD engine

Often banks will "suffer", at least during the initial years after introducing LGD estimation procedures, from insufficient reference datasets of loss observations on certain portfolios. The need to rely on information from various sources, sometimes following different definitions of default and loss, and also having different quality characteristics, can make other, more simple[22] approaches attractive. Capacity as well as time restrictions or priority settings among different portfolio segments are additional reasons why banks may start with these approaches for some portfolios.

Lookup-table based approaches will often provide the basis for LGD estimation procedures in such situations. The purpose here is to tabulate possible values of some variable of the model, for example, a recovery or cost rate, or the resulting LGD numbers themselves, together with the respective selection criteria. For instance, a bank may tabulate recovery rates for unsecured exposures depending on customer type, facility type, seniority, and region (see also Table 2). Given such a

---

[22] While being simple from a pure statistical point of view, setting up a procedure that generates reasonable LGD predictions based on different types of information will nevertheless often remain a demanding task.

table, the bank can generate an estimate for the recovery rate of some exposure by reading the recovery value corresponding to these four characteristics. The development of such a table requires the identification and description of segments of similar values for the considered variable in terms of appropriate explanatory variables and then an estimation of a representative value for each segment. Both steps can be supported by expert judgment or other external information sources if the bank's reference dataset is insufficient.

One should expect such models to capture only a part of the (explicable) variability of LGD figures observed in practice. For example, it will be difficult to describe the dynamics when taking macroeconomic variables into consideration. This can result in higher margins of conservatism and therefore rather conservative LGD estimates. On the other hand, lookup-table based approaches are more intuitively understandable, thus supporting internal communication and acceptance within the bank, which can be advantageous especially during the introduction phase. They may therefore serve as a starting point for some portfolio segments when introducing an LGD estimation procedure. It is then a matter of further developments to successively replace lookup-tables with more sophisticated statistical models wherever sufficient loss data can be made available and one expects significant improvements in the quality of LGD estimates. However, designing an LGD engine in a way that easily supports the migration from a simple to a more sophisticated estimation procedure at a later point in time can be complicated, which can lead to increased follow-up costs.

The following sections consider some aspects of the design of an LGD estimation procedure. The first section considers basic explanatory variables for LGD. Afterwards, approaches to estimate the two main components of LGD, recoveries and costs, are described. The choice of appropriate discount rates is considered next. A last section concludes this part with a short discussion on how the Basel II requirements concerning the conservatism of LGD estimates can be recognized. It is beyond the scope of this article to describe the whole development procedure in detail; the following will therefore skip many technical details in favour of aspects, which might be rather specific for the LGD estimation problem.

6.2.1. Possible Explanatory Variables for LGD Estimation

To identify appropriate explanatory variables, also named risk factors or risk drivers, one can start with a list of possible risk factors resulting from expert judgment, which are then tested during model development for their individual and joint explanatory power. In practice, the limited number of loss observations will sometimes make a statistical analysis difficult or even impossible, and may therefore restrict the set of risk drivers that can be considered in an LGD model.

Table 2 summarizes some possible explanatory variables generally considered as possible risk drivers when developing LGD estimation procedures. Most of them can easily be justified by intuition as being candidates.[23] Furthermore, one will expect some of these variables to have explanatory power not only for single components of LGD but also for PD and EAD, indicating dependencies between these key parameters of credit risk.

Table 2. Examples of possible explanatory variables grouped by categories

Category	Explanatory variables
Borrower	Customer type (sovereign, private entity, SME, corporate, ...), country or region, industry, form of business organisation, capital structure, rating, etc.
Facility	Seniority class (senior, junior, ...), debt type (loan, bond, ...), transaction type (syndicated loan, ...) and number of financing addresses, exposure, financing purpose, degree of standardization, collateralization (LTV,...), etc.
Collateral	Type, current book or market value, value depreciation, age, mobility (immobile, national or international mobile), producer, technical characteristics (for example, engine type of an airplane or gage of a locomotive), etc.
Guarantee	Guarantor (analogous to borrower), warranty clauses, covered risks, value, etc.
Macroeconomic & other external factors	GDP growth rate, unemployment rates, interest rates, FX rates, price indices, legal system and institutions, etc.
Bank internal	Versions of valuation procedures and tools, workout strategy, collateralization strategy, etc.

Borrower and facility characteristics as industry, capital structure, and seniority class may explain recovery rates on unsecured exposures in liquidation scenarios (i.e. from bankrupt's assets). They may also indicate workout intensity as a proxy for workout costs. Depending on the regional distribution of the portfolio, it could be necessary to consider region or country as explanatory variables.[24]

Recoveries from collateral will depend on the possibility of repossessing and selling the respective assets. Depending on the market size and structure observed for a certain asset class, the bank has to accept discounts for distressed sale. Technical characteristics of the respective assets could serve as an indicator for the level of such discounts and may also explain in part the costs of sale. Analogously, the value of a guarantee depends on the credit standing of the respective guarantor as well as on specific warranty clauses. In case the guarantor defaults, recoveries can

---

[23] A comprehensive survey of empirical analyses can be found in Bennett el al. (2005); the following mentions only a few of them.

[24] Altman and Kishore (1996) and Acharaya el al. (2004) found significant differences in recoveries of defaulted bonds belonging to different seniority classes. The same authors report significant differences for only some industry sectors, while Araten el al. (2004) could not find significant impact of industry (or region) on LGDs observed for loans.

be expected to depend to a large degree on the same explanatory variables as mentioned above for unsecured exposures (i.e. borrower characteristics).

The macroeconomic situation at default will generally influence LGD, as was demonstrated by several authors.[25] Basel II explicitly asks to take economic cycles into consideration. Depending on the regional distribution of the institution's portfolio and the considered recovery source (e.g., a certain asset type), one may consider different economic variables. Since default and recoveries from bankrupt's assets and collateral may both depend on the same macroeconomic variables, an appropriate recognition of these dependencies will be important to avoid overestimating recoveries.[26] Other external factors as jurisdiction and legal system can also play a role when explaining lengths and costs of workout activities as well as amount of recoveries.[27]

As a last group of explanatory variables for LGDs, one should consider bank internal characteristics. For instance, the bank's workout strategy will explain recoveries and costs to a certain degree. While especially an initial LGD model may sometimes not require an explicit consideration of these characteristics, this may later change. For example, the version of a valuation tool for some asset types may gain importance as soon as the valuation procedure or its parameters are modified. Such a modification may require a transformation of historical valuations and adjustments in estimated recovery rates for that asset type as well as modifications of the LGD estimation procedure.

6.2.2. Estimating Recoveries

Recoveries are generally the main driver of LGD. With respect to Eqs. (3) – (7), one may define recovery rates as

$$RR_{j,l}(sc_i) = \frac{NPV(CF_{j,l}(sc_i))}{sq_{j,l} \cdot EAD_j} \tag{8}$$

for (un)secured exposures of size $sq_{j,l} \cdot EAD_j$ observed for a loss case[28] j in the respective after-default scenario sc_i. $NPV(CF)$ again denotes the net present value of all cash flows which are observed on the respective exposure. Assume that recovery rates are determined without taking costs into consideration. Instead of applying Eq. (8), one may also determine recovery rates on a nominal basis. Supple-

---

[25] Araten el al. (2004) report correlation of unsecured exposures (but not of secured exposures) with economic cycle. Several authors report dependencies found in bond data, see for example Altman el al. (2003) or Chapter VII.

[26] Several authors have analysed the dependency between default and LGD; see for example Frye (2000a, 2000b), Altman el al. (2003), and Düllmann and Trapp (2004).

[27] See for example Franks el al. (2004) for an analysis of recovery processes and rates in the U.K., France, and Germany. Useful information about doing business in different countries may also be found at www.doingbusiness.org.

[28] A loss case will generally comprise all transactions of a defaulted address.

mented by a reference time period required for realizing the cash flows, the net present value and the recovery rate can then be computed later during ex-ante estimation.[29]

Basel II requires assigning LGDs to each facility (see Section 2.1); however, in practice, recoveries can be observed on different, often higher levels. These are generally addresses (i.e. borrower and guarantors), facilities, and risk mitigation instruments. Ex-post LGD computation as well as ex-ante estimation therefore requires appropriate procedures to allocate recoveries to facilities. Table 3 summarizes recovery sources for the after-default scenarios shown in Table 1.

Table 3. Recovery sources with respect to different after-default scenarios

Scenario sc_i	Unsecured exposure		Secured exposure	
Cure	Recovery = cured facility			A
Restructuring (I) no usage of rmi	Recovery = restructured facility			B
(II) usage of rmi	Recovery = restructured facility	C	Recovery from eligible collateral or guarantee	D
Liquidation	Recovery from bankrupt's assets	E	Recovery from eligible collateral or guarantee	F

Since guarantees require, at least under Basel II, a slightly different treatment, the following considers first exposures, which are either unsecured or secured by collateral. Afterwards, the risk mitigation effect of guarantees is considered in a separate subsection. A concluding third section outlines additional aspects of recovery rate estimation.

Unsecured Exposures and Exposures Secured by Collateral

Consider an exposure collateralized by an asset A_i having a reference value $V_t(A_i)$ at time t. For ex-ante estimation, the reference value will later generally be the result of the most recent valuation of the asset. Ex-post, one may use either the last valuation before default or the valuation performed at default.[30] Assume that asset A_i is of collateral type $k(i)$ and that loss experience indicates a recovery rate $RR_{k(i)}$ for this collateral type or for an exposure collateralized by it, respectively. The bank would then expect a recovery of $V_t(A_i) \cdot RR_{k(i)}$ for the respective reference object, i.e. for a secured exposure or the asset itself. The reference size in Eq. (8) is given by $sq_{j,l(i)} = \min\{1; V_t(A_i)/ EAD_j\}$. One may proceed similarly for unsecured

---

[29] Details of this approach are considered in the next section for collateral recoveries.

[30] In order to estimate PD, EAD, and LGD in a consistent way, one will often apply a cohort approach for all three variables. Therefore the last valuation before default is the more appropriate reference value.

exposures, considering the respective exposure size $sq_0 = \max\{0; 1 - \sum_{l \geq 1} sq_{j,l}\}$ as the "asset" value.

Table 4. Two variants for estimating recovery rates of (un)secured exposures

	Variant 1	Variant 2
Secured exposure	Estimate RR_k of asset type k based on recoveries of $\boxed{A}$, $\boxed{B}$, $\boxed{D}$, and $\boxed{F}$ [a]	Estimate RR_k of asset type k based on recoveries of $\boxed{D}$ and $\boxed{F}$ [a]
Unsecured exposure	Estimate RR_0 based on recoveries of $\boxed{A}$, $\boxed{B}$, $\boxed{C}$, and $\boxed{E}$ [a]	$RR_0 = RR_{total} - \sum_{l \geq 1} sq^*_{j,l}$ with RR_{total} the total recovery of an exposure and $sq^*_{j,l(i)} = \min\{1; RR_{k(i)} \cdot V_t(A_i)/EAD_j\}$

[a] all references with respect to Table 3.

It is usually appropriate to model recoveries on secured and unsecured exposures as separate components. Table 4 shows two approaches to assign the recoveries depicted in Table 3 to unsecured and secured exposures. Recoveries on secured exposures can be expected, at least in principle, to depend not only on collateral but also on facility and borrower characteristics when computed following variant 1.[31] Whenever an institute does not have recovery experience for a certain collateral type, it can therefore be difficult to include external information into the recovery estimate for a secured exposure. The second variant overcomes this problem by considering recoveries from assets separately. It may be justified by stating that (1) recoveries of cure scenarios can generally be expected to be roughly 100% and (2) recoveries from restructurings will (based on economic considerations) generally be at least as high as recoveries on the (whole) exposure in liquidation.[32] In practice, however, this need not always be the case, leading to implausible values for RR_0.

Instead of modelling different components for (un)secured exposures, one may also decide to describe total recoveries on an exposure by a single recovery component. This can be done, for example, by considering the sum of expected asset recoveries, $\sum_{l \geq 1} sq^*_{j,l}$, as an explanatory variable. If exposures are secured by only one asset, as will often be the case, one may also try to incorporate asset values directly as explanatory variables into a recovery model. Since recovery rates generally depend on the respective asset type, such models will probably require considering asset type as an additional explanatory variable.

---

[31] An analogous statement may sometime be true for unsecured exposures.

[32] One may argue that a bank has the option to use the collateral and will therefore agree on a restructuring only in case of higher recovery expectations. The argument, however, does not always hold for several reasons. First, (a priori) recovery expectations may sometimes prove wrong ex-post. Secondly, the economic advantage may not always be measured in terms of the recovery of the current facilities only. Furthermore, a bank may not always be free in its decision-making.

Explicit consideration of after-default scenarios following Section 5 may be applied in loss data analyses as well as LGD estimation for defaulted exposures (see Section 7). Furthermore, explicit consideration of scenarios can sometimes be useful when combining different internal and external data sources or when loss data is missing for some parts of the portfolio. Incorporating external data into the model may require different techniques depending on type and data source. For example, probability of cure depends on the bank's default definition. A separate description of the cure scenario may therefore be of interest for LGD calibration if external data (for example, from a data pooling) is used for estimation purposes or if the bank itself has changed its default criteria over time.[33] As a second example, assume that the bank has a low number of observations for some portfolio segments. It may then try to derive estimates (for example, considering after-default scenarios) for these segments by comparing key characteristics of this portfolio segment with those of other segments where loss observations are available. Thus, the institute may obtain an idea of the recoveries it can expect on the respective portfolios. However, subjective methods as previously outlined can generally only supplement the analysis of external data.

As a third example, consider the estimation of recovery rates for assets.[34] A possible approach for deriving recovery rates for collaterals (in part) from external data can be stated as follows:

1. Estimate the time series of value depreciation for the specified asset type. Sources of information on value depreciation can be market data as well as data from brokers or appraisers.
2. Estimate the time Δt required for repossession or sale. In practice, one may observe time series of cash flows, for example rents or leasing rates followed by one or several cash flows from the observed asset sale. While such cash flow patterns may theoretically also be recognized in a model, it will often be sufficient to assume that the total cash flow arises at one point in time. An exposure-weighted average time often provides a reasonable reference time. If no recovery observations are available, one may refer to experience from similar asset types or rely on expert judgement.
3. Estimate haircuts D for value volatility, distress sale, etc. Again, market data can often be a main source of information. Experience from repossession or sale of similar assets may also provide useful information for estimating haircuts. In addition, one has to determine an appropriate discount factor; see Section 6.2.4.

Having determined these parameters, recovery estimates can be generated as $NPV(V(t_{DF}+ \Delta t)\cdot(1-D))$. To obtain a better idea of the amount of recoveries, one will generally perform scenario analyses or simulations where the input parame-

---

[33] This may sometimes be the case during the introduction of Basel II compliant processes.
[34] For unsecured exposures, recovery estimates may be derived from market LGDs; see Section 4.

ters determined in the three steps are varied in order to reflect certain economic scenarios.

Dependencies between the value of an asset and the default event of the borrower should carefully be taken into account, since they may substantially decrease the effect of risk mitigation (see also BCBS (2004), § 469). It is often helpful to distinguish between general and specific dependencies. The first named recognizes "normal" dependencies which should be recognized by the recovery rates discussed so far. The second type addresses an individual characteristic of a facility-collateral relation, which is generally difficult to detect automatically. It is therefore often sensible to provide credit analysts with the possibility to grade such dependencies manually. These grades can then be used to adjust discounts on recovery rates in an appropriate manner.[35]

Exposures Secured by Guarantees or Credit Derivatives[36]
Since the risk mitigation effect of a guarantee essentially consists of a (partial) transfer of credit risk to a different address, one may explicitly model the guarantor's default probability as a major driver of the guarantee's value, i.e. recoveries from a guarantee can be described as[37]

$$RR_{j,l} = PD(G|B) \cdot RR_{j,l}^{DD} + (1 - PD(G|B)) \cdot RR_{j,l}^{SD} \tag{9}$$

with $PD(G|B)$ the conditional probability of default of the guarantor given the default of a borrower. RR^{SD} and RR^{DD} are the recovery rates a bank may observe in case of a single default (SD) of the borrower or a double default (DD) of both the borrower and guarantor. One may extend Eq. (9) analogously for cases where an exposure is secured by more than one guarantee (for example, in case of a counter-guarantee). The size of a secured exposure, $sq_{j,l}$, can be determined in a similar way as described for collateral above, taking into account that the reference value of a guarantee is generally defined as a maximum amount, $V^{max}(Gar)$, and/ or a certain percentage sq_{Gar} of the exposure.[38]

---

[35] One should be careful to also allow for a grading of negative dependencies, which would lead to an increase in the value of collateral.

[36] The following considers guarantees to simplify the presentation. Credit derivatives can often be treated in a similar way.

[37] Again, j indicates the facility and l the exposure part secured by the guarantee.

[38] In practice, the value of a guarantee may depend on further warranty clauses. To mention a few, guarantees may be restricted to certain parts of the borrower's obligations, for example only interest rate payments or redemption. They may be restricted to protect certain risk classes only (for example, no political risks). Furthermore, they may (partly) protect residual loss after recovery of other collateral and the bankrupt's assets only. This article does not consider the modifications necessary to adequately value such guarantees. Note that some characteristics mentioned above may also be incompatible with Basel II requirements for eligible guarantees and can therefore only be considered in internal models.

In its first versions, Basel II restricted risk mitigation effects of guarantees by requiring that the risk weight resulting from an exposure secured by a guarantee should not be less than that of a comparable exposure with the guarantor in place of the borrower. This approach is known as the substitution approach, indicating the basic idea of replacing the borrower by the guarantor. It has often been criticized for being too conservative. To see why, consider for a moment the borrower as a first guarantor of the contractual cash flows. The guarantor then in fact provides a counter-guarantee for these cash flows. Therefore, the bank faces substantial losses only if the guarantor is unable to pay at the time of the borrower's default, i.e. in case of a double default. Only if one assumes perfect dependency between the two default events, which is generally not the case, a substitution mechanism will describe the credit risk appropriately.

With its recent update in 2005, Basel II now allows for a limited recognition of double default effects in both IRB approaches. Restrictions are defined on the set of eligible instruments, obligors, and guarantors as well as on the method and the correlation parameters.[39] A Merton-style default model (see Merton, 1974) is considered to determine joint default probabilities of guarantor and obligor. Let Y_i be the appropriately normalized asset value of a borrower or guarantor i at a one-year horizon, respectively. With X a systematic risk factor, Z_{BG} a risk factor shared by borrower and guarantor, and E_i a counterparty-specific risk factor, the asset values of both addresses can be described as

$$Y_i = X \cdot \sqrt{\rho_i} + Z_{BG} \cdot \sqrt{1 - \rho_i} \cdot \sqrt{\psi_{BG}} + E_i \cdot \sqrt{1 - \rho_i} \cdot \sqrt{1 - \psi_{BG}} \qquad (10)$$

X, Z_{BG}, and E_i are considered as independent random variables following a standard normal distribution. Furthermore, one assumes that counterparty i defaults if its asset value, Y_i, falls below a threshold κ_i. Given the default probabilities of both addresses, the joint probability can therefore be computed as

$$JPD(B, G) = \Phi\left(\Phi^{-1}(PD(B)), \Phi^{-1}(PD(G)), \rho_{BG}\right) \qquad (11)$$

with $\Phi^{-1}(PD(i)) = \kappa_i$ and $\rho_{BG} = (\rho_B \cdot \rho_G)^{0.5} + \psi_{BG} \cdot ((1 - \rho_B) \cdot (1 - \rho_G))^{0.5}$ the correlation between borrower and guarantor. Stressed default probabilities are determined by conditioning on the systematic risk factor X. For technical details see BCBS (2005) and Heitfield and Barger (2003).

Both Basel II substitution and the double default approach are defined in a way that is most easily implemented in a two-step procedure. Firstly, it is necessary to estimate the LGD of borrower and guarantor considering the risk mitigation effect of collateral only. Afterwards, risk mitigation effects of guarantees are recognized in a second step by appropriately modifying the risk-weight of the secured exposure following the substitution rule or double-default formula.

---

[39] See BCBS (2004), §§ 284 (i) – (iii) and 307 (i), (ii).

For internal purposes, banks may want to relax the restrictions of Basel II or apply their own approach for recognizing double default effects. This can be done, for example, by computing recovery rates based on Eqs. (9) – (11) or, whenever components of LGD are used as input parameters of some simulation model, by directly simulating the risk mitigation effect of guarantees within the simulation.[40] The required information about the dependency structure (i.e. correlations) is often available through the bank's credit portfolio model. Depending on the level of conservatism underlying these correlation estimates, one may want to impose additional margins of conservatism in order to avoid overestimating the effect of risk mitigation by guarantees. As for assets, an institute may provide credit analysts with the possibility of grading specific correlation between guarantor and borrower, which may then, for example, modify the value of ψ_{BG} in Eq. (10).[41] Estimates of the recovery rates RR^{SD} and RR^{DD} can be obtained with only slight changes on the procedures described above for assets.

Further Aspects of Estimating Recovery Rates

Concluding Section 6.2.2, the following outlines additional aspects of recovery rate estimation not yet considered.

- *Participation effects*: By making payments under a guarantee, the guarantor generally acquires the right to pursue the borrower for that money. Furthermore, guarantees may only protect residual loss after recoveries from other risk mitigation instruments, etc. Taking these aspects into account complicates recovery rate estimation since simply adding the recoveries of different instruments may lead to distortion. Furthermore, recovery times of single instruments can change significantly, depending on whether other risk mitigation instruments also protect the same exposure. A tree representation of the transaction and its risk mitigation instruments can be helpful in describing these effects and deriving the respective recovery rates.

- *Allocation of risk mitigation instruments*: Whenever risk mitigation instruments are not clearly assigned to single facilities, the bank may want to optimize the allocation.[42] This can be done following simple heuristics or by solving a (non) linear optimization problem for minimizing risk-weighted assets; see Beckmann and Papazoglou (2004) and Gürtler and Heithecker (2005).

- *Multi-period estimation*: An institute will usually want to generate a multi-period projection of its credit risk numbers. Different techniques like simulation

---

[40] In fact, a bank may use both techniques simultaneously for different purposes. For example, explicit simulation of guarantees may sometimes be too time-consuming so that LGD numbers already including the risk mitigation effect have to be applied instead.

[41] It may sometimes be possible to detect certain dependencies automatically. For example, knowledge on economic integration of different addresses, which may be available in the institute's IT-systems, can be used to decide whether (or to what extent) a guarantee is eligible for a facility of a certain borrower.

[42] The potential for optimization stems from the joint effect of different risk mitigation instruments, possible currency mismatches, changes in exposure class due to risk mitigation, etc.

or scenario computation may be applied for this purpose. As a first step, one may also decide to rely on the conservative assumptions of Basel II (i.e. applying downturn LGDs). To derive future recoveries from collateral, one can proceed similarly as already discussed for estimating recovery rates of assets based on external data. The depreciation profile of the respective asset type provides the basis for estimating a time series of the asset's value. Depending on whether recovery rates are defined as the net present or nominal value of recoveries, estimates can be performed directly by multiplying recovery rate with the predicted future asset value or firstly estimating the time of recovery cash flows. For guarantees, it is necessary to estimate rating migration and cumulative default probability of the guarantor up to the (assumed) default time of the borrower. Furthermore, the value of a guarantee in terms of $V^{max}(Gar)$ and sq_{Gar} may sometimes change over time.

- *Maturity and currency mismatches*: Mismatches in maturity or currency between facility and risk mitigation instruments have to be considered in ex-ante estimates. Maturity mismatches may be recognized by computing a time-weighted average of LGD estimates with and without recoveries of the respective instrument. Currency mismatches are generally recognized by haircuts, which can be derived from an analysis of the volatility of FX rates. This may also require taking individual conversion agreements into account.

6.2.3. Estimating Costs

Similarly, as described for recoveries, costs can generally be assigned to addresses (i.e. borrower and guarantors), facilities, collaterals, and guarantees. It therefore often makes sense to break down the workout costs of a facility j arising in an after-default scenario sc_j into two basic components: (1) general costs $Costs^g_j(sc_i)$, which reflect all costs of the workout process not related to guarantees and collaterals, and (2) specific costs $Costs^s_{j,k}(sc_i)$ arising from a certain exposure part $sq_{j,l}$ from collaterals or guarantees; for example, costs for repossession of an asset. With respect to Eq. (7) one then has

$$Costs_{j,l}(sc_i) = Costs^g_j(sc_i) + \sum_{k\ secures\ sq_{j,l}} Costs^s_{j,k}(sc_i) \tag{12}$$

Alternatively, one may decide to offset costs attributed to collaterals or guarantees directly from the respective recoveries on secured exposures leading to $RR' = \max\{0;\ RR - Costs^s\}$. If a bank plans to use its LGD estimates for IAS/ IFRS purposes as well, the equation should be implemented in a way that allows separating internal and external costs since only the second are generally allowed to enter the respective IAS calculations.

In practice, measuring direct and especially indirect costs can be difficult. The required operations will depend on the institute's cost accounting system, which may not necessarily fulfil the requirements of LGD computation or modelling. Internal costs may therefore at least in part be known only on a level, which is more aggregated than required (for example for workout or restructuring units). As a consequence, model development is complicated by the fact that one does not have the required information regarding internal costs.[43]

Analysis of the institute's workout processes may often serve as a starting point for modelling the cost component of LGD. This comprises firstly identifying key activities or processes causing workout related costs, their respective cost units as well as possible explanatory variables, for all after-default scenarios. A rough classification according to expected cost amounts might be helpful in guiding further development. Expert judgment can play an important role at this stage.

While external costs may be assigned directly to processes, further assumptions are usually required to determine internal costs. Estimates of time required for a certain activity, the number of persons involved, as well as work intensity (i.e. percentage of daily or weekly working hours spend on the task) together with the institute's cost rate per working hour can provide a basis to derive cost estimates for workout activities. Ideally, key activities are recorded by appropriate events within the loss file so that the institute is able to estimate the lengths of its workout activities from past experience. Cost accounting and expert judgment can deliver at least a first estimate of the other parameters, whereas a final model may require a more detailed analysis of a sample of loss cases. Once key costs have been modelled, residual costs can often be distributed proportionally.

If costs are modelled on a borrower, collateral, or guarantee level, which may often be appropriate, LGD computation requires breaking them down to the facility level. This can either be done within the estimation procedure itself, i.e. individually for each address and facility, or a priori during model development. Reasonable distribution keys are in both cases the total exposure of an address' facilities as well as collateral and guarantee values or, alternatively, the number of the respective objects. More realistic estimates can generally be expected from an individual cost distribution during the estimation process. However, the computational effort may be too high with respect to the improvement that can be achieved in the estimate.

6.2.4. Determining Discount Rates

Both recovery and cost estimates require net present value computations to take material discount effects into account. The choice of discount rate(s) will affect the resulting LGD numbers – especially when recovery periods are long. Different approaches have been applied and discussed in the literature before. Basic characteristics for a categorization are: historical vs. present rates, single rates vs. interest rate curves as well as the procedure applied to determine the rates or curves, respectively.

---

[43] Information on external costs will generally be collected in the CLDB. This assures its availability.

Simple approaches, for example, discounting with the contractual loan rate, the effective original loan rate[44], or lender's cost of capital, have been applied in many articles. From a theoretic point of view, it appears most appropriate to discount each cash flow using a discount rate that reflects the respective level of risk as well as the time required for realizing it. Determining an appropriate discount rate curve for each risk class, however, can be difficult. MacIachlan (2004) suggested a procedure based on the CAPM that may be useful in this context.

Discount rates applied in ex-post and ex-ante estimates may differ. Ex-post LGD numbers are generally computed using historical interest rates observed at the time of default. Discount rates chosen for ex-ante estimates will depend on the applied discounted cash flow method. If cash flows are adjusted by margins of conservatism, the risk-adjusted rate should reflect the lower risk profile, i.e. it can sometimes be (almost) the risk free rate. Discount rates applied in downturn LGD estimates should also reflect downturn conditions. For a point-in-time LGD estimate, the current interest rate curves can be relied on to use the most up-to-date information. Combining current interest rates with past loss experience, however, may lead to distorted estimates if dependencies between interest rate and nominal recoveries are not considered adequately.

6.2.5. Determining the Level of Conservatism for LGD Estimates

Basel II requires conservative LGD estimates:

- LGD has to be estimated so as to reflect economic downturn conditions "*where necessary to capture the relevant risk*" (BCBS (2004), § 468).
- LGD cannot be less than the long-time default-weighted average (BCBS (2004), § 468).
- Banks must add a margin of conservatism to their LGD estimates that is related to the likely range of unpredictable errors (BCBS (2004), § 451).
- Institutes must consider dependencies between the risk of the borrower and that of the collateral as well as the collateral provider. Furthermore, currency mismatches have to be considered conservatively (BCBS (2004), § 469).[45]

The kind of (conditional) LGD expectation defined by Basel II will not always correspond to the concepts that institutions may have for their internal risk measurement. Specifically, the required downturn characteristic can be questioned for internal application where one generally wants to recognize the economic cycle in an explicit manner (point-in-time estimate). Depending on the complexity that a bank is willing to accept in its methods, diverging requirements may lead to different models or parameterizations of LGD components applied for regulatory and internal purposes, respectively. One possibility is to apply the concept, proposed

---

[44] Since IAS requires the application of the effective original loan rate, a bank may think about applying this rate in its estimates if LGD numbers are used for IAS purposes as well.

[45] Means of fulfilling this requirement were discussed in Section 6.2.2.

in BCBS (2004) for non-performing exposures, to performing positions as well, i.e. to refer to a best estimate LGD for internal credit risk management[46] while applying a conservative LGD for regulatory purposes. This article will not discuss this rather institution-specific question in more detail.

If LGD estimates are composed from single estimates of their components as discussed in this article, each of the models for these components has to fulfil the requirements mentioned above. When determining the level of conservatism for components, the impact on the resulting level of conservatism for the final LGD estimate should be considered to avoid too conservative estimates.

Downturn conditions can be recognized following different approaches. A first approach is to identify the subset of loss observations reflecting economic downturn and to develop estimation procedures based only on this reference dataset. Time series of macroeconomic variables can be used to identify the respective time intervals reflecting economic downturns. However, with limited reference datasets, this approach will often be a rather theoretical option. Alternatively, one may restrict considerations to the marginal distribution of loss observations for the considered component, i.e. implicitly recognize economic downturn by choosing an appropriately conservative quantile. If the bank intends to develop an LGD model, which explicitly recognizes the impact of economic cycles, a more elegant solution is to estimate downturn LGDs by applying this model with downturn parameters instead of input parameters reflecting the current economic situation.

Margins of conservatism can be derived as percentiles from empirical distributions, based on appropriate parametric distribution assumptions or, for example, from applying resampling techniques as bootstrapping. In practice, observed volatilities can be large, leading to large margins even for lower confidence levels.

Practical problems also arise where loss history may not reflect the characteristics of future losses. If, for example, a bank redesigns its workout processes or changes its workout strategy, future losses may differ from what has been observed in the past. Depending on the portfolio it will take several years until the effect of the modifications becomes visible in loss observations. During that time the bank has the difficult task of recognizing the unknown effect of the modification in its loss estimates in a conservative manner. Similar problems of data aging may arise due to changes in laws, etc.

7. LGD Estimation for Defaulted Exposures

When estimating LGDs for defaulted facilities, an institute faces a slightly different situation than for performing exposures. Besides differences in regulatory requirements (e.g., the need to generate a best estimate and conservative estimate of

---

[46] Volatility of LGD then has to be recognized separately in unexpected loss estimates.

LGD; see Section 2.1) and possible synergies from collaboration with provisioning processes (see Section 2.2), differences in the information basis are a third aspect that should be considered in model development. Information available for defaulted exposures may differ in different aspects from that obtained for performers. Defaulted exposures are generally attended more intensively than performing facilities, resulting in more up-to-date and precise information. The bank will also receive additional information, not available before default. This can be explicit information, for example, from workout processes and markets, or implicit information, as time after default or certain decisions.

Explicit information generally replaces the estimate for some components of LGD. One may therefore think of LGD estimates for defaulted exposures as a transition from ex-ante LGD estimation to ex-post LGD observation. Update-procedures can differ depending on whether the bank keeps default time as the reference time or considers the current date instead. More interesting for practical usage is generally the second variant, which considers only residual loss, i.e.

$$EAD(t) = EAD(t_{DF}) - \sum_{\tau \in [t_{DF}, t)} cf_{\tau}^{Rec} \qquad (13)$$

$$LGD(t) = 1 - \frac{\left[NPV\left(CF_{\tau}^{Rec}, \tau \geq t\right) - NPV\left(CF_{\tau}^{Costs}, \tau \geq t\right)\right]}{EAD(t)}$$

with cf and CF the realized or expected recovery cash flows and costs. While the update-scheme itself has a simple structure, its implementation can become complicated. In particular, the update of EAD and LGD requires that the sources of all cash flows can be automatically identified.

Implicit information, for example, time after default or certain events observed after default, may be used in estimates of NPL-LGDs by considering (abstract) states of information as additional explanatory variables or, more generally, state space models. As an example, consider cure probability as a decreasing function of time after default in a model following Eqs. (3) – (7). While theoretically appealing, estimating such models requires large reference datasets and relatively homogenous portfolios if not (partly) parameterised by expert judgement. Portfolios of standardized retail exposures may therefore be the main field of application.

Purely statistical approaches will often not be able to capture all information available for individual defaulted facilities. For example, recoveries from a bankrupt's assets or collateral as well as costs or payment dates can often be estimated more precisely from knowledge of an individual loss case. The estimate may therefore be improved by allowing overrides for some of the model's input parameters or the resulting LGD estimate. This can also affect the model design.

Since provisioning requires similar information to loss estimation, it can be sensible to link the two processes in order to use a consistent set of information, avoid redundant work, and assimilate provisions and LGD estimates as far as possible, which may also simplify internal communication of these numbers. This type of link can be established in both directions, as depicted in Figure 4 below: A statistical LGD model can deliver information concerning the loss distribution of the facility as well as other useful information, for example, expected collateral recoveries etc. These may serve in a provisioning tool as a basis or reference for determining provisions. During the provisioning process, a credit analyst may then modify or supplement the data based on his knowledge of the respective loss case. These inputs can afterwards be used to improve LGD estimates.

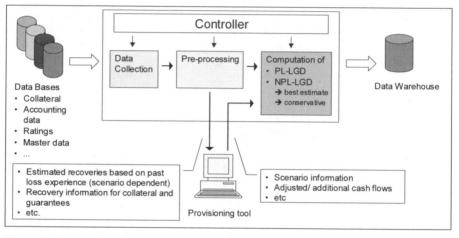

Figure 4. Connection of LGD estimation for nonperforming exposures and provisioning[47]

Before including information from the provisioning process into NPL-LGD estimation, it is necessary to analyse any differences in the respective valuation approaches applied by the bank. It should be kept in mind that coupling the two processes can further complicate the implementation of the estimation process. The decision of whether and how the two processes should cooperate often depends on the respective portfolio. For example, loss experience for standardized or retail portfolios will generally provide a sufficient basis to develop and apply more advanced machine-driven estimation procedures. In this case, the bank may want to derive its provisions from LGD estimates. The opposite will probably become true for individual transactions where expert judgment may prove more valuable than limited empirical loss experience.

Due to regulatory requirements, institutes have to determine a best estimate of loss (LGD^{BE}) as well as a conservative estimate (LGD^{CE}). As discussed in Section

---

[47] (N)PL-LGD is used as an abbreviation for an LGD of a (non)performing exposure.

6.2.5, some banks may apply a similar scheme for performing facilities as well. Since individual information probably enters LGD estimates for defaulted exposures to a larger extend than for performing exposures, it may often be possible to derive estimates of LGD^{CE} by appropriately stressing the best estimate LGD^{BE}. Sometimes, the same or similar stress factors as already used for performing loans can be applied. However, due to better knowledge of the economic situation, one may often expect margins to be smaller than for performing loans. Appropriately stressing human judgment in LGD estimates can be difficult. Depending on its impact on the estimate, one may simply ignore them in conservative LGD estimates.[48]

8. Concluding Remarks

This article provides a general survey of LGD modelling from a practical point of view, giving a snapshot of current practice. Due to the scope of the article, various aspects including most technical details could not be covered. Several aspects of LGD estimation are still topics of discussion and current research. Two important examples are

- *Lack of loss history*: Estimating LGD for exposures of portfolios with little or no defaults is a difficult but common problem. But even for portfolios where loss data is in principle available, it may not always be representative for the future due to internal or external changes, for example, modifications in workout strategy or relevant laws. Some simple approaches to deal with this situation have been outlined in this article; however, additional research is recommended.
- *Validation*: While not considered in detail within this article, model validation forms an important part of LGD methodology. BCBS (2004) requires all institutes applying the advanced IRB approach to validate their rating systems and processes on an annual basis. Little has been published on the validation of LGD models so far; see for example Bennett el al. (2005). Some methods may be taken from PD validation, which already provides more advanced concepts[49]; however, specific characteristics of LGD estimation approaches will probably require adjustments or the development of new validation approaches. The lack of loss data will again complicate the application of quantitative tools for some portfolio segments. A unification of validation techniques, processes, and reports for the risk parameters PD, EAD, and LGD appears reasonable to

---

[48] One may also think about allowing credit analysts to judge the uncertainty of recoveries as well, giving them the possibility to influence stress factors, etc. Any degree of freedom in the applied procedure, however, may not only improve the quality of estimates but also bears the danger of deterioration and generally also complicates the whole procedure – from implementation and workflow aspects up to a later validation.

[49] See for example the articles on PD validation in this book.

reduce costs and promote an understanding of the results within the institute; however, this topic has not been discussed in the literature before.

Many further, less prominent topics arise from daily work within the conflicting fields of statistical significance, degree of detail desired for different applications, and cost-benefit aspects. One may therefore expect and look forward to see many interesting developments within the field of LGD modelling during the next years.

References

Altman E, Brady B, Resti A, Sironi A (2003), A Link between Default and Recovery Rates: Theory, Empirical Evidence and Implications. http://pages.stern.nyu.edu/~ealtman/Link_between_Default_and_Recovery_Rates.pdf

Altman E, Kishore V (1996), Almost Everything You Wanted to Know about Recoveries on Defaulted Bonds, Financial Analysts Journal, November/ December, pp. 57 – 64.

Altman E, Resti A, Sironi A (eds.) (2005), Recovery Risk – The next Challenge in Credit Risk Management, Risk Books, London.

Araten M, Jacobs M, Varshney P (2004), Measuring LGD on Commercial Loans: An 18-Year Internal Study, The RMA Journal, May, pp. 28 – 35.

Basel Committee on Banking Supervision (BCBS) (2004, updated 2005), International Convergence of Capital Measurement and Capital Standards: A Revised Framework, Bank for International Settlements. www.bis.org

Basel Committee on Banking Supervision (BCBS) (2005), The Application of Basel II to Trading Activities and the Treatment of Double Default, Bank For International Settlements. www.bis.org

Committee of European Banking Supervisors (CEBS) (2005, revised 2006), Guidelines on the Implementation, Validation and Assessment of Advanced Measurement (AMA) and Internal Rating Based (IRB) Approaches, CP10. www.c-ebs.org.

Beckmann C, Papazoglou P (2004), Sicherheitenoptimierung nach Basel II, Kreditwesen 3, pp. 146 – 150 (in German).

Bennett RL, Catarineu E, Moral G (2005), Loss Given Default Validation, in: Basel Committee on Banking Supervision, Studies on the Validation of Internal Rating Systems, Working Paper No. 14, Bank For International Settlements, pp. 60 – 93.

Düllmann K, Trapp M (2004), Systematic Risk in Recovery Rates – An Empirical Analysis of US Corporate Credit Exposures, Deutsche Bundesbank Discussion Paper, 02/ 2004.

Franks J, de Servigny A, Davydenko S (2004), A Comparative Analysis of Recovery Process and Recovery Rates for Private Companies in the U.K., France, and Germany, Working Paper, Standard & Poor's Risk Solutions.

Frye J (2000a), Collateral Damage, Risk, April, pp 91 – 94.

Frye J (2000b) Depressing Recoveries, Risk, November, pp. 106 – 111.

Gupton G, Stein R (2005), LossCalc V2: Dynamic Prediction of LGD, Modelling Methodology, Moody's KMV.

Gürtler M, Heithecker D (2005), Sicherheitenoptimierung: adäquate Anrechnung von Bürgschaften, Kreditwesen 17, pp. 926 – 930 (in German).

Hamilton D, Varma P, Ou S, Cantor R (2006), Default and Recovery Rates of Corporate Bond Issuers, 1920 – 2005, Moody's Investor Service, New York.

Heitfield E, Barger N (June 2003), Treatment of Double-Default and Double-Recovery Effects for Hedged Exposures under Pillar I of the Proposed New Basel Capital Accord, A White Paper by the Staff of the Board of Governors of the Federal Reserve System in Support of the Forthcoming Advance Notice of Proposed Rulemaking. www.federalreserve.gov/generalinfo/basel2/docs2003/doubledefault.pdf

International Accounting Standard Board (IASB) (2005), International Financial Reporting Standard (IFRS), IASCF Publications Department, London, UK.

Maclachlan I (2004), Choosing the Discount Factor for Estimating Economic LGD. http://members.dodo.net.au/~maclachl/LGDdiscount.pdf

Merton RC (1974), On the Pricing of Corporate Debt: The Risk Structure of Interest Rates, Journal of Finance, 2, pp. 49 – 71.

IX. Overview of EAD Estimation Concepts

Walter Gruber and Ronny Parchert

1 PLUS i GmbH

1. EAD Estimation from a Regulatory Perspective

1.1. Definition of Terms

The exposure at default (EAD) is defined as the expected amount of a receivable at the time of a default. In order to describe the borrower related risk, the EAD has to be calculated without considering provisions.[1] Bank-internally available provisions serve to cover the equity in the balance sheet in case of losses. Possible losses already have reduced the risk bearing capacity of the bank at the moment of risk identification by the realization of provisions.

The definition shows that in a first step, the EAD is determined by the exact time of default. If observed economically, the expected EAD changes depending on whether the default horizon consists of, e.g. one or of two years. According to regulatory prescriptions, the EAD must not be lower than the book value of a balance sheet receivable.[2] Therefore a regulatory necessity to estimate future EAD for such positions is not given.

Credit Conversion Factors (CCF) have to be estimated for off-balance sheet transactions and credit approvals. They describe the percentage rate of undrawn credit lines (UCL) that have not yet been paid out, but that will be utilized by the borrower until the default happens. Therefore the EAD for an undrawn amount is defined as:

$$EAD = UCL \cdot CCF \tag{1}$$

Concerning credit lines that have not completely been paid out (balance sheet receivables); the EAD for a one year time horizon is defined as illustrated in Figure 1.

---

[1] See BIS (2004), § 308.
[2] See Bundesbank (2005), § 104.

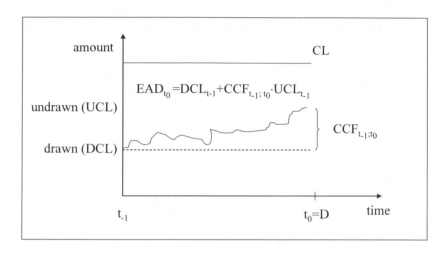

Figure 1. Differences between exposure and credit approval

1.2. Regulatory Prescriptions Concerning the EAD Estimation

Regulatory requirements concerning estimations of loss parameters and related to that also the EAD are mainly given in the regulatory framework of Basel II. Within the equity provisioning requirements that are defined here, three separate approaches for the calculation of risk weighted assets are distinguished. As far as the standardized approach (SA) and the foundation internal ratings-based approach (FIRB) are concerned there is no tolerance regarding the estimation of the EAD/CCF. This is due to the fact that the CCF in relation to classes of receivables is prescribed by regulatory bodies. Specific minimum requirements are defined concerning the advanced internal ratings-based approach (AIRB):[3]

- "EAD for an on-balance sheet or off-balance sheet item is defined as the expected gross exposure of the facility upon default of the obligor. For on-balance sheet items, banks must estimate EAD at no less than the current drawn amount, subject to recognizing the effects of on-balance sheet netting as specified in the foundation approach..."
- "Advanced approach banks must have established procedures in place for the estimation of EAD for off-balance sheet items. These must specify the estimates of EAD to be used for each facility type. Banks estimates of EAD should reflect the possibility of additional drawings by the borrower up to and after the time a default event is triggered. Where estimates of EAD differ by facility type, the delineation of these facilities must be clear and unambiguous."

---

[3] See BIS (2004), § 474 ff.

- "Advanced approach banks must assign an estimate of EAD for each facility. It must be an estimate of the long-run default-weighted average EAD for similar facilities and borrowers over a sufficiently long period of time, but with a margin of conservatism appropriate to the likely range of errors in the estimate. If a positive correlation can reasonably be expected between the default frequency and the magnitude of EAD, the EAD estimate must incorporate a larger margin of conservatism. Moreover, for exposures for which EAD estimates are volatile over the economic cycle, the bank must use EAD estimates that are appropriate for an economic downturn, if these are more conservative than the long run average. For banks that have been able to develop their own EAD models, this could be achieved by considering the cyclical nature, if any, of the drivers of such models. Other banks may have sufficient internal data to examine the impact of previous recession(s). However, some banks may only have the option of making conservative use of external data."

- "The criteria by which estimates of EAD are derived must be plausible and intuitive, and represent what the bank believes to be the material drivers of EAD. The choices must be supported by credible internal analysis by the bank. The bank must be able to provide a breakdown of its EAD experience by the factors it sees as the drivers of EAD. A bank must use all relevant and material information in its derivation of EAD estimates. Across facility types, a bank must review its estimates of EAD when material new information comes to light and at least on an annual basis."

- "Due consideration must be paid by the bank to its specific policies and strategies adopted in respect of account monitoring and payment processing. The bank must also consider its ability and willingness to prevent further drawings in circumstances short of payment default, such as covenant violations or other technical default events. Banks must also have adequate systems and procedures in place to monitor facility amounts, current outstandings against committed lines and changes in outstandings per borrower and per grade. The bank must be able to monitor outstanding balances on a daily basis."

Apart from that specific minimal estimation, periods are defined concerning classes of receivables. Regulatory prescriptions clearly show the high qualitative and quantitative demands banks have to meet when using the AIRB. In practice, the utilization of a bank's internal model to bring the estimation method for the EAD into unison with the other loss parameters probability of default (PD) and loss given default (LGD), is independent of the question whether the model is utilized for internal or for regulatory requirements or for both.

1.3. Delimitation to Other Loss Parameters

Next to a clear definition of the specific parameters and the best possible data quality, a uniform definition of default is most important for a methodologically correct internal estimation of loss parameters for the credit risk. The first primary loss parameter is the PD which describes the probability of default of a borrower within a predefined period, usually one year. The statistical methods for estimating the PD are described in Chapters I, II, and III.

The estimation period of the PD is identical with the estimation period of the EAD, in general one year. The difference between those two parameters lies in the data base needed for estimation. When estimating the PD, it is necessary to forecast how many of the customers who are alive today will default over the next period. Therefore, the overall portfolio has to be considered. Concerning the CCF estimation, the data base is reduced and only those credit lines where the default took place within the period of observation can be regarded ex post. In an economic point of view concerning amortization effects, all receivables have to be taken into account for the EAD estimation.

LGD describes the rate of the defaulted amount of receivables (EAD) that leads to a loss for the creditor. It is the third major component of credit risk and expected loss (EL), which is computed as $EL = EAD \cdot PD \cdot LGD$. The LGD estimation, similar to the estimation of CCF, depends on the defaults that have already taken place. Only on the basis of the defaulted receivables, can it be measured empirically which part of the default-volume will lead to an economic loss for the bank. The estimation of the empirical LGD suffers from the relatively limited amount of data and additionally from the long duration of the estimation period. Whereas PD and EAD/CCF with an estimation horizon of one year already assume a very long period compared to market price risk parameters, LGD estimation periods on average reach 3 to 5 years. The experience within banks shows that the administration of defaulted engagements - including the realization of collateral – takes a long time. Due to this, the backtest of LGD estimations becomes increasingly difficult or nearly impossible. Figure 2 shows the relations between EAD-CCF-LGD in a scheme.

The figure shows that LGD always refers to EAD. Concerning estimations, a simple motto might be derived from this fact. Everything that takes place until the default happens has to be considered in the EAD. All payments after this event only influence the LGD.

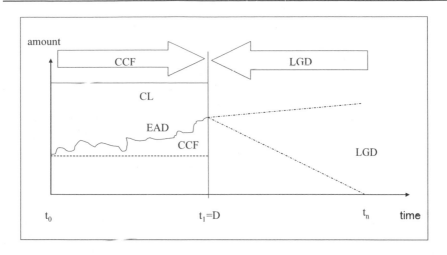

Figure 2. Relation between EAD-CCF-LGD

1.4. EAD Estimation for Derivative Products

If we examine derivative products like interest rate swaps, caps, floors, swaptions, cross currency swaps, equity swaps, or commodity swaps; two kind of counterparty risks have to be considered: settlement and pre-settlement risk.

Settlement risks occur if the payments are not synchronous: This is for example the case if bank A has paid a EUR cash flow in a cross currency swap to bank B before it has received the USD cash flow. Here the risk consists in missing the USD cash flow. If bank B defaults, a loss of the amount of this cash flow would occur. Settlement risks are mostly of short term character.

Much more important are the pre-settlement risks. Characteristic for pre-settlement risks is the following situation: Bank A expects in the future a rising interest rate. For hedging the loan portfolio, bank A makes a payer swap with bank B. This transaction eliminates the interest rate risk but creates a counterparty risk. If bank B defaults during the lifetime of the interest rate swap, bank A has to look for a new counterparty to make the same payer swap with this new counterparty. If in the meantime, the interest rate has moved up, the replacement with an identical swap will only be possible by paying an upfront payment to the new counterparty. Pre-settlement risks are of a long term nature because they may occur during the whole life time of the derivative product.

When calculating the EAD for derivative products, it has to be noted that the EAD consists of two parts:

- *The current exposure (CE)*: These are the replacement costs of derivative transactions, if the counterparty defaults immediately. This is given by the market value of the instrument, if this market value is positive. If the market value is negative, it is zero: CE = max{market value; 0}.
- *The potential future exposure (PFE)*: This an estimate for the increase in market value to a pre-specified time horizon (e.g. one year). In practice, it is calculated by assuming a future distribution of the risk factors on which the specific instrument depends. From this distribution of the risk factors, a distribution of future market values can be inferred. From this distribution, PFE can be estimated, e.g. as a quantile of the distribution. For calculating the PFE for regulatory purposes, fixed add-on factors, which have to be applied to the nominal amount of the contract, are used.

So the EAD is given by: max{market value; 0} + PFE. The figure below demonstrates the calculation of the EAD for derivative products in the regulatory context:

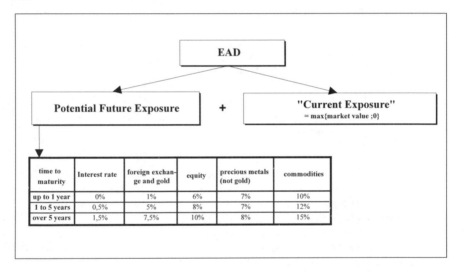

Figure 3. EAD calculation for derivative products in the regulatory context

The height of the add-on factors, which are given in the regulatory framework, should correspond on the one hand to the volatilities of the various risk factor groups (e.g. interest rate section, fx section). On the other hand, the sensitivity of a derivative product increases with its time-to-maturity, which is taken into consideration because the add-on-factors for derivative products are higher for long-term than for short term-products.

The regulatory EAD calculation can be illustrated with a simple example. Consider an interest rate swap with a notional of 1,000,000 Euro, a market value of

10,000 Euro, and a time to maturity of seven years. For this instrument the EAD is given by:

$$10.,000 \ EUR + 1.5\% \cdot 1,000,000 \ EUR = 25,000 \ EUR$$

If there is a netting agreement with the counterparty, the negative and positive market values of all derivative contracts, which are integrated in the netting agreement, can be offset against each other and the current exposure of all these contracts is then given by:

$$CE = \max\left\{\sum_i market \ value_i; 0\right\} \tag{2}$$

For the potential future exposure, a total offsetting of the various PFE's of the various contracts is not allowed. A so called "PFE-floor" which is given by 40% of the sum of the PFE's of the various derivative contracts must be provided. The remaining 60% depend on the "market value structure" of the bilateral derivative portfolio. The total value of the PFE under a netting agreement is given by:

$$PFE = 0,4 \cdot \sum_i PFE_i + 0,6 \cdot \left\{\sum_i PFE_i\right\} \cdot \frac{\max\left\{\sum_i market \ value_i; 0\right\}}{\sum_i \max\{market \ value_i; 0\}} \tag{3}$$

Again we provide a small illustrative example. Consider the portfolio of interest rate swaps given in Table 1.

Table 1. Example portfolio of interest rate swaps

position:	market value:	nominal amount:	time-to-maturity:	add-on-factor:	PFE:
1	10.000	10.000.000	3	0,50%	50.000
2	20.000	15.000.000	5	0,50%	75.000
3	15.000	20.000.000	7	1,50%	300.000
4	-20.000	10.000.000	1	0,00%	0
5	-15.000	7.000.000	8	1,50%	105.000

For this portfolio, the EAD is computed in the following steps

$$CE = 10,000$$

$$PFE = 0.4 \cdot 530,000 + 0.6 \cdot 530,000 \cdot \frac{10,000}{45,000} = 282,667$$

$$EAD = CE + PFE = 292,667$$

If there are further collateral agreements, the EAD can be reduced by the amount of the collateral.

Below the following shortcomings concerning the methodology, how the EAD for derivative portfolios is calculated, can be stated:

- The add-on-factors are static. The volatilities and correlations of the risk factors are not taken into account.
- The specific product structure is neglected in the add-on-factors, e.g. for an interest rate swap and an interest rate cap, the add-on factor is the same as long as both instruments fall into the same maturity time band.
- There is no offsetting between negative market values and the PFE allowed. So an interest rate swap with market value 0 and an interest rate swap with a negative market value will lead to the same EAD.
- There is a very rough distinction concerning the add-on factors for products with different maturities, e.g. an interest rate swap with a maturity of 6 years has the same add-on factor as an interest rate swap with a maturity of 30 years, although the two products react completely different to changes in the interest rate curve.
- There is no recognition of an amortization effect. In the described "regulatory proceeding", that cash flows of a product which are paid before the proposed default point (e.g. 1 year), should not be considered in the CE.

Banks who use the AIRB may use more elaborate techniques for calculating the EAD of derivative portfolios. These techniques will be explained in Section 2.2.

2. Internal Methods of EAD Estimation

2.1. Empirical Models

The delimitation between the loss parameters fulfils the main requirement concerning the creation of an internal empirical data collection model for the EAD. In addition to the open credit lines, an empirical model should also generally contain balance sheet exposures even if the respective information cannot be integrated into the regulatory equity provisioning.

In general, variations in the EAD are not to be underestimated concerning balance sheet exposures. This can be illustrated by a short example. Two credits utilized at the level of 100 EUR and that bear an interest rate of 6% are given. For credit A, an annual repayment of 12% and for credit B a monthly repayment of 1% are agreed upon. Assume that both borrowers stop paying their annual repayments after 11 months, meaning that after 90 days a default in accordance with the Basel II default definitions occurs. This means for credit A that at the time of default a total amount of receivables of 100 EUR is given. Apart from this, 6% interest = 6 EUR for one year and the interest for the 90-days-period of about 1.6 EUR have not been paid. This adds up to a total receivables amount (EAD) of 107.6 EUR. For credit B, this means that 11 repayments and interest payments have been duly effected and therefore, the remaining amount of receivables equals 89 EUR. Interest payments for the 12th month and for the excess period of 1.75 EUR have to be added. The total amount of receivables demanded from the customer adds up to about 90.75 EUR. This delimitation is also of prior importance concerning the LGD-estimation. Assume that customer B pays back the total receivable amount of 90.75 EUR and all administration related costs. In this case, the bank does not incur an economic or a balance sheet loss. But if we assume the regulatory EAD-definition for balance sheet receivables, the EAD adds up to 100 EUR and a loss (LGD) of about 10% occurs.

The regulatory approach assumes that the effects of cases A and B cancel each other out. This can be accepted as far as equity provisioning is concerned, but should not be accepted as far as an economic observation is given. Figure 1 therefore has to be adapted concerning balance sheet receivables as follows.

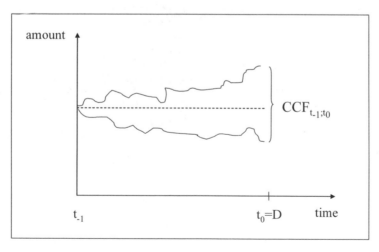

Figure 4. Development of the exposure concerning receivables on the balance sheet

While constructing empirical models it makes sense to define the EAD in cash values. In case A, the customer pays interest of 6%. If we assume that one year before default, 5% was the risk adjusted interest rate for this customer, a cash-value of more than 100% results. Within an economic observation, this claim to profits is not realizable for the bank. An eventual refinancing loss starting from the date of default has to be considered in the frame of the LGD.

After fixing the mentioned methodological framework for an internal empirical model, its creation is relatively simple. In general, the following requirements must be observed:

- Saving all EAD and CL related information at least for one year and concerning all accounts, if necessary including market interest rates, conditions, cash flow structures, etc.
- Segmentation of classes of receivables to create pools for the EAD/CCF estimation, i.e. loans for home construction, current account overdrafts, guarantees, etc.
- Classification according to classes, e.g. receivables, ratings, etc.

The last two points refer to the necessity of a clear definition of the aggregation level of the survey. The schemes of those are depicted in Figure 5. For a detailed treatment of techniques for estimating conversion factors we refer to Chapter X.

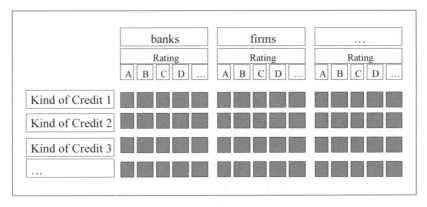

Figure 5. Levels of aggregation of the EAD-survey

2.2. Internal Approaches for EAD Estimation for Derivative Products

As we have seen in Section 1.4, the regulatory proceeding for estimating EAD for derivative products has a lot of shortcomings and should not be used if the EAD is to be measured in an economically sensible way. Therefore, banks that use the AIRB in Basel II would use more elaborate techniques where these shortcomings do not occur. Below we present such techniques.

2.2.1. EAD Estimation Using Sensitivity Approaches

A simple way to calculate EAD estimates for derivative products is to use the variance-covariance approach for calculating the PFE. Here, the PFE is defined as the maximum increase in the market value of a derivative instrument during a certain holding period given the confidence level α.

Expressing this in formulas gives us the PFE by[4]:

$$PFE = \sqrt{x^T \cdot C \cdot x} \tag{4}$$

with:

$$x = \begin{pmatrix} VaR_1 \\ ... \\ VaR_n \end{pmatrix}$$

the vector of the risk factor-specific VaR and the correlation matrix C.

If we assume that the various risk factors are normally distributed, then the VaR for a single risk factor i which has a certain risk factor sensitivity, holding period t_0, und confidence level α is given by:

$$VaR = \sqrt{t_0} \cdot q_\alpha \cdot \sigma_i \cdot Sensititivity_i \tag{5}$$

Then the EAD for a derivative product is given by:

$$EAD = \max\{market\ value + PFE; 0\} \tag{6}$$

If we use a sensitivity approach (like described above) for estimating the EAD for derivative products approach still some shortcomings remain:

- Amortization effects are not recognised appropriately (Section 1.4)
- Second-order-risks of options are ignored.

Banks are increasingly using Monte-Carlo techniques to estimate the EAD for derivative portfolios.[5] Before these techniques are presented some general remarks concerning Monte-Carlo techniques are made.[6]

---

[4] For a deeper explanation of the various VaR-approaches for measuring market risk see Jendruschewitz (1997).

[5] Seelhof (1999)

[6] For a detailed description of Monte-Carlo techniques see Vose (1997).

2.2.2. EAD Estimation using Monte-Carlo Techniques

Basic Remarks

It is generally said that in a Monte-Carlo simulation, future risk factors are "diced" using:

- A specific stochastic process for the risk factors[7] (e.g. geometrical Brownian motion) which results in distributions of the risk factors at specific time horizons (e.g. log-normal distribution).
- Estimations of the parameters of these stochastic processes, e.g. volatilities and correlations.

Further distinctions have to be made between:

- Path-independent and path-dependent Monte-Carlo simulations
  - In a path-independent Monte-Carlo simulation, the risk factor(s) are simulated to one future time horizon (Figure 6).
  - In a path-dependent Monte-Carlo simulation, the risk factor(s) are simulated for various pre-specified future time horizons (Figure 7).
- Univariate and multivariate Monte-Carlo
  - In a univariate Monte-Carlo simulation, each risk factor is separately simulated.
  - In a multivariate Monte-Carlo simulation, all risk factors are simultaneously simulated under consideration of the correlation matrix. This is achieved by the so called Cholesky decomposition (Figure 8 and Figure 9).

In the following, we need two types of Monte-Carlo-paths:

- For estimating the EAD for a bilateral derivative portfolio for a certain time horizon, we need a multivariate path-independent Monte-Carlo simulation.
- For estimating the EAD for a bilateral derivative portfolio for its whole lifetime, we need a multivariate path-dependent Monte-Carlo simulation.

---

[7] For an overview, regarding which stochastic processes could be used for the various risk factor categories see Rebonato (1997).

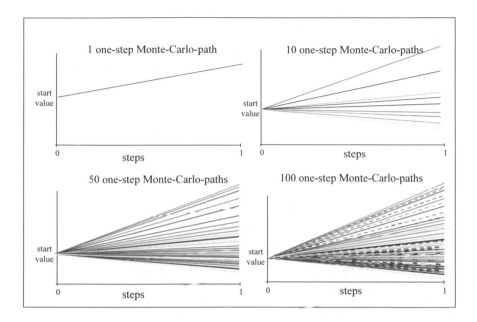

Figure 6. Creation of one-step Monte-Carlo-paths

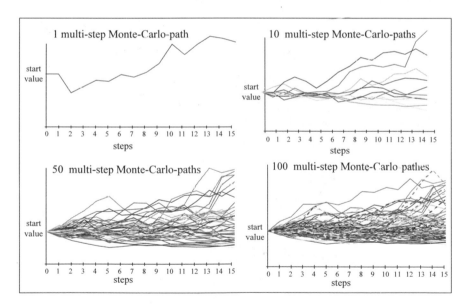

Figure 7. Creation of multi-step Monte-Carlo-paths

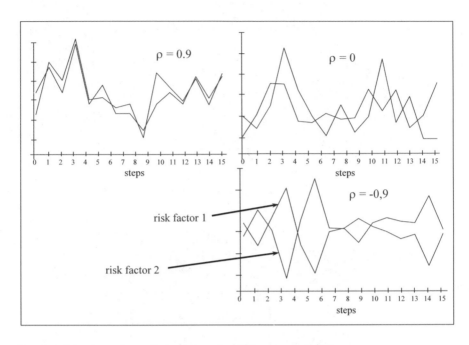

Figure 8. Bivariate Monte-Carlo-paths using different correlations

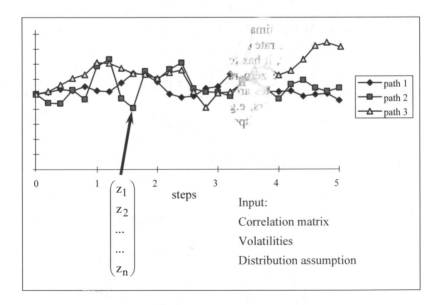

Figure 9. Multivariate Monte-Carlo-paths

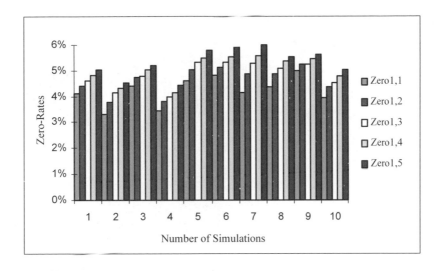

Figure 10. Simulated zero-rates for a one-year time horizon

Multivariate One-Step Monte-Carlo for EAD Estimation for a Specific Time Horizon

The basic methodology for est   ting EAD for derivative contracts will be explained by a six year interest   wap. If the EAD for the time horizon of one year should be measured first   to be stated that the fair value of the interest rate swap is a function of the   tes $z_1, ...,z_5$, which will hold in one year. Therefore, only the five zero ra   simulated to one year, using a specific stochastic process and its paramete   the volatilities and the correlation matrix (Figure 10). We do not focus on a s ecific stochastic process here but explain the general principles.

For each simulation i of interest rates we get a specific swap value SV_i (Figure 11).

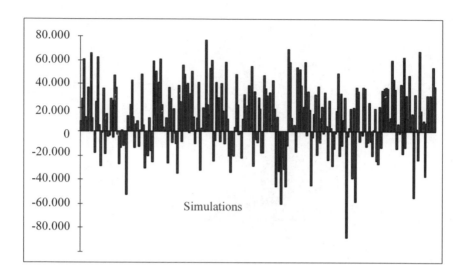

Figure 11. Simulated fair values for an interest rate swap for a one-year time horizon

Because an exposure is always positive, the exposure for a certain simulation is the swap value, if the simulation led to a positive value and 0 otherwise (Figure 12). If we look at the frequency distribution (Figure 13), there are three possibilities for defining the EAD. It could be defined as the average exposure as in (7).

$$EAD_{Av} = \frac{1}{n}\sum_{i=1}^{n}\max\{SV_i;0\}$$ (7)

Other possibilities are defining EAD as the maximum exposure as in (8) or as the quantile exposure to the confidence level α as in (9).

$$EAD_{max} = \max_{i=1}^{n}[\max\{SV_i;0\}]$$ (8)

$$EAD_{\alpha} = \alpha\text{ - quantile of }[\max\{SV_i;0\}, i=1,...,n]$$ (9)

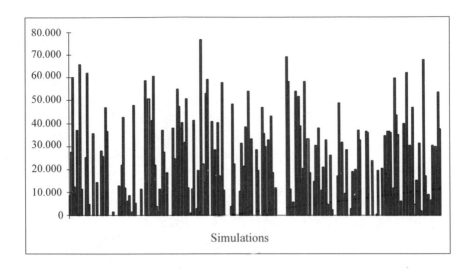

Figure 12. Simulated future exposures for an interest rate swap for a one-year time horizon

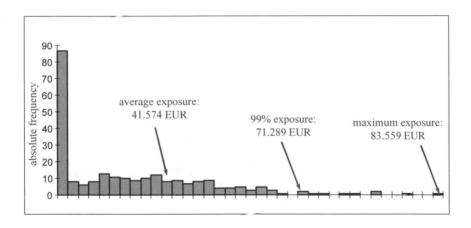

Figure 13. Average, 99%, and maximum exposure for an interest rate swap for a one-year-time horizon

Multivariate Multi-Step Monte-Carlo for EAD Estimation for the Total Lifetime

The next step is to calculate the different EAD-types now for arbitrary time horizons along the whole lifetime. If we do this for our six year interest rate swap and we look at $EAD(t)$, then we see two opposite effects:

- *Diffusion effect*: The further the time horizon is in the future, the more volatile are the risk factors and therefore the bigger is the EAD.
- *Amortization effect*: The further the time horizon is in the future, the more cash flows of the swaps are paid by the counterparty and are no longer part of the exposure.

Putting both effects together, we see the so-called Sydney curves for the swap (Figure 14), which represent average, maximum and quantile exposure during the lifetime of the product.

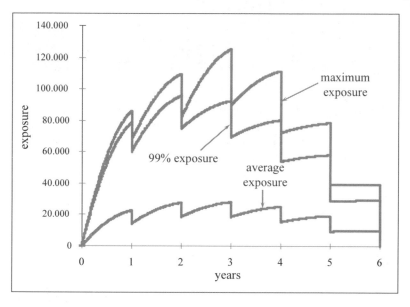

Figure 14. Average, 99%, and maximum exposure for an interest rate swap for its lifetime

On the basis of the quantile exposure $EAD_\alpha(t)$, a limit system for the derivative position along its lifetime could be established. Alternatively, the so called peak-exposure which is just the maximum of $EAD(t)$ is used for limitation purposes.

This technique can now be extended for a whole bilateral derivative portfolio under recognition of netting and collateral agreements. Here we use a multivariate path-dependent Monte-Carlo simulation, which is based on all risk factors that influence the whole bilateral portfolio. The resulting Sydney curve gives the $EAD(t)$ under netting and collateral agreements. An easy example of two opposite interest rate swaps is presented in Figure 15.

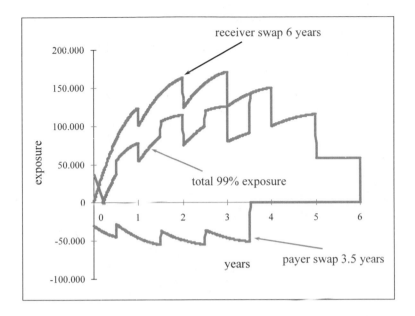

Figure 15. 99% exposure for a portfolio of two interest rate swaps

3. Conclusion

This article presented basic concepts for estimating EAD for balance-sheet and off-balance-sheet financial products. We started with the description of the methods, which are delivered by the regulatory framework. If we look at the various shortcomings of the regulatory methods, we motivated how internal methods for EAD-estimation should be designed to avoid these disadvantages and create more elaborate techniques to estimate the EAD in an economic sense. For estimating the EAD for derivative portfolios various Monte-Carlo techniques can be applied.

References

BIS (2004), International Convergence of Capital Measurement and Capital Standards, Basel Committee on Banking Supervision, June 2004.

Bundesbank (2005), Entwurf zur Solvabilitätsverordnung, Bundesbank, May 2005.

Gruber W (2001), Konzepte zur Messung von Markt- und Kreditrisiken, in: Eller R, Gruber W, Reif M (eds.): Handbuch Gesamtbanksteuerung, Schäffer-Poeschel-Verlag, Stuttgart.

Gruber W (2005), Praxisorientierte Bepreisung von einfachen und strukturierten Credit Default Swaps, in: Gruber J, Gruber W, Braun H (eds.): Praktikerhandbuch Asset-Backed-Securities und Kreditderivate, Schäffer-Poeschel-Verlag, Stuttgart.

Jendruschewitz B (1997), Value-at-Risk, Hochschule für Bankwirtschaft.

Rebonato R (1997), Interest Rate Option Models, John Wiley & Sons.

Seelhof M (1999), Messung von Ausfallrisiken aus derivativen Instrumenten mit dynamischen Simulationstechniken, in: Eller R, Gruber, W., Reif, M. (eds.): Handbuch Kreditrisikomodelle und Kreditderivate, Schäffer-Poeschel-Verlag, Stuttgart.

Vose D (1997), Quantitative Risk Analysis, John Wiley & Sons.

X. EAD Estimates for Facilities with Explicit Limits

Gregorio Moral

Banco de España[1]

1. Introduction

The estimation of exposure at default, EAD, for a facility with credit risk, has received a lot of attention, principally in the area of counterparty risk and has focused on situations where the variability of the exposure is due to: the existence of variability in the underlying variables of a derivative; the use of a fixed nominal amount not expressed in the presentation currency; or the existence of collateral whose value (variable over time), reduces the exposure. Less attention has been given to the case of loan commitments with explicit credit limits. In this case, the source of variability of the exposure is the possibility of additional withdrawals when the limit allows this. The implementation of Basel II is forcing credit institutions to address this problem in a rigorous, transparent and objective manner. Moreover, Basel II imposes a set of minimum conditions on the internal EAD estimates in order to allow the use of these as inputs in the calculation of the minimum capital requirement. Currently, credit institutions have problems meeting the requirements of both the data and the methodologies.

This chapter analyses various methods for estimating EAD for facilities with explicit limits and tries to assess their optimality from both an internal and a regulatory point of view. It focuses on objective methods, based on a reference data set (RDS) extracted from observed defaulted facilities, which are frequently used in practice by banks. Section 2 presents the definition of realised conversion factors (realised CFs) that are the basic input in most of the estimation procedures. Section 3 describes several approaches for computing realised CFs: "Fixed Time Horizon", "Cohort Approach", and "Variable Time Horizon" and summarises their pros and cons. Section 4 explores issues that have to be addressed before estimating EADs such as: structure and scope of the reference data set (RDS); data cleaning; treatment of observations with negative or greater than one CFs; and risk drivers. Section 5 focuses on EAD estimates. First, it establishes the equivalence

---

[1] The views expressed in this paper are the responsibility of the author and do not necessarily reflect those of Banco de España.

between EAD estimators and CF estimators under certain conditions. Second, the most common methods used by banks in practice are presented as special cases of optimisation problems. It concludes that these methods are solutions for regression problems with quadratic and symmetric loss functions. Section 6 discusses issues related to the optimality of the estimates and introduces a different kind of loss function, one that is linear and asymmetric. These loss functions are naturally linked to Basel II capital requirements and they are used to derive optimal estimators that, consequently, could be more appropriate when the estimates are used for computing capital requirements under Advanced Internal Ratings-Based approaches (AIRB). Section 7 illustrates issues discussed in the previous sections and the consequences of using different estimation methods with a stylised but realistic example. Finally, Section 8 summarises the current practice on CF and EAD estimation, highlights problematic aspects, suggests possible improvements and concludes that traditional methods, based on averages, are less conservative than those based on quantiles.

2. Definition of Realised Conversion Factors

In practice, when estimating the EAD for a non-defaulted facility, f, with an explicit credit limit[2], there are two main classes of methods in terms of the basic equation used to link the estimated EAD with the limit:

- In the first class, estimates of the EAD are based on a suitable conversion factor for the total limit of the facility, $EAD(f) = CCF(f) \cdot Limit(f)$.
- In the second class, estimates of the EAD are based on another factor[3] applied to the undrawn part of the limit, $EAD(f) = Current\ Exposure(f) + LEQ(f) \cdot Undrawn\ Limit(f)$[4].

As it is shown in Section 5, both approaches are equivalent and the problem of $EAD(f)$ estimation can be reduced to the estimation of suitable conversion factors $CF(f)$ ($CCF(f)$ or $LEQ(f)$).

---

[2] For example, credit lines which are committed, i.e. the borrower can draw additional amounts until a limit $L(t)$ is reached.

[3] In the Revised Framework and the Capital Directive such factors are called Credit Conversion Factors (CCFs) and Conversion Factors (CFs) respectively. In the drafts of Rules for Implementation of Basel II in the US the factor used is called LEQ factor and the Guidelines by CEBS uses the term Conversion Factors (CFs). In this chapter, for clarity, conversion factors that are applied to the undrawn amount are called Loan Equivalent (LEQ) factors and the term Credit Conversion Factor, CCF, is reserved for the factor related to the total limit.

[4] This is the approach required for these types of facilities in the Revised Framework, the Capital Directive, the drafts of Rules for Implementation of Basel II in the US, and in the CEBS Guidelines.

In order to obtain the CF estimates, banks use as basic data, a set of observations at specific dates prior to the default time, of defaulted facilities. Most of the estimation methods used are based on certain statistics, related to the increase in the usage of the facility[5] between a reference date and the default date, computed from the former observations. One of these statistics is called the realised LEQ factor and is defined below.

Consider a defaulted facility g with an exposure variable over time, given by $E(t)$ and a credit limit given by $L(t)$. Figure 1 presents the evolution of the exposure.

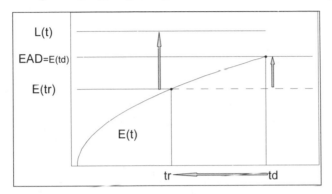

Figure 1. Definition of realised LEQ factor

If the facility has a default date td, given a reference date $tr < td$, the pair $i = \{g, tr\}$ is called index of the observation. If EAD_i stands for the observed exposure at default[6], $E(td)$, this can be expressed in terms of the exposure and the limit of the facility observed at the reference date, assuming that $L(tr) \neq E(tr)$, as:

$$EAD_i = E(tr) + LEQ_i \cdot (L(tr) - E(tr)) \tag{1}$$

Where LEQ_i is given by:

$$LEQ_i = \frac{E(td) - E(tr)}{L(tr) - E(tr)} \tag{2}$$

---

[5] Throuhgout this chapter the term "usage" refers to the usage of the facility in euros (sometimes the terms exposure, drawn amount or utilization are used with the same meaning).

[6] In this chapter, it is assumed that a precise definition of observed EAD for defaulted facilities, EAD_i, has been established previously and that it is applied consistently across facilities and over time for different internal purposes. To understand why an explicit definition of observed EAD is necessary see Araten (2001, p.37), where two situations are cited when the simple definition of EAD_i ("*final amounts shown at the time of default*") is not adequate: charge-offs or seizures of collateral occurred just prior to the default date.

or:

$$LEQ_i = \frac{\dfrac{E(td)}{L(tr)} - \dfrac{E(tr)}{L(tr)}}{1 - \dfrac{E(tr)}{L(tr)}} = \frac{ead_i - e(tr)}{1 - e(tr)} \qquad (3)$$

Therefore, given an observation, O_i, characterised by a pair $i = \{g, tr\}$, with $L(tr) \neq E(tr)$, the former formulae can be used to compute a realised LEQ factor. We denote the realised LEQ factor associated with the observation O_i by LEQ_i, and by $LEQ(tr)$ when the focus is on the reference date tr.

There are three limitations when using this statistic as the basic input for estimation procedures:

- It is not defined when $L(tr) = E(tr)$. This implies that it is not possible to estimate directly $EAD(f)$ based on the value of this statistic for facilities that at the current date exhibit percent usage, $e(tr)$, equal to one.[7]
- It is not stable when $L(tr) \cong E(tr)$. This means that realised LEQ factors are not very informative when percent usage is close to one. As shown in Section 4.2.2, the different behaviour of realised LEQ factors, depending on the level of credit percent usage at the reference date, has important practical consequences.
- It does not take into account changes in the limit over time. In formulae (2) and (3) realised LEQ factors have been defined without taking into account possible changes in the limit of the facility between the reference date and the default date[8]. As it is shown in detail in Section 4.2.3, this is only one of the causes that justifies the existence of realised LEQ_i factors greater than one.

For these reasons, banks sometimes use other statistics as their basis for estimating EADs. For example, an obvious possibility is to define realised CCFs similarly to realised LEQ factors. By using an equation analogous to (1) the expression for this statistic is given by the percent exposure at default:

$$CCF_i = \frac{EAD_i}{L(tr)} = ead_i \qquad (4)$$

Although this statistic is less used in practice than LEQ_i for these types of facilities, it has two advantages:

---

[7] This limitation applies when the estimates are used for internal purposes because, in principle, internal uses do not need to assume that $LEQ(f) \geq 0$, or equivalently, that the $EAD(f)$ estimate has to be greater or equal than the current exposure of this facility, $E(f)$.

[8] Some banks define realised LEQ factors by using $E(td)/L(td)$, percent usage at default, instead of $ead_i = E(td)/L(tr)$, percent exposure at default, in (3). The aim of this definition is to take into account changes in the credit limit after the reference date and to avoid computing realised LEQ factors greater than 1. It is straightforward to show that the former definition is consistent with equation (1) if EAD_i is multiplied by the factor $L(tr)/L(td)$.

- The realised CCF is well defined even when $L(tr) = E(tr)$.
- It is stable even when $L(tr) \cong E(tr)$.

Sometimes it is said that with this statistic, if the facility g had a constant limit $L(g)$, it is not necessary to specify a reference date. However, as it is shown in Section 4, data sets for estimating procedures need to include the values of certain risk drivers that vary over time and therefore it is necessary to consider an explicit reference date.

Additional useful statistics are introduced in Section 5; until then it is assumed that realised LEQs are used as the basis for the estimation process.

3. How to Obtain a Set of Realised Conversion Factors

Given a set of defaulted facilities, there are several approaches frequently employed by banks to obtain realised conversion factors or other statistics[9] that can be used, in addition with other information, to obtain estimates for the EAD of non defaulted facilities. All these approaches are based on observations of defaulted facilities at specific reference dates previous to the default date. Depending on the rule used for selecting these reference dates we refer to these approaches as: Fixed Time Horizon, Cohort Approach or Variable Time Horizon.

3.1. Fixed Time Horizon

In this approach, first a time horizon, T, is selected and second, for each defaulted facility with $L(td-T) \neq E(td-T)$, a realised LEQ factor is computed by using $td-T$ as the reference date:

$$LEQ(td-T) = \frac{E(td) - E(td-T)}{L(td-T) - E(td-T)}$$
(5)

In practice, T is frequently set to one year.

---

[9] As is shown in Section 5, in addition to the realised CFs, the percent increase in usage between the reference date and the default date or the increase in exposure between those dates are statistics that can be used to estimate CFs or EADs.

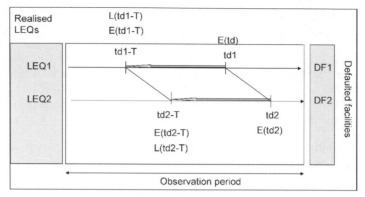

Figure 2. Realised LEQ with the fixed time horizon approach

Drawbacks:

- The fixed time horizon, T, is conventional.
- It is not possible to include directly defaulted facilities when the age of the facility at the date of default is less than T.
- It does not take into account all the relevant information because for each facility g defaulted during the observation period, only the observation $\{g, td - T\}$ is used.
- It does not take into account the possibility that current exposures can default at any moment during the following year. Implicitly, estimates based on this approach assume that the default date for each facility that will default over the following twelve months, will be the end of this period. This assumption could introduce bias into the estimates.

Advantages:

- Dispersion of reference dates.
- The use of a common horizon, $T = td - tr$, contributes to the homogeneity of the realised LEQs.

3.2. Cohort Method

First, the observation period[10] is divided into intervals of a fixed length (cohorts), for example one-year intervals. Second, the facilities are grouped into cohorts according to the interval that includes their default dates. Third, in order to compute a realised LEQ factor associated with each facility, the starting point of the time interval that contains its default date is used as the reference date, $\{t1, t2, ..., ti, ..., tn\}$:

---

[10] The period of time covering the data is the observation period.

$$LEQ(ti) = \frac{E(td) - E(ti)}{L(ti) - E(ti)}$$ (6)

This is illustrated in Figure 3 below.

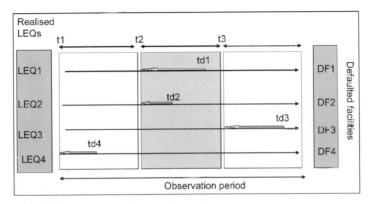

Figure 3. Realised LEQ with the cohort approach

Drawbacks:

- The length of cohorts is conventional
- The reference dates are conventional
- It does not use all the relevant available information because for each facility g defaulted during the observation period (and included in a cohort with initial date t_j) only the observation $\{g, t_j\}$ is used
- The reference dates are concentrated
- The realised LEQs are less homogenous than those computed by using a fixed time horizon. The reason is that this approach computes LEQ_i factors with very different values for the horizon $(td - tr)$.

Advantages:

- It does take into account the possibility that current exposures can default at any moment during the following year.

3.3. Variable Time Horizon

First, a range for horizon values (e.g., one year) for which we are going to compute LEQ_i factors is fixed. Second, for each defaulted facility we compute the realised LEQ factors associated with a set of reference dates, (for example[11], one month, two months,..., twelve months before default).

---

[11] Although with this approach, in theory, it is not necessary to use monthly observations, from now on it is assumed that the reference dates are the end of each month from the

The rationale for this method is to take into account a broader set of possible default dates than in the other approaches when estimating a suitable LEQ factor for a non-defaulted facility conditional on the default during the following year.

$$\{LEQ(td - j) = \frac{E(td) - E(td - j)}{L(td - j) - E(td - j)}, \quad j = 1,...,12 \text{ months}\} \tag{7}$$

In principle[12], twelve realised LEQs could be associated with each defaulted facility. However, these LEQ factors are clearly not homogenous in the sense that some of these values are computed by using observations very close to the default date ($i = \{g, td - 1\}$) and others are based on observations one year before default ($j = \{g, td - 12\}$). This means that it is necessary to recognise these differences via risk drivers. As shown in Section 4.3, the key point is to take into account when the bank identified the facilities as non-normal and, consequently for the purpose of obtaining estimates for facilities in a "normal status", to use only observations meeting this requirement. The main reason is that near to default, borrowers are in general, classified in a non-normal internal class (in the following the variable that identifies these different internal classes is called "status"). This means that a facility is subject to close monitoring and, in general, the borrower can not make additional drawdowns under the same conditions as before. For example, in retail portfolios during the last three months before default, since the first impairment, it is very difficult for the borrower to make further drawdowns and, in general, only interest and other internal charges are allowed. Therefore, it is necessary to identify when a defaulted facility was labelled as non-normal and only use the realised LEQs associated with previous dates when estimating LEQ factors to normal facilities. In practice, for retail portfolios, at least six dates can frequently be used, and as a maximum, nine dates. On the other hand, for corporate portfolios, the status of the facilities is closely linked to the internal rating of the borrower, and therefore there could be cases in which the normal status applies until it is known that the borrower has defaulted.

---

first month before the default date ($td - tr = 1$) to twelve months before ($td - tr = 12$). This choice may be adequate for most of the product types and, in many cases, compatible with the information currently available in banks.

[12] For example, if a facility is only 4 months old when it defaults, then we will have at most four associated LEQ factors.

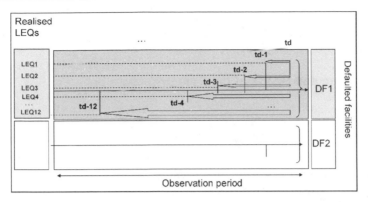

Figure 4. Realised LEQs with the variable time horizon method

In general, it is necessary to take into account the twelve separate LEQ_i factors associated with the same facility because the values of the risk drivers can be different for each reference date.

Advantages:

- It takes into account more observations than the previous methods.
  - Those facilities with $L(tr) = E(tr)$, that in the previous methods were not taken into account, can now be used for those reference dates when $L(td{-}i) \neq E(td{-}i)$ for some $i{=}1,...,12$.
  - Each facility could produce up to twelve LEQ_i associated with twelve different observations.
- In principle, estimate procedures based on these data should produce more stable (it uses more observations) and accurate (it uses more information) estimates.

Drawbacks:

- Banks have to store more data for each defaulted facility (up to twelve observations)
- It is necessary to use a variable (status) that contributes to identifying homogenous LEQ_i factors.

4. Data Sets (RDS) for Estimation Procedures

This section discusses the ideal requirements for the reference data set (RDS) which includes the available information that can be used for estimation procedures. It focuses on those RDS based on historical information from facilities that defaulted over an observation period. First, it presents a general structure for this RDS that facilitates the implementation of estimation procedures and then it enumerates some fields that should be included in the RDS. Second, it lists certain scope requirements. Finally, it comments on several adjustments and decisions that have to be made before the estimation phase.

4.1. Structure and Scope of the Reference Data Set

4.1.1. Structure

Given the focus on estimation procedures based on observations of defaulted facilities at certain reference dates, it is useful to have a structure for the reference data set adapted to this approach. Consequently, the data structure should contain the relevant information on the basis of observations O_i which have associated a unique pair formed by a defaulted facility, g, and a valid reference date, $tr < td$, (more specifically, the mentioned pair $i = (g, tr)$ should be the primary key of the reference data set). Each of these observations, O_i, includes:

- The values of certain static characteristics of g, $I(g)$
- The values of a set of observable variables related to g at the reference date tr, that are going to be used as explanatory variables or Risk Drivers, $RD(tr)$
- The observed EAD_i and default date td.

In summary, a very general structure for the RDS is given by:

$$RDS = \left\{ O_{i=(g,tr)} \right\}; \; O_{i=(g,tr)} = \left\{ (g, tr), I(g), RD(tr), EAD_i = E(td) \right\} \tag{8}$$

With regard to the fields that contain the information associated with each observation, in practical implementations, as a minimum, the following data are required:

- Static characteristics, $I(g)$: identifier of facility, NF ; type of facility, TF ; identifier of portfolio, TP; and identifier of borrower, NB
- Risk drivers, RD: reference date, tr; default date, td; reference exposure, $E(tr)$; reference limit, $L(tr)$; facility status, $S(tr)$; and rating class or pool, $R(tr)$.

If other potential risk drivers for the EAD were identified, the RDS should contain fields for the values of these potential RD at the reference date tr. For example, it is worth considering the inclusion of macroeconomic indicators, MI that can be used to increase the forward looking character of the estimates and the predictive ability of the estimators. In symbols:

$$RD(tr) = \{E, L, S, R, td, MI, Other\}$$

$$I(g) = (NF, NB, TF, TP, Other) \tag{9}$$

Risk drivers are discussed in more detail in Section 4.3.

4.1.2. Scope and Other Requirements on the RDS

In addition to a structure for the RDS suitable for the estimation procedures, the RDS has to meet certain internal and external requirements related to the scope of the RDS.

- The scope of the RDS has to be defined without ambiguity. As a minimum, it is necessary:
  - To define the type of facilities, type of borrowers and type of portfolios
  - To make explicit the definition of default used and the observation period covered
  - To identify and describe the source (or sources) of the data.
- The RDS should include observations for all the facilities that have defaulted during the observation period and meet the other scope requirements (type of facilities, portfolios, etc). All the exclusions should be identified and justified
- The definition of default used should be consistent with the ones used for PD and LGD estimation purposes
- The observation period should be long enough to include observations of facilities defaulted under very different general economic circumstances, ideally covering an entire economic cycle
- Additionally, to use the estimates in capital requirements under AIRB approaches:
  - The definition of default should be consistent with the IRB default definition
  - The observation period should cover at least seven years for corporate portfolios and five for retail portfolios
  - When necessary, the observation period should contain a period with downturn conditions.

4.2. Data Cleaning

As well as other more general issues related to data cleaning (identification and treatment of outliers, elimination of poor quality data, etc.), before to the estimation phase it is necessary to make certain decisions that could affect the observations included in the RDS. Some of these issues are analysed in the next sections.

4.2.1. Treatment of Multiple Credit Facilities with a Single Obligor

Although it is clear that realised CFs and the other relevant information included in the RDS are computed or observed at facility level, under certain circumstances, to produce sensible estimates, it could be necessary or appropriate to group together, within the same observation, information from different facilities associated with the same borrower. There are at least two situations to be considered:

- If there are two or more observations of similar credit facilities with the same borrower and the same risk drivers' values, excluding current usages and other values that are a function of $L(t)$ and $E(t)$, then it could be appropriate to group these observations in a new observation as[13]:

$$\left.\begin{array}{l}\{(h,tr),E(h,tr),L(h,tr),B(h),RD(h,tr)\}\\\{(g,tr),E(g,tr),L(g,tr),B(g),RD(g,tr)\}\end{array}\right\} \Rightarrow \{(h+g,tr)\}$$

(10)

$$\{(h+g)\} = \{(h+g,tr),E(h,tr)+E(g,tr),L(h,tr)+L(g,tr),B,RD(tr)\}$$

- For certain portfolios and facilities, it is common for the maturity to be one year. However, in most cases, the bank approves a new facility (maybe with a different limit), when the old facility expires. In these circumstances, facilities default with age less than twelve months and therefore it is not possible to obtain twelve observations for the RDS. However, if this facility was approved at the time of the expiration of a non-defaulted facility of the same type with the same borrower, it could be useful to chain these facilities together. Using this procedure, more observations can be included in the RDS.

Depending on the characteristics of the portfolio, these decisions could be made on a case by case basis or following a mechanical rule.

4.2.2. Treatment of Observations with Negative Realised LEQ Factors[14]:

As Figure 5 shows, it is possible to obtain negative realised LEQ factors associated with defaulted facilities.

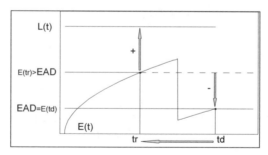

Figure 5. Negative realised LEQ factors

Arithmetically, negative realised LEQs arise when $EAD_i = E(td) < E(tr)$. This situation is especially frequent when $td - tr$ is large and the credit percent usage at the reference date, $e(tr)$, is close to one, moreover some of these values are very large in absolute value. It is very important to note that:

---

[13] This procedure is mentioned in Araten (2001, p.36).

[14] From a formal point of view, this discussion is similar to that related to realised LGDs. However, there are substantial differences in the reasons that justify the existence of negative realised values between both cases.

- The empirical distributions of realised LEQ factors conditional on the percent usage at the reference date, $e(tr)$, are very different
- These empirical distributions are highly asymmetrical, especially for percent usage values close to one.

To illustrate these points, from definition (3) it can be seen that a small increment of $e(tr)$ affects the realised LEQ factor following:

$$\frac{\partial LEQ_i}{\partial e(tr)} = -\frac{1-e(td)}{(1-e(tr))^2} \tag{11}$$

Therefore, the sensitivity of realised LEQ factors to small changes in the percent usage at the reference date depends critically on the level of $e(tr)$. The smaller is $(1-e(tr))^2$, the larger tends to be the variability of LEQ conditional on $e(tr)$.

Moreover, if LEQ_i is expressed in terms of a percent realised exposure at default ead_i proportional to the percent usage at the reference date, from definition (3) the following is obtained:

$$LEQ_i(\Delta) = \frac{e(tr) \cdot (1+\Delta) - e(tr)}{(1-e(tr))} = \Delta \frac{e(tr)}{1-e(tr)} \tag{12}$$

and for large values of $e(tr)$ there is no possibility of large values of Δ, but it is possible to find negative large values for Δ.

The former asymmetries among LEQ_i for low and large percent usage values and the existence of more observations with large negative LEQ_i than with large positive values have practical importance. The main reason is that, as is shown in Section 5, banks frequently use averages of LEQ_i as estimators for $LEQ(f)$ and these sample means are severely affected by both circumstances. The former points suggest that, as a minimum, these averages should be restricted to those observations with similar percent usage levels or, in other words, percent usage level should be a risk driver for $LEQ(f)$.

As a consequence, it is important to clarify the treatment of those observations with negative realised LEQ factors. In practice, there are several possibilities:

- Censoring[15] the data (the LEQ_i factors) to impose certain restrictions:
  - Some banks change the definition of realised LEQ to force the non-negativity: $LEQ_i^+ = \max[0, LEQ_i]$
  - In other cases, banks change the definition of the realised EAD used in LEQ$_i$ computations directly (observed EAD): $EAD_i^+ = \max[EAD_i, E(tr)]$.

---

[15] It is necessary to use of this terminology (censoring and truncation) carefully because these words are not used consistently in the literature. For example, Araten (2001, p.36), uses the term truncation for describing what in this paper is referred to as censoring. The terminology employed in the text follows that used in Working Paper No. 14 BCBS (2005, p. 66).

As discussed previously, negative LEQ_i can be associated with valid observations of defaulted facilities. To justify this practice, banks argue that, ceteris paribus, this adjustment introduces a conservative bias into the estimates.

- Truncation: this practice consists of the removal of the observations associated with negative LEQ_i factors. It is difficult to find a rationale for the truncation of observations with negative or zero realised LEQs. In principle, this truncation could be a practical method to generate a stressed distribution of LEQ_i factors. However, this procedure presents at least two important drawbacks:
  - The elimination of observations with $LEQ_i \leq 0$ could introduce inconsistencies with the RDS used for obtaining LGD estimates because some of those observations could be associated with facilities with high realised losses.
  - When the estimation method uses sample averages, the LEQ estimates based on a truncated RDS could be very unstable with changes in the RDS depending on the number of observations with LEQ_i factors close to zero.
- Do nothing with the realised LEQ factors (but set a floor to the estimates[16], $LEQ(f) \geq 0$).This is the most natural decision.

As proved in Section 6.3.1, if the constraint on the estimators given by $LEQ(f) \geq 0$ is imposed and a specific model for the estimated LEQ based on minimising the estimation errors (measured in terms of a special loss function) is adjusted then the same estimates are produced by using the original or the censored data.

4.2.3. Treatment of Observations with Realised LEQ Factors Greater than One

In principle, given the definition of LEQ_i factors (2) it would be natural to expect LEQ_i factors to be less or equal to one in a bank with an adequate control environment. However, the existence of LEQ_i factors greater than one is not in all cases an indicator of a failure in the controls established by the bank to ensure that credit limits are effective. There are situations in which LEQ_i factors greater than one naturally arise. For example:

- In some cases, banks use unadvised limits[17] instead of the nominal limits of the facilities to manage the risk internally. The possibility of additional drawdowns for the borrower only stops when the exposure is greater than the unadvised limit
- In some products, for example credit cards or current account overdrafts, such problems are difficult to avoid because there is typically a time lag between the current exposure and the figure used by the bank to establish controls

---

[16] As a minimum, this floor is a requirement when the estimates are used for regulatory purposes.

[17] Frequently, these unadvised limits are computed as a percentage or a fixed amount above the explicit advised limits.

- Sometimes the exposure at default includes the last liquidation of interest (and fees) and this amount is charged to the account even when the limit had been previously reached.

The former excesses over the nominal limits are typically small. In these cases, it would be appropriate to treat these observations as any other cases. However, in other circumstances there are observations with large realised LEQ factors that are the result of several causes completely different, such as:

- Changes in the limit after the reference date and previous to the knowledge of difficulties in the facilities
- Explicit or implicit change of limit at the date of default or when difficulties with the facility have already arisen
- Inadequate control environment and existence of human errors or frauds that could be treated as operational risk events.

In spite of the diversity of the former circumstances, some banks cap all the realised EADs at one. In general, this rule is neither adequate for internal use nor for regulatory use and, on the contrary, a detailed analysis of the causes behind these observations is necessary before making acceptable decisions for each situation. In any case, coherence with the procedures used when calculating realised LGDs is a prerequisite.

4.3. EAD Risk Drivers

In practice, risk drivers (RD) affect the estimates in two different ways. First, certain qualitative and quantitative characteristics are used to segment the portfolio under analysis into homogenous classes. Among these risk drivers, different studies state as a minimum:

- Facility type: the importance of this characteristic is because there is a spectrum of facilities with explicit limits and different conditions for drawdowns, ranging from facilities with unconditional limits, to facilities in which each drawdown requires approval.
- Covenants: frequently the bank can deny additional drawdowns when specific circumstances occur. The clauses which detail these circumstances are called covenants.[18] Typically, these covenants are related to objective situations that are indicators of credit deterioration of the borrower such as: downgrades, drops in profitability or changes in certain key financial ratios below explicit thresholds.[19]

Second, once we have identified a class including facilities that, in principle, are homogenous enough for the proposal of designing a common explanatory EAD

---

[18] Sometimes these clauses are called Material Adverse Changes (MAC) clauses. See Lev (2004, p.14).

[19] For more details on covenants, see Sufi (2005, p.5).

model, it is necessary to select an appropriate set of explanatory (quantitative) variables (risk drivers). Among these quantitative risk drivers, different studies, based on private data bases, suggest it is convenient to consider as a minimum:

- Commitment size $L(tr)$
- The drawn and undrawn amounts, $E(tr)$ and $L(tr) - E(tr)$
- The credit percent usage at the reference date $e(tr)$. As discussed in 4.2.2, this percent usage value has discriminative power with regard to realised LEQ factors
- The time to default td–tr: ex-post analysis shows that this variable has significant explanatory power, at least close to default
- The rating class at the reference time $R(tr)$: this variable is in general relevant, but different studies have found a significant positive correlation between credit quality and CF in some cases and a significant negative correlation in others. It seems that the role of the rating as a relevant risk driver is linked to the type of portfolio, the dynamic of each rating system and the uses of the rating for internal purposes
- Status of the facility at the reference date $S(tr)$: most banks, in addition to rating or scoring systems, have warning systems that focus on early identification of liquidity problems and other short term borrower difficulties. The basic difference with the rating is that these warning systems are more dynamic and identify problems before the rating[20] does. As a result of these systems, certain facilities are classified into certain broad classes, typically: normal status and a few grades under special vigilance. This means that once a facility has been identified as linked to a problematic borrower the level of monitoring and, in some cases; the practical conditions for additional drawdowns are changed[21]. Therefore, the status is a critical risk driver when estimating EAD
- Macro indicators.

For the observations in the RDS, the values of the above listed risk drivers are in general, known. For a non-defaulted facility, the values of these variables are computed using the current date t, as the reference date tr. With regard to the time to default, there is a problem because, for a non defaulted facility, the time to default is unknown. In the Basel II context, the interest is in EAD estimates subject to the condition that the facility defaults during a period of one year. Therefore, in

---

[20] The most common relationship between these early warning systems and the ratings is that certain changes of status trigger the processes for a new evaluation of the borrower rating.

[21] § 477. "Due consideration must be paid by the bank to its specific policies and strategies adopted in respect of account monitoring and payment processing. The bank must also consider its ability and willingness to prevent further drawings in circumstances short of payment default, such as covenant violations or other technical default events. Banks must also have adequate systems and procedures in place to monitor facility amounts, current outstandings against committed lines and changes in outstandings per borrower and per grade. The bank must be able to monitor outstanding balances on a daily basis.", BCBS (2004).

this context, the interest is in the influence of this variable when the value ranges from one to twelve months.

5. EAD Estimates

5.1. Relationship Between Observations in the RDS and the Current Portfolio

This section presents different methods of assigning a one-year EAD estimate to a non-defaulted facility f at the date t, included in the current portfolio, based on a subset of a RDS which comprises observations (of defaulted facilities) similar to f at t. We denote this subset by $RDS(f)$.

The process of assigning a subset of the RDS to each facility in the portfolio is called "mapping" and this allows the current portfolio to be classified by grouping facilities with the same or "similar" $RDS(f)$. Conversely, some banks segment the portfolio of current exposures into classes comprising "similar" facilities. This approach could be reduced to the previous one because after this classification of exposures, each class C has to be mapped into a $RDS(C)$ which is used to estimate $EAD(f)$ for all f included in C.

5.2. Equivalence between EAD Estimates and CF Estimates

Given a non-defaulted facility f and an estimator $EAD(f)$, if $L(f) \neq E(f)$, the estimate can be expressed in terms of a $LEQ(f)$ factor following the equation:

$$EAD(f) = E(f) + LEQ(f) \cdot (L(f) - E(f)) \tag{13}$$

if $LEQ(f)$ is given by:

$$LEQ(f) = \frac{EAD(f) - E(f)}{L(f) - E(f)} = \frac{ead(f) - e(f)}{1 - e(f)} \tag{14}$$

Additionally, if we are interested in $EAD(f)$ estimates that satisfy $EAD(f) \geq E(f)$, then from Equation (13):

- If $L(f) > E(f)$ then $EAD(f) \geq E(f)$ if and only if $LEQ(f) \geq 0$
- If $L(f) < E(f)$ then $EAD(f) \geq E(f)$ if and only if $LEQ(f) \leq 0$.

Therefore, without any additional hypothesis, for facilities that verify $L(f) \neq E(f)$, it has been shown that to estimate $EAD(f)$, it is sufficient to focus on methods that estimate suitable conversion factors $LEQ(f)$ based on the observations included in the reference data set, $RDS(f)$ and afterwards to employ Equation (13) to assign individual EAD estimates.

Finally, the simplest procedure to estimate a class EAD is to add the individual EAD estimates for all the facilities included in the class.

For example, for certain facility types, some banks assign EADs by using a previously estimated $CCF(f)$, and then applying the formula:

$$EAD(f) = CCF(f) \cdot L(f) \tag{15}$$

This method is sometimes called Usage at Default Method[22]. If $e(f) \neq 1$, this case can be reduced to the general method, given in equation (13), by assigning a $LEQ(f)$ factor given by:

$$LEQ(f) = \frac{CCF(f) \cdot L(f) - E(f)}{L(f) - E(f)} = \frac{CCF(f) - e(f)}{1 - e(f)} \tag{16}$$

Conversely, if a $LEQ(f)$ is available, from Equation (16), an expression for an equivalent $CCF(f)$ can be found, given by:

$$CCF(f) = LEQ(f) \cdot \left(1 - e(f)\right) + e(f) \tag{17}$$

Therefore, the EAD estimation method based on $LEQ(f)$ and the one based on CCF(f) are equivalent, with the exception of those facilities with $e(f) = 1$.

In the following sections, several methods that are normally used in practice by banks to estimate LEQ factors are presented from a unified perspective. This is used later to analyse the optimality of the different approaches. Additionally, the formulae most used in practice are derived as special cases of the previous methods when a specific functional form has been assumed for $LEQ(f)$.

5.3. Modelling Conversion Factors from the Reference Data Set

This section presents several methods for estimating conversion factors based on regression problems starting with the following basic equation:

$$EAD(f) - E(f) = LEQ(f) \cdot (L(f) - E(f)) \tag{18}$$

These methods try to explain the observed increases in the exposure between the reference date and the default date and they can be grouped into three approaches depending on how these increases are measured: as a percentage of the available amount (focus on realised LEQ factors); as a percentage of the observed limit (fo-

---

[22] This method is called Momentum Method in CEBS Guidelines (2006, §§ 253 and 254).

cus on percent increase in usage); or finally in absolute value (focus on increase in exposure).

Model I. Focus on realised LEQ factors

Dividing (18) by $L(f) - E(f)$, it is obtained:

$$\frac{ead(f) - e(f)}{1 - e(f)} = \frac{EAD(f) - E(f)}{(L(f) - E(f))} = LEQ(f) \tag{19}$$

In this approach, the rationale is to determine a function of the risk drivers $LEQ(RD)$ which "explains" the LEQ_i factors associated with $RDS(f)$, $LEQ_i = (EAD_i - E_i)/(L_i - E_i)$, in terms of $LEQ(RD_i)$. This can be made starting with an expression for the error associated with $LEQ_i - LEQ(RD_i)$ and solving a minimisation problem. In practice, a quadratic and symmetric error function is almost universally used. As a consequence of this choice, the minimisation problem to solve is given by (Problem P.I):

$$\underset{LEQ}{Min}\left\{\sum_i (LEQ_i - LEQ(RD_i))^2\right\} = \underset{LEQ}{Min}\left\{\sum_i \left(\frac{EAD_i - E_i}{L_i - E_i} - LEQ(RD_i)\right)^2\right\} \tag{20}$$

Or:

$$\overline{LEQ(f)} = \underset{LEQ}{Min}\left\{\sum_i \frac{1}{(L_i - E_i)^2}\cdot(EAD_i - E_i - LEQ(RD_i)\cdot(L_i - E_i))^2\right\} \tag{21}$$

Model II. Focus on the increase of the exposure as a percentage of the observed limit (focus on percent increase in usage).

Dividing the basic Equation (18) by $L(f)$, it is obtained:

$$\frac{EAD(f) - E(f)}{L(f)} = LEQ(f)\cdot\frac{L(f) - E(f)}{L(f)} \tag{22}$$

Therefore, using this approach, the observable amounts to be explained are $(EAD_i - E_i) / L_i$ and the explanatory values are $LEQ(RD_i) \cdot (L_i - E_i) / L_i$. Following the same reasoning as in the previous approach, the minimisation problem to solve is given by (Problem P.II):

$$\underset{LEQ}{Min}\left\{\sum_i \left(\frac{EAD_i - E_i}{L_i} - LEQ(RD_i)\cdot(\frac{L_i - E_i}{L_i})\right)^2\right\} \tag{23}$$

Or:

$$\overline{LEQ(f)} = \underset{LEQ}{Min}\left\{\sum_i \frac{1}{L_i^2}\cdot(EAD_i - E_i - LEQ(RD_i)\cdot(L_i - E_i))^2\right\} \tag{24}$$

Model III. Focus on increases in the exposure

Directly from the basic equation, it is obtained:

$$EAD(f) - E(f) = LEQ(f) \cdot \big(L(f) - E(f)\big) \qquad (25)$$

In this case, the amounts to explain are $EAD_i - E_i$ and the explanatory variable is $LEQ(RD_i) \cdot (L_i - E_i)$. As in the other cases, the associated minimization problem is given by (Problem P.III):

$$\overline{LEQ}(f) = \underset{LEQ}{Min}\left\{ \sum_i \big(EAD_i - E_i - LEQ(RD_i) \cdot (L_i - E_i)\big)^2 \right\} \qquad (26)$$

From equations (21), (24) and (26), these problems can be reduced to a more general (Problem P.IV):

$$\underset{LEQ}{Min}\left\{ \sum_i \left(\frac{EAD_i - E_i}{\omega_i} - LEQ(RD_i) \cdot \frac{(L_i - E_i)}{\omega_i} \right)^2 \right\} \qquad (27)$$

where ω_i stands for $L_i - E_i$ in Model I, L_i in Model II, and 1 in Model III. If F^* denotes the empirical distribution of $(EAD - E) / \omega$ associated with the observations included in $RDS(f)$, the Problem P.IV can be expressed as:

$$\overline{LEQ}(f) = \underset{LEQ}{Min}\left\{ \underset{F^*}{E}\left\langle \left(\frac{EAD - E}{\omega} - LEQ(RD) \cdot \frac{(L - E)}{\omega} \right)^2 \right\rangle \right\} \qquad (28)$$

In the most general case, assuming that $(L - E) / \omega$ is constant for observations in $RDS(f)$, the solution to (28) is given by[23]:

$$\overline{LEQ}(f) = \underset{F^*}{E}\left\langle \left(\frac{EAD - E}{\omega} \right)\bigg\| RD(f) \right\rangle \cdot \frac{\omega(f)}{L(f) - E(f)} \qquad (29)$$

As a consequence, the practical problem is to find out methods to approximate these conditional expectations.

If a parametric form for LEQ is assumed, the problem becomes:

$$\overline{LEQ}(f) = LEQ(\hat{a}, \hat{b}, ...),$$

$$\{\hat{a}, \hat{b}, ...\} = \underset{\{a, b, ...\}}{Min}\left\{ \underset{F^*}{E}\left\langle \left(\frac{EAD - E}{\omega} - LEQ(a, b, ...) \cdot \frac{(L - E)}{\omega} \right)^2 \right\rangle \right\} \qquad (30)$$

---

[23] See Appendix B.

If the parametric functional form is linear in the parameters, the problem becomes a linear regression problem.

In summary, traditional methods can be classified as regression models that focus on the minimization of quadratic errors in the forecasts of: LEQ_i factors; EAD_i in percentage of the limit; or EAD_i. These methods produce different $EAD(f)$ estimates based on $LEQ(f)$ estimates proportional to conditional expectations. At first glance, the approach that focuses directly on LEQ factors (Model I) seems the most natural, the method that focuses on percent increases in usage (Model II) seems more stable than the previous one and, as is shown in detail in Section 6, the approach based on EAD increases (Model III), could present advantages when the estimates are used in regulatory capital computations because of the link between capital requirements and EAD.

5.4. LEQ = Constant

Problem P.I: The Sample Mean

In practice[24], banks frequently use, as an estimator for $LEQ(f)$ at t, the sample mean of realised LEQ_i, restricted to those observations $i=\{g,t\}$ similar to $\{f,t,RD\}$. Assuming that the conversion factor is a constant for observations similar to $\{f, t\}$, $LEQ(f) = LEQ$, and solving the Problem P.I the following is obtained:

$$\overline{LEQ} = \underset{LEQ \in R}{Min}\left\{\sum_i\left(\frac{EAD_i - E_i}{(L_i - E_i)} - LEQ\right)^2\right\} = \frac{1}{n}\sum\frac{EAD_i - E_i}{(L_i - E_i)} = \frac{1}{n}\sum LEQ_i \qquad (31)$$

In other cases, banks use a sample weighted mean that tries to account for a possible relationship between size of the exposures (or limits) and LEQ. If in Problem P.I a weight w_i is introduced, and it is assumed that LEQ is constant for observations similar to $\{f, t\}$, then:

$$\overline{LEQ} = \underset{LEQ \in R}{Min}\left\{\sum_i w_i\left(\frac{EAD_i - E_i}{(L_i - E_i)} - LEQ\right)^2\right\} = \frac{\sum w_i \cdot LEQ_i}{\sum w_i} \qquad (32)$$

When the reason for incorporating the weighting is to take into account a LEQ risk driver, this approach is inconsistent. The reason for this is that the weighted average is the optimum solution only after assuming that LEQ = constant, i.e. no risk drivers are considered.

---

[24] At least this is the case in models applied by some Spanish banks at present (2006).

Problem P.II: The Regression without Constant

Another method widely used by banks is to use the regression estimator for the slope of the regression line based on Model II, assuming that LEQ is a constant. Under these conditions the expression for the regression estimator is given by:

$$\overline{LEQ} = \underset{LEQ \in R}{Min} \left\{ \sum_i \left(\frac{EAD_i - E_i}{L_i} - LEQ \cdot \left(\frac{L_i - E_i}{L_i} \right) \right)^2 \right\}$$

$$= \frac{\sum \dfrac{(EAD_i - E_i)(L_i - E_i)}{L_i^2}}{\sum \left(\dfrac{L_i - E_i}{L_i} \right)^2} = \frac{\sum (ead_i - e_i)(1 - e_i)}{\sum (1 - e_i)^2} \qquad (33)$$

Problem P.III: Sample weighted mean

If in P.III it is assumed that LEQ = constant it can be expressed as:

$$\overline{LEQ}(f) = \underset{LEQ \in R}{Min} \left\{ \sum_i (L_i - E_i)^2 \left(\frac{EAD_i - E_i}{(L_i - E_i)} - LEQ \right)^2 \right\} \qquad (34)$$

And the optimum is given by:

$$\overline{LEQ} = \frac{\sum w_i \cdot LEQ_i}{\sum w_i}, \text{ with } w_i = (L_i - E_i)^2 \qquad (35)$$

Therefore, using this approach, a weighted mean naturally arises. However, it is worth noting that these weights $(L_i - E_i)^2$ are different from those currently proposed by some banks (based on L_i or E_i).

5.5. Usage at Default Method with CCF = Constant (Simplified Momentum Method):

This method is sometimes used by banks that try to avoid the explicit use of realised negative LEQ factors, or for facilities for which the current usage has no predictive power on EADs. It estimates the EAD for a non-defaulted facility, $EAD(f)$, by using Equation (15) directly and a rough CCF estimate, for example, the sample mean of the realised CCFs computed from a set of defaulted facilities C.

$$\overline{EAD}(f) = \overline{CCF}(C) \cdot L(f) \qquad (36)$$

From Equation (16) and assuming that CCF = constant, a specific functional form for $LEQ(e(f))$ is founded, given by:

$$\overline{LEQ}(f) = \frac{\overline{CCF} \cdot L(f) - E(f)}{L(f) - E(f)} = \frac{\overline{CCF} - e(f)}{1 - e(f)} \tag{37}$$

In general, two facilities with the same estimated CCF and with different values for current percent usage, $e(t)$, will have different LEQ estimates following the former Equation (37).

The main drawback with the procedure based on Equation (36) is that experience shows that, in general, drawn and undrawn limits have strong explanatory power for the EAD. For this reason, this method (with CCF=constant) does not seem to meet the requirement of using all the relevant information[25] (because it does not take into account the drawn and undrawn amounts as explanatory variables in the EAD estimating procedure) for most of the types of facilities that arise in practice.

6. How to Assess the Optimality of the Estimates

To assess the optimality of the different CF estimates associated with a reference data set and a portfolio, it is necessary to be more precise about some elements in the basic problem. The first element requiring clarification is the type of estimates according to the role of macroeconomic risk drivers in the estimation method. The second element is how to measure the errors associated with the estimates and to motivate that particular choice. This can be done by introducing a loss function that specifies how the differences between the estimated values for the EAD and the actual values are penalised.

6.1. Type of Estimates

Focusing on the use of the macroeconomic risk drivers, the following types of estimates can be distinguished:

- *Point in Time estimates* (*PIT*): these estimates are conditional on certain values of the macroeconomic risk drivers, for example, values close to the current ones. This allows the estimates to be affected by current economic conditions and to vary over the economic cycle. In theory, this is a good property for the internal estimates banks need for pricing and other management purposes. The main problem with PIT estimates is that they are based on less data than long-run estimates (LR estimates, defined below) and therefore, in practice, they are less stable than LR estimates and harder to estimate.

---

[25] § 476. "The criteria by which estimates of EAD are derived must be plausible and intuitive, and represent what the bank believes to be the material drivers of EAD. The choices must be supported by credible internal analysis by the bank. [...] A bank must use all relevant and material information in its derivation of EAD estimates. [...]", BCBS (2004).

- *Long-run estimates* (*LR*): These are unconditional macroeconomic estimates, i.e. the macroeconomic risk drivers are ignored. The main advantage is that they are more robust and stable than PIT estimates. These LR estimates are required in AIRB approaches[26], except for those portfolios in which there is evidence of negative dependence between default rates and LEQ factors. Currently, these LR estimates are also used by banks for internal purposes.
- *Downturn estimates* (*DT*): these are specific PIT estimates based on macroeconomic scenarios (downturn conditions) in which the default rates for the portfolio are deemed to be especially high. When there is evidence of the existence of adverse dependencies between default rates and conversion factors, this could be the type of estimates that, in theory, should be used in IRB approaches[27]. In practice, the use of DT estimates is difficult because, in addition to the difficulties associated with PIT estimates, it is necessary to identify downturn conditions and to have sufficient observations in the RDS restricted to these scenarios.

In the following, it is assumed that the focus is on long run estimates.

6.2. A Suitable Class of Loss Functions

The objective of this section is to determine a type of loss function that meets the basic requirements for the EAD estimation problem when it is necessary to obtain EAD estimates adequate for IRB approaches. Therefore, it makes sense to specify the loss associated with the difference between the estimated value and the real one in terms of the error in the minimum regulatory capital (computed as the difference between the capital requirements under both values). By using the regulatory formula, at the level of the facility, the loss associated with the difference between the capital requirement under the estimated value of the exposure $K(EAD(f))$ and the real one K(EAD), could be expressed as follows[28]:

$$L(\Delta K(f)) = L(K(EAD) - K(EAD(f))) =$$
$$L(\phi(PD) \cdot LGD \cdot (EAD - EAD(f))) = L(\phi(PD) \cdot LGD \cdot \Delta(EAD(f)))$$

(38)

---

[26] § 475. "Advanced approach banks must assign an estimate of EAD for each facility. It must be an estimate of the long-run default-weighted average EAD for similar facilities and borrowers over a sufficiently long period of time, [...] If a positive correlation can reasonably be expected between the default frequency and the magnitude of EAD, the EAD estimate must incorporate a larger margin of conservatism. Moreover, for exposures for which EAD estimates are volatile over the economic cycle, the bank must use EAD estimates that are appropriate for an economic downturn, if these are more conservative than the long-run average.", BCBS (2004).

[27] This can be interpreted in the light of the clarification of the requirements on LGD estimates in Paragraph 468 of the Revised Framework, BCBS (2005).

[28] In the following it is assumed that a *PD* = PD(*f*) and an *LGD* = LGD(*f*) have been estimated previously.

Additionally, at least from a regulatory point of view, underestimating the capital requirement creates more problems than overestimating such a figure. For this reason, it is appropriate to use asymmetric loss functions that penalises more an underestimation of the capital requirement than an overestimation of the same amount. The simplest family of such functions is given by (39), where $b > a$:

$$L(\Delta K) = \begin{cases} a \cdot \Delta K & \text{iff } \Delta K \geq 0 \\ b \cdot \Delta K & \text{iff } \Delta K < 0 \end{cases} \tag{39}$$

These loss functions quantify the level of conservatism. The larger b/a (relative loss associated with an underestimation of K), the larger is the level of conservatism imposed. For example, if $a = 1$ and $b = 2$, the loss associated with an underestimation of the capital requirement ($\Delta K < 0$) is twice the loss for an overestimation of the same amount.[29] The graphic of the loss function is presented in Figure 6.

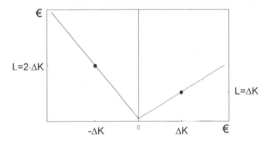

Figure 6. Linear asymmetric loss function

By using this specific type of loss function (39), and assuming that $LGD \geq 0$, a simpler expression for the error in K in terms of the error in EAD is obtained:

$$L(\Delta K(f)) = \phi(PD) \cdot LGD \cdot L(\Delta(EAD(f))) \tag{40}$$

The loss associated with an error in the capital requirement is proportional to the loss associated with the error in terms of exposure and the units of the loss are the same as those of the exposure ($€$).

6.3. The Objective Function

Once the loss function has been determined, it is necessary to find the most natural objective function for the estimation problem.

---

[29] To the best of my knowledge, the first application of such a loss function in the credit risk context was proposed in Moral (1996). In that paper the loss function is used to determine the optimal level of provisioning as a quantile of the portfolio loss distribution.

6.3.1. Minimization at Facility Level of the Expectation in the Capital Requirement Error

If the expected error in the minimum capital requirement at the level of exposure is used as an objective function, by using Equation (40) the following is obtained:

$$\underset{LEQ}{Min}\{E[L(\Delta K(f))]\} = \phi(PD) \cdot LGD \cdot \underset{LEQ}{Min}\{E[L(\Delta(EAD(f)))]\} \qquad (41)$$

This means that Problem P.III in Section 5.3 arises with a different loss function:

$$\underset{LEQ}{Min}\left\{ \underset{F^*}{E}\left\langle L\big(EAD - E - LEQ(RD)\cdot(L - E)\big)\right\rangle\right\} \qquad (42)$$

or in terms of the sample

$$\underset{LEQ}{Min}\left\{\sum_i L\big(EAD_i - E_i - LEQ(RD_i)\cdot(L_i - E_i)\big)\right\} \qquad (43)$$

and a solution is given[30] by:

$$\overline{LEQ}(f) = \underset{F^*}{Q}\left\langle EAD - E, \frac{b}{a+b}\bigg| RD(f)\right\rangle \cdot \frac{1}{L(f) - E(f)}, \qquad (44)$$

where $Q(x, b/(a+b))$ stands for a quantile of the distribution $F(x)$ such that[31] $F(Q) = b/(a+b)$. When $a = b$, the loss function (39) is symmetric and the former quantile is the median and for values of $b/a > 1$ the associated quantile is placed to the right of the median and, therefore, a more conservative estimate of $LEQ(f)$ is obtained. It is interesting to note that (44), with $b > a$, penalises uncertainty[32].

An important consequence of using the former loss function L is that the problems M.I and M.II described in equations (45) and (46) are equivalent[33].

Problem M.I:

$$\underset{LEQ}{Min}\left\{\sum_i L\big(EAD_i - E_i - LEQ(RD_i)\cdot(L_i - E_i)\big)\right\} \qquad (45)$$

$$\text{Subject to}: 0 \le LEQ(RD) \le 1$$

---

[30] See Appendix B.

[31] In practice, it is necessary to be more precise when defining a q-quantile because the distribution $F(x)$ is discrete. A common definition is: a "q-quantile" of $F(x)$ is a real number, $Q(x,q)$, that satisfies $P[X \le Q(x,q)] \ge q$ and $P[X \ge Q(x,q)] \ge 1-q$. In general, with this definition there is more than a q-quantile.

[32] § 475. "Advanced approach banks must assign an estimate of EAD for each facility. It must be an estimate […] with a margin of conservatism appropriate to the likely range of errors in the estimate.", BCBS (2004).

[33] The proof follows from the proposition in Appendix A.

Problem M.II:

$$\underset{LEQ}{Min}\left\{\sum_i L\left(Min\left[Max\left[EAD_i,E_i\right],L_i\right]-E_i-LEQ(RD_i)\cdot\left(L_i-E_i\right)\right)\right\}$$

(46)

Subject to : $0 \le LEQ(RD) \le 1$

This means that an estimator meeting the constraint $0 \le LEQ(f) \le 1$ that is optimal when using the original data is also optimal when using data censored to show realised LEQ factors between zero and one.

6.3.2. Minimization of the Error in the Capital Requirement at Facility Level for Regulatory Classes

Sometimes, in spite of the existence of internal estimates for LEQ factors at facility level, it could be necessary to associate a common LEQ with all the facilities included in a class comprising facilities with different values for the internal risk drivers. This could occur due to difficulties in demonstrating with the available data, that discrimination at an internal level of granularity is justified. In this case, for regulatory use, it is necessary to adopt a less granular structure for the risk drivers than the existing internal one. Therefore, the problem of finding an optimal estimator for regulatory use can be solved by using the regulatory structure for the risk drivers. In other words, the procedure is to compute new estimates using the same method and a less granular risk driver structure. In general, the new estimator is not a simple or weighted average of the former more granular estimates.

7. Example 1

This example[34] illustrates the pros and cons of using the methods explained in the former sections for estimating LEQ factors and EADs. The focus is on long run estimates for the EAD of a facility f in normal status by using as basic risk drivers the current limit $L(f)$ and exposure $E(f)$.

7.1. RDS

7.1.1. Characteristics

The main characteristics of the reference data set, used in this example, are described below:

---

[34] Although this example could be representative for certain SME portfolios comprising credit lines, it is not a portfolio taken from a bank.

- Source of the RDS: the observations were obtained from a set of defaulted facilities from a portfolio of SMEs
- Observation period: 5 years
- Product types: credit lines with a committed limit of credit, that is known for the borrower, given by $L(t)$
- Exclusions: It does not include all the internal defaults which took place during the observation period because several filters had been applied previously. As a minimum, the following facilities were excluded from the data set:
  - defaulted facilities with $L(td-12) < E(td-12)$ and
  - those with less than twelve monthly observations before the default date
- Number of observations, O_i: #RDS = 417·12 = 5004 observations, which are associated with 417 defaulted facilities and dates 1, 2,...,12 months before the default date
- Structure of the reference data set: the structure proposed in (8) but, for simplicity, only a basic set of risk drivers is considered:

$$O_i = \left\{ i, (f, tr), RD_i = \{L(tr), E(tr), S(tr)\}, EAD, td, tr \right\} \tag{47}$$

- Status of a facility at the reference date, $S(tr)$: there is no information about the status of the facilities. The bank has implemented a warning system that classifies the exposures on four broad classes: N = normal monitoring and controls; V = under close monitoring for drawdowns; I = current exposure greater than the limit and implies tight controls making additional drawdowns impossible without a previous approval; D = defaulted, no additional drawdowns are possible, but sometimes there are increases in the exposures due to the payment of interest and fees. However, in this example, in order to take into account the status, $S(tr)$, as a risk driver, observations with $S(tr) = N$ are approximated using the following procedure:
  - First, all the observations with $L(tr) < E(tr)$ are marked as in a non-normal status
  - Second, after analysing the empirical distributions of realised LEQ factors (and other information) it was decided to consider all the observations with $td - tr$ less than five months as if they were in a non-normal status and to eliminate all the observations with $td - tr = 7$ months (see next section).

In practice, the use of the values of the variable status is necessary, because the early identification of problematic borrowers and the subsequent changes in the availability of access to the nominal limit have important consequences in the observed EADs. For this reason, observations up to five months before default for which $E(tr) \leq L(tr)$ are considered in normal status. In this case, the number of observations with $S(tr) = N$ is: #RDS(N) = 2,919.

7.1.2. Empirical distributions of certain statistics

Distribution of realised LEQ factors

Figure 7 summarises the empirical variability of the realised LEQ factors associated with 2,442 observations for which it is possible to compute this statistic[35].

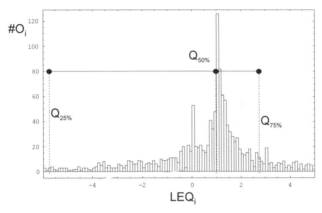

Figure 7. Histogram of realised LEQ factors

It shows that the distribution is asymmetric with a high number of observations outside of [0,1] which is the natural range for LEQ factors. The sample mean is about -525 due to the existence of many observations with large negative values and it highlights one of the main issues when a sample mean is used as the estimator. The median is 0.97 and this value, in contrast with the former sample mean value, highlights the advantages of using statistics less dependent on the extreme values of the distribution for estimation purposes.

Joint distribution of realised LEQ factors and percent usage at the reference date

To reduce the variability in the observed realised LEQ factors, it is necessary to consider a variable that exhibits explanatory power, at least, for the range of values of realised LEQ factors. For example, the joint empirical distribution presented in Figure 8 shows that the variable percent usage at the reference date is important for limiting the variability of realised LEQ factors. Black points at the top of Figure 8 represent the observations in the space $\{1 - e(tr), LEQ_i\}$.

---

[35] Observations associated with, the horizon value, $td - tr = 7$ were removed from the RDS as it is explained later on.

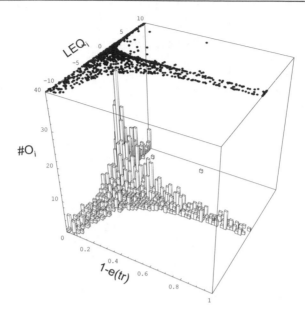

Figure 8. Joint distribution of LEQ_i and percent usage at the reference date tr

Influence of $td - tr$ in the basic statistics

Figure 9 presents the empirical distributions of realised LEQs associated with a fixed distance in months between the default and reference dates for $td - tr = 1,\ldots,12$.

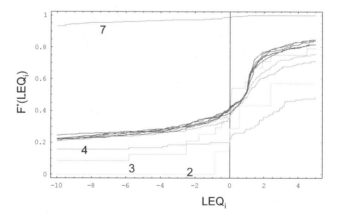

Figure 9. Empirical distributions of LEQ_i conditional on different $td - tr$ values

The distributions associated with $td - tr = 1, 2, 3, 4$ are very different from the others. The distribution conditional on $td - tr = 7$ months is totally anomalous and the reason for that is an error in the processes that generated these data.

Figure 10 presents the empirical distributions of the percent increase in usage between the reference and the default dates, $ead_i - e(tr)$, associated with a fixed distance in months between the default and reference dates for $td - tr = 1,...,12$. Again, the differences among the distributions conditional on reference dates near to default and far from default are obvious and the existence of anomalous values for the case $td - tr = 7$ is evident.

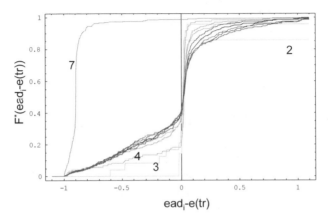

Figure 10. Empirical distributions of percent increase in usage since the reference date

Finally, Figure 11 shows the empirical distributions of the increase in exposure, $EAD_i - E(tr)$, between the reference and the default dates.

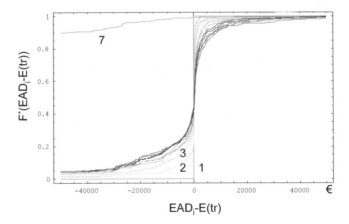

Figure 11. Empirical distributions of the increase in exposure from tr to td

7.2. Estimation Procedures

7.2.1. Model II

Original Data and Fixed Time Horizon

Some banks use Model II assuming a constant LEQ, and a fixed time horizon approach, $T = 12$ months. This means that they adjust a linear regression model without an independent term, given by:

$$\frac{EAD_i}{L(td-12)} - \frac{E(td-12)}{L(td-12)} = k \cdot \left(1 - \frac{E(td-12)}{L(td-12)}\right) \tag{48}$$

Therefore, in these cases, the bank's approach focuses on the minimisation of the quadratic error in the increase of the exposure expressed in percentage terms of the limit. The results with this method are summarised below:

By using the *original data,* the estimated LEQ factor is LEQ= 0.637 and the adjusted R^2 is 0.13. Therefore, the final estimate for the EAD of a facility, f, in normal status is given by the formula:

$$EAD(f) = E(t) + 0.637 \cdot (L(t) - E(t)) \tag{49}$$

Figure 12 presents, for each observation in the $RDS(td-12)$, the values of the pairs $\{1 - e(td-12),\ ead_i - e(td-12)\}$. The upper shadow zone in Figures 12, 13, 14 are associated with points with $LEQ_i > 1$.

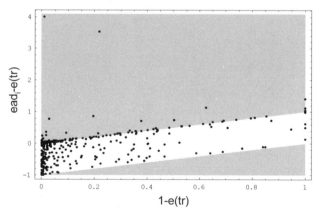

Figure 12. Percent increase in usage from tr, to td and percent usage at the reference date

From analysis of the distribution of these points and the results of the regression it is clear that, at least:

1. It is necessary to carry out an explicit RDS cleaning process before the estimation phase. For example, it is necessary to analyse the observations associated with the points above the line $y = x$ and afterwards to make decisions about which observations have to be removed from the RDS.
2. The degree of adjustment is very low. Most of the points (those with $1 - e(tr)$ closer to zero) have little influence on the result of the regression model because of the constraint that there is no independent term.
3. In order to assess the reliability of the estimated LEQ it is necessary to identify outliers and influential observations and to perform stability tests. In this case, given the functional form of the model, $y = k \cdot x$, and the low number of points associated with large values of $1 - e(tr)$, these observations are influential points.[36] It is easy to understand that changes in these points affect the result of the regression and therefore the LEQ estimate.
4. In order to get more stable results, it is necessary to get more observations (for example by using a variable time horizon approach).

Censored Data and Fixed Time Horizon
Sometimes banks use *censored data* to force realised LEQ factors to satisfy the constraint $0 \le LEQ_i \le 1$. Using censored data, the estimated LEQ factor is 0.7 and the R^2 increase to 0.75. In this case, all the points are in the white triangular region of Figure 13 and it is clear that the existence of very influential points (those with large values of $1 - e(r)$) introduces instability. Figure 13 presents the censored observations and the regression line.

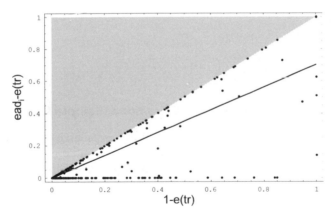

Fig. 13. Linear regression in Model II and censored data

The EAD estimator is in this case:

$$EAD(f) = E(t) + 0.7 \cdot (L(t) - E(t)) \tag{50}$$

---

[36] Influential points have a significant impact on the slope of the regression line which, in Model II, is precisely the LEQ estimate.

Original Data and Variable Time Approach

By using a *variable time approach*, based on observations with $tr = td - \{12, 11, 10, 9, 8\}$, the estimated LEQ factor is LEQ = 0.49 and the R^2 is 0.06. Figure 14 presents, for each observation in the RDS, the pairs $\{1 - e(tr), ead_i - e(tr)\}$ and the regression line associated with this extended data set and Model II.

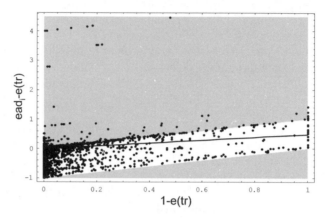

Fig. 14. Linear regression in Model II and variable time approach

In Model II, the use of a time variable approach does not increase the degree of adjustment (which is very low due to the functional form assumed in the model), but increases the stability of the results.

The EAD estimator in this case is:

$$EAD(f) = E(t) + 0.49 \cdot (L(t) - E(t)) \tag{51}$$

7.2.2. The Sample Mean and the Conditional Sample Mean

If Model I is used and a constant LEQ for facilities "similar" to f is assumed, an estimate for $EAD(f)$ is obtained by computing the sample mean of the realised LEQ conditional on observations in $RDS(f)$ as the $LEQ(f)$ estimate and then applying Equation (13). With regard to $RDS(f)$, in this example, two possibilities are analysed:

- $RDS(f) = RDS$ or equivalently to use a global sample mean as estimator.
- $RDS(f) = \{O_i$ such as percent usage e_i is similar to $e(f)\}$ or equivalently to use as estimator a function based on different local means depending on $e(f)$.

Case $RDS(f) = RDS$, Use of a Global Sample Mean

If the sample mean of all the realised LEQ factors associated with the observations in the RDS is computed, the result is a nonsensical figure:

$$LEQ(f) = LEQ = \frac{1}{n} \sum_i LEQ_i = -578 \tag{52}$$

The problems that arise when using this global average arc due to:

1. Instability of certain realised LEQ factors: when $1 - E(f)/L(f)$ is small the real-ised LEQs are not informative.
2. Very high values for certain observations, in some cases several times $L(tr) - E(tr)$. The treatment of these observations needs a case by case analysis.
3. Asymmetries in the behaviour of positive and negative realised LEQ factors.
4. Evidence of a non-constant LEQ_i sample mean depending on the values of $1 - E(f)/L(f)$.

Figure 15 represents the distribution of the realised LEQ factors and undrawn amounts as a percentage of the limit, $1 - E(f)/L(f)$ and it can help to increase under-standing of the main problems associated with this method:

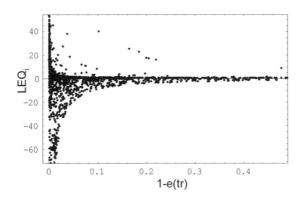

Figure 15. Realised LEQ factors and percent usage at the reference date

Figure 16 focuses on observations associated with values of realised LEQ factors less than 2. It is clear that there are observation realised LEQ factors greater than one, (upper shadow zones in Figures 16 and 17) across the range of percent usage values, although such observations are much more common when the percent us-age values are large (small values of $1 - e(tr)$).

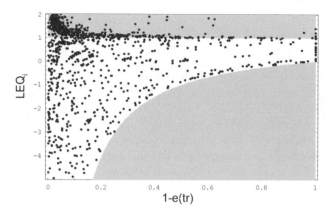

Figure 16. Realised LEQ factors smaller than two

For these reasons, before using this procedure, it is necessary to make some decisions after analysing the observations in the RDS, for example:

- To eliminate from the RDS those anomalous observations with large LEQ_i factors
- To censor other observations associated with LEQ_i factors greater than one
- To remove observations with very low values of $E(f) - L(f)$ from the RDS, because their LEQ_i values are not informative.

In this example, observations with $1 - E(tr)/L(tr) \leq 0.1$ and those with $LEQ_i \geq 2$ were removed from the reference data set. After these modifications of the RDS, the new LEQ_i sample mean is:

$$LEQ(f) = LEQ = \frac{1}{m}\sum_i LEQ_i = 0.08 \qquad (53)$$

It is clear that this global estimate of 8% is very low for most of the facilities in the portfolio because of the weight in the global average of the negative realised LEQ factors associated with observations with low values of $1 - e(f)$.

An improvement to the former estimate is to eliminate outliers, i.e observations associated with very large (in absolute terms) realised LEQ factors. If observations with LEQ factors below the 10th percentile and above the 90th are considered outliers, the average restricted to the RDS without outliers is about 33% and this value is stable when the former percentiles are changed.

$$LEQ(f) = LEQ = \frac{1}{r}\sum_i LEQ_i = 0.33 \qquad (54)$$

However, it is clear that local averages are very different and therefore this global estimate of 33% for the LEQ is not adequate. For this reason, it is necessary to consider different estimates for the LEQ factor for different values of $1 - E(f)/L(f)$.

Case $RDS(f) = \{O_i$ such as percent usage e_i is similar to $e(f)\}$

In this case, the $RDS(f)$ comprises all the observations O_i with $1 - e(tr) \in [1 - e(f) - 0.2,\ 1 - e(f) + 0.2]$ and the average of the realised LEQ factors restricted to observations in the $RDS(f)$ is used as the estimate of $LEQ(f)$. To select a functional form for $LEQ(f)$, first the estimated values for different $1 - e(tr)$ values are computed and second, a regression model is adjusted using $1 - e(tr)$ as the explanatory variable, and the local sample mean as the dependent variable. After rejecting different models and using intervals of width 0.4 an expression for the "local"[37] sample mean of LEQ factors based on $a + b \cdot \sqrt{(1 - e(tr))}$ is obtained as:

$$LEQ(f) = -0.82 + 1.49 \cdot \sqrt{1 - E(f)/L(f)} \qquad (55)$$

with an adjusted R^2 equal to 0.94. Figure 17 represents the realised LEQ factors, the local averages and the adjusted function (with the constraint $LEQ(f) \geq 0$).

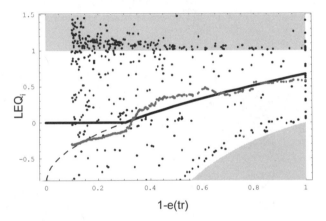

Figure 17. Approximation for $E[LEQ|1 - e(tr)]$ and the adjusted regression curve

Therefore an estimator for $EAD(f)$ of a facility f in normal status is given by:

$$EAD(f) = E(f) + Max\left[0, \left(-0.82 + 1.49 \cdot \sqrt{1 - E(f)/L(f)}\right) \cdot \left(L(f) - E(f)\right)\right] \qquad (56)$$

7.2.3. The Median and the Conditional Quantiles

The rationale under Model III is to explain directly the increase in exposure from the reference date to the default date. Therefore, it is necessary to explain $EAD_i - E(tr)$ in terms of $LEQ(RD_i) \cdot (L(tr) - E(tr))$. For simplicity, it is assumed that $RD_i = \{S(tr),\ L(tr) - E(tr)\}$ and the focus is on observations with status $S(tr) =$

---

[37] The "local" condition is to consider only those observations in an interval centred on $1 - E(f)/L(f)$ and with length 0.4.

"normal" and the only quantitative variable that is taken into account is the current undrawn amount $L(f) - E(f)$. Moreover, the loss function proposed in (39) is used to determine the optimal estimates and therefore as shown in Section 6.3.1, the solution is to approximate the quantile $Q[b/(a+b)]$ of the distribution of $EAD_i - E(tr)$ conditional on those observations which satisfy $L(tr) - E(tr) = L(f) - E(f)$. To approximate that quantile for each value of $EAD(f) - E(f)$, the process is similar to the one explained in the previous section. First, $RDS(f)$ is defined as all the observations such as $(L(tr) - E(tr)) \in [(L(f) - E(f)) \cdot 0.8, (L(f) - E(f)) \cdot 1.2]$. Second, for each value of $L(tr) - E(tr)$ the optimal quantile is computed. Third, a linear regression model that uses $L(tr) - E(tr)$ as the explanatory variable and the optimal quantile as the dependent variable is adjusted and, finally, the estimator for $LEQ(f)$ is obtained by using formula (44).

Figure 18 represents, for each observation in the RDS with $tr = td - \{12, 11, 10, 9, 8\}$, the pairs $\{L(tr) - E(tr), EAD_i - E(tr)\}$ in the range of values of $L(tr) - E(tr)$ given by $[0, 17000]€$, for which it is considered there exists sufficient number of observations. The shadow zones in Figures 18 and 19 are defined as $EAD_i \geq L(tr)$.

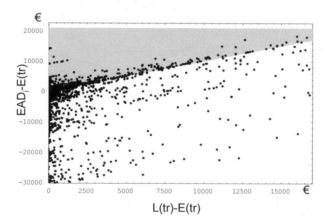

Figure 18. Observations in Model III

The results of the regression model for the local medians (case $a = b$) and for the 66.6^{th} percentile (case $2 \cdot a = b$) produces the following results:

$$Median[EAD(f) - E(f)] = 86.8 + 0.76 \cdot (L(f) - E(f))$$

$$Quantile[EAD(f) - E(f), 0.666] = 337.8 + 0.92 \cdot (L(f) - E(f)) \tag{57}$$

With adjusted R^2 equal to 0.95 and 0.99 respectively. Therefore, the associated LEQ estimates, obtained dividing (57) by $L(f) - E(f)$, are almost constant (close to 0.76 and 0.92 respectively) and have values larger than the previous estimates.

Figure 19 represents the local medians ($Q_{50\%}$ line) and local 66.6 percentiles ($Q_{66\%}$ line) obtained from the original points, the regression lines associated with (57) (dotted line for the adjusted 66.6 percentiles, thick line for the adjusted local medians).

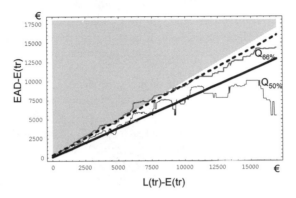

Figure 19. Quantiles conditional on the undrawn amount and adjusted $EAD - E(tr)$ values

8. Summary and Conclusions

The following points summarise the current practice on CF and EAD estimates and highlight some problematic aspects:

- The CF and EAD estimators applied by banks can be derived from special cases of regression problems, and therefore these estimators are based on conditional expectations
- Implicitly, the use of these estimators assumes the minimisation of prediction errors by using a quadratic and symmetric loss function that is neither directly correlated with the errors in terms of minimum capital requirements nor penalises uncertainty. The way in which these errors are measured is crucial because they are very large
- In most of the cases, the EAD estimates are based on the unrealistic assumption of a constant LEQ factor mean
- Frequently, the basic statistics for the estimation process are censored to obtain realised LEQ factors between zero and one
- Banks frequently use "Cohort Approaches" or "Fixed Time Horizon Approaches" to select the observations included in the estimation process. These approaches do not take into account all the relevant information because they only focus on a conventional reference date for each defaulted facility
- With regard to risk drivers, the focus is on the rating at the reference date.

Other approaches and some comments on different aspects:

- For regulatory use, it seems appropriate for the estimators to be solutions to optimisation problems that use a loss function directly related with errors in terms of capital requirements
- For example, a logical choice is to use a simple linear asymmetric loss function applied at the level of facility. This loss function enables banks or supervisors to quantify the level of conservatism implicit in the estimates
- Using this loss function, the derived estimators are based on conditional quantiles (for example, the median for internal purposes and a more conservative quantile for regulatory use)
- If the estimates are based on sample means LEQ factors, as a minimum, should depend on the level of the existing availability of additional drawdowns: $LEQ(1-e(tr))$
- The common practice of censoring the realised LEQ factors to [0, 1], is not justified and, in general, it is not possible to conclude ex ante if the associated LEQ estimates are biased in a conservative manner
- However, under certain hypotheses, the use of censored data does not change the optimal estimator for LEQ
- The estimates should be based on observations at all the relevant reference dates for defaulted facilities, "Variable Time Approach"
- With regard to risk drivers, if there is a warning system for the portfolio, it is important to focus on the status of the facility at the reference date rather than on the rating
- The example presented here suggests that:
  - Estimates based on sample means are less conservative than those based on conditional quantiles above the median
  - The CF estimates obtained by using these conditional quantiles, are so large that the use of downturn estimates in this case might not be a priority.

References

Araten M, Jacobs M (2001), Loan Equivalents for Revolving Credits and Advised Lines, The RMA Journal, pp. 34-39.
Basel Committee on Banking Supervision (2005), Guidance on Paragraph 468 of the Framework Document.
Basel Committee on Banking Supervision (2004), International Convergence of Capital Measurement and Capital Standards, a Revised Framework.
Basel Committee on Banking Supervision (2005), Studies on the Validation of Internal Rating Systems, Working Paper No. 14.
CEBS (2006), Guidelines on the implementation, validation and assessment of Advanced Measurement (AMA) and Internal Ratings Based (IRB) Approaches, CP 10 revised.
Lev B, Rayan S (2004) Accounting for commercial loan commitments.
Moral G (1996), Pérdida latente, incertidumbre y provisión óptima, Banco de España, Boletín de la Inspección de ECA.

Office of the Comptroller of the Currency (OCC), Treasury; Board of Governors of the Federal Reserve System (Board); Federal Deposit Insurance Corporation (FDIC); and Office of Thrift Supervision (OTS), Treasury. Federal (2003), Draft Supervisory Guidance on Internal Ratings-Based Systems for Corporate Credit (corporate IRB guidance). Register / Vol. 68, No. 149.

Office of the Comptroller of the Currency (OCC), Treasury; Board of Governors of the Federal Reserve System (Board); Federal Deposit Insurance Corporation (FDIC); and Office of Thrift Supervision (OTS), (2004), Proposed supervisory guidance for banks, savings associations, and bank holding companies (banking organizations) that would use the internal-ratings-based (IRB) approach to determine their regulatory capital requirements for retail credit exposures. Treasury. Federal Register / Vol. 69, No. 207.

Pratt J, Raiffa H, Schlaifer R (1995) Introduction to Statistical Decision Theory. The MIT Press.

Sufi A. (2005) Bank Lines of Credit in Corporate Finance: An Empirical Analysis University of Chicago Graduate School of Business.

Appendix A. Equivalence Between two Minimisation Problems

Proposition: Consider a set of observations $O = \{(x_i, y_i)\}_{i=1,\ldots,n}$ and the problem G.I given by:

$$Minimise_{g \in G}\left[\sum_{i=1}^{n} L(y_i - g(x_i))\right] \tag{58}$$

Subject to $f(x) \geq g(x) \geq h(x)$

where the error is measured in terms of the function L that satisfies:

$$L(x + y) = L(x) + L(y) \quad if \ x \cdot y \geq 0 \tag{59}$$

then, g is a solution of Problem G.I if and only if it is a solution of Problem G.II given by:

$$Minimise_{g \in G}\left[\sum_{i=1}^{n} L\big(Min[Max[y_i, h(x_i)], f(x_i)] - g(x_i)\big)\right] \tag{60}$$

Subject to $f(x) \geq g(x) \geq h(x)$

Proof: The set O can be partitioned into three classes $O = O^+ \amalg O^- \amalg O^=$, where:

$$O^+ = \{(x_i, y_i) \big| y_i > f(x_i)\}, \ O^- = \{(x_i, y_i) \big| y_i < h(x_i)\} \tag{61}$$

For observations in O^+:

$$\left(y_i - f(x_i)\right) \cdot \left(f(x_i) - g(x_i)\right) \geq 0 \tag{62}$$

Therefore, from (59) and (62), the error in Problem G.I associated with an observation in O^+ can be expressed in terms of the error in Problem G.II plus an amount independent of g:

$$
\begin{aligned}
err\left[GI, \left(x_i, y_i\right)\right] &= L\left(y_i - g(x_i)\right) = L\left(y_i - f(x_i) + f(x_i) - g(x_i)\right) \\
&= L\left(y_i - f(x_i)\right) + L\left(f(x_i) - g(x_i)\right) \\
&= L\left(y_i - f(x_i)\right) + L\left(Min\left[Max\left[y_i, h(x_i)\right], f(x_i)\right] - g(x_i)\right) \\
&= L\left(y_i - f(x_i)\right) + err\left[GII, \left(x_i, y_i\right)\right]
\end{aligned} \tag{63}
$$

But the O^+ set does not depend on the function g, therefore for these observations, and for all g, the error in Problem G.I can be decomposed in a fixed amount, independent of the g function, given by $\sum L\left(y_i - f(x_i)\right)$, where the index i applies at the observations in O^+ and the error in Problem G.II.

Similarly, for observations in O^-, the error in Problem G.I is equal to the error in Problem G.II plus the fixed amount $\sum L\left(h(x_i) - y_i\right)$.

Finally, for the observations in $O^=$ the errors in Problem G.I and in Problem G.II are the same.□

Appendix B. Optimal Solutions of Certain Regression and Optimization Problems

Let X and Y be random variables with joint distribution given by $F(x,y)$, then we get in the case of a quadratic loss function

$$d^*(x) = E\langle Y|X\rangle = \underset{d(x)}{Min}\left\{ \underset{F^*}{E}\left\langle (Y - d(X))^2 \right\rangle \right\}. \tag{64}$$

In the case of the linear asymmetric loss function:

$$L(x) = \begin{cases} a \cdot x & \text{iff } x \geq 0 \\ b \cdot x & \text{iff } x < 0 \end{cases} \tag{65}$$

The following is found

$$d^*(x) = Q\left\langle Y \middle| X, \frac{b}{a+b} \right\rangle = \underset{d(x)}{Min}\left\{ \underset{F^*}{E}\langle L(Y - d(X)) \rangle \right\} \qquad (66)$$

See, for example, Pratt (1995, pp. 261-263).

Therefore, a solution for (28) can be obtained from (64), and taking into account:

$$Y = \frac{EAD - E}{\omega}; \, d(X = RD) = LEQ(RD) \cdot h(RD); \text{ where } h(RD) = \frac{L - E}{\omega} \qquad (67)$$

Then, d^* is given by (64) and assuming that $h(RD) = h(f)$ for observations in $RDS(f)$:

$$d^*(X = RD(f)) = E\left\langle \frac{EAD - E}{\omega} \middle| RD \right\rangle = \overline{LEQ}(RD(f)) \cdot \frac{L(f) - E(f)}{\omega(f)} \qquad (68)$$

The result showed in (29) is obtained from the former equation.□

Appendix C. Diagnostics of Regressions Models

Model II (Section 7.2.1)

- By using original data:

$$\frac{EAD_i}{L(td - 12)} - \frac{E(td - 12)}{L(td - 12)} = 0.64 \cdot \left(1 - \frac{E(td - 12)}{L(td - 12)} \right) \qquad (69)$$

		Estimate	SE	TStat	Pvalue
Parameter Table	x	0,64	0,08	8,03	0

Degree of adjustment	Rsquared	ADjustedRSquared	EstimatedVariance
	0,13	0,13	0,21

			ANOVATable		
	DF	SumOfSq	MeanSq	FRatio	Pvalue
Model	1	13,5	13,54	64,45	0
Error	416	87,41	0,21		
Total	417	100,95			

- By using censored data:

$$\frac{EAD_i}{L(td - 12)} - \frac{E(td - 12)}{L(td - 12)} = 0.7 \cdot \left(1 - \frac{E(td - 12)}{L(td - 12)} \right) \qquad (70)$$

Parameter Table		Estimate	SE	TStat	Pvalue
	x	0,7	0,02	35,07	0

Degree of adjustment	Rsquared	ADjustedRSquared	EstimatedVariance
	0,75	0,75	0,013

			ANOVATable		
	DF	SumOfSq	MeanSq	FRatio	Pvalue
Model	1	16,49	16,49	1229,67	0
Error	416	5,58	0,013		
Total	417	22,05			

- By using a variable time approach:

$$\frac{EAD_i}{L(tr)} - \frac{E(tr)}{L(tr)} = 0.49 \cdot \left(1 - \frac{E(tr)}{L(tr)}\right) \tag{71}$$

Parameter Table		Estimate	SE	TStat	Pvalue
	x	0,49	0,04	13,86	0

Degree of adjustment	Rsquared	ADjustedRSquared	EstimatedVariance
	0,06	0,06	0,19

			ANOVATable		
	DF	SumOfSq	MeanSq	FRatio	Pvalue
Model	1	35,92	16,49	1229,67	0
Error	2918	545,3	0,19		
Total	2919	581,2			

Model I (Section 7.2.2)

- By using Model I, variable time approach:

$$LEQ(f) = -0.82 + 1.49 \cdot \sqrt{1 - E(f)/L(f)} \tag{72}$$

The diagnostics for this regression model are:

		Estimate	SE	TStat	Pvalue
Parameter	1	-0,82	0,009	-93,09	0
Table	x^0,5	1,49	0,014	104,57	0

Degree of adjustment	Rsquared	ADjustedRSquared	EstimatedVariance
	0,94	0,94	0,006

			ANOVATable		
	DF	SumOfSq	MeanSq	FRatio	Pvalue
Model	1	66,13	66,13	10934,1	0
Error	663	4,01	0,006		
Total	664	70,14			

Model III (Section 7.2.3)

- By using a variable time approach:

$$Median[EAD(f) - E(f)] = 86.8 + 0.76 \cdot (L(f) - E(f)) \qquad (73)$$

$$Quantile[EAD(f) - E(f), 0.666] = 337.8 + 0.92 \cdot (L(f) - E(f))$$

With the diagnostics given by:

		Estimate	SE	TStat	Pvalue
Parameter	1	86,8	11,23	7,73	0
Table	x	0,76	0,003	222,74	0

Degree of adjustment	Rsquared	ADjustedRSquared	EstimatedVariance
	0,95	0,95	227741

			ANOVATable		
	DF	SumOfSq	MeanSq	FRatio	Pvalue
Model	1	1,13*10^10	1,13*10^10	49611	0
Error	2370	5,40*10^8	227741		
Total	2371	1,18*10^10			

and for the quantile:

		Estimate	SE	TStat	Pvalue
Parameter	1	337,8	5,14	65,7	0
Table	x	0,92	0,002	594,6	0

Degree of adjustment	Rsquared	ADjustedRSquared	EstimatedVariance
	0,99	0,99	47774,6

			ANOVATable		
	DF	SumOfSq	MeanSq	FRatio	Pvalue
Model	1	1,69*10^10	1,7*10^10	353621	0
Error	2370	1,13*10^8	47774,6		
Total	2371	1,7*10^10			

Appendix D. Abbreviations

AIRB	Advanced internal ratings-based approach
CCF	Credit conversion factor
CF	Conversion factor
EAD	Exposure at default
$EAD_i = E(td)$	Realised exposure at default associated with O_i
$EAD(f)$	EAD estimate for f
ead_i	Realised percent exposure at default, associated with O_i
$E(t)$	Usage or exposure of a facility at the date t
$e(t)$	Percent usage of a facility at the date t
$e_i = e(tr)$	Percent usage associated with the observation $O_{i=\{g, tr\}}$
f	Non-defaulted facility
g	Defaulted facility
$i = \{g, tr\}$	Index associated with the observation of g at tr
IRB	Internal ratings-based approach
LEQ	Loan equivalent exposure
$LEQ(f)$	LEQ estimate for f
LEQ_i	Realised LEQ factor associated with the observation O_i
LGD	Loss given default
$L(t)$	Limit of the credit facility at the date t
O_i	Observation associated with the pair i=\{g, tr\}
PD	Probability of default
$Q_a = Q(x, a)$	Quantile associated with the a% of the distribution F(x)
RDS	Reference data set
$RDS(f)$	RDS associated with f
RD	Risk drivers
$S(tr)$	Status of a facility at the reference date tr
t	Current date
td	Default date
tr	Reference date
$td - tr$	Horizon

XI. Validation of Banks' Internal Rating Systems - A Supervisory Perspective

Stefan Blochwitz and Stefan Hohl

Deutsche Bundesbank and Bank for International Settlements (BIS)[1]

1. Basel II and Validating IRB Systems

1.1. Basel's New Framework (Basel II)

'Basel II' is associated with the work recently undertaken by the Basel Committee on Banking Supervision (BCBS)[2]. This aimed to secure international convergence on revisions to supervisory regulations on capital adequacy standards of internationally active banks. The main objective of the 1988 Accord[3] and its revision is to develop a risk-based capital framework that strengthens and stabilises the banking system. At the same time, it should provide for sufficient consistency on capital adequacy regulation across countries in order to minimize competitive inequality among international banks. In June 2004, the BCBS issued 'Basel II', titled 'International Convergence of Capital Measurement and Capital Standards: A Revised Framework', carefully crafting the balance between convergence and differences in capital requirements.

This paper presents pragmatic views on validating IRB systems. It discusses issues related to the challenges facing supervisors and banks of validating the systems that generate inputs into the internal ratings-based approach (IRBA) used to calculate the minimum regulatory capital for credit risk, based on internal bank information.

---

[1] The views expressed are those of the authors and do not necessarily reflect those of the Bank for International Settlements (BIS), the Basel Committee of Banking Supervision, or the Deutsche Bundesbank.

[2] The Basel Committee on Banking Supervision is a committee of banking supervisory authorities that was established by the central bank governors of the Group of Ten countries in 1975. It consists of senior representatives of bank supervisory authorities and central banks from Belgium, Canada, France, Germany, Italy, Japan, Luxembourg, the Netherlands, Spain, Sweden, Switzerland, the United Kingdom, and the United States.

[3] see BIS (1988)

The key role of Banks as financial intermediaries highlights their core compe-
tences as lending, investing and risk management. In particular, analysing and
quantifying risks is a vital part of efficient bank management. An appropriate corporate structure is vital to successful risk management. Active credit risk management is indispensable for efficiently steering a bank through the economic and
financial cycles, despite the difficulties stemming from a lack of credit risk data.

A well-functioning *credit risk measurement system* is the key element in every
bank's internal risk management process. It is interesting to note that the debate
about the new version of the Basel Capital Accord (Basel II), which establishes
the international minimum requirements for capital to be held by banks, has
moved this topic back to the centre of the discussion about sound banking. The
proper implementation of the IRBA is at the heart of a lively debate among bankers, academics and regulators. At the same time a paradigm shift has taken place.

Previously, credit risk assessment used only the experience, intuition and powers
of discernment of a few select specialists. The new process is more formalised,
standardised and much more objective by bank's internal rating systems.   The
human element has not been entirely discounted, however; now both human
judgement and rating systems each play an equally important role in deciding the
credit risk of a loan.

Since the IRBA approach will be implemented in most of the G10-countries in the
very near future, the debate on the IRBA has shifted its accent. More emphasis is
now given to the problem of validating a rating system, rather than how to design
a rating system. Both the private sector and banking supervisors need well-
functioning rating systems. This overlap of interests and objectives is reflected in
the approach towards validation of rating systems; even if different objectives imply different priorities in qualifying and monitoring the plausibility of such systems.

We will discuss some of the challenges faced by banks and supervisors, aware that
we have only scratched the surface. This is followed by a discussion of some of
the responses given by the BCBS. We then will discuss a pragmatic approach towards validating IRB systems while touching on some issues previously raised.
However, we would like to stress that implementation of Basel II, and especially
the validation of IRB systems (and similarly AMA models for operational risk)
requires ongoing dialogue between supervisors and banks. This article, including
its limitations, offers a conceptual starting point to deal with the issues related to
the validation of IRB systems.

1.2. Some Challenges

The discussion on validation has to start with a discussion of the structure and usage of internal rating systems within banks. The two-dimensional risk assessment
for credit risk as required in Basel II, aims to quantify borrower risk, via the prob-

ability of default (PD) for a rating grade, and the facility risk by means of the Loss Given default (LGD). The third dimension is the facility's exposure at default (EAD).

The broad structure of a bank-internal rating system is shown in Figure 1. First, the information, i.e. the raw data on the borrower to be rated have to be collected in accordance with established banking standards. Accordingly, the data is used to determine the potential borrower's credit risk. In most cases, a quantitative rating method which draws on the bank's previous experience with credit defaults is initially used to determine a credit score. Borrowers with broadly similar credit scores, reflecting similar risk characteristics, are typically allocated to a preliminary risk category, i.e. rating grade. Usually, a loan officer then decides the borrower's final rating and risk category, i.e. this stage involves the application of qualitative information.

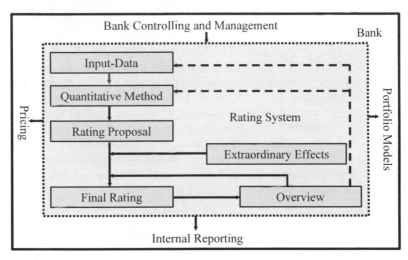

Figure 1. Schematic evolution of a rating process and its integration in the bank as a whole

A well-working rating system should demonstrate that the risk categories differ in terms of their risk content. The quantification of risk parameters is based on the bank's own historical experience, backed by other public information and to certain extent, private information. For example, the share of borrowers in a given rating category who have experienced an occurrence defined as a credit default[4]

---

[4] What constitutes credit default is a matter of definition. For banks, this tends to be the occurrence of an individual value adjustment, whereas at rating agencies, it is insolvency or evident payment difficulties. The IRBA included in the new Basel Capital Accord is based on an established definition of default. Compared with individual value adjustments, the Basel definition of default provides for a forward-looking and therefore relatively early warning of default together with a retrospective flagging of payments that are 90 days overdue.

within a given time-frame, usually one year, will be used for the estimation process. The described standardisation of ratings allows the use of quantitative models where sufficient borrower data is available and highlights the need for high-quality, informative data.

For consumer loans, the BCBS also allows risk assessment on the level of homogenous retail portfolios that are managed accordingly by the bank on a pool basis. The challenge for banks is to identify such homogenous portfolios exhibiting similar risk characteristics. This leads to the importance of using bank-internal data, which plays a crucial role in both the segmentation process used to find homogenous portfolios, and the quantification process used for the risk parameters. One of the techniques used for segmentation and quantification is the utilisation of so-called "roll rates"[5], where different delinquency stages are defined (for example 30 days, 60 days etc.). Counting the roll rate from one delinquency stage to another and filling the migration matrix would serve as a basis for estimating the PDs for those exposures.

There are a couple of issues related to this procedure. Firstly, there is the issue of segmentation, i.e. do roll rates take into account all relevant risk drivers as required in the Basel II framework? Secondly, for quantification purposes, how will roll rates be translated into PDs, more specifically, which delinquency class should be used (to comply with the Basel II framework), and to what extent can these PDs be validated? Lastly, in many instances a quicker reaction of current conditions, sometimes coupled with a longer time horizon, might be needed for purposes of risk management and pricing, especially for retail exposures. How would such quantification processes for PDs (and LGDs) be rectified with the application of the use-test as required in Basel II?

Another issue relates to the modification performed by a credit officer of the automated rating proposal, i.e. a qualitative adjustment. This may question the rigidity needed for validation, especially in cases where documentation may be insufficient, and the information used is more qualitatively based, the latter being a general problem in credit assessments.

A simple, but important, question is who has the responsibility for validating a rating system in the context of Basel II, given that the calculation of minimum regulatory capital is legally binding and set by the supervisors. In addition, a valid point in this regard is that some requirements, for example, the quantification process focussing on long-term averages to reduce volatility of minimum regulatory capital requirements, are not fully in line with bank practice. This may lead to a different quantification process, i.e. a second process for the sole purpose of meeting supervisory standards, or even to a different risk management process as suggested above in the retail portfolios. In sum, the use-test requirement, the extent to which an internal rating system is used in daily banking business, will play

---

[5] Fritz et al. (2002)

a crucial role in assessing compliance with Basel II implementation including the validation of IRB systems.

Since a bank's internal rating systems are individual, and in the best case, fully tailored to the bank's necessities; validation techniques must be as individual as the rating system they are used for. As an example, we highlight the so-called Low-Default-Portfolios. As the IRB framework in Basel II is intended to apply to all asset classes, there are naturally portfolios which exhibit relatively low or even no default at all.[6] This makes the quantification, required to be grounded in historical experience, of PDs and LGDs, extremely challenging. Thus, a straightforward assessment based on historic losses would not be sufficiently reliable for the quantification process of the risk parameters, but conservative estimates serving as an upper benchmark may be derived (cf. Chapter V).

Some of the issues raised in this section have been discussed by the BCBS.

1.3. Provisions by the BCBS

The Subgroup on Validation (AIGV)[7] of the BCBS' Accord Implementation Group (AIG) was established in 2004. The objective of the AIGV is to share and exchange views related to the validation of IRB systems. To the extent possible, the groups should also narrow gaps between different assessments of the New Framework by the different supervising agencies represented in the AIGV. The objective of the validation of a rating system is to assess whether a rating system can – and ultimately does – fulfil its task of accurately distinguishing and measuring credit risk. The common view describes the term 'validation' as a means to combine quantitative and qualitative methods. If applied together, it should indicate whether a rating system measures credit risks appropriately and is properly implemented in the bank in question.

The BCBS newsletter No. 4, January 2004, informs about the work of the AIGV in the area of validation in Basel II. The most important information provided was the relatively simple answer to the question, "what aspects of validation will be looked at?" Despite the importance of validation as a requirement for the IRB approach, the New Framework does not explicitly specify what constitutes validation. Consequently, the Subgroup reached agreement on that question. In the context of rating systems, the term "validation" encompasses a range of processes and

---

[6] See BCBS newsletter No 6, "for example, some portfolios historically have experienced low numbers of defaults and are generally—but not always—considered to be low-risk (e.g. portfolios of exposures to sovereigns, banks, insurance companies or highly rated corporate borrowers)".

[7] The Validation Subgroup is focusing primarily on the IRB approach, although the principles should also apply to validation of advanced measurement approaches for operational risk. A separate Subgroup has been established to explore issues related to operational risk (see BCBS newsletter No 4.).

activities that contribute to assessing whether ratings adequately differentiate risk, and importantly, whether estimates of risk components (such as PD, LGD, or EAD) appropriately characterise and quantify the relevant risk dimension.

Starting with this definition, the AIGV developed six important principles (see Figure 2), on validation that result in a broad framework for validation. The validation framework covers all aspects of validation, including the goal of validation (principle 1), the responsibility for validation (principle 2), expectations on validation techniques (principles 3, 4, and 5), and the control environment for validation (principle 6). Publishing these principles was a major step in clarifying the ongoing discussions between banks and their supervisors about validation for at least three reasons:

1. The principles establish a broad view on validation. Quite often, validation was seen as being restricted to only dealing with aspects related to backtesting. The established broad view on validation reinforces the importance of the minimum requirements of the IRBA, as well as highlighting the importance of risk-management. The debate around the IRBA was too often restricted to solely risk quantification or measurement aspects. We think that this balanced perspective, including the more qualitative aspects of the IRBA, reflects the shortcomings in establishing and validating rating systems, especially given the data limitations. This clarification also formed the basis for the development of validation principles for the so-called "Low Default Portfolios (LDPs)" as proposed in the BCBS newsletter No. 6 from August 2005.
2. The responsibility for validation and the delegation of duties has also been clarified. The main responsibility lies rightfully with the bank, given the importance of rating systems in the bank's overall risk management and capital allocation procedures. Since validation is seen as the ultimate sanity-check for a rating system and all its components, this task clearly *must* be performed by the bank itself, including the final sign-off by senior management. It should be noted that only banks can provide the resources necessary to validate rating systems.
3. Principles 3 - 5 establish a comprehensive approach for validating rating systems. This approach proposes the key elements of a broad validation process, on which we will elaborate more in the next section.

Principle 1: *Validation is fundamentally about assessing the predictive ability of a bank's risk estimates and the use of ratings in credit processes*

The two step process for ratings systems requires banks to firstly discriminate adequately between risky borrowers (i.e. being able o discriminate between risks and its associated risk of loss) and secondly calibrate risk (i.e. being able to accurately quantify the level of risk). The IRB parameters must, as always with statistical estimates, be based on historical experience which should form the basis for the forward-looking quality of the IRB parameters. IRB validation should encompass the processes for assigning those estimates including the governance and control procedures in a bank.

Principle 2: *The bank has primary responsibility for validation*

The primary responsibility for validating IRB systems lies with the banks itself and does not remain with the supervisor. This certainly should reflect the self-interest and the need for banks having a rating system in place reflecting its business. Supervisors obviously must review the bank's validation processes and should also rely upon additional processes in order to get the adequate level of supervisory comfort.

Principle 3: *Validation is an iterative process*

Setting up and running an IRB system in real life is by design an iterative process. Validation, as an important part of this circle, should therefore be an ongoing, iterative process following an iterative dialogue between banks and their supervisors. This may result in a refinement of the validation tools used.

Principle 4: *There is no single validation method*

Many well-known validation tools like backtesting, benchmarking, replication, etc are a useful supplement to the overall goal of achieving a sound IRB system. However, there is unanimous agreement that there is no universal tool available, which could be used across portfolios and across markets.

Principle 5: *Validation should encompass both quantitative and qualitative elements*

Validation is not a technical or solely mathematical exercise. Validation must be considered and applied a broad sense, its individual components like data, documentation, internal use and the underlying rating models and all processes which the rating system uses are equally important.

Principle 6: *Validation processes and outcomes should be subject to independent review*

For IRB systems, there must be an independent review within the bank. This specifies neither the organigram in the bank nor its relationship across departments, but the review team must be independent of designers of the IRB system and those who implement the validation process.

Figure 2. The six principles of validation

2. Validation of Internal Rating Systems in Detail

According to the BCBS elaboration on the term "validation", we consider three mutually supporting ways to validate bank internal rating systems. This encompasses a range of processes and activities that contribute to the overall assessment and final judgement. More specifically, this can be directly related to the application of principle 4 and principle 5 of the BCBS newsletter as discussed above.

1. *Component-based validation:* - analyses each of the three elements – data collection and compilation, quantitative procedure and human influence – for appropriateness and workability.
2. *Result-based validation* (also known as backtesting): - analyses the rating system's quantification of credit risk ex post.
3. *Process-based validation:* - analyses the rating system's interfaces with other processes in the bank and how the rating system is integrated into the bank's overall management structure.

2.1. Component-based Validation

2.1.1. Availability of High-quality Data

Ensuring adequate data quality is the key task which, for at least two reasons, must be addressed with the greatest urgency. First, as the rating is based primarily on individual borrowers' current data, it can only be as good as the underlying data. Second, the quantitative component of the rating process requires a sufficiently reliable set of data, including a cross-sectional basis, which is crucial for calibration of the risk parameters. Accordingly, both historical data and high-quality recent data are essential to ensure that a rating system can be set up adequately, and will also be successful in the future. Clearly, the availability of data, i.e. financial versus account specific information, and its use for different borrower characteristics, - wholesale versus consumer – is dissimilar. Activities in consumer finance may produce more bank-specific behavioural data whereas financial information for large wholesale borrowers should be publicly available. However, the availability of reliable and informative data, especially for the mid-size privately owned borrowers, may frequently not be met for at least several reasons:

- Data compilation and quality assurance incur high costs because they require both qualified staff and a high-performance IT infrastructure. In addition, these tasks seem to have little to do with original banking business in its strict sense, and their usefulness may only become apparent years later. Clearly, proper investment is needed, adding pressure to costs and competition.
- Similarly, it is a costly exercise in staffing and resource allocation in credit departments. However, the Basel II efforts may have helped to allocate more resources to capturing adequate and reliable credit data.

- In reality, borrowers also are often reluctant to supply the requested data. This may be because, especially at smaller enterprises, this data is not readily available. Admittedly, because of the predominant classic "house bank" system in Germany, this information historically had not been requested. Also, potential misuse of data and reluctance on the part of firms to provide information on their own economic situation seems to be a widespread concern. Sometimes, data is passed on to a very limited number of third parties only.[8]
- Further concentration in the banking industry is also contributing to the problem. Owing to the lack of uniform standards for banks, in the event of a merger, different sets of data have to be synchronized – this adds a new dimension to the problem and is, again, no quick and easy task to do.

A thorough knowledge of the IT systems underlying the rating approach is necessary for the proper assessment of data quality; in addition the following may help to provide a realistic evaluation:

- *Ensuring data quality*: The sheer existence and quality of bank internal guidelines, including tests around them, is an indication of the importance banks place on good data quality. Whether a bank takes its own guidelines seriously can be gauged from day-to-day applications. For instance, data quality assurance can reasonably be expected to be as automated as possible to ensure that a uniform standard is applied throughout the bank. Also, comparison with external sources of data seems to be necessary to ensure data plausibility.
- *Bank-wide use of the data*: The extent to which data are used allows assessing the confidence that the bank has in its data. This leads to two consequences. On the one hand, frequent and intensive use of specific data within a bank exposes inconsistencies which might exist. On the other hand, where larger numbers of people are able to manually adjust data, the more likely is its potential contamination, unless suitable countermeasures are taken.

2.1.2. The Quantitative Rating Models

The second facet of the rating process, in the broadest sense, is the mathematical approach which can be used to standardise the use of data. The aim is to compress data collected in the first stage to prepare and facilitate the loan officer's decision on the credit risk assessment of a borrower. In recent years, the analysis and development of possible methods has been a focus of research at banks and in microeconomics.

The second stage methods attribute to each borrower, via a rating function f_{Rat}, a continuous or discrete risk measure Z, a rating score, which is dependent on both

---

[8] An indication of this attitude, which is widespread in Germany, is, for example, the approach that is adopted to the obligation laid down in Section 325 of the German Commercial Code for corporations to publish their annual accounts. No more than 10% of the enterprises concerned fulfil this statutory obligation.

the individual features of each borrower $X_1, X_2, ..., X_N$ – also denoted as risk factors – and free, initially unknown model parameters $\alpha_1, \alpha_2, ..., \alpha_M$:

$$Z = f_{Rat}(\alpha_1, \cdots \alpha_M; X_1, \cdots, X_N)$$

The value of Z permits the suggested rating to be derived from the quantitative analysis of the borrower concerned, in that each value of Z is allocated precisely to one of Y various rating categories. The methods suitable for this kind of quantitative component can be classified as:

- *Statistical methods*: This is probably the best known and the most widespread group of methods. They are used by almost all banks in both corporate and private sector business. The best known of such methods are discriminatory analyses (primarily in corporate business) and logit regressions (used mainly as scorecards in private sector business). Generalised regression and classification methods (such as neural networks) also belong in this category, even if they are rarely used in practice.
- *Rule-based systems*: Such systems model the way in which human credit experts reach a decision and are used in corporate business. They comprise a set of predetermined "if ... then" rules (i.e. expert knowledge). Each enterprise is first graded according to these rules. The next stage is for the rules matched by the firm to be aggregated in order to give a risk rating.
- *Benchmarking methods*: In these methods, observable criteria, such as bond spreads, are used to compare borrowers with unknown risk content with rated borrowers with known risk content – the so-called benchmarks.
- *Applied economic models*: Option price theory models are the most widely known. They enable, for example, an enterprise's equity capital to be modelled as a call option on its asset value and thus the concepts used in option price theory to be applied to credit risk measurement. The starting point for the development of these models was the Merton model; KMV has been successful in its further development offering its Public Firm Model for listed enterprises and a Private Firm Model for unlisted enterprises (Crosbie and Bohn, 2001).

Another classification distinguishes between *empirical models*, where the parameters are determined from data of known borrowers by using mathematical or numerical optimisation methods, and *expert methods*, where the parameters are specified by credit experts based on their experience. Basically, the difference lies in the specification of the model parameters $\alpha_1, \alpha_2, ..., \alpha_M$.

2.1.3. The Model Itself

Transparency, intelligibility and plausibility are crucial for validating the appropriateness of the rating process. Clearly, either with the set of rules for expert systems or with the underlying model in the case of benchmarking methods and applied economic models, these requirements seem to be easily fulfilled. The situation regarding statistical models is somewhat more complex – as there is no economic theory underlying these models. However, certain basic economic requirements should also be incorporated in using statistical models. For example, experience has shown that many risk factors are invariably more marked among "good" borrowers than "bad" borrowers. Likewise, if a requirement of risk measure Z is invariably larger among better borrowers than among worse borrowers, the direct consequence is that the monotony of the risk factor must also be evident in the monotony of the risk measure. Therefore, for the i-th risk factor X_i, the following applies:

$$\frac{\partial Z}{\partial X_i} = \frac{\partial f_{Rat}(\alpha_1, \cdots \alpha_M; X_1, \cdots, X_N)}{\partial X_i} > 0$$

Economic plausibility leads to the exclusion of "non-monotonous" risk factors in linear models. Non-monotonous risk factors are, for example, growth variables, such as changes in the balance sheet total, changes in turnover etc. Experience shows that both a decline and excessively high growth of these variables imply a high risk. Such variables cannot be processed in linear models, i.e. in models like $Z = \alpha_0 + \alpha_1 \cdot X_1 + \ldots + \alpha_N \cdot X_N$, because, owing to

$$\frac{\partial Z}{\partial X_1} = \alpha_i = \text{const.},$$

the plausibility criterion in these models cannot be fulfilled for non-monotonous features.[9] Further economic plausibility requirements and sensitivity analysis should be considered in a causal relationship with economic risk, for example the creditworthiness of an enterprise cannot be derived from the managing director's shoe size!

The commonly applied statistical standards must be observed for all empirical models (statistical models, specific expert systems and applied economic models). Non-compliance with these standards is always an indication of design defects, which generally exhibit an adverse effect when applied. Without claiming completeness, we consider the following aspects to be vital when developing a model:

- *Appropriateness of the random sample for the empirical model*: The appropriateness of the random sample is the decisive factor for all empirical and statistical models. This is also relevant to applied economic models, as is illustrated by the KMV models. These models have been based on data on US firms, meaning that they draw on developments in the US markets only and solely reflect US accounting standards. Not all data which is important in this system is available when other accounting standards are used, with the result that when the models are transferred to other countries, one has to work with possibly questionable approximations. This has a bearing on certain characteristics of the models such as lack of ambiguity and the stability of the results.

---

[9] Moody's RiskCalc (Falkenstein et al., 2000) provides one way of processing non-monotonous risk factors by appropriate transformation in linear models. Another one can be found in Chapter II.

- *Over-parameterising the model*: A mistake, frequently observed, is to include too many risk factors in the design of a rating system. The reasons for this include an overly cautious approach when developing the system, i.e. each conceivable risk factor, or those which credit experts seem to consider obvious, are to be fed into the system. On the other hand, rating systems are often developed by committees and these would naturally like to see their particular "babies" (mostly a "favourite variable" or a special risk factor) reflected in the rating design. Neither approach is optimal from the statistical perspective as there is an upper limit to the number of parameters to be calculated, depending on the size of the sample and the model used. If this rule is breached, errors are made which are called "overfitting".

- *Statistical performance of the estimated model*: The performance of the model in a statistical sense is generally provided as a type-1 or a type-2 error, applying measures of inequality such as Gini coefficients or entropy measures (Falkenstein et al., 2000), or other statistical measures which can be determined either for the sample or the entire population. These variables quantify the rating system's ability to distinguish between good and bad borrowers and thus provide important information about the capability of the rating model with regard to discriminating between risks. These variables are especially important during the development of a rating system as they allow comparison of the performance of various models within *the same* data set. However, we think that these tools are only of minor importance for ongoing prudential monitoring. First, owing to the concave form of the risk weighting function in the new Basel Accord, which provides logical incentives so that systems which discriminate more finely, are less burdened by regulatory capital than coarser systems. Second, the absolute size of the probability of default is the variable relevant for banking supervision as it is linked to the size of the regulatory capital.

- *Modelling errors, precision and stability*: Certain modelling errors are inevitably part of every model because each model can depict only a part of economic reality in a simplified form. In order to be able to use a model correctly, one has to be aware of these limitations. However, in addition to these limitations, which are to a certain extent a "natural" feature of each model, the modelling errors caused by using an optimisation or estimation procedure also need to be considered. These estimation errors can be quantified for the model parameters from the confidence levels of the model parameters. Given certain distribution assumptions, or with the aid of cyclical or rotation methods, these confidence levels can be determined analytically from the same data which is used to estimate the parameters (Fahrmeir et al., 1996). If error calculation methods frequently used in the natural sciences are applied, it is possible to estimate the extent to which measurement bias of the individual model parameters affects the credit score Z. The stability of a model can be derived from the confidence levels of model parameters. Determining the stability of a model seems to be particularly important, i.e. the responsiveness to portfolio changes. A more critical issue is model precision. In some methods, model parameters are determined – though illogically – with a precision that is several orders of magnitude higher than for the risk parameters.

2.1.4. Role of the Loan Officer – or Qualitative Assessment

Loan officers play an important role in both setting up a rating system as well as using it in practice. We think that qualitative assessments should be included in the final rating assignment, by allowing the loan officer to modify the suggested credit rating provided by the quantitative model.[10] This is certainly necessary for exposures above a certain size; retail loans may be dependent on the business activities and risk management structures in the bank. The sheer size of mass financing of consumer loans certainly results in less influence for the loan officer, rather, they rely on correct procedures to check the automated rating proposal and the input provided by the sales officer. We discuss three important aspects accordingly:

- *The loan officer's powers*: Any manual modification of the automated rating proposal should be contained within a controlled and well-documented framework. The loan officer's discretion should be set within clearly defined limits which specify at least the conditions permitting a deviation from the automated rating proposal and the information that the loan officer used additionally. One way to look at discretion is the use of a deviation matrix of final and suggested ratings, showing for each rating category, how many suggested ratings (generated by the quantitative rating tool) are changed by manual override: more specifically, the share M_{ij} of borrowers assigned by the quantitative system to the i-th category which loan officers finally place in category j. In a well-defined, practicable rating system, a high match between suggested ratings and final ratings should be expected in most cases, so in each line the values of M_{ii} should be the largest and M_{ij} should decrease the more the final ratings diverge from the suggestions. Clearly, greater deviations should lead to careful analysis of the shortcomings of the rating model, either indicating data issues or problems with the model itself.

- *Monitoring the ratings over time*: Any rating system must ideally be monitored continuously and be able to process incoming information swiftly; however, ratings must be updated at least annually. This does also apply for consumer loans. However, the focus is on ensuring that loans and borrowers are still assigned to the correct pool, i.e. still exhibiting the loss characteristics and the delinquency status of the previously assigned pool. As such, different methodologies may be used, for example by using an account-specific behavioural score. For wholesale loans, it may be helpful to analyse the frequency distribution of the time-span between two successive ratings of all borrowers in a specific portfolio. The expected pattern is shown in Figure 3: most borrowers are reevaluated at regular intervals, roughly once every 12 months, but in between, "ad hoc ratings" are based on information deemed to be important and their frequency increases with the amount of time that has elapsed since the first rating. Between the two regular re-ratings, a whole group of the same type of borrowers (e.g. enterprises in one sector) may occasionally be re-rated because in-

---

[10] The normal transformation of qualitative information like family status, gender, etc into numerical variables for the assessment of consumer loans would not replace such a qualitative oversight.

formation relevant to the rating of this group has been received. It should be possible to explain any divergent behaviour which, in any case, provides insights into the quality of the rating process.

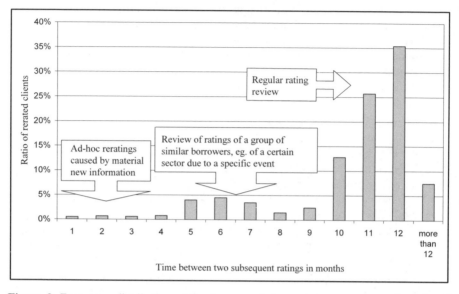

Figure 3. Frequency distribution of the time-span between two successive ratings for all borrowers in one portfolio

- *Feedback mechanisms of the rating process*: A rating system must take account of both the justified interests of the user – i.e. the loan officer – whose interest is driven by having a rating process which is lean, easy to use, comprehensible and efficient. On the other hand, the model developer is interested in a rating model which is theoretically demanding and as comprehensive as possible. Where interests conflict, these will need to be reconciled. It is all the more important that a rating system is checked whilst in operational mode, to ascertain whether the model which the process is based on is appropriate and sufficiently understood by the users. In any case, procedures must be implemented according to which a new version – or at least a new parameterisation — of the rating model is carried out.

2.2. Result-based Validation

In 1996, the publication of capital requirements for market risk for a bank's trading book positions as an amendment to the 1988 Basel Accord, was the first time that a bank's internal methodology could be used for purposes of regulatory capital. The output of bank internal models, the so-called Value-at-Risk (VaR) which is the most popular risk measure in market risk, is translated into a minimum capital requirement, i.e. three times VaR. The supervisory challenge for most countries, certainly Germany, was to establish an appropriate supervisory strategy to finally permit these bank internal models for calculating regulatory capital. In addition to the supervisory assessment of the qualitative market risk environment in a bank, another crucial element of the strategy was the implementation of an efficient "top-down" monitoring approach for banks and banking supervisors. The relatively simple comparison between ex-ante estimation of VaR and ex-post realisation of the "clean" P&L[11] of a trading book position, excluding extraneous factors such as interest payments, was the foundation for the quantitative appraisal.

The concept for backtesting in the IRBA as introduced in paragraph 501 of the New Framework is relatively similar. In the IRB approach, according to market risk, the probability of default (PD) per rating category or, in special cases, the expected loss (EL) in the case of consumer loans, must be compared with the realised default rate or losses that have occurred.

Despite the basic features common to market risk and credit risk, there are also important differences, most importantly the following two. First, the conceptual nature is different; in market risk the forecasted VaR is a percentile of the "clean" P&L distribution. This distribution can be generated from the directly observable profit and losses, and thus the VaR can be directly observed. By contrast, in credit risk only realised defaults (and losses) according to a specific definition can be observed directly instead of the forecasted PD (and EL).

A common and widespread approach for credit risk is the application of the law of large numbers and to infer from the observed default rate, the probability of default.[12] To our knowledge, almost all backtesting techniques for PD (or EL) rely on this statistical concept. However, a proper application requires that borrowers are grouped into grades exhibiting similar default risk characteristics.[13] This is necessary even in the case of direct estimates of PD, when each borrower is assigned an individual PD.

---

[11] There are different interpretations among different supervisors on this issue.

[12] Beside the fact, that an application of the law of large numbers would require that defaults are uncorrelated, there is another subtle violation in the prerequisites for applying the law of large numbers. It is required that the defaults stem from the same distribution. This requirement cannot be seen to be fulfilled for different borrowers. To give a picture: The difference for the task of determining the probability of throwing a six is like approximating this probability either by throwing the same dice 1,000 times and calculating the ratio of sixes to the total number of throws or throwing 1,000 dices once and calculating the ratio of sixes to the number of dices thrown.

[13] We believe that validation of rating systems, i.e. the calibration of PDs is almost impossible without the grouping of borrowers to grades with the same risk profile; which is also one of the key requirements of Basel II.

The second main difference relates to the available data history on which the comparison is based. In market risk, the frequency is at least 250 times a year in the case of daily data. By contrast, in credit risk there is only one data point per annum to be assumed. To make it more complex, there is an additional problem arising from measuring credit default, which is the key variable for the quantification and therefore the validation. The definition of credit default is largely subjective. The New Framework suggests retaining this subjective element as the basis of the IRB approach, albeit with a forward-looking focus and a back-stop ratio of 90 days past due. This may be justified, not least by the fact that a significant number of defaulted borrowers seem to have a considerable influence on the timing of the credit default.

Correspondingly, the criteria and – more importantly – the applied methodology are also different. In market risk, the challenge is to provide a clean P&L and to store the corresponding data. This differs significantly from the necessary compilation of the rating history and credit defaults over time. Depending on the required reproducibility of the results, considerable time and effort may be needed and it is difficult to estimate what requirement is most important for what area, thus entailing higher costs for the bank. Owing to the volume of available data points in market risk, the simplicity and multiplicity of the applicable methods are impressive. This naturally poses an apparently insuperable challenge for credit risk.

A further problem is the impact of a rating philosophy on backtesting. The rating philosophy is what is commonly referred to as either Point-in-Time (PIT) or Through-the-Cycle (TTC) ratings. PIT-ratings measure credit risk given the current state of a borrower in its current economic environment, whereas TTC-ratings measure credit risk taking into account the (assumed) state of the borrower over a "full" economic cycle. PIT and TTC mark the ends of the spectrum of possible rating systems. In practice, neither pure TTC nor pure PIT systems will be found, but hybrid systems, which are rather PIT or rather TTC. Agency ratings are assumed to be TTC, whereas bank internal systems – at least in most cases in Germany – are looked at as PIT.

The rating philosophy has an important impact on backtesting. In theory, for TTC systems borrower ratings, i.e. its rating grade, are stable over time, reflecting the long-term full cycle assessment. However, the observed default rates for the individual grades are expected to vary over time in accordance with the change in the economic environment. The contrary is the case for PIT systems. By more quickly reacting to changing economic conditions, borrower ratings tend to migrate through the rating grades over the cycle, whereas the PD for each grade is expected to be more stable over time, i.e. the PD is more independent from the current economic environment. The Basel Committee did not favour a special rating philosophy. Both PIT systems as well as TTC systems are fit for the IRBA. However, it seems to be reasonable to look at risk parameters as a forecast for their realisations which can be observed within a one year time horizon. This reasoning is reflected in the first validation principle of the AIGV, where a forward looking element is required to be included in the estimation of Basel's risk parameters.

In the special case of consumer loans, the estimation and validation of key parameters is extremely dependent on the approach taken by a bank. A similar rating system as used for wholesale borrowers, leads to an analogous assessment for purposes of validation. In contrast, instead of rating each borrower separately, the BCBS clusters loans in homogenous portfolios during the segmentation process (see above). This segmentation process should include assessing borrower and transaction risk characteristics like product type etc., as well as identifying the different delinquency stages (30 days, 60 days, 90 days etc.). Subsequently, the risk assessment on a (sub-) portfolio level could be based on its roll rates, transaction moving from one delinquency stage to another.

The implications of these rather general considerations and possible solutions for the problems raised here are discussed in detail in Chapter VIII.

2.3. Process-based Validation

Validating rating processes includes analysing the extent to which an internal rating system is used in daily banking business. The use test and associated risk estimates is one of the key requirements in the BCBS' final framework. There are two different levels of validation. Firstly, the plausibility of the actual rating in itself, and secondly, the integration of ratings output in the operational procedure and interaction with other processes:

- *Understanding the rating system*: It is fundamental to both types of analysis that employees understand whichever rating methodology is used. The learning process should not be restricted to loan officers. As mentioned above, it should also include those employees who are involved in the rating process. In-house training courses and other training measures are required to ensure that the process operates properly.
- *Importance for management*: Adequate corporate governance is crucial for banks. In the case of a rating system, this requires the responsibility of executive management and to a certain extent the supervisory board, for authorising the rating methods and their implementation in the bank's day-to-day business. We would expect different rating methods to be used depending on the size of the borrower[14], and taking account of the borrowers' different risk content and the relevance of the incoming information following the decision by senior management.

---

[14] In the Basel Committee's new proposals in respect of the IRB approach, small enterprises may, for regulatory purposes, be treated as retail customers and, unlike large corporate customers, small and medium-sized enterprises are given a reduced risk weighting in line with their turnover.

- *Internal monitoring processes*: The monitoring process must cover at least the extent and the type of rating system used. In particular, it should be possible to rate all borrowers in the system, with the final rating allocated before credit is granted. If the rating is given after credit has been granted, this raises doubts about the usefulness of internal rating. The same applies to a rating which is not subject to a regular check. There should be a check at least annually and whenever new information about the debtor is received which casts doubt on their ability to clear their debts. The stability of the rating method over time, balanced with the need to update the method as appropriate, is a key part of the validation. To do this, it is necessary to show that objective criteria are incorporated so as to lay down the conditions for a re-estimation of the quantitative rating model or to determine whether a new rating model should be established.
- *Integration in the bank's financial management structure*: Unless rational credit risk is recorded for each borrower, it is impossible to perform the proper margin calculation taking into account standard risk costs. If this is to be part of bank management by its decision-making and supervisory bodies, a relationship must be determined between the individual rating categories and the standard risk costs. However, it must be borne in mind that the probability of default is simply a component of the calculation of the standard risk costs and, similarly to the credit risk models, other risk parameters, such as the rate of debt collection and the size of the exposure in the event of a credit default, the maturity of the loan, transfer risk and concentration risks should also be recorded. Ultimately the gross margin, which approximates to the difference between lending rates and refinancing costs, can act as a yardstick for including the standard risk costs. In order to determine the concentration risks at portfolio level more appropriately, it seems essential to use credit risk models and thus to be in a position to allocate venture capital costs appropriately. Therefore, if net commission income is added to the gross margin, the operational costs netted out, and also the venture capital costs taken into account, it is possible to calculate the result of lending business. It is naturally advisable to include as part of the management of the bank, all other conventional instruments of credit risk measurement, such as employee bonus systems, portfolio optimisation.

In principle, the Basel Committee requires these mainly portfolio-based methods in the second pillar of the new Accord as part of the self-assessment of capital adequacy required of the banks in the Capital Adequacy Assessment Process (CAAP). This frequently leads to problems when integrating banks' own rating systems into credit risk models purchased from specialist providers. In our view, this may ultimately increase the complexity for banks and banking supervisors and at the same time entail considerable competitive distortions if the rating is less objective.

3. Concluding Remarks

To set up and to validate bank-internal rating systems is a challenging task and requires a considerable degree of sensitivity (Neale, 2001). Our analysis started with the comparatively more difficult data situation and the availability of public and private information in order to quantify credit risk of banks' borrowers in a structured way including its subsequent validation. The advantage of the structured credit risk assessment, when applying an automated rating process, is its objectivity. This is true for the rating method and for the selection of the risk factors in the rating model, including their effectiveness in generating a rating proposal. The final integration of the qualitative credit assessment, based on a subjective decision by the loan officer, is more difficult in the structured assessment.

The final rating outcome comprises an array of individual observations, which may provide very different results. Ultimately, our suggested approach to validation takes this complexity into account by highlighting the importance of the rating process. This interdependence is reflected in the ongoing cycle of setting up and monitoring the rating system. Individual observations during the monitoring process are frequently integrated quickly into a revision of the methodological process.

The validation method is analogous to a jigsaw puzzle. Only if the many individual pieces are being assembled properly, will the desired result be achieved. The individual pieces of the puzzle seem unimpressive and often unattractive at first, but they eventually contribute to the ultimate picture. This may, for example, be an appropriate description when setting up the system and conducting ongoing checks on the quality of the data management or the ongoing adjustment of banks' internal credit standards. Each piece of the puzzle is crucial, to both component-based and process-based validation. One crucially important piece is the process-based component. All conventional methods of quantitative validation should encompass the assessment of the rating tool's economic meaningfulness as well as its compliance with statistical standards.

Transparency and comprehensibility of the chosen methods at each stage of development, as well as its plausibility, are fundamental requirements of a sound rating system. The advantage of using empirical statistical approaches is that these models are comprehensible and that defects or statistical shortcomings can be detected by simple statistical tests. By contrast, rule-based systems and applied economic models are more heavily model-dependent and therefore point to model risk. In the case of benchmarking methods; however, the choice of the peer group with known risk content is decisive, although the instability of such models, in particular, can be a problem. Despite the differences, most applied methods can fulfil all requirements initially, albeit to a differing degree.

The broad use and the interplay of different quantitative plausibility and validation methods is the basis of a quantitative analysis of the methods used. Backtesting using a simple retrospective comparison of estimated default probabilities with actual default rates is crucial, and therefore a decisive element in the validation of the results.[15] Complementary methods are also needed, particularly in the development stage of rating models, in order to ensure the plausibility of the selected methods. These include techniques which underscore the stability and accuracy of the methods, although caution is required with regard to quantification and especially with regard to methods used to measure accuracy.

The validation of internal rating systems underscores the importance of using a formalised process when devising them and in their daily application. This covers both the formalised keying in of data and the criteria for subjectively "overruling" the rating proposal. Unless internal ratings are used on a regular basis and in a structured manner over time, banks and banking supervisors by referring to the "use-test" will find difficulties in accepting such a rating system.

References

Basel Committee on Banking Supervision (2005), International Convergence of Capital Measurement and Capital Standards: A Revised Framework, BIS, Updated November 2005. http://www.bis.org/publ/bcbs107.htm

Basel Committee on Banking Supervision (2005a), Validation, Newsletter No. 4. www.bis.org/publ/bcbs_nl4.htm

Basel Committee on Banking Supervision (2005b), Validation of Low Default Portfolios, Newsletter No. 6. www.bis.org/publ/bcbs_nl4.htm

Basel Committee on Banking Supervision (2005c), The Application of Basel II to Trading Activities and the Treatment of Double Default Effects. http://www.bis.org/publ/bcbs116.htm

Basel Committee on Banking Supervision (1988): International Convergence of Capital Measurement and Capital Standards. http://www.bis.org/publ/bcbs04a.htm

Crosbie PJ, Bohn JR: Modelling Default Risk, KMV LLC 2001. http://www.kmv.com/ insight/index.html

Deutsche Bundesbank (2003): The new "Minimum requirements for the credit business of credit institutions" and Basel II, Monthly Report, January 2003, 45–58.

Falkenstein E, Boral A, Carty LV (2000), RiskCalc™ for Private Companies: Moody's Default Model, Moody's Investor Service May 2000. http://www.moodys.com/cust/research/venus/Publication/Rating%20Methodology/noncategorized_number/56402.pdf

Fritz S, Popken L, Wagner C (2002), Scoring and validating Techniques for Credit Risk Rating Systems, in "Credit Ratings", Risk books, London.

Koyluoglu, U, Hickman A (1998), Reconcilable Differences, Risk Magazine, October, pp. 56-62.

Neale C (2001), The Truth and the Proof, Risk Magazine, March, pp 18-19.

Wilde T (2001), IRB Approach Explained, Risk Magazine, May, pp. 87-90.

---

[15] We thus concur with the Basel Committee on Banking Supervision.

XII. Measures of a Rating's Discriminative Power – Applications and Limitations

Bernd Engelmann

Quanteam AG

1. Introduction

A key attribute of a rating system is its discriminative power, i.e. its ability to separate good credit quality from bad credit quality. Similar problems arise in other scientific disciplines. In medicine, the quality of a diagnostic test is mainly determined by its ability to distinguish between ill and healthy persons. Analogous applications exist in biology, information technology, and engineering sciences. The development of measures of discriminative power dates back to the early 1950's. An interesting overview is given in Swets (1988).

Many of the concepts developed in other scientific disciplines in different contexts can be transferred to the problem of measuring the discriminative power of a rating system. Most of the concepts presented in this article were developed in medical statistics. We will show how to apply them in a ratings context.

Throughout the article, we will demonstrate the application of all concepts on two prototype rating systems which are developed from the same data base. We consider only rating systems which distribute debtors in separate rating categories, i.e. the rating system assigns one out of a finite number of rating scores to a debtor. For both rating systems, we assume that the total portfolio consists of 1000 debtors, where 50 debtors defaulted and 950 debtors survived. Both rating systems assign five rating scores 1, 2, 3, 4, and 5 to debtors where 1 stands for the worst credit quality and 5 for the best. Table 1 summarizes the rating scores that were assigned to the non-defaulting debtors by both rating systems.

Table 1 tells us precisely the distribution of the non-defaulting debtors on the two rating systems. For example, we can read from Table 1 that there are 40 non-defaulting debtors who were assigned into rating category 4 by Rating 1 while they were assigned into rating category 5 by Rating 2. The other numbers are interpreted analogously. The distribution of the defaulting debtors on the two rating systems is given in Table 2. Both tables provide all information needed to apply the concepts that will be introduced in the subsequent sections of this article.

Table 1. Distribution of the non-defaulting debtors in Rating 1 and Rating 2

		Rating 1					
		1	2	3	4	5	Total
	1	90	60	15	10	5	180
	2	45	90	30	20	15	200
Rating	3	10	35	100	45	20	210
2	4	5	10	30	100	70	215
	5	0	5	10	40	90	145
	Total	150	200	185	215	200	

Table 2. Distribution of the defaulting debtors in Rating 1 and Rating 2

		Rating 1					
		1	2	3	4	5	Total
	1	20	5	0	3	0	28
	2	4	7	0	0	0	11
Rating	3	3	0	2	0	0	5
2	4	0	0	0	2	2	4
	5	0	2	0	0	0	2
	Total	27	14	2	5	2	

We introduce the notation we will use throughout this article. We assume a rating system which consists of discrete rating categories. The rating categories[1] are denoted with $R_1, ..., R_k$ where we assume that the rating categories are sorted in increasing credit quality, i.e. the debtors with worst credit quality are assigned to R_1 while the debtors with the best credit quality are assigned to R_k. In our example in Table 1 and Table 2 we have $k=5$ and $R_1=1, ..., R_5=5$. We denote the set of defaulting debtors with D, the set of non-defaulting debtors with ND, and the set of all debtors with T. The number of debtors in the rating category R_i is denoted with $N(i)$ where the subscript refers to the group of debtors. If we discuss a specific rating we make this clear by an additional argument. e.g. for Rating 1 the number of defaulters in rating category 4 is $N_D(4;1) = 5$, or the total number of debtors in rating category 2 is $N_T(2;1) = 214$. Since the event 'Default' or 'Non-default' of a debtor is random, we have to introduce some random variables. With S we denote random distribution of rating scores while the subscript will indicate the group of debtors the distribution function corresponds to, e.g. S_D denotes the distribution of the rating scores of the defaulting debtors. The empirical distribution of the rating scores, i.e. the distribution of the rating scores that is realised by the observed defaults and non-defaults is denoted by $\hat{S}$, where the subscript again refers to the group of debtors. For example, for Rating 1

---

[1] The terminology rating category or rating score is used interchangeably throughout this chapter.

$$\hat{S}_D(3;1) = 2/50 = 0.04,$$

$$\hat{S}_{ND}(2;1) = 200/950 = 0.21,$$

$$\hat{S}_T(5;1) = 202/1000 = 0.20.$$

The cumulative distribution of S is denoted with C, i.e. $C(R_i)$ is the probability that a debtor has a rating score lower than or equal to R_i. The specific group of debtors the distribution function is referring to is given by the corresponding subscript.

The empirical cumulative distribution function is denoted by $\hat{C}$, e.g. the empirical probability that a non-defaulting debtor's rating score under Rating 2 is lower than or equal to '4' is given by

$$\hat{C}_{ND}(4;2) = (180 + 200 + 210 + 215)/950 = 0.847.$$

Finally, we define the common score distribution of two rating systems Rating 1 and Rating 2 by S^{12}. The expression $S^{12}(R_i, R_j)$ gives the probability that a debtor has rating score R_i under Rating 1 and a rating score R_j under Rating 2. Again the index D, ND, T refers to the set of debtors to which the score distribution corresponds. The cumulative distribution is denoted with C^{12}, i.e. $C^{12}(R_i, R_j)$ gives the probability that a debtor has a rating score less than or equal to R_i under Rating 1 and less than or equal to R_j under Rating 2. Again, examples are given for the corresponding empirical distributions using the data of Table 1:

$$\hat{S}_D^{12}(2,2) = 7/50 = 0.14,$$

$$\hat{S}_{ND}^{12}(2,4) = 10/950 = 0.0105,$$

$$\hat{C}_D^{12}(2,3) = (20 + 5 + 4 + 7 + 3 + 0)/50 = 0.78.$$

Having defined the notation we will use throughout this chapter, we give a short outline. In Section 2 we will define the measures, Cumulative Accuracy Profile (CAP) and Receiver Operating Characteristic (ROC), which are the most popular in practice and show how they are interrelated. In Section 3 we will focus on the statistical properties of the summary measures of the CAP and the ROC. The final section discusses the applicability and the correct interpretation of these measures.

2. Measures of a Rating System's Discriminative Power

We will define the measures of discriminative power that are of interest to us in this section. We will focus on the Cumulative Accuracy Profile (CAP) and the Receiver Operating Characteristic (ROC). These are not the only measures described in the literature but the most important and the most widely applied in practice. Examples of measures that are not treated in this article are entropy measures. We refer the reader to Sobehart et al. (2000) for an introduction to these measures. Besides the basic definitions of the CAP and the ROC and their summary measures, we will show how both concepts are connected and explore some extensions in this section.

2.1. Cumulative Accuracy Profile

The definition of the Cumulative Accuracy Profile (CAP) can be found in Sobehart et al (2000). It plots the empirical cumulative distribution of the defaulting debtors $\hat{C}_D$ against the empirical cumulative distribution of all debtors $\hat{C}_T$. This is illustrated in Figure 1. For a given rating category R_i, the percentage of all debtors with a rating of R_i or worse is determined, i.e. $\hat{C}_T(R_i)$. Next, the percentage of defaulted debtors with a rating score worse than or equal to R_i, i.e. $\hat{C}_D(R_i)$, is computed. This determines the point A in Figure 1. Completing this exercise for all rating categories of a rating system determines the CAP curve. Therefore, every CAP curve must start in the point (0,0) and end in the point (1,1).

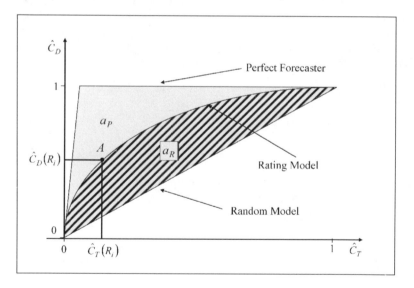

Figure 1. Illustration of Cumulative Accuracy Profiles

There are two special situations which serve as limiting cases. The first is a rating system which does not contain any discriminative power. In this case, the CAP curve is a straight line which halves the quadrant because if the rating system contains no information about a debtor's credit quality it will assign $x\%$ of the defaulters among the $x\%$ of the debtors with the worst rating scores ('Random Model' in Figure 1). The other extreme is a rating system which contains perfect information concerning the credit quality of the debtors. In this case, all defaulting debtors will get a worse rating than the non-defaulting debtors and the resulting CAP curve raises straight to one and stays there ('Perfect Forecaster' in Figure 1).

The information contained in a CAP curve can be summarised into a single number, the Accuracy Ratio (AR) (this number is also known as Gini Coefficient or Power Statistics). It is given by

$$AR = \frac{a_R}{a_P},$$ (1)

where a_R is the area between the CAP curve of the rating model and CAP curve of the random model (grey/black area in Figure 1) and a_P is the area between the CAP curve of the perfect forecaster and the CAP curve of the random model (grey area in Figure 1). The ratio AR can take values between zero and one.[2] The closer AR is to one, i.e. the more the CAP curve is to the upper left, the higher is the discriminative power of a rating model.

We finish this subsection by calculating the CAP curves of Rating 1 and Rating 2. Since both rating systems have five rating categories, we can compute four points of the CAP curve in addition to the points (0,0) and (1,1). To get a real curve, the six points of each CAP curve able to be computed have to be connected by straight lines. We illustrate the procedure with Rating 1. Starting at the left, we have to compute $\hat{C}_T(1;1)$ and $\hat{C}_D(1;1)$, which we get from Table 1 and Table 2 as

$$\hat{C}_T(1;1) = 177/1000 = 0.177,$$

$$\hat{C}_D(1;1) = 27/50 = 0.540.$$

In the next step, we compute $\hat{C}_T(2;1)$ and $\hat{C}_D(2;1)$ which results in

$$\hat{C}_T(2;1) = (177 + 214)/1000 = 0.391,$$

$$\hat{C}_D(2;1) = (27 + 14)/50 = 0.820.$$

The remaining points are computed analogously. The procedure for Rating 2 is similar. The resulting CAP curves are illustrated in Figure 2. We see that the CAP curve of Rating 1 is always higher than the CAP curve of Rating 2, i.e. the discriminative power of Rating 1 is higher. This is also reflected in the AR values of both rating models. For Rating 1, we find an AR of 0.523 while for Rating 2, the AR is calculated as 0.471.

---

[2] In principle, AR could be negative. This would be the case when the ranking of the debtors by the rating system is wrong, i.e. the good debtors are assigned to the rating categories of the poor debtors.

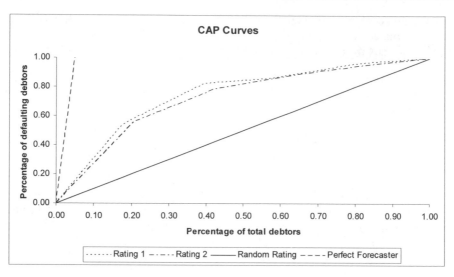

Figure 2. CAP curves for Rating 1 and Rating 2

2.2. Receiver Operating Characteristic

The concept of the Receiver Operating Characteristic (ROC) was developed in signal detection theory, therefore the name. It was introduced to rating systems in Sobehart and Keenan (2001). The concept is illustrated in Figure 3. This figure shows the distributions of the rating scores for defaulting and non-defaulting debtors. It can be seen that the rating system has discriminative power since the rating scores are higher for non-defaulting debtors. A cut-off value V, provides a simple decision rule to classify debtors into potential defaulters and non-defaulters. All debtors with a rating score lower than V are considered as defaulters while all debtors with a rating score higher than V are treated as non-defaulters. Under this decision, rule four scenarios can occur which are summarised in Table 3.

Table 3. Outcomes of the simple classification rule using the cut-off value V

		Default	Non-default
Rating Score	below cut-off value	correct prediction (hit)	wrong prediction (false alarm)
	above cut-off value	wrong prediction (error)	correct prediction (correct rejection)

If a debtor with a rating score below V defaults, the rating system's prediction was correct. We call the fraction of correctly forecasted defaulters the "hit rate". The same is true for non-defaulters with a rating score above V. In this case, a non-defaulter was predicted correctly. If a non-defaulter has a rating score below V, the decision was wrong. The rating system raised a false alarm. The fourth and final case is a defaulter with a rating score above V. In this case the rating system missed a defaulter and made a wrong prediction.

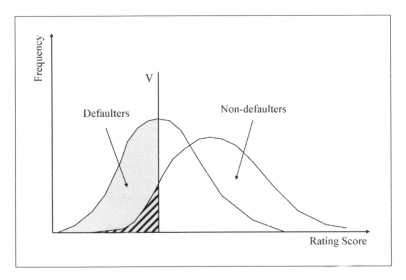

Figure 3. Rating score distributions for defaulting and non-defaulting debtors

For a given cut-off value V, a rating system should have a high hit rate and a low false alarm rate. The Receiver Operating Characteristic curve is given by all pairs (false alarm rate, hit rate), which are computed for every reasonable cut-off value. It is clear that the ROC curve starts in the point $(0,0)$ and ends in the point $(1,1)$. If the cut-off value lies below all feasible rating scores both the hit rate and the false alarm rate is zero. Similarly, if the cut-off value is above all feasible rating scores, the hit rate and the false alarm rate are equal to one. The concept of the ROC curve is illustrated in Figure 4 above.

In our setting, the cut-off points V are defined by the rating categories. Therefore, we get in total k-1 cut-off points. Consider the point B in Figure 4. To compute this point we define the decision rule: *A debtor is classified as a defaulter if he has a rating of R_i or worse, otherwise he is classified as a non-defaulter.* Under this decision rule, the hit rate is given by $\hat{C}_D(R_i)$, which is the fraction of all defaulters with a rating of R_i or worse. Similarly, the false alarm rate is given by $\hat{C}_{ND}(R_i)$, which is the fraction of all non-defaulters with a rating of R_i or worse. The ROC curve is obtained by computing these numbers for all rating categories.

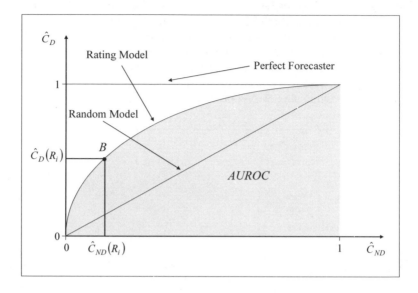

Figure 4. Illustration of Receiver Operating Characteristic curves

Again, we have the two limiting cases of a random model and the perfect fore-caster. In the case of a random model where the rating system contains no dis-criminative power, the hit rate and the false alarm rate are equal regardless of the cut-off point. In the case of the perfect forecaster, the rating scores distributions of the defaulters and the non-defaulters of Figure 3 are separated perfectly. There-fore, for every value of the hit rate less than one the false alarm rate is zero and for every value of the false alarm rate greater than zero, the hit rate is one. The corre-sponding ROC curve connects the three points (0,0), (0,1), and (1,1) by straight lines.

Similar to the CAP curve, where the information of the curve was summarized in the Accuracy Ratio, there is also a summary statistic for the ROC curve. It is the area below the ROC curve (AUROC). This statistic can take values between zero and one, where the AUROC of the random model is 0.5 and the AUROC of the perfect forecaster is 1.0. The closer the value of AUROC is to one, i.e. the more the ROC curve is to the upper left, the higher is the discriminative power of a rat-ing system.[3]

We apply the concept of the ROC curve to the example in Table 1 and Table 2. We proceed in the same way as in the previous subsection, when we computed the CAP curve. Since we have five rating categories, we can define four decision rules

---

[3] A rating system with an AUROC close to zero also has a high discriminative power. In
   this case, the order of good and bad debtors is reversed. The good debtors have low rating scores while the poor debtors have high ratings.

in total which gives us four points in addition to the points (0,0) and (1,1) on the ROC curve. To get a curve, the points have to be connected by straight lines. We compute the second point of the ROC curve for Rating 2 to illustrate the procedure. The remaining points are computed in an analogous way. Consider the decision rule that a debtor is classified as a defaulter if he has a rating of '2' or worse and is classified as a non-defaulter if he has a rating higher than '2'. The corresponding hit rate is computed as

$$\hat{C}_D(2;2) = (28 + 11)/50 = 0.78,$$

while the corresponding false alarm rate is given by

$$\hat{C}_{ND}(2;2) = (180 + 200)/950 = 0.40.$$

The remaining points on the ROC curve of Rating 2 and Rating 1 are computed in a similar fashion. The ROC curves of Rating 1 and Rating 2 are illustrated in Figure 5. Computing the area below the ROC curve, we get a value of 0.762 for Rating 1 and 0.735 for Rating 2.

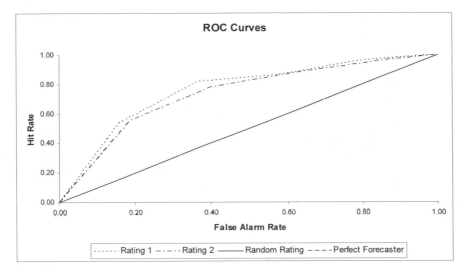

Figure 5. ROC curves for Rating 1 and Rating 2

We finish this subsection by exploring the connection between AR and AUROC. We have seen that the CAP curve and the ROC curve are computed in a similar way. In fact, it can be shown that both concepts are just different ways to represent the same information. In Appendix A, we proof the simple relation between AR and AUROC

$$AR = 2 \cdot AUROC - 1. \tag{2}$$

From a practical perspective, both concepts are equivalent and it is a question of preference as to which one is used to evaluate the discriminative power of a rating system. In Section 3, we will see that AUROC allows for an intuitive probabilistic interpretation which can be used to derive various statistical properties of AUROC. By (2) this interpretation carries over to AR. However, it is less intuitive in this case.

2.3. Extensions

CAP curves and ROC curves only allow a meaningful evaluation of some rating function's ability to discriminate between 'good' and 'bad' if there is a linear relationship between the function's value and the attributes 'good' and 'bad'. This is illustrated in Figure 6. The figure shows a situation where the rating is able to discriminate perfectly between defaulters and non-defaulters. However, the score distribution of the defaulters is bimodal. Defaulters have either very high or very low score values. In practice, when designing corporate ratings, some balance sheet variables like growth in sales have this feature.

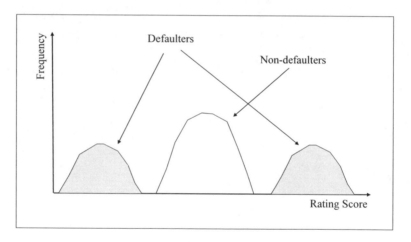

Figure 6. Score distribution of a non-linear rating function

A straight forward application of the ROC concept to this situation results in a misleading value for AUROC. The ROC curve which corresponds to the rating distribution of Figure 6 is shown in Figure 7. It can be seen that the AUROC corresponding to the score distribution in Figure 6 is equal to 0.5. In spite of the rating system's ability to discriminate perfectly between defaulters and non-defaulters, its AUROC is the same as the AUROC of a rating system without any discriminative power. This is due to the non-linearity in the relationship between the rating score and credit quality of the debtors.

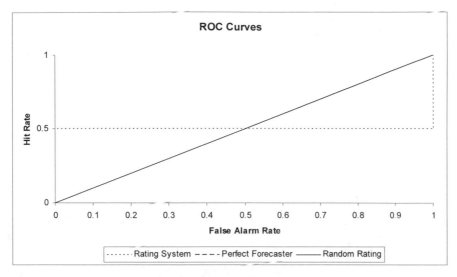

Figure 7. ROC curve corresponding to the score distribution of Figure 6

To obtain meaningful measures of discriminatory power also in this situation, Lee and Hsiao (1996) and Lee (1999) provide several extensions to the AUROC measure we have introduced in Section 2.2. We discuss only one of these extensions, the one which could be most useful in a rating context.

Lee (1999) proposes a simple modification to the ROC concept which delivers meaningful results for score distributions as illustrated in Figure 6. For each rating category the likelihood ratio L is computed as

$$L(R_i) = \frac{S_D(R_i)}{S_{ND}(R_i)}. \tag{3}$$

The likelihood ratio is the ratio of the probability that a defaulter is assigned to rating category R_i to the corresponding probability for a non-defaulter. To illustrate this concept, we compute the empirical likelihood ratio $\hat{L}$ which is defined as

$$\hat{L}(R_i) = \frac{\hat{S}_D(R_i)}{\hat{S}_{ND}(R_i)} \tag{4}$$

for the rating systems Rating 1 and Rating 2. The results are given in Table 4.

In the next step, the likelihood ratios are sorted from the highest to the least. Finally, the likelihood ratios are inverted to define a new rating score.[4] In doing so,

---

[4] The inversion of the likelihood ratios is not necessary. We are doing this here just for didactical reasons to ensure that low credit quality corresponds to low rating scores throughout this article.

we have defined a new rating score that assigns low score values to low credit quality. The crucial point in this transformation is that we can be sure that after the transformation, low credit quality corresponds to low score values even if the original data looks like the data in Figure 6.

Table 4. Empirical likelihood ratios for Rating 1 and Rating 2

		Rating Category				
		1	2	3	4	5
Rating 1	$\hat{S}_D(R_i;1)$	0.54	0.28	0.04	0.10	0.04
	$\hat{S}_{ND}(R_i;1)$	0.16	0.21	0.19	0.23	0.21
	$\hat{L}(R_i;1)$	3.42	1.33	0.21	0.44	0.19
Rating 2	$\hat{S}_D(R_i;2)$	0.56	0.22	0.10	0.08	0.04
	$\hat{S}_{ND}(R_i;2)$	0.19	0.21	0.22	0.23	0.15
	$\hat{L}(R_i;2)$	2.96	1.05	0.45	0.35	0.26

We compute the ROC curves for the new rating score. They are given in Figure 8.

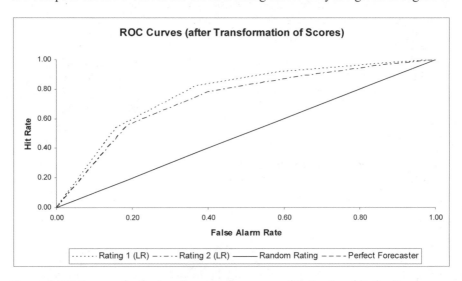

Figure 8. ROC curves for the transformed rating scores of Rating 1 and Rating 2

Note that there is no difference to the previous ROC curve for Rating 2 because the sorting of the likelihood ratios did not change the order of the rating scores. However, there is a difference for Rating 1. The AUROC of Rating 1 has increased slightly from 0.7616 to 0.7721. Furthermore, the ROC curve of Rating 1 is concave everywhere after the transformation. As pointed out by Tasche (2002), the non-concavity of a ROC curve is a clear sign that the rating model does not reflect the information contained in the data in an optimal way. With this simple transformation, the quality of the rating model can be improved.

A practical problem in the construction of rating models is the inclusion of variables that are non-linear in the credit quality of debtors (e.g. Figure 6). As pointed out in Hayden (2006) in this book, these variables can offer a valuable contribution to a rating model provided that they are transformed prior to the estimation of the rating model. There are several ways to conduct this transformation. Computing likelihood ratios and sorting them as was done here is a feasible way of producing linear variables from non-linear ones. For further details and an example with real data, refer to Engelmann et al. (2003b).

3. Statistical Properties of AUROC

In this section we will discuss the statistical properties of AUROC. We focus on AUROC because it can be interpreted intuitively in terms of a probability. Starting from this interpretation we can derive several useful expressions which allow the computation of confidence intervals for AUOC, a rigorous test if a rating model has any discriminative power at all, and a test for the difference of two rating systems' AUROC. All results that are derived in this section carry over to AR by applying the simple relation (2) between AR and AUROC.

3.1. Probabilistic Interpretation of AUROC

The cumulative distribution function of a random variable evaluated at some value x, gives the probability that this random variable takes a value which is less than or equal to x. In our notation, this reads as

$$C_D(R_i) = P(S_D \leq R_i),$$
$$C_{ND}(R_i) = P(S_{ND} \leq R_i),$$

(5)

or in terms of the empirical distribution function

$$\hat{C}_D(R_i) = P(\hat{S}_D \leq R_i),$$
$$\hat{C}_{ND}(R_i) = P(\hat{S}_{ND} \leq R_i),$$

(6)

where $P(.)$ denotes the probability of the event in brackets $(.)$.

In Appendix B, we show that AUROC can be expressed in terms of empirical probabilities as

$$AUROC = P\left(\hat{S}_D < \hat{S}_{ND}\right) + \frac{1}{2}P\left(\hat{S}_D = \hat{S}_{ND}\right). \tag{7}$$

To get further insight, we introduce the Mann-Whitney statistic U as

$$U = \frac{1}{N_D \cdot N_{ND}} \sum_{(D,ND)} u_{D,ND},$$

$$u_{D,ND} = \begin{cases} 1, & \text{falls } \hat{s}_D < \hat{s}_{ND} \\ \frac{1}{2}, & \text{falls } \hat{s}_D = \hat{s}_{ND} \\ 0, & \text{falls } \hat{s}_D > \hat{s}_{ND} \end{cases} \tag{8}$$

where $\hat{s}_D$ is a realisation of the empirical score distribution $\hat{S}_D$ and $\hat{s}_{ND}$ is a realisation of $\hat{S}_{ND}$. The sum in (8) is over all possible pairs of a defaulter and a non-defaulter. It is easy to see that

$$U = P\left(\hat{S}_D < \hat{S}_{ND}\right) + \frac{1}{2}P\left(\hat{S}_D = \hat{S}_{ND}\right), \tag{9}$$

what means the area below the ROC curve and the Mann-Whitney statistic are measuring the same quantity.

This gives us a very intuitive interpretation of AUROC. Suppose we draw randomly one defaulter out of the sample of defaulters and one non-defaulter out of the sample of non-defaulters. Suppose further we should decide from the rating scores of both debtors which one is the defaulter. If the rating scores are different, we would guess that the debtor with the lower rating score is the defaulter. If both scores are equal we would toss a coin. The probability that we make a correct decision is given by the right-hand-side of (9), i.e. by the area below the ROC curve.

Throughout this article, we have introduced all concepts and quantities with the data set given in Tables 1 and 2. However, the data set of Tables 1 and 2 is only one particular realisation of defaults and non-defaults from the underlying score distributions which are unknown. It is not the only possible realisation. In principle, other realisations of defaults could occur which lead to different values for AUROC and U. These different possible values are dispersed about the expected values of AUROC and U that are given by

$$E[AUROC] = E[U] = P\left(S_D < S_{ND}\right) + \frac{1}{2}P\left(S_D = S_{ND}\right). \tag{10}$$

To get a feeling of how far the realised value of AUROC deviates from its expected value, confidence intervals have to be computed. This is done in the next subsection.

Finally, we remark that the AR measure can also be expressed in terms of probabilities. Applying (2) we find

$$E[AR] = P(S_D < S_{ND}) - P(S_D > S_{ND}).$$ (11)

The expected value of AR is the difference between the probability that a defaulter has a lower rating score than a non-defaulter and the probability that a defaulter has a higher rating score than a non-defaulter. It is not so clear how to give an intuitive interpretation of this expression.

3.2. Computing Confidence Intervals for AUROC

To get a feeling for the accuracy of a measure obtained from a data sample, it is customary to state confidence intervals to a confidence level α, e.g. $\alpha = 95\%$. In the first papers regarding measuring the discriminative power of rating systems, confidence intervals were always computed by bootstrapping.[5] These papers mainly used the measure AR. Bootstrapping requires the drawing of lots of portfolios with replacement from the original portfolio. For each portfolio, the AR has to be computed. From the resulting distribution of the AR values, confidence intervals can be computed. The main drawback of this method is its computational inefficiency.

A more efficient method is based on the application of well-known properties of the Mann-Whitney statistic introduced in (8). The connection between AR and a slightly modified Mann-Whitney statistic is less obvious[6] than for AUROC which might be the reason for the inefficient techniques that were used in those early papers.

From mathematical statistics it is known that an unbiased estimator of the variance σ_U^2 of the Mann-Whitney statistic U in (8) is given by

$$\hat{\sigma}_U^2 = \frac{1}{4 \cdot (N_D - 1) \cdot (N_{ND} - 1)} \cdot \left(\hat{P}_{D \neq ND} + (N_D - 1) \cdot \hat{P}_{D,D,ND} \right.$$
$$\left. + (N_{ND} - 1) \cdot \hat{P}_{ND,ND,D} - 4 \cdot (N_D + N_{ND} - 1) \cdot (U - 0.5)^2 \right)$$ (12)

where $\hat{P}_{D \neq ND}$, $\hat{P}_{D,D,ND}$, and $\hat{P}_{ND,ND,D}$ are estimators for the probabilities $P(S_D \neq S_{ND})$, $P_{D,D,ND}$, and $P_{ND,ND,D}$ where the latter two are defined as

---

[5] Efron and Tibshirani (1998) is a standard reference for this technique.

[6] In (8) the ½ has to be replaced by 0, and the 0 has to be replaced by -1 to get the corresponding Mann-Whitney statistic for the AR.

$$P_{D,D,ND} = P\left(S_{D,1}, S_{D,2} < S_{ND}\right) + P\left(S_{D,1} < S_{ND} < S_{D,2}\right)$$
$$- P\left(S_{D,2} < S_{ND} < S_{D,1}\right) + P\left(S_{ND} < S_{D,1}, S_{D,2}\right),$$
$$P_{ND,ND,D} = P\left(S_{ND,1}, S_{ND,2} < S_D\right) - P\left(S_{ND,1} < S_D < S_{ND,2}\right) \tag{13}$$
$$- P\left(S_{ND,2} < S_D < S_{ND,1}\right) + P\left(S_D < S_{ND,1}, S_{ND,2}\right),$$

where $S_{D,1}$ and $S_{D,2}$ are two independent draws of the defaulter's score distribution and $S_{ND,1}$ and $S_{ND,2}$ are two independent draws of the non-defaulter's score distribution.

Using (12) confidence intervals can be easily computed using the asymptotic relationship

$$\frac{AUROC - E[AUROC]}{\hat{\sigma}_U} \xrightarrow{N_D, N_{ND} \to \infty} N(0,1). \tag{14}$$

The corresponding confidence intervals to the level α are given by

$$\left[AUROC - \hat{\sigma}_U \Phi^{-1}\left(\frac{1+\alpha}{2}\right), AUROC + \hat{\sigma}_U \Phi^{-1}\left(\frac{1+\alpha}{2}\right) \right], \tag{15}$$

where Φ denotes the cumulative distribution function of the standard normal distribution.

The asymptotic relation (14) is valid for large number N_D and N_{ND}. The question arises how many defaults a portfolio must contain to make the asymptotic valid. In Engelmann et al. (2003a, 2003b) a comparison between (14) and bootstrapping is carried out. It is shown that for 50 defaults a very good agreement between (14) and bootstrapping is achieved. But even for small numbers like 10 or 20 reasonable approximations for the bootstrapping results are obtained.

We finish this subsection by computing the 95% confidence interval for the AUROC of our examples Rating 1 and Rating 2. We start with Rating 1. First we compute $\hat{P}_{D \neq ND}$. It is given by the fraction of all pairs of a defaulter and a non-defaulter with different rating scores. It is computed explicitly as

$$\hat{P}_{D \neq ND} = 1 - \hat{P}_{D=ND} = 1 - \left(\sum_{i=1}^{5} \hat{S}_D(i;1) \cdot \hat{S}_{ND}(i;1)\right) / (N_D \cdot N_{ND})$$

$$= 1 - (2 \cdot 200 + 5 \cdot 215 + 2 \cdot 185 + 14 \cdot 200 + 27 \cdot 150) / (50 \cdot 950) = 0.817$$

The estimators for $P_{D,D,ND}$ and $P_{ND,ND,D}$ are more difficult to compute than for $P_{D \neq ND}$. To estimate $P_{D,D,ND}$ it is necessary to estimate three probabilities, $P(S_{D,1}, S_{D,2} < S_{ND})$, $P(S_{D,1} < S_{ND} <, S_{D,2})$ (which is equal to $P(S_{D,2} < S_{ND} <, S_{D,1})$), and $P(S_{ND} < S_{D,1}, S_{D,2})$. We illustrate the procedure for $P(S_{D,1}, S_{D,2} < S_{ND})$. The other probabilities are computed analogously.

A naïve way to compute $P(S_{D,1}, S_{D,2} < S_{ND})$ is to implement a triple loop, two loops over all defaulters and one loop over all non-defaulters. For each triple, one has to check if the scores of both defaulters are less than the score of the non-defaulter. The probability $P(S_{D,1}, S_{D,2} < S_{ND})$ is then estimated as the number of triples where this condition is fulfilled by the total number of all triples. However, this procedure is very time consuming when the number of non-defaulters is large. It is much more efficient to exploit the sorting of the debtors in their score values. We get the results

$$P(\hat{S}_{D,1}, \hat{S}_{D,2} < \hat{S}_{ND}) = \sum_{i=2}^{5} \hat{C}_D^2(i-1) \cdot \hat{S}_{ND}(i),$$

$$P(\hat{S}_{D,1} < \hat{S}_{ND} < \hat{S}_{D,2}) = \sum_{i=1}^{5} \hat{C}_D(i-1) \cdot \hat{S}_{ND}(i) \cdot \hat{C}_D(i+1),$$

$$P(\hat{S}_{ND} < \hat{S}_{D,1}, \hat{S}_{D,2}) = \sum_{i=1}^{4} \hat{S}_{ND}(i) \cdot \hat{C}_D^2(i+1).$$

Similar estimation formulas can be derived for $P(S_{ND,1}, S_{ND,2} < S_D)$, $P(S_{ND,1} < S_D < S_{ND,2})$, and $P(S_D < S_{ND,1}, S_{ND,2})$. Applying these formulas to the rating system Rating 1 we get

$$P(\hat{S}_{D,1}, \hat{S}_{D,2} < \hat{S}_{ND}; 1) = 0.554, \quad P(\hat{S}_{D,1} < \hat{S}_{ND} < \hat{S}_{D,2}; 1) = 0.051,$$

$$P(\hat{S}_{ND} < \hat{S}_{D,1}, \hat{S}_{D,2}; 1) = 0.044, \quad \hat{P}_{D,D,ND} = 0.497,$$

$$P(\hat{S}_{ND,1}, \hat{S}_{ND,2} < \hat{S}_D; 1) = 0.069, \quad P(\hat{S}_{ND,1} < \hat{S}_D < \hat{S}_{ND,2}; 1) = 0.046,$$

$$P(\hat{S}_D < \hat{S}_{ND,1}, \hat{S}_{ND,2}; 1) = 0.507, \quad \hat{P}_{ND,ND,D} = 0.483.$$

Finally, we have all ingredients for (12) and compute the variance of U as $\hat{\sigma}_U^2 = 0.001131$. Finally we compute the confidence interval to the level 95% which results in $[0.69573, 0.82754]$. A similar calculation for Rating 2 leads to a 95% confidence interval of $[0.66643, 0.80431]$. We see that both confidence intervals are rather broad. This is due to the relatively low number of debtors in our example rating systems.

3.3. Testing for Discriminative Power

The 95% confidence intervals of the AUROC of Rating 1 and Rating 2 are far away from the value 0.5. This suggests that the discriminative power of both rating systems is statistically significant. To confirm this we apply a rigorous statistical test.

The null hypothesis of our test is that a rating system does not contain any discriminative power. Under this null hypothesis, (12) can be simplified considerably. If a rating system has no discriminative power, the score distributions of the defaulters and the non-defaulters are identical. We get the identity

$$P(S_D \neq S_{ND})/3 = P(S_{D,1}, S_{D,2} < S_{ND}) = P(S_{D,1} < S_{ND} < S_{D,2})$$

$$= P(S_{ND} < S_{D,1}, S_{D,2}) = P(S_{ND,1}, S_{ND,2} < S_D) \qquad (16)$$

$$= P(S_{ND,1} < S_D < S_{ND,2}) = P(S_D < S_{ND,1}, S_{ND,2})$$

This leads to the simplified formula for the variance of the Mann-Whitney statistic

$$\sigma_U^2 = \frac{P(D \neq ND) \cdot (1 + N_D + N_{ND})}{12 \cdot (N_D - 1) \cdot (N_{ND} - 1)} \qquad (17)$$

If we make a two-sided test the p-value of this test given by solving (15) for one minus the confidence level α. This calculation results in

$$\text{p} - \text{value} = 2 - 2 \cdot \Phi\left(\frac{U - 0.5}{\hat{\sigma}}\right). \qquad (18)$$

The application of (18) with the variance of (17) leads to a p-value of $8.23 \cdot 10^{-12}$ for Rating 1. The corresponding value for Rating 2 is $5.36 \cdot 10^{-10}$. This means both rating systems have a highly significant discriminatory power. This confirms our conjecture at the beginning of this subsection.

3.4. Testing for the Difference of two AUROCs

Throughout this article we always considered two rating models, Rating 1 and Rating 2. We have seen so far that Rating 1 has a slightly higher AUROC than Rating 2. The question arises whether this difference is significant from a statistical point of view. To answer this question, we discuss a test on the difference of two AUROCs that was developed by DeLong et al. (1988).

Comparing the confidence intervals of the AUROC of Rating 1 and Rating 2, we find that they overlap widely. Therefore, we would suppose that there is no significant difference between both AUROCs. However, when comparing confidence levels only, we are neglecting correlations between both AUROCs. To carry out a rigorous statistical test, we need in addition to the variances of both AUROCs, the covariance between them.

The estimator for the covariance is more complex than the estimator for the variance. It is given by

$$\hat{\sigma}_{U_1,U_2} = \frac{1}{4 \cdot (N_D - 1) \cdot (N_{ND} - 1)} \Big[\hat{P}^{12}_{D,D,ND,ND} + (N_D - 1) \cdot \hat{P}^{12}_{D,D,ND}$$

$$+ (N_{ND} - 1) \cdot \hat{P}^{12}_{ND,ND,D} - 4 \cdot (N_D + N_{ND} - 1) \cdot (U_1 - 0.5) \cdot (U_2 - 0.5) \Big], \tag{19}$$

where $\hat{P}^{12}_{D,D,ND,ND}$, $\hat{P}^{12}_{D,D,ND}$, and $\hat{P}^{12}_{ND,ND,D}$ are estimators for the probabilities $P^{12}_{D,D,ND,ND}$, $P^{12}_{D,D,ND}$, and $P^{12}_{ND,ND,D}$ which are defined as

$$P^{12}_{D,D,ND,ND} = P\!\left(S^1_D > S^1_{ND}, S^2_D > S^2_{ND}\right) + P\!\left(S^1_D < S^1_{ND}, S^2_D < S^2_{ND}\right)$$

$$- P\!\left(S^1_D > S^1_{ND}, S^2_D < S^2_{ND}\right) - P\!\left(S^1_D < S^1_{ND}, S^2_D > S^2_{ND}\right),$$

$$P^{12}_{D,D,ND} = P\!\left(S^1_{D,1} > S^1_{ND}, S^2_{D,2} > S^2_{ND}\right) + P\!\left(S^1_{D,1} < S^1_{ND}, S^2_{D,2} < S^2_{ND}\right)$$

$$- P\!\left(S^1_{D,1} > S^1_{ND}, S^2_{D,2} < S^2_{ND}\right) - P\!\left(S^1_{D,1} < S^1_{ND}, S^2_{D,2} > S^2_{ND}\right), \tag{20}$$

$$P^{12}_{ND,ND,D} = P\!\left(S^1_D > S^1_{ND,1}, S^2_D > S^2_{ND,2}\right) + P\!\left(S^1_D < S^1_{ND,1}, S^2_D < S^2_{ND,2}\right)$$

$$- P\!\left(S^1_D > S^1_{ND,1}, S^2_D < S^2_{ND,2}\right) - P\!\left(S^1_D < S^1_{ND,1}, S^2_D > S^2_{ND,2}\right),$$

where the quantities S^i_D, $S^i_{D,1}$, $S^i_{D,2}$ are independent draws from the score distribution of the defaulters. The index i indicates whether the score of Rating 1 or of Rating 2 has to be taken for this defaulter. The meaning of S^i_{ND}, $S^i_{ND,1}$, $S^i_{ND,2}$ is analogous for the score distributions of the of non-defaulters under Rating 1 and Rating 2.

Under the null hypothesis that both AUROCs are equal it is shown in DeLong et al. (1988) that the test statistic T which is defined as

$$T = \frac{(U_1 - U_2)^2}{\hat{\sigma}^2_{U_1} + \hat{\sigma}^2_{U_2} - 2\hat{\sigma}_{U_1,U_2}}. \tag{21}$$

is asymptotically χ^2 distributed with one degree of freedom. This asymptotic relationship allows us the computation of critical values given a confidence level α.

We finish this section by computing the p-value of the test for difference of the two AUROCs of Rating 1 and Rating 2. The variances for both AUROC values have already been computed in Section 3.2. It remains to compute the covariance between both AUROCs. We show explicitly how to compute estimators for $P^{12}_{D,D,ND,ND}$, and $P^{12}_{D,D,ND}$. The estimator for $P^{12}_{ND,ND,D}$ is computed in a similar way as for $P^{12}_{D,D,ND}$.

We start with the computation of $\hat{P}^{12}_{D,D,ND,ND}$. To compute this estimator, four probabilities have to be calculated from the sample. Consider the probability $P\left(S^1_D > S^1_{ND}, S^2_D > S^2_{ND}\right)$. A naïve way to calculate this probability would be to implement a loop over all defaulters and a loop over all non-defaulters. This probability is then given by the fraction of all pairs where both Rating 1 and Rating 2 assign a higher rating score to the defaulter. This can be done in a more efficient way by using the sorting of debtors in score values. The four probabilities needed for the computation of $\hat{P}^{12}_{D,D,ND,ND}$ can be calculated by

$$P\left(\hat{S}^1_D > \hat{S}^1_{ND}, \hat{S}^2_D > \hat{S}^2_{ND}\right) = \sum_{i=1}^{5}\sum_{j=1}^{5} \hat{S}^{12}_{ND}(i,j)\cdot \sum_{k=i+1}^{5}\sum_{l=j+1}^{5}\hat{S}^{12}_D(k,l),$$

$$P\left(\hat{S}^1_D < \hat{S}^1_{ND}, \hat{S}^2_D < \hat{S}^2_{ND}\right) = \sum_{i=1}^{5}\sum_{j=1}^{5} \hat{S}^{12}_{ND}(i,j)\cdot \sum_{k=1}^{i-1}\sum_{l=1}^{j-1}\hat{S}^{12}_D(k,l)$$

$$P\left(\hat{S}^1_D > \hat{S}^1_{ND}, \hat{S}^2_D < \hat{S}^2_{ND}\right) = \sum_{i=1}^{5}\sum_{j=1}^{5} \hat{S}^{12}_{ND}(i,j)\cdot \sum_{k=i+1}^{5}\sum_{l=1}^{j-1}\hat{S}^{12}_D(k,l)$$

$$P\left(\hat{S}^1_D < \hat{S}^1_{ND}, \hat{S}^2_D > \hat{S}^2_{ND}\right) = \sum_{i=1}^{5}\sum_{j=1}^{5} \hat{S}^{12}_{ND}(i,j)\cdot \sum_{k=1}^{i-1}\sum_{l=j+1}^{5}\hat{S}^{12}_D(k,l)$$

Evaluating these formulas with the data of Table 1 leads to

$$P\left(\hat{S}^1_D > \hat{S}^1_{ND}, \hat{S}^2_D > \hat{S}^2_{ND}\right) = 0.0747, \quad P\left(\hat{S}^1_D < \hat{S}^1_{ND}, \hat{S}^2_D < \hat{S}^2_{ND}\right) = 0.5314,$$

$$P\left(\hat{S}^1_D > \hat{S}^1_{ND}, \hat{S}^2_D < \hat{S}^2_{ND}\right) = 0.0357, \quad P\left(\hat{S}^1_D < \hat{S}^1_{ND}, \hat{S}^2_D > \hat{S}^2_{ND}\right) = 0.0506,$$

$$\hat{P}^{12}_{D,D,ND,ND} = 0.5197$$

In the next step we consider the estimation of $P^{12}_{D,D,ND}$. Again, four probabilities have to be estimated. A naïve way to estimate for instance, the probability $P\left(S^1_{D,1} > S^1_{ND}, S^2_{D,2} > S^2_{ND}\right)$ is the implementation of a triple loop, two loops over the defaulters and one loop over the non-defaulters. This probability is then estimated as the fraction of all triples where the first defaulter has a higher rating score than the non-defaulter under Rating 1 and the second defaulter has a higher score than the non-defaulter under Rating 2. A more efficient procedure is given by the formulas

$$P\left(\hat{S}^1_{D,1} > \hat{S}^1_{ND}, \hat{S}^2_{D,2} > \hat{S}^2_{ND}\right) = \sum_{i=1}^{5}\sum_{i=1}^{5} \hat{S}^{12}_{ND}(i,j) \cdot \left(1 - \hat{C}_D(i;1)\right) \cdot \left(1 - \hat{C}_D(j;2)\right),$$

$$P\left(\hat{S}^1_{D,1} < \hat{S}^1_{ND}, \hat{S}^2_{D,2} < \hat{S}^2_{ND}\right) = \sum_{i=1}^{5}\sum_{i=1}^{5} \hat{S}^{12}_{ND}(i,j) \cdot \hat{C}_D(i-1;1) \cdot \hat{C}_D(j-1;2),$$

$$P\left(\hat{S}^1_{D,1} > \hat{S}^1_{ND}, \hat{S}^2_{D,2} < \hat{S}^2_{ND}\right) = \sum_{i=1}^{5}\sum_{i=1}^{5} \hat{S}^{12}_{ND}(i,j) \cdot \left(1 - \hat{C}_D(i;1)\right) \cdot \hat{C}_D(j-1;2),$$

$$P\left(\hat{S}^1_{D,1} < \hat{S}^1_{ND}, \hat{S}^2_{D,2} > \hat{S}^2_{ND}\right) = \sum_{i=1}^{5}\sum_{i-1}^{5} \hat{S}^{12}_{ND}(i,j) \cdot \hat{C}_D(i-1;1) \cdot \left(1 - \hat{C}_D(j;2)\right).$$

An application of these formulas to the data of Table 1 leads to

$$P\left(\hat{S}^1_{D,1} > \hat{S}^1_{ND}, \hat{S}^2_{D,2} > \hat{S}^2_{ND}\right) = 0.0389, \quad P\left(\hat{S}^1_{D,1} < \hat{S}^1_{ND}, \hat{S}^2_{D,2} < \hat{S}^2_{ND}\right) = 0.4949,$$

$$P\left(\hat{S}^1_{D,1} > \hat{S}^1_{ND}, \hat{S}^2_{D,2} < \hat{S}^2_{ND}\right) = 0.0620, \quad P\left(\hat{S}^1_{D,1} < \hat{S}^1_{ND}, \hat{S}^2_{D,2} > \hat{S}^2_{ND}\right) = 0.0790,$$

$$\hat{P}^{12}_{D,D,ND} = 0.3930.$$

A similar calculation for $P^{12}_{ND,ND,D}$ leads to $P^{12}_{ND,ND,D} = 0.3534$.

Taking everything together and evaluating (21) leads to $T = 0.57704$. This corresponds to a p-value of 0.4475. This means that the difference in the AUROC values of Rating 1 and Rating 2 is not statistically significant. This result is not surprising given the low number of debtors.

4. Correct Interpretation of AUROC

In this section we want to give some guidelines on how to interpret AUROC values.[7] When discussing rating systems, one is often confronted with the opinion that a good rating system should have some minimum value for the AUROC. Sometimes people are happy that their rating system has a higher AUROC than the rating model of others, or a company wants to achieve an AUROC of $x\%$ during the next five years for its rating systems.

In this section we explain why all these opinions and goals are unreasonable. Consider a hypothetical portfolio with identical debtors only, e.g. a portfolio of companies with identical balance sheets. No rating model has a chance to discriminate anything in this situation because there is nothing to discriminate. This means that the AUROC does not depend on the rating model only, but also the portfolio. This

---

[7] See also Blochwitz et al. (2005)

can be proven formally. Hamerle et al. (2003) show that for a portfolio of N debtors the expected AUROC is given by

$$E(AUROC) = \frac{0.5}{1-PD_P}\left(\frac{2}{N_T^2 \cdot PD_P}\left(1 \cdot PD_1 + 2 \cdot PD_2 + \ldots + N_T PD_{N_T}\right) - PD_P - \frac{1}{N_T}\right) \quad (22)$$

where debtor i has a default probability PD_i and the average default probability of the portfolio is denoted with PD_P. Furthermore, it is assumed that the debtors are sorted from the worst credit quality to the best.

A further example is provided. Consider two rating systems with two rating categories for different portfolios. They are given in Table 5.

Table 5. Two rating systems on different portfolios

		Rating Category	
		1	2
Rating A	Number of Debtors	500	500
	Default Probability	1%	5%
Rating B	Number of Debtors	500	500
	Default Probability	1%	20%

We assume that both rating models are perfect, i.e. they assign the correct default probability to each rating model. Then we find for the expected AUROC values

$$E[AUROC_A] = 0.6718,$$

$$E[AUROC_B] = 0.7527.$$

We see that there is a huge difference in the AUROC values in spite of the fact that both ratings are perfect. This demonstrates that a comparison of AUROC values for different portfolios is meaningless.

The same applies to a comparison of the AUROC on the same portfolio in different time points. Because of changes in the portfolio structure over time, i.e. changes in the default probabilities of the debtors, the rating model is being compared on different portfolios. However, this analysis could be helpful in spite of this. If the AUROC of a rating model worsens over time, one should find out if this is due to changes in the portfolio structure or if the quality of the rating model has indeed deteriorated and a new estimation is necessary.

We conclude that a comparison of the AUROC of two rating models is meaningful only if it is carried out on the same portfolio at the same time. It does not make sense to compare AUROCs over different portfolios or to try to achieve a target AUROC. As demonstrated in the example in Table 5, achieving a higher AUROC could require the inclusion of more poor debtors into the portfolio, a business strategy not every credit institution might want to follow.

References

Blochwitz S, Hamerle A, Hohl S, Rauhmeier R, Rösch D (2005), Myth and Reality of Discriminatory Power for Rating Systems, Wilmott Magazine, January, pp.2-6.

DeLong E, DeLong D, Clarke-Pearson D (1988), Comparing the Areas under Two or More Correlated Receiver Operating Characteristic Curves: A Nonparametric Approach, Biometrics 44, pp. 837-845.

Efron B, Tibshirani RJ (1998), An Introduction to the Bootstrap, Chapman & Hall Boca Raton.

Engelmann B, Hayden E, Tasche D (2003a), Testing Rating Accuracy, Risk 16 (1), pp. 82-86.

Engelmann B, Hayden E, Tasche D (2003b), Measuring the Discriminative Power of Rating Systems, Working Paper. http://www.quanteam.de/papers/Discrimination.pdf

Hamerle A, Rauhmeier R, Rösch D (2003), Uses and Misuses of Measures for Credit Rating Accuracy, Working Paper.

Hayden E (2006), Estimation of a Rating Model for Corporate Exposures, in: Engelmann B, Rauhmeier R (eds.), The Basel II Risk Parameters: Estimation, Validation and Stress Testing, Springer, Berlin Heidelberg New York, pp. 13-26.

Lee, WC, Hsiao, CK (1996), Alternative Summary Indices for the Receiver Operating Characteristic Curve, Epidemiology 7, pp. 605-611.

Lee WC (1999), Probabilistic Analysis of Global Performances of Diagnostic Tests: Interpreting the Lorenz Curve-based Summary Measures, Statistics in Medicine 18, pp. 455-471.

Sobehart JR, Keenan SC (2001), Measuring Default Accurately, Risk, pp. S31-S33.

Sobehart JR, Keenan SC, Stein RM (2000), Benchmarking Quantitative Default Risk Models: A Validation Methodology, Moody's Investors Service.

Swets JA (1988), Measuring the Accuracy of Diagnostic Systems, Science 240, pp. 1285-1293.

Tasche D (2002), Remarks on the Monotonicity of Default Probabilities, Working Paper. http://www-m1.ma.tum.de/m4/pers/tasche/quant.pdf

Appendix A. Proof of (2)

We introduce the shortcut notation $\hat{C}_D^i = \hat{C}_D(R_i)$, $\hat{C}_{ND}^i$ and $\hat{C}_T^i$ have a similar meaning. Furthermore, we denote the sample default probability by $\hat{p}$. Note that $\hat{C}_T^i$ can be written in terms of $\hat{C}_{ND}^i$ and $\hat{C}_D^i$ as

$$\hat{C}_T^i = \hat{p} \cdot \hat{C}_D^i + (1 - \hat{p}) \cdot \hat{C}_{ND}^i. \tag{23}$$

By computing simple integrals, we find for AUROC, $a_R + 0.5$, and a_P the expressions

$$AUROC = \sum_{i=1}^{k} 0.5 \cdot \left(\hat{C}_D^i + \hat{C}_D^{i-1} \right) \cdot \left(\hat{C}_{ND}^i - \hat{C}_{ND}^{i-1} \right),$$

$$a_R + 0.5 = \sum_{i=1}^{k} 0.5 \cdot \left(\hat{C}_D^i + \hat{C}_D^{i-1} \right) \cdot \left(\hat{C}_T^i - \hat{C}_T^{i-1} \right), \qquad (24)$$

$$a_P = 0.5 \cdot (1 - \hat{p}).$$

Plugging (23) into the expression for $a_R + 0.5$ and simplifying leads to

$$a_R + 0.5 = \sum_{i=1}^{k} 0.5 \cdot \left(\hat{C}_D^i + \hat{C}_D^{i-1} \right) \cdot \left(\hat{C}_T^i - \hat{C}_T^{i-1} \right)$$

$$= \sum_{i=1}^{k} 0.5 \cdot \left(\hat{C}_D^i + \hat{C}_D^{i-1} \right) \cdot \left(\hat{p} \cdot \left(\hat{C}_D^i - \hat{C}_D^{i-1} \right) + (1 - \hat{p}) \cdot \left(\hat{C}_{ND}^i - \hat{C}_{ND}^{i-1} \right) \right)$$

$$= (1 - \hat{p}) \cdot \sum_{i=1}^{k} 0.5 \cdot \left(\hat{C}_D^i + \hat{C}_D^{i-1} \right) \cdot \left(\hat{C}_{ND}^i - \hat{C}_{ND}^{i-1} \right) \qquad (25)$$

$$+ \hat{p} \cdot \sum_{i=1}^{k} 0.5 \cdot \left(\hat{C}_D^i + \hat{C}_D^{i-1} \right) \cdot \left(\hat{C}_D^i - \hat{C}_D^{i-1} \right)$$

$$= (1 - \hat{p}) \cdot AUROC + 0.5 \cdot \hat{p} \cdot \sum_{i=1}^{k} \left(\left(\hat{C}_D^i \right)^2 - \left(\hat{C}_D^{i-1} \right)^2 \right)$$

$$= (1 - \hat{p}) \cdot AUROC + 0.5 \cdot \hat{p}.$$

Taking (24) and (25) together leads to the desired result

$$AR = \frac{a_R}{a_P} = \frac{(1 - \hat{p}) \cdot (AUROC - 0.5)}{0.5 \cdot (1 - \hat{p})} = 2 \cdot AUROC - 1 . \square$$

Appendix B. Proof of (7)

Using the same shortcut notation as in Appendix A, we get

$$AUROC = \sum_{i=1}^{k} 0.5 \cdot \left(\hat{C}_D^i - \hat{C}_D^{i-1} \right) \cdot \left(\hat{C}_{ND}^i - \hat{C}_{ND}^{i-1} \right)$$

$$= \sum_{i=1}^{k} 0.5 \cdot \left(P\left(\hat{S}_D \leq R_i \right) + P\left(\hat{S}_D \leq R_{i-1} \right) \right) \cdot P\left(\hat{S}_{ND} = R_i \right)$$

$$= \sum_{i=1}^{k} \left(P\left(\hat{S}_D \leq R_{i-1} \right) + 0.5 \cdot P\left(\hat{S}_D = R_i \right) \right) \cdot P\left(\hat{S}_{ND} = R_i \right)$$

$$= \sum_{i=1}^{k} P\left(\hat{S}_D \leq R_{i-1} \right) \cdot P\left(\hat{S}_{ND} = R_i \right) + 0.5 \cdot \sum_{i=1}^{k} P\left(\hat{S}_D = R_i \right) \cdot P\left(\hat{S}_{ND} = R_i \right)$$

$$= P\left(\hat{S}_D < \hat{S}_{ND} \right) + 0.5 \cdot P\left(\hat{S}_D = \hat{S}_{ND} \right)$$

which proves (7).□

XIII. Statistical Approaches to PD Validation

Stefan Blochwitz, Marcus R. W. Martin, and Carsten S. Wehn

Deutsche Bundesbank and DekaBank[1]

1. Introduction

When developing an internal rating system, besides its calibration, the validation of the respective rating categories and associated probabilities of default plays an important role. To have a valid risk estimate and allocate economic capital efficiently, a credit institution has to be sure of the adequacy of its risk measurement methods and of the estimates for the default probabilities. Additionally, the validation of rating grades is a regulatory requirement to become an internal ratings based approach bank (IRBA bank).

We discuss different methods of validating estimates for probabilities of defaults (PDs). We start by outlining various concepts used to estimate PDs and the assumptions in rating philosophies including point-in-time and through-the-cycle approaches, a distinction necessary for a proper validation. Having discussed this, several common statistical tests used for the validation of PD estimates are introduced. These tests include the binomial test, the normal test and goodness-of-fit-type tests like the χ^2-test. Also, the incorporation of descriptive measures linked to density forecast methods is discussed. For every test, the question of respective quality is raised. An alternative approach starts with the one factor model and gives an intuitive validation tool, the so-called extended traffic light approach. We conclude with a discussion of the approaches introduced, especially with respect to possible limitations for the use in practice and to their respective usefulness.

2. PDs, Default Rates, and Rating Philosophy

The meaning of "Validation of PDs" or backtesting in credit risk can be described quite simply. In the words of the Basel Committee on Banking Supervision, it is to "compare realized default rates with estimated PDs for each grade of a rating system and to assess the deviation between the observed default rates and the esti-

---

[1] This Chapter represents the personal opinions of the authors and cannot be considered as representing the views of the Deutsche Bundesbank or DekaBank.

mated PD," (cf. Basel Committee on Banking Supervision (2004), § 501). Here, backtesting is defined as a statistical task which hopefully can be solved with the existing means and tools. However, performing such backtesting in practice raises some issues. Before we discuss the statistical means we want to draw readers' attention to some more general aspects:

- *Recognition of defaults*: Validation of PDs is fundamental in the recognition of defaults. A correct count of defaults is a necessary prerequisite for a correctly determined default rate, and the measurement of default events is the underlying concept of risk for determining PDs. A default of a borrower, however, is not objective event. On the one hand, there is the fact that a reasonable number of defaulted borrowers seem to have a considerable influence on the timing of the credit default. On the other hand, there is the observation that declaring a borrower as defaulted leaves room for judgement. Therefore, the definition of credit default is to a considerable degree, subjective, and even the new Basel framework retains this subjective element as the basis of the IRBA. However, a forward-looking focus and a limit of 90 days past due which is objective, is implemented into the definition of default, (cf. Basel Committee on Banking Supervision (2004), §§ 452 and 453). The requirement is that the definition of default – with all its subjective elements – has to be applied consistently to guarantee that the conclusions drawn from the validation of PDs are correct.

- *Inferring from default rates to PDs*: A common and widespread approach for credit risk is the application of the law of large numbers, and to infer from the observed default rate the probability of default. An application of the law of large numbers would require that the defaults are independent and occur in the same distribution. This requirement cannot be seen to be fulfilled for different borrowers. To tell it in a picture: The difference for the task of determining the probability of throwing a six is like approximating this probability either by throwing the same dice 1,000 times and calculating the ratio of sixes to the total number of throws or throwing 1,000 dices once and calculating the ratio of sixes to the number of dices thrown. In any case, a proper application requires that borrowers are grouped into grades exhibiting similar default risk characteristics. Thus, the validation of PDs in most cases is preceded by grouping the borrowers to grades with the same risk profile (for an exemplary exception, the Spiegelhalter statistics, cf. Chapter XIV) This is necessary even in the case of direct estimates of PD, when each borrower is assigned an individual PD.

- *PDs in their context*: An immediate consequence of the issues raised is that PDs have a meaning just in a certain context, namely in the portfolio. In our opinion, there is no such thing as an objective PD which can be measured with a rating system like temperature can be measured with a thermometer. Let us assume we rate the same borrower with two different rating systems: One with good discriminatory power resulting in different grades, which are assumed to be calibrated perfectly, and the other – very simple system – assigning all borrowers to the same grade, calibrated with the portfolio PD. Applying these two rating systems to the same borrower would result in different PDs; either in the PD of the respective grade or in the portfolio PD. However, both systems can claim to be right and there is no method of deciding what the "true" PD of that borrower might be. The example works exactly the same for two rating systems with similar discriminatory power and the same numbers of grades, providing both systems are calibrated with two different portfolios. Let us assume there is a subset of borrowers, which appears in both portfolios. If the remainder of the respective portfolios is different in terms of risk, then the same borrower in general will be assigned to grades with different PDs, and again, both systems can claim to be right.

- *Rating philosophy*: Rating philosophy is what is commonly referred to as either point-in-time (PIT) or through-the-cycle (TTC) ratings. PIT-ratings measure credit risk given the current state of a borrower in its current economic environment, whereas TTC-ratings measure credit risk taking into account the (assumed) state of the borrower over a whole economic cycle. PIT and TTC mark the ends of the spectrum of possible rating systems. In practice, neither pure TTC nor pure PIT systems will be found, but hybrid systems, which are rather PIT or rather TTC. Agency ratings are assumed to be TTC, whereas bank internal systems – at least in most cases in Germany – are looked at as PIT. The underlying rating philosophy definitely has to be assessed before validation results can be judged, because the rating philosophy is an important driver for the expected range for the deviation between PDs and default rates. Jafry and Schuermann (2004) have introduced the equivalent average migration as a tool for assessing rating philosophy. According to Jafry and Schuermann (2004), the rescaled Euclidean–distance mobility metric is equal to the average migration, which describes the average number of borrowers migrating from one rating grade to another grade. This average migration gives an impression at which end of the spectrum a rating system can be found, if it is 0, then the rating system has no migration at all – a PIT system in its purest form – if it is 1, then on average, no borrower stays in a rating grade. To level off credit risk measurement for PIT systems as well as for TTC systems, the Basel Committee has clarified that estimation of PDs for regulatory purposes needs to include a forward looking element (cf. Principle 1 of Newsletter No. 4, Basel Committee on Banking Supervision, 2005a). In practice, this would mean that for regulatory purposes in respect of risk quantification of their grades, PIT and TTC systems are a bit closer.

3. Tools for Validating PDs

This section is devoted to a brief overview on statistical tests that can be performed to validate the so-called calibration of a rating system, i.e. the assignment of a probability of default (PD) to a certain rating grade or score value.

In order to draw the right conclusions, in most cases – due to insufficient obligors or defaults to obtain reliable statistical implications – a purely statistical validation of a rating system is not sufficient to ensure the validity of the rating system. It has to be complemented by alternative qualitative approaches such as, e.g., shadow rating systems or plausibility checks by credits experts (cf. OeNB / FMA (2004, pp. 94), or Basel Committee on Banking Supervision, 2004 and 2005b).

Furthermore, we implicitly assume that the validation of the rating system's discriminatory power and stability is to be also checked by a validation procedure which should be part of an integrated process covering calibration, discriminatory power and stability of the rating system (cf. Blochwitz and Hohl (2003), Tasche (2005, pp. 32), or OeNB / FMA (2004) which also includes some numerical examples).

We describe the rating system to be validated as follows: Let N denote the total number of borrowers classified within a portfolio by application of the rating system. Moreover, N_k denotes the number of obligors in this portfolio which were associated to the rating grade $k \in \{1,\ldots,K\}$. Hence, we have

$$N = \sum_{k=1}^{K} N_k \, .$$

Finally, let each rating grade be assigned a probability of default forecast PD_k.

The statistical tests presented in this section can be classified rather approximately either by validation period (single- versus multi-period tests) or by the number of rating grades undergoing the test (single- versus multi-grade tests). By construction, TTC rating systems are based on much longer time horizons than PIT rating systems. Therefore, the validation methodologies set out in this section will, in practice, be more applicable to PIT rather than to TTC rating systems.

3.1. Statistical Tests for a Single Time Period

We start by considering tests that are usually applied to a single time period case, i.e. starting about one and a half years after the first introduction of a rating system and in the annual validation process that follows.

The most prominent example for this kind of test is the binomial test (as well as its normal approximation) which is the most often applied single-grade single-period test in practice. On the other hand, the Hosmer-Lemeshow- or χ^2-test provides an example of a single-period multi-grade test that can be used to check the adequacy of PD forecasts for several rating grades simultaneously.

3.1.1. Binomial Test

To apply the binomial test, we consider one single rating grade over a single time period, usually one year. Therefore, we fix a certain rating grade by

(B.1)   choosing a fixed rating grade $k \in \{1,\ldots,K\}$ throughout this subsection, and, additionally,

(B.2)   assume independence of default events between all credits within the chosen rating grade k.

The last assumption readily implies that the number of defaults in rating grade $k \in \{1, \ldots, K\}$ can be modelled as a binomially distributed random variable X with size parameter $n := N_k$ and "success" probability $p := PD_k$. Thus, we can assess the correctness of the PD forecast for one time period by testing the null hypothesis

H0:   The estimated PD of the rating category is conservative enough, i.e. the actual default rate is less than or equal to the forecasted default rate given by the PD

against the alternative hypotheses

H1:   The estimated PD of the rating category is less than the actual default rate.

Thereby, the null hypothesis **H0** is rejected at a confidence level α whenever the number of observed defaults d in this rating grade is greater than or equal to the critical value

$$d_\alpha = \min\left\{ d \ : \ \sum_{j=d}^{N_k} \binom{N_k}{j} PD_k^j \left(1 - PD_k\right)^{N_k - j} \leq 1 - \alpha \right\}.$$

According to Tasche (2005), the binomial test is the most powerful test among all tests at a fixed level and the true type I error (i.e. the probability to reject erroneously the hypothesis of an adequate PD forecast) can be much larger than the nominal level of the test if default events are correlated.

In fact, assumption **(B.2)** is not realistic at all and turns out to completely disagree with all empirical experiences: In practice, default correlations in a range between 0 % and 3 % do occur. The Basel II framework assumes asset correlation between 12 % and 24 %. Despite this, we should particularly mention two recent results eg.: For well diversified German retail portfolios, indications exist that *asset correlations* are in a range between 0 % and 5 % which in turn would imply that default correlations are even smaller fractions of these (cf. Hamerle et al. (2004) and Huschens and Stahl, 2005).

Therefore, one gets a realistic early warning tool using the binomial test and its rather complicated expression for the critical number of defaults. Another aspect worth considering is that one should rely on consistency between the modelling of correlation for risk measurement within the internally applied credit portfolio model on the one hand and the validation on the other to derive consistent confidence intervals.

3.1.2. Normal Approximation to the Binomial Test

One possibility of obtaining an easier (but only approximate) expression for the number of critical defaults within a fixed rating grade $k \in \{1,\ldots,K\}$, is to apply the central limit theorem: In short, we take advantage of the limiting properties of the binomial distribution and assume it approaches a normal distribution in the limit as the number of obligors N_k becomes large (enough). Hence, we obtain

$$\tilde{d}_{\alpha} = N_k \cdot PD_k + \Phi^{-1}(\alpha) \cdot \sqrt{N_k \cdot PD_k \cdot (1 - PD_k)}$$

as a critical value where $\Phi^{-1}(\cdot)$ denotes the inverse of the cumulative standard normal distribution function.

To apply this asymptotic approximation by the normal distribution, we necessarily have to ensure that either the condition (sometimes also called Laplace's rule of thumb)

$$N_k \cdot PD_k \cdot (1 - PD_k) > 9$$

or the following less restrictive condition

$$N_k \cdot PD_k > 5 \text{ and } N_k \cdot (1 - PD_k) > 5$$

holds. In most cases of practical importance, the approximation seems to be valid already for not too large numbers of N_k (while some numerical examples indicate that even for figures of N_k as low as 50, the approximation works reasonably well). Note that for low default probabilities and a low numbers of credits in the individual rating classes, these prerequisites for using the normal approximation imply implausible high numbers of obligors.

The same approach as the one used to derive the normal approximation to the binomial test was applied by Stein (2003) to get a lower estimate for the number of defaults necessary for validating the accuracy of the PD forecasts. Stein (2003) also discusses the question of sample size (closely related to the *finite population correction* by Cochran, 1977) as well as the influence of correlated defaults which we address in the following subsection, too.

3.1.3. A Modified Binomial Test Accounting for Correlated Defaults

The assumption of uncorrelated defaults **(B.2)** for the binomial test generally yields an overestimate of the significance of deviations in the realized default rate from the forecast rate. In particular, this is true for *risk underestimates*, i.e. cases in which the realized default rate is higher than the forecasted rate. Therefore, from a purely conservative risk assessment point of view, overestimating significance is not critical in the case of risk underestimates. This means that it is entirely possible to operate under the assumption of uncorrelated defaults. Clearly, persistent overestimates of significance will lead to more frequent recalibration of the rating model. In addition, this can have negative effects on the model's stability over time. It is therefore necessary to determine at least the approximate extent to which default correlations influence PD estimates.

Similar to the one-factor approach underlying the risk-weight functions of the IRB approach of Basel II, default correlations can be modelled on the basis of the dependence of default events on common (systematic) and individual (specific or idiosyncratic) random factors (cf. Tasche, 2003 and 2005). For correlated defaults, this model also enables us to derive limits for assessing deviations in the realized default rate from its forecast as significant at certain confidence levels.

On a confidence level α, the null hypothesis **H0** is rejected under the assumptions **(B.1)** and **(B.2)** whenever the number of observed defaults d in rating grade $k \in \{1,...,K\}$ is greater than or equal to the critical value

$$d_\alpha := q + \frac{2q-1}{2N_k} - \frac{q(1-q)}{\varphi\left(\frac{\sqrt{\rho}\Phi^{-1}(1-\alpha)+\Phi^{-1}(PD_k)}{\sqrt{\rho(1-\rho)}}\right)} \cdot \frac{(1-2\rho)\Phi^{-1}(1-\alpha)-\sqrt{\rho}\Phi^{-1}(PD_k)}{2N_k \cdot \sqrt{\rho(1-\rho)}}$$

where

$$q := \Phi^{-1}\left(\frac{\sqrt{\rho}\Phi^{-1}(\alpha)+\Phi^{-1}(PD_k)}{\sqrt{1-\rho}}\right)$$

and ρ denotes the default correlation. This adjustment takes into account that due to unsystematic risk correlation with the systematic risk factor, the respective quantile lies a little further in the tail than without this further uncertainty and thus needs to be corrected.

Tasche (2005) shows that assumption **(B.2)** is not robust for higher percentiles, i.e.: Small deviations from a zero correlation already lead to dramatic changes in the critical value of the test which is – of course – not a desirable feature of a test. Furthermore, Tasche (2005) concludes that taking into account dependence by incorporating a one factor dependence structure generated by a Vasicek dynamic and Gordy's granularity adjustment, yield tests of rather moderate power. This is the case even for such low correlation levels as typical for the problem of correlated defaults.

Clearly, the normal approximation is also applicable in this context and yields an easier expression for the critical number of defaults.

Up to now, only single rating grades k were validated separately. The next test by Hosmer and Lemeshow will close this gap by an approach to validating more than a single rating grade simultaneously.

3.1.4 Goodness-of-fit Type Tests: χ^2- or Hosmer-Lemeshow-test

The two-sided Hosmer-Lemeshow-test provides an alternative approach in a single-period validation environment to check the adequacy of PD forecasts for several rating grades simultaneously. Recall that PD_k denotes the PD forecast for rating grade $k \in \{1,\ldots,K\}$.

For this purpose, let us pose the following assumptions:

(LH.1) The forecasted default probabilities PD_k and the default rates $p_k := d_k / N_k$ are identically distributed.

(LH.2) All the default events within each of the different rating grades as well as between all rating grades are independent.

Let us define the statistic

$$S_K^{\chi^2} := \sum_{k=1}^{K} \frac{(N_k \cdot PD_k - d_k)^2}{N_k \cdot PD_k \cdot (1 - PD_k)}$$

with $d_k = p_k \cdot N_k$ denoting the number of defaulted obligors with rating $k \in \{1,\ldots,K\}$. By the central limit theorem, when $N_k \to \infty$ simultaneously for all $k \in \{1,\ldots,K\}$, the distribution of S_K will converge in distribution towards a χ^2-distribution with $K-2$ degrees of freedom because of assumptions **(LH.1)** and **(LH.2)**.

Again, a limiting distribution is used to assess the adequacy of the PD forecasts of the rating system by considering the p-value of a χ^2_{K-2}-test: The closer the p-value is to zero, the worse the estimation is. A further problem arises when the PD_k are very small: In this case the rate of convergence to the χ^2_{K-2}-distribution may be very low as well. Furthermore, relying on the p-value enables under certain circumstances (e.g. comparability of underlying portfolios) a direct comparison of forecasts with different numbers of rating categories.

The construction of the test is based on the assumption of independence and a normal approximation again. Therefore, the Hosmer-Lemeshow-test is also likely to underestimate the true type I error (as the binomial test).

3.1.5. Brier Score

Another method to validate a rating system across all rating grades is to calculate the average quadratic deviation of the forecasted PD and the realized default rates. Here, in contrast to the preceding statistical tests, it is about an exploratory method. The resulting score between zero and one is called Brier score (cf. Brier, 1950) and is defined in the context of N debtors associated to the K rating grades by

$$B = \frac{1}{N} \sum_{k=1}^{K} \left[d_k (1 - PD_k)^2 + (N_k - d_k) PD_k^2 \right]$$

$$= \frac{1}{N} \sum_{k=1}^{K} N_k \left[p_k (1 - PD_k)^2 + (1 - p_k) PD_k^2 \right]$$

where PD_k denotes the probability of default assigned to each obligor in rating grade k and $p_k = d_k / N_k$ is the observed default rate within the same rating grade (cf. OeNB / FMA, 2004). The closer the Brier score is to zero, the better is the forecast of default probabilities.

Note that, by definition, the Brier score does not measure directly the difference of the default probability forecast and the true conditional probability of default. Hence, the Brier score is in fact not a measure of calibration accuracy alone. Since the Brier score can be decomposed as

$$B = p(1-p) + \frac{1}{N} \sum_{k=1}^{K} N_k (PD_k - p_k)^2 - \frac{1}{N} \sum_{k=1}^{K} N_k (p - p_k)^2$$

(cf. Murphy & Winkler, 1992) whereby $p = d / N$, a separate analysis is in principle possible:

- The first term describes the variance of the default rate observed over the entire sample. Here, PD denotes the default frequency of the overall sample. This value is independent of the rating procedure's calibration and depends *only* on the observed sample itself. It represents the minimum Brier score attainable for this sample with a perfectly calibrated but also "trivial rating model", which forecasts the observed default rate precisely for each obligor, but only comprises *one* rating class for the whole sample, i.e. $PD = PD_k = p_k = d_k / N_k$ for all $k \in \{1, \ldots, K\}$. In this case the expected Brier score is equal to the variance of the default indicator, i.e. the first of the 3 terms in the representation above, $B = \overline{B} := p \cdot (1 - p)$.
- The second term represents the average quadratic deviation of forecast and realized default rates in the K rating classes. A well-calibrated rating model will show lower values for this term than a poorly calibrated rating model. The value itself is thus also referred to as the "calibration".
- The third term describes the average quadratic deviation of observed default rates in individual rating classes, from the default rate observed in the overall sample. This value is referred to as "resolution". While the resolution of the trivial rating model is zero, it is not equal to zero in discriminating rating systems. In general, the resolution of a rating model rises as rating classes with clearly differentiated observed default probabilities are added. Resolution is thus linked to the discriminatory power of a rating model.

An additional caveat is the different signs preceding the calibration and resolution terms. These make it more difficult to interpret the Brier score as an individual value for the purpose of assessing the classification accuracy of a rating model's calibration. Moreover, the numerical values of the calibration and resolution terms are generally far lower than the total variance.

One of the main drawbacks of the Brier score is its performance for small default probabilities. In this case the "trivial rating model" yields a rather small Brier score. By "trivial rating model" we mean that all debtors are assigned the realized default rates p, of the overall sample. In this case, the expected Brier score is equal to the variance of the default indicator, i.e. the first of the 3 terms in the representation above,

$$\overline{B} = p \cdot (1 - p).$$

Evidently, for $p \to 0$ the Brier score also converges to zero. The only possibility of applying this score in a meaningful way is to compute the Brier score relative to the "trivial score" $\overline{B}$ since the absolute values are very close together for cases with few defaults.

3.2. Statistical Multi-period Tests

While the binomial test and the χ^2-test are usually restricted to a single-period validation framework, the normal test and the extended traffic lights approach are devoted to overcoming the assumption of independence inherent to most single-period tests by assuming a dependence structure throughout a time horizon of several years.

3.2.1. Normal Test

The normal test for a given rating grade k, is a multi-period test of correctness of a default probability forecast for a single rating grade. It can be applied under the assumption that the mean default rate does not vary too much over time and that default events in different years are independent. Mathematically speaking, the fundamental assumptions for the normal test are given by

(N)   The random variables $PD_{k,t} = D_{t,k} / N_{t,k}$ that describe the forecasted probabilities of default for a single rating grade $k \in \{1,...,K\}$ over the years $t \in \{1,...,T\}$ are independent with means $\mu_{t,k}$ and common variance $\sigma_k^2 > 0$.

In this case, the central limit theorem can be applied to prove that the standardized sum S_k^N with

$$S_k^N = \frac{\sum\limits_{t=1}^{T}\left(PD_{k,t} - \mu_{t,k}\right)}{\sigma_k \cdot \sqrt{T}}$$

will converge to the standard normal distribution as $T \to \infty$. Since the rate of convergence is extremely high, even small values of T yield acceptable results. Consequently, to apply the normal test to the PD forecasts $PD_{k,t}$ and corresponding observed percentage default rates $\mu_{t,k}$, one has to estimate the variance σ_k^2. The classical estimator

$$\hat{\sigma}_{0,k}^2 = \frac{1}{T-1} \cdot \sum\limits_{t=1}^{T}\left(\mu_{t,k} - PD_{k,t}\right)^2$$

is unbiased only if the forecasted PDs exactly match the default rates $\mu_{t,k}$. Otherwise, the classical estimator will be reasonably upwardly biased, hence one should choose

$$\hat{\sigma}_k^2 = \frac{1}{T-1} \cdot \left[\sum\limits_{t=1}^{T}\left(\mu_{t,k} - PD_{k,t}\right)^2 - \frac{1}{T}\left(\sum\limits_{t=1}^{T}\left(\mu_{t,k} - PD_{k,t}\right)\right)^2\right]$$

instead. This alternative estimator $\hat{\sigma}_k^2$ is unbiased under the hypothesis of exact forecasts, too, but less upwardly biased than the classical estimator otherwise.

Now, we can test the null hypothesis

HN: None of the realized default rates in the years $t \in \{1,...,T\}$ is greater than its corresponding forecast $PD_{k,t}$.

Therefore, the null hypothesis **HN** is rejected at a confidence level α whenever

$$S_k^N > z_\alpha$$

where z_α denotes the standard-normal α-quantile.

Note that cross-sectional dependence is admissible in the normal test. Tasche (2003, 2005) points out that the quality of the normal approximation is moderate but exhibits a conservative bias. Consequently, the true type I error tends to be lower than the nominal level of the test. This means that the proportion of erroneous rejections of PD forecasts will be smaller than might be expected from the formal confidence level of the test. Furthermore, the normal test seems even to be, to a certain degree, robust against a violation of the assumption that defaults are independent over time. However, the power of the test is moderate, in particular for short time series (for example five years).

3.2.2. Extended Traffic Light Approach

Dating back to the approval of market risk models for regulatory purposes, the idea of using a traffic light approach for model validation seems to be a considerable exploratory extension to statistical tests. In the Basel Committee on Banking Supervision (1996), for value at risk outliers produced by market risk models, a binomial test with green, yellow and red zones is implemented that leads eventually to higher capital charges against potential risks.

Tasche (2003) picks up the idea of a traffic light approach for the validation of default probabilities. The basic idea is to introduce probability levels $\alpha_{low} = 0.95$ and $\alpha_{high} = 0.999$ (note, that the exemplary levels are similar to Basel Committee on Banking Supervision, 1996) with respective critical values c_{low} and c_{high}, that assure with the model used, that the ex post observed number of defaults exceeds the level c_{low} by only a probability of $1 - \alpha_{low}$ (and for c_{high} by probability $1 - \alpha_{high}$ respectively). First, the modified binomial test is introduced as above. Furthermore, the Vasicek model with asset correlation ρ, independent standard normal random variables X, and $\xi_1,\ldots,\xi_n$ and a threshold c is given by (see also Martin et al., 2006).

$$d_k = \sum_{i=1}^{N_k} 1_{(-\infty,c]}(\sqrt{\rho}X + \sqrt{1-\rho}\xi_i).$$

Now, to determine critical values, the choice of asset correlation is of crucial importance as the critical values are given for a level α by

$$c_{crit} = \min\{i : P(d_k \geq i) \leq 1-\alpha\}$$

Two approaches are introduced, one based on a granularity adjustment and one based on moment matching, see above. It can be concluded that, for high values of asset correlation, the respective critical values change clearly.

Blochwitz et al. (2005) propose an alternative approach for implementing a traffic light based judgment that does not need an explicit specification of asset correlations emphasizing the accessibility for practitioners. They use a heuristic approach to the validation of rating estimates and to identify suspicious credit portfolios or rating grades.

Starting again with assumptions **(B.1)** and **(B.2)**, the number of defaults can be determined to be binomially distributed. Using the results given in Section 3.1.2, they obtain

$$P_{max} = PD_k + \Phi^{-1}(\alpha_{bin})\sqrt{\frac{PD_k(1-PD_k)}{N_k}}$$

for some given level of confidence α_{bin}. A similar consideration for the one-factor model (cf. Vasicek (1987) among others) with asset correlation ρ yields

$$p_{max} = \Phi\left(\frac{\sqrt{\rho}\Phi^{-1}(\alpha_{asset})+\Phi^{-1}(PD_k)}{\sqrt{1-\rho}}\right)$$

The next step is to compare the second order error for the statistics of these two approaches. Using $\beta_* := 1-\alpha_*$ with β_{bin} and β_{asset} as the values for the respective models, they derive:

$$PD_k + \Phi^{-1}(1-\beta_{bin})\sqrt{\frac{PD_k(1-PD_k)}{N_k}} = \Phi\left(\frac{\sqrt{\rho}\Phi^{-1}(1-\beta_{asset})+\Phi^{-1}(PD_k)}{\sqrt{1-\rho}}\right)$$

A comparison shows that for low levels of asset correlation covering many relevant situations, there is no significant difference in the second order errors. Therefore, for good reason, the subsequent considerations can be based on the normal approximation.

To compare the adequacy of eventually time changing forecasts for probabilities of default, the application is based on a relative distance between observed default rates and forecasted probabilities of default. Motivated by the considerations above and by taking into account the expression

$$\sigma(PD_k,N_k) = \sqrt{PD_k(1-PD_k)/N_k} \ ,$$

Blochwitz et al. (2005) establish four coloured zones to analyse the deviation of forecasts and realisations by setting

Green if $p_k < PD_k$

Yellow if $PD_k \le p_k < PD_k + K^y\sigma(PD_k,N_k)$

Orange if $PD_k + K^y\sigma(PD_k,N_k) \le p_k < PD_k + K^o\sigma(PD_k,N_k)$

Red   if $PD_k + K^o\sigma(PD_k,N_k) \le p_k$.

The parameters K^y and K^o have to be chosen carefully as they strongly influence the results of the later application to a given data set. Practical considerations lead to the conclusion that the respective probability for the colours green, yellow, orange and red to appear should decline. But in contrast, K^o should not be chosen too large as in the tail of the distribution, asset correlation influences results much more than in the centre of it. Hence, a proper choice could be $K^y = 0.84$ and $K^o = 1.64$, which corresponds to a probability of observing green of 0.5, observing yellow with 0.3, orange with 0.15 and red with 0.05.

Being in the comfortable situation to include more than one period into the evaluation framework, a potential enhancement is the application to a multi period. Now, a labelling function is given by

$$\Lambda[L_g, L_y, L_o, L_r] = 1000L_g + 100L_y + 10L_o + L_r$$

A possible weighting function is

$$\Omega[L_g, L_y, L_o, L_r] = P_g L_g + P_y L_y + P_o L_o + P_r L_r$$

with L_g denoting the number of observed green periods, L_y the respective yellow number and so on and P_g, P_y, P_o, and P_r the associated probabilities (i.e. 0.5, 0.3, 0.15, and 0.05 respectively).

With the help of the weighting function, it is possible to assign a mixed colour for more then one observed period. By numerical analysis and by application to rating agencies' data, it is concluded that for many relevant cases, the deducted extended traffic light approach gives clear indications for a review of the forecasts for probability of defaults.

According to Blochwitz et al. (2004), it is also possible to apply a multi-period null hypothesis which is in fact a continuation of the null hypothesis as in the normal test **(HN)**: Reject the hypothesis at a level β if $\Lambda[L_g, L_y, L_o, L_r] \leq c_\beta$, where

$$c_\beta = \max\{c \mid P(\Lambda[L_g, L_y, L_o, L_r] \leq c) < 1 - \beta\}.$$

Numerical studies to check the robustness with respect to the adequacy of neglecting correlations show that the extended traffic light approach is a useful tool in the jigsaw of validation.

3.2.3. Some Further Readings and Remarks

In Chapter V a PD estimation method applicable even for low default portfolios is suggested. The main idea is to use the *most prudent estimation principle*, i.e. to estimate the PD by upper confidence bounds while guaranteeing at the same time, a PD ordering that respects the differences in credit quality indicated by the rating grades. Unfortunately, the application of the proposed methodology for backtesting or similar validation tools would not add much additional information, as the (e.g. purely expert based) average PDs per rating grade would normally be well below the quantitative upper bounds proposed using the most prudent estimation principle.

Other approaches to estimating non-zero PDs for high-quality rating grades are based upon Markov chain properties of rating migrations matrices (cf. Schuermann and Hanson (2004) or Jafry and Schuermann, 2004). Therefore, a qualitative study of the evolution of these transition matrices across several years can shed light on possible problems in a rating system. After all, we still lack reliable statistical validation methods for low default portfolios or high-quality rating grades.

For further discussions concerning backtesting issues, refer to Frerichs and Löffler (2003) or Bühler et al. (2003) and the references therein.

3.3. Discussion and Conclusion

All the above mentioned tests focus on comparisons between the forecasted probabilities of default and the afterwards observed default rates. For all statistical tests, the eventual correlation (i.e. asset or default correlation) between different obligors plays a crucial role and thus influences the possibilities for the use of the test in practice. Some tests neglect correlation, for others, it is necessary to specify it. It is common understanding, that to test correlation itself, the database is insufficiently comprehensive. Hence, it is highly important to keep in mind the respective assumptions used by the different tests.

Further work can be done on integrating different rating categories into one test and with respect to the ranking of statistical tests for their use in practice. In the validation process to be established in a bank, the use of the statistical tests and exploratory means introduced herein can thus only be one piece of the puzzle among others.

4. Practical Limitations to PD Validation

For several reasons, backtesting techniques of PDs, as described here, have their limitations:

- *Precision of measurement*: Calibrating a rating system is comparable to measuring a physical property. If – as a rule of thumb in measurement theory – a standard deviation is taken as a reasonable size of the measurement error, the figures are rather disappointing. A lower bound for the measurement error of the k-th rating grade is given by the standard deviation of the uncorrelated binomial distribution. As a numerical example: Setting $N_k = 500$ and $PD_k = 1\%$ yields $\sigma(PD_k, N_k) = 0.45\%$, resulting in a relative error of measurement of 45 %, which is an extraordinary high error compared to physical properties measured. This argument can be turned as well: If it is assumed, that the PD had been estimated precisely, then there would have been no surprise in default rates fluctuating with a standard deviation around the PD.[2]

---

[2] Under the settings of the normal approximation of the binomial test in Section 3.1.2 there is a more than 15%-chance, that the default rate exceeds the PD by more than a standard deviation.

- *Limited data*: Backtesting relies on data. All statistical methods discussed here need a certain number of defaults to be observed before they can be applied. This challenge can be illustrated with a numerical example. For investment grade portfolios with PDs of less than 10 bps, a size of more than 1,000 borrowers is necessary to observe an average one default per year. These portfolios often are much smaller in size, and empirical evidence shows in most years no default at all. In these cases, backtesting would not provide any information, because neither evidence for a right calibration nor for an insufficient calibration can be found, because for PDs larger than zero, default rates of zero are observed. The implication of limited default data on the validation of rating systems and specifically on backtesting issues, are discussed in the Basel Committee on Banking Supervision (2005b).
- *Impact of stress*: Rating systems are designed to work in 'normal' times. In general they are calibrated to a more or less conservative estimated expected value of the PD for a longer time horizon. However, from time to time, unforeseeable events - often called 'stress' - result in a sudden increase of default rates, which may be interpreted as a result of a sudden and likewise unforeseeable increase of PDs caused by that event. Usually, banks utilize credit risk models and the correlations modelled therein, yielding measures like Credit Value at Risk (CVar). In the Basel framework, this is implemented in the risk weight function, which can be looked at as a kind of stressed PD: The expected value of the PD is "translated" by this function into a stressed PD, which is expected to appear once in 1,000 years, see Basel Committee on Banking Supervision (2005c). If PDs are estimated as expected values, then in periods of stress, any validation technique of PDs that compares a calibrated long run average PD to observed default rates will fail, because as a result of the stress to which the rated borrowers are exposed, the default rates will exceed that type of PD heavily.

Further, when rating systems are backtested, two aspects need to be balanced: (i) One period tests make a statement about the current performance of a rating system's calibration. However, this statement must be judged carefully, because it may be misleading for reasons already mentioned. (ii) Multi period tests as suggested in this article provide a more robust statement about a rating system's performance, but these tests have another drawback: They need a time series of four years at minimum. In four years time, however, a rating system has undergone some revisions, triggered by the experience a bank has collected by using the rating system. That's why multi-period tests may infer using outdated information, and in the extreme, make a statement on a rating system which has ceased to exist.

Our conclusion is that backtesting techniques as described here have to be carefully embedded into a comprehensive validation approach of rating systems. Validation of PDs should be the first element in a top down validation approach, since a successful – keeping in mind its limits – backtesting is just a necessary prerequisite for a well functioning rating system. Backtesting may reveal deficiencies in a rating system, but the final conclusion as to whether the rating system works as designed or not can be drawn only if the entire rating system is looked at.

References

Basel Committee on Banking Supervision (1996), Supervisory framework for the use of 'backtesting' in conjunction with the internal models approach to market risk capital requirements. www.bis.org

Basel Committee on Banking Supervision (2004), International Convergence of Capital Measurement and Capital Standards, a Revised Framework. www.bis.org

Basel Committee of Banking Supervision (2005a), Update on work of the Accord Implementation Group related to validation under the Basel II Framework, Newsletter No. 4. www.bis.org/publ/bcbs_nl4.htm

Basel Committee of Banking Supervision (2005b), Validation of Low Default Portfolios, Newsletter No. 6. www.bis.org/publ/bcbs_nl6.htm

Basel Committee on Banking Supervision (2005c), An Explanatory Note on the Basel II IRB Risk Weight Functions. www.bis.org

Brier G (1950), Verification of forecasts expressed in terms of probability, Monthly Weather Review 78 (1), pp. 1-3.

Blochwitz S, Hohl S (2003), Validation of bank's internal rating systems. www.gloriamundi.org

Blochwitz S, Hohl S, Tasche D, Wehn CS (2004), Validating Default Probabilities on Short Time Series, Capital & Market Risk Insights (Federal Reserve Bank of Chicago), December issue.

Blochwitz S, Hohl S, Wehn CS (2005), Reconsidering Ratings, Wilmott Magazine, May 2005, pp. 60-69.

Bühler W, Engel C, Korn O, Stahl G (2002), Backtesting von Kreditrisikomodellen, in: Oehler A (ed.): Kreditrisikomanagement Kernbereiche, Aufsicht und Entwicklungstendenzen, Schäffer-Poeschel, 2nd edition.

Cochran (1977), Sampling techniques, John Wiley New York.

Frerichs H, Löffler G (2003), Evaluating credit risk models using loss density forecasts, Journal of Risk 5 No. 4.

Jafry Y, Schuermann T (2004), Measurement, estimation and comparison of credit migration matrices, Journal of Banking & Finance 28, pp. 2603-2693.

Hamerle A, Liebig T, Scheule H (2004), Forecasting Portfolio Risk, Deutsche Bundesbank, Discussion Paper.

Huschens S, Stahl G (2005), A General Framework for IRBA Backtesting, Bankarchiv, Zeitschrift für das gesamte Bank- und Börsenwesen 53, pp. 241-248.

Martin RW, Reitz S, Wehn CS (2006), Kreditderivate und Kreditrisikomodelle: Eine mathematische Einführung, Vieweg Verlag.

Murphy A, Winkler R (1992), Diagnostic verification of probability forecasts, International Journal of Forecasting 7, pp. 435-455.

OeNB / FMA (2004), Guidelines on Credit Risk Management – Rating Models and Validation. www.oenb.at or www.fma.gv.at

Schuermann T, Hanson S (2004), Estimating Probabilities of Default, Staff report no. 190, Federal Reserve Bank of New York.

Stein RM (2003), Are the probabilities right? – A first approximation on the number of observations required to test for default rate accuracy, KMV Moody's Technical Report #030124

Tasche D (2003), A Traffic Lights Approach to PD Validation, Deutsche Bundesbank, Working Paper.

Tasche D (2005), Rating and Probability of Default Validation, In: Studies on the Validation of Internal Rating Systems, Working Paper no. 14, Basel Committee on Banking Supervision.

Vasicek O (1987), Probability of loss on loan portfolios, KMV Corporation, Working Paper.

XIV. PD-Validation – Experience from Banking Practice

Robert Rauhmeier

Dresdner Bank AG[1]

1. Introduction

This chapter deals with statistical hypothesis tests for the quality of estimates of probabilities of defaults (PDs). The focus is on the practical application of these tests in order to meet two main targets. Firstly, bank internal requirements have to be met, assuming that PDs from bank internal rating systems are an essential element of modern credit risk management. Secondly, under the future regime of the Basel II framework, regular recurrent validations of bank internal rating systems have to be conducted in order to get (and retain!) the approval of banking supervisors for the purpose of calculating the regulatory capital charge.

The theoretical findings are illustrated by an empirical validation study with real world rating data from bank internal models. We want to illustrate how validation - or more accurately, statistical backtesting - could be conducted with real world rating data in banking practice.

We organised this article as follows. In the second section we describe briefly how rating systems are commonly used in the banking industry. Some basic notation is introduced in Section three. In the fourth section, common statistical tests like the exact and the approximated binomial test, the Hosmer-Lemeshow test and the Spiegelhalter test, are discussed. These tests are suitable for testing the absolute quality of a rating system presuming that the final outcome of the analyzed rating system is a forecast of default probabilities. For comparing two rating systems - a further central issue in rating praxis - additional tests are required. In validation practice, these tests can be used to analyze whether using expert human opinion, which is usually applied subsequent to the pure machine rating, significantly improves the quality of the rating. The application of the tests discussed in this article is limited by assumptions, e.g. independence of the default events or high numbers of obligors in order to fulfil the central limit theorem. Section five presents some practical guidance to tackle these challenges by simulation techniques.

---

[1] The views expressed in this article are those of the author and do not necessarily reflect those of Dresdner Bank AG.

Additional research on the issue, including which of the suggested tests performs best under certain portfolio compositions is presented. Furthermore, results on the analysis regarding the test power (β- error) under practical, near to reality conditions are shown. In Section six, we introduce the concept of creating backtesting samples from databases found in banking practice. Section seven illustrates the theoretical considerations developed in previous sections by real world rating data and Section eight concludes.

2. Rating Systems in Banking Practice

2.1. Definition of Rating Systems

Firstly, we define the outcome of a rating system. In this article, a rating system forecasts a 1-year default probability of a (potential) borrower. It is not just a rank order of creditworthiness, nor an estimate of overall (expected) losses, nor the prediction of specific default events.[2] The latter means that we suppose that defaults are the realisation of random variables and a rating system consequently can at best forecast accurate probabilities for an event but not the event itself.[3] Secondly, it needs to be specified what is meant by a default. In this article and especially in the empirical example we refer to the Basel II default definition.[4]

2.2. Modular Design of Rating Systems

Often, bank internal rating systems are designed in a modular way, which is sketched in Figure 1. The first module is often called 'machine rating', because a mechanical algorithm generates a first proposal for the borrower's PD. Typically, this algorithm is based on statistical models as described in the initial chapters of this book. Usually this module is composed of a quantitative element, which consists of hard risk drivers (e.g. balance sheet ratios, legal form, gender, profession, age) and a qualitative element consisting of soft risk drivers, which have to be assessed by the loan manager or rating analyst (e.g. management quality, competitiveness of the borrower).

The second module, 'expert-guided adjustments', allows for the adjustments of the rating by the analyst subject to obligor specific details not or not sufficiently reflected in the 'machine rating'. Usually this is done in a standardised form, for ex-

---

[2] We use the phrase *forecast* instead of *estimation* in order to emphasis that at the time the rating for a certain borrower is done, the regarding event, namely the default, is in the future.

[3] We will come to this later in Section 3.

[4] See BCBS (2005), §§ 452ff.

ample, possibly by selecting predefined menu items and evaluating their severity. This is in contrast to the qualitative part of module 1, where the weights of the respective risk drivers are fixed by the algorithms and only the value has to be assessed (for example "good", "average" or "bad"). In module 2, even the weight of the risk driver can be determined by upgrading or downgrading in full rating grades (Section 2.4). As an interim result, we obtain the stand-alone-rating of the borrower.

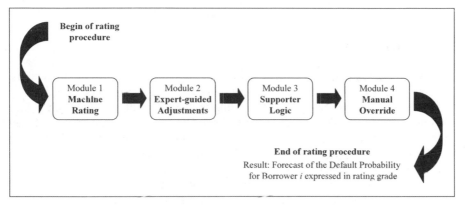

Figure 1. Modular Design of Rating Systems

Module 3 'supporter logic' captures effects arising from a potential backing of a borrower close to default. This module is especially important for rating systems designed for corporates and banks.[5] Here, often expert guided weightings of borrower ratings and potential supporter ratings are used, flanked with some reasonable guidelines. Like the first two modules, module 3 is also tightly standardised. These three modules have to be subsequently passed through and will result in a rule-based proposal for the PD. Since it is impossible to foresee every eventuality affecting the creditworthiness of a borrower in the model building process and the ultimate goal of the bank is to forecast the PD as accurately as possible for each individual borrower, the rating system might allow an override of the rule based rating. In our modular rating approach this refers to module 4 'manual override'. Overrides should be of exceptional character and must be well documented, founded and approved by a senior management board. Additionally, Basel II requires separate monitoring of overrides.[6] Therefore, we suggest incorporating monitoring of overrides into the annual validation process. Frequent reasons for

---

[5] Contrary to the extensive opinion, the term 'supporter' has not to be taken literally because the supporter could even have negative influence on the PD of the borrower. Further on all parties with strong direct influence on the PD of the borrower should be considered here. Popular is the influence of the corporate group where the regarding borrower is embedded, but also essential other (one-sided) dependencies could be taken into account. For example an automobile manufacturer might support his most important supplier in case of an imminent default in order to ensure his own medium-term interests.

[6] See BCBS (2005a), § 428.

overrides could lead to a refinement of the rule-based modules of the rating system.

It has to be stressed that the detailed design of the sketched modular set-up of a rating system may strongly vary in practice and even one or more modules will be omitted if they are irrelevant, impractical or even too cost-intensive in relation to the expected benefits. A good example here is retail business with credit cards, where often the machine module is used exclusively.

2.3. Scope of Rating Systems

A rating model is a model of the real world process that generates default events. This process is called 'default generating process' (DGP) and can be thought of as a function of various risk drivers The rating model takes into account only a limited number of selected key risk drivers of the DGP. Since borrowers of different portfolio segments follow different DGPs it is a consequence that there have to be as many different rating systems as portfolio segments to cover the whole portfolio.[7] But all rating systems have the same intrinsic aim, namely to forecast the 1-year–PD of a borrower as good as possible. With this in mind, the introduced backtesting methods are applicable in general for all rating systems as long as they are forecasting 1-year-PDs and realisations of defaults or non-defaults could be observed. Certainly, there are constraints regarding the number of borrowers (and the number of associated defaults).[8] These constraints affect the significance of the results of the statistical backtesting, but not the methodology itself.

2.4. Rating Scales and Master Scales

It is common banking practice to use rating scales. This means that there is only a limited number of possible PD forecasts (associated with the corresponding rating grades) rather than a continuum of PD forecasts. Usually, there is a bank wide rating scale called a 'master scale' which all rating systems are mapped into. An example of a master scale is illustrated in Table 1.

The table is to be interpreted as follows. If the machine rating module, assuming a logistic regression model is used, produces a forecast PD of 0.95%, then it fits into the PD range of rating grade 8 and for the sake of keeping things simple, we round this forecast to 1.05% as it is the (geometrical) mean of the boundaries.

---

[7] Strictly speaking every borrower follows its own specific DGP but in practice borrowers following similar DGPs can be pooled into portfolio segments.

[8] See Chapter V where low default portfolios are treated.

Table 1. Illustration of a Master Scale

Rating Grade	PD Range	PD of Grade
1	...	...
...	...	...
4	...	0.11%
...	...	...
8	0.80% to 1.40%	1.05%
...	...	...
14	...	...

We could interpret this kind of loss of measurement accuracy simply as rounding-off difference. Using a master scale has certain advantages. For example, it is easier to generate reports and figures and for bank internal communication in general. Moreover, for some people it is easier to think in a few discrete values instead of a continuous measurement scale. This is especially relevant when adjustments of ratings coming from the pure machine rating within module 2 are completed by upgrading or downgrading rating grades. But there are obvious pitfalls accompanying the use of a master scale which arises from solely thinking in rating grades and neglecting the fact that these grades are just proxies or aliases of forecast PDs. For instance, downgrading a borrower from grade 4 to grade 8 does not mean a doubling of the PD. Because of the exponential relationship of grades and corresponding PDs, this means nearly a tenfold increase in the forecast PD.

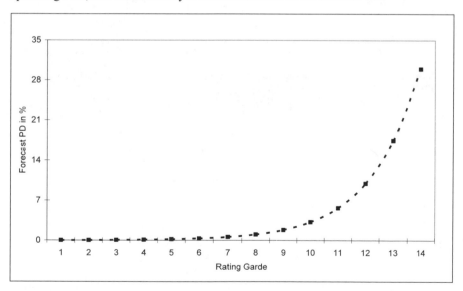

Figure 2. Typical Master Scale – exponential run of the curve

As seen in Figure 2, master scales often have the attribute that the PD according to the rating grades increases roughly exponentially.[9] Two reasons may explain this. First, master scales are sometimes inspired by the scale of the rating agencies and the derived default rates for these grades. Second, banks want (and supervisors claim, see BCBS (2005), § 403) to have a meaningful distribution of their borrowers across their rating grades.

As noted above, a master scale is used group wide. Rating grades of the master scale mean the same across different portfolios. For example a rating grade 8 means the same - namely a forecast PD of 1.05% - no matter whether it is assigned to a large corporate or a retail customer. Additionally we assume that rating grades of the master scale mean the same across time. A rating grade 8 means the same no matter if it is assigned in 1998 or 2005. This definition is often referred to as Point-in-Time (PIT) rating approach.

2.5. Parties Concerned by the Quality of Rating Systems

In general we can distinguish three groups of stakeholders of a bank's internal rating system as illustrated in Figure 3.

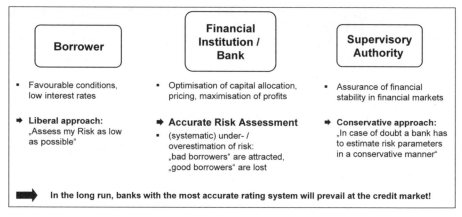

Figure 3. Parties concerned by the quality of rating systems

First of all, there is the supervisory authority with the main objective of ensuring the stability of credit markets and financial markets in general. Therefore, the solvency of the bank itself has to be assured. Transferring this intention to the field of testing the quality of rating systems supervisors will accept forecast PDs that are too high compared to the true PDs. But they will intervene, if the default risk is significantly underestimated. But supervisory authority tends to follow a rather conservative approach which is understandable from its position.

---

[9] Thinking in a logarithmic world, ln(PD) of the master scale grows almost linearly in the grades.

The opposite holds for the (possible) borrower, who is interested in low interest rates and favourable credit conditions. Assuming the price for the credit or at least the credit accommodation itself depends on the PD (beside the other risk parameters LGD and EAD), the borrower calls for a low PD assessment. So an underestimation of his PD is all right for the borrower, but an overestimation of his PD is not acceptable from his point of view.

The third party is the bank itself. Each kind of misjudgement of the creditworthiness harms an optimal capital allocation, a good pricing system, and, in consequence, the maximisation of profits. Therefore, we conclude that neither an underestimation nor an overestimation of risk is satisfactory. In terms of statistical test theory, supervisors and borrowers would perform one-sided statistical hypothesis tests whereas the bank prefers two-sided tests.

We introduce some notation in the next section and describe the theoretical framework.

3. Statistical Framework

We have obligors $i = 1,...,N$ each with a true, but unfortunately unknown probability of default $\pi_i \in [0;1]$. The main intention of the rating system is to forecast each π_i as accurately as possible. We denote a forecast by $\hat{\pi}_i$.

We want to start with the description of the theoretical framework of the default generating process (DGP). Therefore, we mainly refer to the well known model of categorical regression in its variations, logistic regression or probit regression. These topics are explained in detail in Chapter I.

The standard method used to describe a binary outcome variable y_i depending on one or more variables x_i is the categorical regression model. The model equation is

$$\pi_i(x_i) = P(y_i = 1 \mid x_i) = F(x_i'\beta) \tag{1}$$

The outcome variable y_i takes the value $y_i = 1$ if a default is observed and $y_i = 0$ if a non-default is observed. In the vector x_i all kinds of risk drivers are included. These may be financial ratios, obligor specific indicators like age or status of marriage, macroeconomic risk factors like GDP-growth-rate or interest rates, and even variables describing trends in industrial sectors. These variables mainly depend on the specific segment of obligors that is considered and on the data that is in general available for this segment[10]. Note that in equation (1), the probability of de-

---

[10] In more sophisticated models like panel models or hazard rate models (see Chapter I) the time index t has to be incorporated beside index i in order to account for the time de-

fault for obligor i, π_i, is the outcome of the model and not the forecast of the outcome event itself. Therefore, it fits perfectly into our basic understanding what a rating system should do as described in Section 1. The probability that obligor i gets in the status non-default is simply

$$1 - \pi_i(x_i) = P(y_i = 0 \mid x_i) = 1 - F(x_i'\beta) \tag{2}$$

The specification of the cumulative distribution function $F(.)$ denotes whether we assume a logistic model

$$\pi_i(x_i) = P(y_i = 1 \mid x_i) = \frac{e^{x_i'\beta}}{1 + e^{x_i'\beta}} \tag{3}$$

or a probit model.

$$\pi_i(x_i) = P(y_i = 1 \mid x_i) = \Phi(x_i'\beta) \tag{4}$$

where $\Phi(.)$ denotes the cumulative standard normal distribution function. Other specifications for $F(.)$ exist.

Often $x_i'\beta$ is called linear predictor or simply score. The vector β consists of the weights for the risk drivers in x used to obtain the score. Because $F(.)$ represents a cumulative distribution function, a monotonic relationship between $x_i'\beta$ and π_i is assured.

Some conceptional background should explain (3) and (4), the models of the categorical regression: Suppose that behind the observable dichotomy of the depending variable y_i, there is a non observable, meaning latent, continuous variable $\tilde{y}_i$. The value of $\tilde{y}_i$ depends on the value of the risk drivers x_i. If the latent variable $\tilde{y}_i$ falls below the also latent threshold θ_i the status $y_i = 1$ is observable, otherwise the status $y_i = 0$ is realised:

$$y_i = 1 \Leftrightarrow \tilde{y}_i = x_i'\beta + \tilde{\varepsilon}_i \leq \theta_i$$
$$y_i = 0 \Leftrightarrow \tilde{y}_i = x_i'\beta + \tilde{\varepsilon}_i > \theta_i \tag{5}$$

The error term $\tilde{\varepsilon}_i$ allows for randomness and is needed to account for idiosyncratic risk factors not covered in x_i. The random error term $\tilde{\varepsilon}_i$ follows a cumulative distribution function $F(.)$ and it is found

---

pendency of the risk drivers. In rating practice it is often assumed that the risk drivers in x are time-lagged (e.g. x_{t-1}) explaining the default of borrower i in t. For the reason of keeping things simple we neglect this time-series component in this chapter.

$$\pi_i(x_i) = P(y_i = 1 \mid x_i) = P(\tilde{y}_i \leq \theta_i) =$$
$$= P(\tilde{\varepsilon}_i \leq \theta_i - x_i'\beta) = F(\theta_i - x_i'\beta) = F(\tilde{\theta}_i) \tag{6}$$

The latent threshold θ_i can be combined with the constant β_0 in β and we obtain our starting point equation (1). Depending on the cumulative distribution function that is assumed for $\tilde{\varepsilon}_i$, a logit (3) or probit (4) model is obtained.

Further on, we will restrict ourselves to the standard normal distribution function. For example for a borrower i with a rating grade $k = 8$ - accompanied with a probability of default $\pi_{i,k=8} = 0.0105$ - we will acquire

$$\tilde{\theta}_{i,k=8} = \Phi^{-1}(0.0105) = -2.3080 .$$

So $\tilde{\theta}_{i,k}$ is determined by the PDs of the master scale grades.

As a next step, we want to extend the model in order to integrate the possibility of modelling dependencies in the DGP. A widely used approach is the one-factor model[11] which is also the basis of the Basel II formula for the risk weighted assets.

We split up the error term $\tilde{\varepsilon}_i$ in equation (5) in the components ε_i and f and get

$$y_i = 1 \Leftrightarrow \tilde{y}_i = x_i'\beta + \sqrt{\rho} \cdot f + \sqrt{1-\rho} \cdot \varepsilon_i \leq \theta_i$$
$$y_i = 0 \Leftrightarrow \tilde{y}_i = x_i'\beta + \sqrt{\rho} \cdot f + \sqrt{1-\rho} \cdot \varepsilon_i > \theta_i \tag{7}$$

where $f \sim N(0,1)$ and $\varepsilon_i \sim N(0,1)$ are normally distributed random variables with mean zero and standard deviation one. The random variable ε_i represents the idiosyncratic risk and f represent the so called systematic risk. It is assumed that idiosyncratic risk and systematic risk are independent and idiosyncratic risk is independent for two different borrowers. Therefore, the integration of the systematic factor f, models dependencies in the DGP of two borrowers and ρ is called the asset correlation:[12]

$$\sigma_i^2 = Var(\tilde{y}_i) = (\sqrt{\rho})^2 + (\sqrt{1-\rho})^2 = 1$$

$$\sigma_{ij} = Cov(\tilde{y}_i, \tilde{y}_j) = (\sqrt{\rho})^2 = \rho \tag{8}$$

$$\rho_{ij} = Corr(\tilde{y}_i, \tilde{y}_j) = \frac{Cov(\tilde{y}_i, \tilde{y}_j)}{Var(\tilde{y}_i) \cdot Var(\tilde{y}_j)} = \rho$$

---

[11] See for example Finger (2001).
[12] The asset correlation can be transformed in default correlations as shown in several papers, see e.g. BCBS (2005b, Chapter III).

Conditional on the realisation f of the common random factor, the (conditional) default probability becomes

$$\pi_i(\boldsymbol{x}_i, f) = P(y_i = 1 \mid \boldsymbol{x}_i, f) = P(\tilde{y}_i \leq \theta_i) =$$

$$= P\left(\boldsymbol{x}_i'\boldsymbol{\beta} + \sqrt{\rho} \cdot f + \sqrt{1-\rho} \cdot \varepsilon_i \leq \theta_i\right) =$$

$$= F\left(\varepsilon_i \leq \frac{\theta_i - \boldsymbol{x}_i'\boldsymbol{\beta} - \sqrt{\rho} \cdot f}{\sqrt{1-\rho}}\right) = \tag{9}$$

$$= \Phi\left(\frac{\tilde{\theta}_i - \sqrt{\rho} \cdot f}{\sqrt{1-\rho}}\right)$$

Up to now, this detailed annotation may seem to be purely academic, but we will see its practical benefits in Section 5 where we extend the (standard) statistical hypothesis test being introduced in the following section by using this simple but very useful model variant in order to account for dependent default events.

4. Central Statistical Hypothesis Tests Regarding Calibration

As should become apparent, the realisation $y_i = 1$ or $y_i = 0$, respectively, is the result of a random process (the DGP), which is expressed by including the random variable ε_i in our approach. This means that even if the parameters of the model $\boldsymbol{\beta}$ are specified perfectly correct, some unpredictable randomness still remains. Hence it is clear, that a certain realization of the default event could not be forecast, because this would imply that the rating system could exactly predict the realization of the random variable ε_i. This situation could easily be compared to the well known random experiment of throwing a dice. Even if you know that a six-sided dice is not bogus, you cannot predict the result. The best you can specify is the probability of throwing a certain number, in this example this is 1/6. By analogy, the best a rating system can do is to forecast the probability of default most exactly for each obligor i.

In the following, sometimes the term "calibration" is used. In our context calibration means a property of a rating system and not an action. The later interpretation as action - "to calibrate a model" - means to estimate the parameter of the (statistical) model, e.g. to estimate by means of OLS or a maximum likelihood estimator the coefficients in the equation of the logistic regression. But in this article "calibration" is more in the sense of "to be calibrated". The phrase refers to the outcomes of the rating systems and is a property of the rating system. This means that each forecast probability of default is right: $\hat{\pi}_i = \pi_i \; \forall i$. Therefore, we introduce several approaches how to perform tests on calibration next.

4.1. Binomial Test

4.1.1. Exact Binomial Test

Someone whose task is to validate the hypothesis whether the PDs predicted by a rating system are consistent with observed default events, will most likely perform the well known binomial test, as presented in standard statistical textbooks, as a first step.

Suppose we have N_g obligors in rating grade g, and all of them have the same (true but unknown) probability of default π_g. If we assume that the realisations are independent from each other, (we will drop this constraint at a later stage), then the number of defaults in grade g, $N_{g,y=1}$, follows a binomial distribution with

$$P\left(N_{g,y=1} \mid N_g, \pi_g\right) = \binom{N_g}{N_{g,y=1}} \cdot \pi_g^{N_{g,y=1}} \cdot \left(1 - \pi_g\right)^{N_g - N_{g,y=1}} \tag{10}$$

Based on this, we could perform a statistical hypothesis test with the null hypothesis

$$H_0 : \pi_g = \hat{\pi}_g \tag{11}$$

and the alternative

$$H_1 : \pi_g \neq \hat{\pi}_g \tag{12}$$

where $\hat{\pi}_g$ denotes the forecast derived from the rating system. The test statistic is the observed number of defaults $N_{g,y=1}$ and we reject the null hypothesis if the incidence of observing $N_{g,y=1}$ under H_0 is too unlikely. What is meant by "too unlikely" is defined by the confidence level α. Knowing the distribution of $N_{g,y=1}$ under H_0 we can calculate these critical region as

$$N_{g,y=1} \leq b\left(\alpha/2\right)$$
$$\text{or} \tag{13}$$
$$N_{g,y=1} \geq b\left(1 - \alpha/2\right)$$

where $b(.)$[13] is the quantile of the cumulative distribution function of the binomial distribution $B(N_g, \pi_g)$.

Figure 4 illustrates an example with $N_g = 350$ in rating grade 8. If we will observe at least 9 defaults or no default at all this is too unlikely under the null hypothesis.

---

[13] It has to hold for $b\left(\alpha/2\right)$: $B\left(b\left(\alpha/2\right) \mid N_g; \pi_g\right) \leq \alpha/2 < B\left(b\left(\alpha/2\right)+1 \mid N_g; \pi_g\right)$ and for $b\left(1-\alpha/2\right)$: $1 - B\left(b\left(1-\alpha/2\right)-1 \mid N_g; \pi_g\right) \leq \alpha/2 < 1 - B\left(b\left(\alpha/2\right)-2 \mid N_g; \pi_g\right)$.

In this case we would reject the correctness of the null hypothesis knowing that we made a wrong decision with probability of $\alpha = 0.05$.

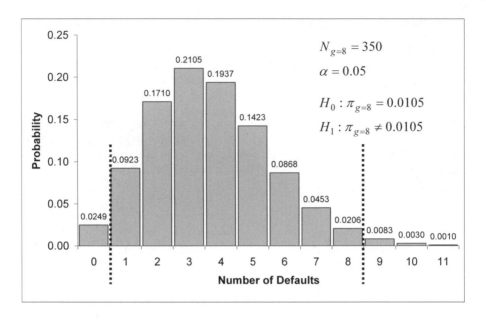

Figure 4. Illustrative binomial test with marked rejection areas

4.1.2. Normal Approximation of the Binomial Test

The normal approximation of the exact binomial test is often applied in practice, using the fact that the exact discrete binomial distribution converges to the normal distribution for increasing sample sizes. As a rule of thumb, this approximation may be sound if $N_g \cdot \pi_g \geq 10$ and at the same time $N_g \cdot \pi_g \cdot (1-\pi_g) \geq 10$ holds.[14] The number of defaults is normally distributed $N_g \sim N(N_g \cdot \pi_g \,; N_g \cdot \pi_g \cdot (1-\pi_g))$ and the test statistic has to be constructed as

$$Z_{bin} = \frac{N_g \cdot \bar{y}_g - N_g \cdot \pi_g}{\sqrt{N_g \cdot \pi_g \cdot (1 - \pi_g)}} \sim N(0,1) \tag{14}$$

and follows a standard normal distribution, where $\bar{y}_g = N_{g,y=1}/N_g$ denotes the observed default rate in rating grade g. Performing the two-sided hypothesis test, the critical values can easily be derived as the $\alpha/2$ and $1-\alpha/2$ - quantile of the standard normal distribution.

---

[14] This rule of thumb may vary depending on what statistical text book is consulted.

4.2. Spiegelhalter Test (SPGH)

Up to now, we have presented very standard approaches. But these approaches have a shortfall, namely they are primarily suited for testing a single rating grade but not several or all rating grades simultaneously.

Spiegelhalter (1986) introduced a further generalisation we call Spiegelhalter test (SPGH). Originally it was used in the context of clinical statistics and the validation of weather forecasts.

The starting point is the Mean Square Error (MSE), also known as Brier Score[15]

$$MSE = \frac{1}{N} \sum_{i=1}^{N} (v_i - \hat{\pi}_i)^2 \tag{15}$$

representing the squared difference of the default ($v_i = 1$) and non-default ($v_i = 0$) indicators, respectively, and the corresponding default probability forecast $\hat{\pi}_i$ [16] averaged across all obligors.

Obviously the MSE gets small, if the forecast PD assigned to defaults is high and the forecast PD assigned to non-defaults is low. Generally speaking, a small value of MSE indicates a good rating system. The higher the MSE the worse is the performance of the rating system (keeping other things equal).

The MSE can be interpreted as a weighted average of independent Bernoulli distributed random variables. Spiegelhalter derived an approach which allows us to test whether an observed MSE is significantly different from its expected value or not. Again the hypotheses are

$$H_0 : \ \pi_i = \hat{\pi}_i \ \ \forall \ i$$
$$\text{and} \tag{16}$$
$$H_1 : \text{not } H_0$$

Then under H_0 the MSE has an expected value of

$$E(MSE_{\pi_i = \hat{\pi}_i}) = \frac{1}{N} \sum_{i=1}^{N} \pi_i \cdot (1 - \pi_i) \tag{17}$$

and variance

$$Var(MSE_{\pi_i = \hat{\pi}_i}) = \frac{1}{N^2} \sum_{i=1}^{N} (1 - 2\pi_i)^2 \cdot \pi_i \cdot (1 - \pi_i) \tag{18}$$

---

[15] See Brier (1950)

[16] $\hat{\pi}_i = \hat{\pi}_g$ if obligor i is rated in rating grade g.

It is obvious from (17) that the expected value of the MSE under the null hypothesis is greater than zero[17], and a function of the true (but unknown) probabilities of defaults. Therefore the absolute value of the MSE is not a meaningful performance index of the rating system because its value is constrained by the quality of the rating system <u>and</u> the portfolio structure i.e. the true but unknown default probabilities.

Using the central limit theorem, it can be shown that under the null hypothesis the test statistic

$$
Z_S = \frac{MSE - E(MSE_{\pi_i = \hat{\pi}_i})}{Var(MSE_{\pi_i = \hat{\pi}_i})^{0,5}} = \frac{\dfrac{1}{N}\sum_{i=1}^{N}(y_i - \pi_i)^2 - \dfrac{1}{N}\sum_{i=1}^{N}\pi_i \cdot (1 - \pi_i)}{\sqrt{\dfrac{1}{N^2}\sum_{i=1}^{N}(1 - 2\pi_i)^2 \cdot \pi_i \cdot (1 - \pi_i)}}
\tag{19}
$$

follows a standard normal distribution and the familiar steps coming to a test decision have to be conducted.

It can be shown that a forecaster (in our case the rating system) minimizes its expected MSE when he or she forecasts the probability of default for each obligor equal to its true default probability.[18] There is no way of improving the MSE by modifying the forecast probabilities away from the true probabilities. Thus it can be stated that the MSE rewards honest forecasting. This is known as a proper scoring rule.[19]

As a special case of the SPGH statistic, namely if there is just one single probability of default in the entire portfolio, then the SPGH statistic Z_S is exactly equal to the Z_{bin} of the approximated binomial test.[20]

The major advantage of the SPGH test over the binomial test is that with the former all rating grades can be tested simultaneously on the property of calibration within one step.[21]

4.3. Hosmer-Lemeshow-χ^2 Test (HSLS)

The same can be done with an approach introduced by Hosmer and Lemeshow (1980, 2000). Their test statistic has its origin in the field of categorical regression

---

[17] As long as we do not consider the special case of a deterministic DGP, where all true PDs are zero or one.

[18] See De Groot and Fienberg (1983)

[19] See e.g. Murphy and Dann (1985)

[20] See Appendix A

[21] Rauhmeier and Scheule (2005) show that by factorising the MSE more rating properties could be derived and how they influence Basel II capital.

and is often used in the process of model finding as a performance measure for "goodness-of-fit".

The SPGH test penalizes squared differences between realised event indicators (default or non-default) and PD forecasts on an individual level.[22] In contrast, the basic idea of the Hosmer-Lemeshow test (HSLS) is to penalize squared differences of forecast default rates from realised default rates on a group level as could be seen from numerator terms in (20).

$$\chi^2_{HL} = \sum_{g=1}^{G} \frac{(N_g \cdot \overline{y}_g - N_g \cdot \hat{\pi}_g)^2}{N_g \cdot \hat{\pi}_g \cdot (1 - \hat{\pi}_g)} = \sum_{g-1}^{G} N_g \cdot \frac{(\overline{y}_g - \hat{\pi}_g)^2}{\hat{\pi}_g \cdot (1 - \hat{\pi}_g)} \tag{20}$$

Originally the groups come from arranging individual forecasts into e.g. ten centiles or by using the number of covariate patterns in the logistic regression model. In this context, the groups are defined by the rating grades.[23] When using the HSLS test statistic as a means of backtesting, χ^2_{HL} is approximately χ^2-distributed with G degrees of freedom.[24, 25] This can easily be seen because χ^2_{HL} consists in fact of G independent squared standard normal distributed random variables if

$$H_0: \pi_g = \hat{\pi}_g \quad \forall\, g \tag{21}$$

holds. It can be shown that in an extreme case, when there is just one rating grade at all, the HSLS test statistic and the (squared) SPGH test statistic and the (squared) approximated binomial test statistic are identical.

4.4. A Test for Comparing Two Rating Systems: The Redelmeier Test

Up to now we have introduced approaches adequate for testing whether the final outcomes of the rating system - forecasts of PDs for each obligor - are statistically in line with their realisations. This is unquestionably the main objective of statistical backtesting. But, more questions arise when dealing with rating systems in

---

[22] See (19)

[23] Hosmer et al. (1988) allude to some approximation conditions, e.g. that in about 4/5 of all groups the expected number of defaults should exceed the number of five and in no group the number of defaults should be smaller than one.

[24] G denotes the number of rating grades with $N_g > 1$, i.e. with at least one obligors being rated in this class.

[25] When using the HSLS statistic as a measure of fit in the process of model finding, then we say "in-sample", because the model estimation sample and the sample on which the measure of fit is computed are identically. In this case the distribution is χ^2 with $G - 2$ degrees of freedom. When using the HSLS statistic for backtesting, we say "out-of-sample", because there is no observation coexistent in the estimation sample and the validation sample.

practice. One might be interested in knowing whether the quality of the rating system is significantly enhanced when e.g. using so called human expertise in a module subsequent to the machine rating module. This interest might arise from a purely statistical perspective, but in banking practice, the rating systems which are to be implemented and maintained, are cost intensive. These costs may include salaries for the rating analysts as well as IT-related costs for operating systems and data storage.

First of all we want to stress that only a comparison of two or more rating systems by means of the same rating data is meaningful as mentioned in Section 3.2 and in Chapter XII. This means the same obligors (by name) in the same time period and with the same default indicator definition have to be used.[26] Therefore, while it is in general not feasible to compare ratings across banks - one should think of business confidentiality and protection of data privacy - this may be done in the context of pooling[27], or especially when comparing two rating modules of the same rating system of a bank. We may primarily attend to the latter.

The basic idea of the approach introduced by Redelmeier et al. (1991) is to compare two MSEs calculated on the same data basis. A test statistic is derived which allows us to test whether the deviation of a realised MSE from its expected value is significantly different of the deviation of another realised MSE of its expected value derived by an other module on the same data basis. As described in Section 3.2 the module with the lower MSE is the better one.

The test statistic[28] is

$$
Z_R = \frac{\sum_{i=1}^{N}\left[\left(\hat{\pi}_{i,m1}^2 - \hat{\pi}_{i,m2}^2\right) - 2\left(\hat{\pi}_{i,m1} - \hat{\pi}_{i,m2}\right)\cdot y_i\right]}{\left[\sum_{i=1}^{N}\left[\left(\hat{\pi}_{i,m1} - \hat{\pi}_{i,m2}\right)^2\left(\hat{\pi}_{i,m1} + \hat{\pi}_{i,m2}\right)\left(2 - \hat{\pi}_{i,m1} - \hat{\pi}_{i,m2}\right)\right]\right]^{0,5}} \tag{22}
$$

and follows a standard normal distribution under the hypotheses:

$$
H_0 : E\left[\left(E\left(MSE_{m1}\right) - MSE_{m1}\right) - \left(E\left(MSE_{m2}\right) - MSE_{m2}\right)\right] = 0
$$
$$
\text{and} \tag{23}
$$
$$
H_1 : E\left[\left(E\left(MSE_{m1}\right) - MSE_{m1}\right) - \left(E\left(MSE_{m2}\right) - MSE_{m2}\right)\right] \neq 0
$$

Note that it only makes sense to compare two MSE derived from two modules when each module passes a test of calibration like the SPGH test for example. Otherwise, comparing two MSE with respect to the property calibration is useless

---

[26] See Chapter XII and Hamerle et al. (2005).

[27] Here we mean cooperation of autonomous banks organized in a project structure with the object of gathering data in order to enlarge the common data basis by merging banks individual data bases.

[28] See Appendix B for details.

knowing that at least one of the two modules is not fulfilling the premise to be in line with the forecasts.

We stress that we do not pay attention to theoretical considerations on statistical tests regarding discriminatory power as presented in Chapter XII, but we use them in our empirical analysis in Section 7.

5. The Use of Monte-Carlo Simulation Technique

As mentioned previously, the statistical tests introduced to date are based on crucial assumptions like independent realisations of defaults and / or a large number of observations in order to ensure that the central limit theorem holds. Using a simulation technique, which is sometimes referred to as Monte-Carlo-Simulation, allows us to drop these limiting assumptions. Fortunately, the basic ideas of the approaches discussed in Section 4 could be taken up and be combined with the default generation process of Section 3.

Furthermore, these techniques could be used to derive some results on the analysis regarding the test power (β- error) under practical, near to reality conditions. This is a fundamental concept in order to highlight the chance of a non-detection of a low quality rating system.

5.1. Monte-Carlo-Simulation and Test Statistic: Correction of Finite Sample Size and Integration of Asset Correlation

The fundamental idea is to derive the distribution of the test statistic (e.g. SPGH Z_S, HSLS χ^2_{HL}) under the null hypothesis by simulation, that means by replication of a random experiment several times. If basic assumptions like independent default events or infinite sample size are not fulfilled, we can implement those circumstances in our simulation process and substitute the theoretical test statistic (e.g. normal distribution in the case of the SPGH test), by the one obtained by the simulation. All test decisions are then based on the "new" simulated distribution of the test statistic. The more simulation runs are used, the more accurately the new simulated distribution can be determined.

Our approach is very similar to the one in Balthazar (2004) and could be interpreted as an extension, as his focus was on tests for a single rating grade whereas we want to use tests for all grades simultaneously.

Firstly, we consider the simulation under $H_0 : \hat{\pi}_k = \pi_k$: The simulation approach could be best illustrated in eight steps starting with equation (6):

1. Calculate the threshold $\widetilde{\theta}_{i,k} = \Phi^{-1}(\pi_k)$ depending on which rating grade the obligor i is rated into ($\widetilde{\theta}_{i,k} = \theta_i - x_i'\beta$). Constitute the asset correlation ρ before the start of the simulation.[29]

2. Generate a realisation of the random variable $f \sim N(0,1)$. This represents the common factor of the DGP, the systematic risk.

3. For each obligor $i = 1,\ldots,N$ in the examined portfolio: generate a realisation of the random variable $\varepsilon_i \sim N(0,1)$. This represents the idiosyncratic, unsystematic risk.

4. Calculate the value of $\widetilde{y}_i$ under consideration of ρ.

5. Calculate whether obligor i defaults in this simulation run according to (7).

6. Calculate all the test statistics of interest.

7. Repeat steps two to six, say about 1 Mio times (i.e. 1 Mio simulation runs) and generate a simulated distribution of the test statistic (based on the simulated defaults).

8. Having a simulated distribution of the test statistic, the rejection areas of the H_0 can be calculated and by comparison with the observed test statistic value, a test decision could be derived for each test considered.

This approach permits a very flexible application because according to requirements, several values for the asset correlation could be analysed with respect to their impact on the distribution of the test statistic. Secondly, the impact of the portfolio size may be studied but this is not our focus as in normal backtesting situations the portfolio is given. Nevertheless, someone might get a feeling for the variance caused by low numbers of obligors and / or the impact of the supposed asset correlation ρ.

5.1.1. The Simultaneous Binomial Test (Sim Bin)

The above described eight steps are sufficient to generate the simulated χ^2-HSLS test statistic and the simulated SPGH-Z_S[30] in order to backtest a whole rating system - all grades simultaneously - under more practical situations. Considering the exact binomial test a further challenge arises. Whereas the binomial test by means of the simulation has been extended for integration of correlation, (the number of defaults under the simulation scenario divided by the number of obligors in the rating grade generates the simulated test distribution), there still is the problem of using the results of the grade-wise conducted binomial tests for the backtesting of all grades simultaneously. Our aim is to draw a conclusion for the whole rating system and not just for a single grade.

---

[29] We will discuss this point in detail later.

[30] We have to emphasis that the simulated HSLS test statistic is generally not χ^2 distributed as well as the simulated Spiegelhalter test statistic is not standard normal distributed but for convenience we maintain the termini χ^2 and Z_S.

The starting point of our consideration is the fact that for a rating system of 14 grades and a binomial test done with $\alpha = 0.10$, we have to expect that for 1.4 grades, the correct null hypothesis will be rejected. Someone who assumes that a rating system is "good" only if the statistical test fails for no grade, is off the track.

Therefore, we suggest a two-staged approach within our simulation framework when the binomial test is used. The two steps are:

1. Generate the rejection areas for each grade individually (maybe regarding some correlation with help of the Monte-Carlo-simulation) on a certain α - level and conduct the test decision.
2. Count the number of "grade-wise rejections" per simulation run (introduce a step 7b in our 8 step approach) and use them to generate the distribution of the "sum of grade-wise rejections". When the $1 - \alpha_{sb}$-percentile of this distribution is exceeded (i.e. the critical value) by the observed sum of rejections of the individual grade-wise test, the rating system as a whole would fail the quality check.[31] Note that we perform a one-sided test in this second level. The reason is that, assuming very low numbers of grade-wise rejections indicates a high quality of a rating system and too many grade-wise rejections are a signal of a low quality rating system.

5.1.2. Remarks on the Adherence of the α-Level with Using the Exact Binomial Test

We would like to point out that because of the discreteness of the binomial distribution, the α - level that is in fact being held is lower than the ascertained α would suggest. We call this phenomenon "effect of dilution". Therefore, a binomial test is in general "too less conservative" as could be seen for example in Figure 4 where the probability of being in the non-rejection area (1 - 8 defaults) is 96.24% and therefore the real α - level is 3.76% which is evidently lower as the composed level of 5%. The (correct) null hypothesis is rejected in much fewer cases than expected.

This is especially true for samples with a low number of borrowers. The effect disappears when the exact binomial distribution converges to the normal distribution with a growing number of borrowers or to any other continuous distribution generated by simulation as described above.

The effect of dilution intensifies when using the simultaneous binomial test in stage two as a discrete distribution is also used here (see e.g. Table 2).

---

[31] We use α_{sb} to label the simultaneous binomial test. We point out that the α - level of the individual tests and the α_{sb} - level of the distribution of the sum of the grade-wise rejections (simultaneous binomial test) need not to be the same value.

5.1.3. Simulation Study A: Impact of Portfolio Size and Correlation

To demonstrate our theoretical findings above, we perform a small simulation study. We have three portfolios, each with the same relative distribution over the grades as shown in Figure 5, but with different absolute size. We start with a small portfolio, with $N = 200$ obligors representing for example a portfolio of large corporates or financial institutions, next we have a portfolio of $N = 1000$ acting as an example for a portfolio of middle sized corporates and finally we analyse a portfolio consisting of $N = 10,000$ obligors which could be seen as a portfolio of small business clients.

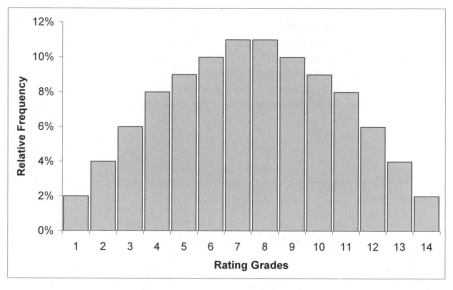

Figure 5. Distribution of the borrowers over the rating grades in simulation study A

The distribution we applied is bell-shaped[32] as could be seen from Figure 5 with an average probability of default $\bar{\pi} = 0.0308$ and π_g's according to the master scale of Section 2.4 (e.g. $\pi_{g=8} = 0.0105$). All tests are done with $\alpha = 0.05$.

In Table 2 the results of our simulation study are presented. We show the lower and upper bound of the SPGH for the three portfolio sizes and furthermore, for three assumed asset correlations $\rho = 0.00$, $\rho = 0.01$ and $\rho = 0.10$. For the HSLS it is sufficient that we show only the upper bound because the lower bound is fixed at zero. We also report in the column titled "Identical decisions" how often the SPGH and HSLS came to the same test decision as we want to analyse whether someone has to await different (and therefore confusing) test decisions when ap-

---

[32] Often in banking practice the master scale is constituted in the way that many obligors are rated in the grades in the middle of the master scale and fewer in the very good or very bad grades.

plying both tests. As we can see from our study, in 95% to > 99%, the HSLS and SPGH reach the same test decision.

In general, we can state, that when ρ increases, the distribution gets broader and therefore the bounds of the non-rejection areas move outwards. Especially for the exact binomial test and the simultaneous binomial test, this effect is somewhat diluted because of the discrete character of these distributions.

Table 2. Results from the simulation study A, non-rejection areas, 1 million runs, $\alpha = 0.05$

	Portfolio Size		SPGH		HSLS	Identical decisions	Sim Bin[33]	Exact Bin, $g = 8$	
ρ	N	$N_{g=8}$	lower bound	upper bound	upper bound	in %[34]	upper bound[35]	lower bound	upper bound
0.00			-1.7551	2.1437	34.40	95.74	1	0.0000	0.0455
0.01	200	22	-1.8448	2.4306	35.64	95.93	1	0.0000	0.0455
0.10			-2.0505	4.7912	54.98	99.45	1	0.0000	0.0909
0.00			-1.8697	2.0403	33.05	95.48	2	0.0000	0.0364
0.01	1000	110	-2.5659	3.1637	36.21	96.09	2	0.0000	0.0364
0.10			-4.6298	9.5255	93.89	97.51	2	0.0000	0.0455
0.00			-1.9569	1.9665	28.91	95.39	2	0.0046	0.0164
0.01	10,000	1100	-6.1455	7.7193	65.90	98.05	2	0.0036	0.0200
0.10			-14.0278	29.2670	527.55	97.50	4	0.0000	0.0391

When we look at the SPGH under $\rho = 0.00$, we clearly see how the approximation to the standard normal distribution is improved when the number of observations is increased. For $N = 10,000$ we get very close to the $Z_S = \Phi^{-1}(0.025) \approx -1.96$ (lower bound) and $Z_S = \Phi^{-1}(0.975) \approx +1.96$ (upper bound) we expect. The same is true in principle for the HSLS but the convergence is much slower, as it holds $\chi(0.95,14) \approx 23.68$.

What is interesting is that in the presence of asset correlation ($\rho > 0.00$), an increased in N leads seemingly not to a convergence of the boundaries to any value. Instead, when we extend from $N = 1,000$ to $N = 10,000$, the non-rejection area increases dramatically from [-4.6298 ; +9.5255] to [-14.0278 ; +29.2670] by $\rho = 0.10$. The same holds for HSLS and Sim Bin but not for the exact binomial test.

---

[33] In the first and the second step we used a $\alpha = 0.05$ regarding the simultaneous binomial test.

[34] In percent of the 1 million simulation runs

[35] Marks the upper bound of the non-rejection area. For example in the first row ($\rho = 0.00$ and $N = 200$), simultaneous binomial test: If 2 or more grade-wise rejections are observed, the rating system as a whole would be rejected.
Exact binomial test for rating grade 8: If a default rate of more than 0.0455 is observed (more than $22 \cdot 0.0455 = 1$ default) the null hypothesis can be rejected.

Now, we turn to the Sim Bin as we reported the simulation details in Table 3. As stated already above, we expect using $\alpha = 0.05$, a number of $0.05 \cdot 14 = 0.7$ grade-wise rejections on average (expected value). Because of the effect of dilution, this value was not achieved as could be calculated from Table 3: For $\rho = 0.01$ and $N = 10,000$, we get 0.57 whereas the effect of dilution is quite higher for $\rho = 0.00$, as we get just 0.49. Therefore, the effect of dilution on step one and step two is weakened when correlation is taken into account.

Table 3. Simultaneous binomial test, portfolio size $N = 10,000$, $\alpha = 0.05$

Number of grade-wise rejections	$\rho = 0.10$	$\rho = 0.00$
0	86.1791	60.7638
1	5.9460	30.8927
2	1.6888	7.2325
3	0.9566	1.0092
4	0.6389	0.0952
5	0.5221	0.0067
6	0.4445	-
7	0.4462	-
8	0.4679	-
9	0.5172	-
10	0.5810	-
11	0.6455	-
12	0.5681	-
13	0.3122	-

We conclude this subject with the proposition that all of the three tests conducted within our simulation framework are appropriate for means of backtesting. It is somewhat a question of flavour which test is preferred for banks' backtesting. We tend to suggest SPGH because of its "most continuous" distribution generated by the simulation.

5.1.3. Remarks on the Asset Correlation

As can be seen from Table 2, the extent of the asset correlation ρ has a very high impact on the distributions of the test statistics and therefore finally on the test decisions itself. We feel it is worthwhile to think twice which asset correlation to use. Though we do not want to describe how asset correlations can be estimated in detail, we discuss some basic considerations regarding the right choice of asset correlations and its impact on PD validation.

First of all, the asset correlations used in the backtesting of the bank's internal rating model should be in line with the asset correlations used in other fields of the bank wide (credit) risk management systems as in the credit portfolio model. This guarantees a consistent bank wide risk assessment.

In practice, asset correlations are often not estimated on bank internal data, but based on empirical studies on external data which serve as a guideline. For example, Hamerle et al. (2003) report that asset correlations in a point-in-time rating framework are in a range of roughly 0.01 to 0.02. This is slightly higher than assuming no asset correlation at all - the most conservative approach regarding statistical backtesting - but much lower than the asset correlations used in the Basel II framework. In the latter, the asset correlation depends on the corresponding exposure class and varies from $\rho = 0.04$ (exposure class: Qualifying Revolving Retail) over $\rho = 0.15$ (Residential Mortgage) up to $\rho = 0.16$ (Other Retail), $\rho = 0.24$ (Corporates, Sovereigns and Banks), and even $\rho = 0.30$ for High Volatile Commercial Real Estate. These Basel II asset correlations might not be taken as best estimators of asset correlations by nature, but rather are assessed by political regulatory concerns in the light of being conservative.

5.2. Assessing the Test Power by Means of Monte-Carlo-Simulation

5.2.1. Theoretical Background

As mentioned above, a further application of the Monte-Carlo-Simulation is the assessment of the type II error or the pendant, called test power. Our aim is to derive an approach for getting an idea of how well our tests work with respect to the test power. In general, the power of a statistical hypothesis test measures the test's ability to reject the null hypothesis when it is actually false - that is, to make a correct decision.

Table 4 gives an overview of the possibilities of correct and incorrect decisions one can make with statistical hypothesis tests.

Table 4. Types of test decisions and its consequences

		Test Decision	
		H_0	H_1
Reality	H_0 is true	Correct decision	Type I Error (α-Error)
	H_1 is true	Type II Error (β-Error)	Correct decision

The type II error (β- error) is defined as the probability of not rejecting H_0 when in fact H_1 is right. The power of a statistical hypothesis test is defined as the probability of not committing a type II error. It is calculated by subtracting the probability of a type II error from one: power = $(1 - \beta)$.

Whereas we can control the α-error by setting α to a specific value (usually 0.01, 0.05 or 0.10), we have no control of the β-error simultaneously. The reason is that the β-error depends on the hypothesis H_1. We will not go into theoretical details, but demonstrate it with an example.

We refresh the example for the exact binomial test of Section 3.1.1 with H_0: $\pi_{g=8} = 0.0105$ and H_1: $\pi_{g=8} \neq 0.0105$. With this pair of hypotheses, there are an infinite number of possibly alternative hypotheses. Therefore, we have to pick out one of these. For example, we can specify H_1: $\pi_{g=8} = 2 \cdot 0.0105 = 0.0210$. Thus, we can calculate the possibility of detecting a false H_0 when the true PD of the grade is twice as high as predicted.

The grey bars in Figure 6 mark the distribution under H_1. The area outside of the non-rejection area of H_0 (no default and at least 9 defaults) and under the H_1-distribution determines the test power.

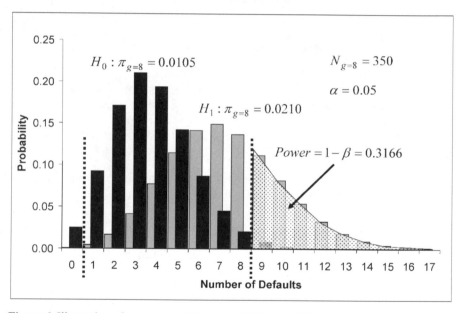

Figure 6. Illustration of α-error and β-error with the exact binomial test

In our example, we get a power of 0.3166. In general - ceteris paribus - the power of a test rises if

- the number of borrowers rises,
- the distance of values under H_0 and H_1 (here the PDs) rises,
- the α-level is raised.

5.2.2. Simulation Study B: What is the "best test"?

The concept of assessing the test power is obviously not restricted to the exact binomial test but applicable to other statistical tests and in particular, the SPGH test and the HSLS test and even the simultaneous binomial test. Furthermore, the concept works well in our framework which allows correlations.

In the following, we take the simulation framework of Section 5.1 and add more steps in order to analyze the test power. Now, steps one to eight have to be done under H_0 and again under H_1. Finally the area outside the non-rejection area of H_0 has to be calculated under the H_1 distribution.[36]

The focus is twofold:

- First, we want to analyse how the power reacts under certain conditions such as varying numbers of borrowers and / or asset correlations.
- Second, we want to analyse which of our tests – SPGH, HSLS or simultaneous binomial - performs best.

We call test A better than another test B if it has more power (a lower type II error), with respect to an alternative hypothesis H_1, but at the same time holds the assumed α - level.[37, 38]

We emphasise that we do not want to carry out a stringent mathematical proof, but merely provide an initial glance within our simulation framework.

This chapter is strongly orientated towards real banking practice and we continue this approach in this subsection: We distinguish three modes which may serve as point alternative hypothesis H_1:

- Mode 1: a fraction $1 - q$ of all borrowers is assumed to be classified in the correct grade where the fraction q is randomly distributed over all rating grades.
- Mode 2: all borrowers are graded up by s grades
- Mode 3: all borrowers are graded down by s grades[39]

Whereas Mode 2 and Mode 3 describe a systematic, monotonic error in the rating system,[40] Mode 1 represents a mixture of incorrect ratings and might be the most realistic problem in backtesting rating systems.

---

[36] We assume hereby again that the relative frequency resulting from the 1 million runs is a good enough approximation for the probability.

[37] This is similar but - not identical - to the concept of "uniformly most powerful test". A test is called a "uniformly most powerful test" to a level α if under a given initial situation it maximizes the probability of rejecting the H_0 on all distributions or parameter values belonging to the alternative hypothesis H_1.

[38] The latter is fulfilled automatically as we derived the boundaries if the non-rejection area within the simulation.

[39] Rating grade 1 (14) has an upper (lower) 'absorbing boundary' which means that a borrower in the first (last) rating grade remains in it and cannot become better (worse).

Table 5. Results from the simulation study B, Power, 1 million runs, $\alpha = 0.05$

ρ	N	SPGH	HSLS	Sim Bin
		Mode 1: $q = 0.5$		
0.00		0.1746	0.2408	0.1071
0.01	200	0.1482	0.2345	0.1066
0.10		0.0686	0.1595	0.1071
0.00		0.7644	0.9987	0.9763
0.01	1000	0.4345	0.9954	0.9763
0.10		0.1001	0.8239	0.9759
0.00		> 0.9999	> 0.9999	> 0.9999
0.01	10,000	0.6839	> 0.9999	> 0.9999
0.10		0.1111	0.9606	> 0.9999
		Mode 2: all borrowers graded up by $s = 1$		
0.00		0.1927	0.0203	0.0015
0.01	200	0.1863	0.0200	0.0016
0.10		0.0036	0.0204	0.0016
0.00		0.7605	0.0291	0.0139
0.01	1000	0.4697	0.0228	0.0138
0.10		0.1369	0.0130	0.0138
0.00		> 0.9999	> 0.9999	0.9996
0.01	10,000	0.7510	0.6141	0.9996
0.10		0.1543	0.0078	0.9996
		Mode 3: all borrowers graded down by $s = 1$		
0.00		0.3428	0.1699	0.1568
0.01	200	0.2836	0.1719	0.1563
0.10		0.1217	0.1385	0.1560
0.00		0.9119	0.4875	0.4277
0.01	1000	0.5854	0.4275	0.4282
0.10		0.1362	0.1905	0.4295
0.00		> 0.9999	> 0.9999	> 0.9999
0.01	10,000	0.7771	0.8669	> 0.9999
0.10		0.1388	0.2212	> 0.9999

Table 5 shows the result of our simulation study. As expected, an increase in portfolio size leads, ceteris paribus, generally to an increase in power. This is true for the three tests and for the three modes regarded. Further on, an increase in asset correlation - leaving the portfolio size constant - decreases the power.

---

[40] Within the master scale we use (see Section 2.4) the PD from one rating grade to the next worse grade increases by a factor between 1.75 and 2 depending on the specific grade.

It is remarkable that when looking at the SPGH already at $N = 1,000$ and by $\rho = 0.01$ or lower for all three modes, a power near to or over 0.5 is achieved. But the picture is quite mixed when regarding the HSLS or Sim Bin. These two tests perform worse in comparison to SPGH especially for Mode 2 and a small portfolio size.

Analysing the relative competitiveness of the SPGH, HSLS and Sim Bin the picture is not unambiguous. Regarding Mode 1, which stands for an interchange of obligors' assessed rating, HSLS seems to be the best choice. SPGH outperforms when the systematic up-grade by one grade is analysed as an alternative hypothesis. Even the Sim Bin in some situations has the highest power.

What can we learn from this simulation study about power and what are the consequences for practical backtesting? We conclude that unfortunately none of the statistical test we analysed clearly outperforms the others in all circumstances. For practical issues, all tests should be performed when an assessment of the probability of non-detecting a low quality rating system is required.

What is most important at all is that especially the higher management should be aware that there is[41] a (perhaps significant) probability that in fact H_0 is wrong, but the statistical tools did not reveal this. Our simulation approach can be interpreted as an instrument to fulfil this purpose.

6. Creating Backtesting Data Sets – The Concept of the Rolling 12-Month-Windows

Up to now we have shown some concepts for statistical backtesting, but when dealing with real data, the first step is always to create a specific sample on which a meaningful analysis can be carried out.

In banking practice ratings are performed continually over the year, for instance, when a new customer must be evaluated, a credit line requires extension, new information (e.g. financial figures) concerning a borrower already in the portfolio comes up, or questions of any fields regarding the creditworthiness are recognised.

We propose an approach for creating backtesting samples clearly in line with
- the definition of what a rating is, namely a forecast for the 1-Year-PD.
- what could be found in the IT-database at any point of time we may look into it.
- the general concept a bank manages its credit risks including the calculation of Basel II risk capital.

---

[41] This is true even if the hypothesis H_0 "The rating system forecasts the PD well." could not be rejected at a certain level α.

From these guidelines, it follows that whenever we look into the rating database we find the bank's best assessment of the borrower's probability of default for the next year. This is irrespective of how old the rating is at the time we look into the database. This is because when the bank has an inducement that when there is a noteworthy change in the creditworthiness of the borrower (its PD), the bank has to alter the rating immediately[42]. This means that a re-rating just once a year, for example whenever new annual accounts are available, might be not adequate in the case when other, relevant information regarding the PD in any form is made available. When there is no change in the rating, it remains valid and predicates each day the same, namely the forecast of the 1-year-PD from the day we found it in the database.

In the same way, the second essential variable, the defaults and non-defaults, have to be collected.

The termination of the backtesting sample is done according to the principle of reporting date. We call this approach 'cutting slices' or 'rolling 12-months-window' (compare to Figure 7).

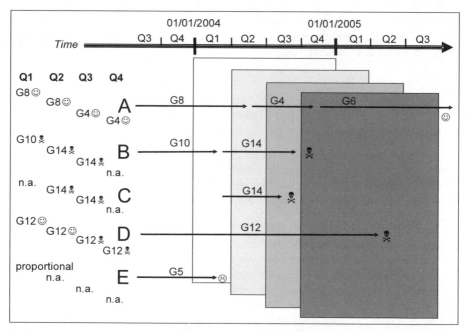

Figure 7. Concept of the rolling 12-Months-Windows – the backtesting slices

We start with the first slice called 'Q1/2004', which begins at January 2004. We look in the database and find borrower A with rating grade 8. He was rated with grade 8 a few months before (and gets other ratings after 1st January 2004), but

[42] See BCBS (2005a), § 411 and § 449.

has grade 8 at the beginning of January 2004. Within the next 12 months (up to the end of December 2004) he did not get into default, this was indicated with a ☺. He enters the slice 'Q1/2004', as non-default and rating grade 8 ($y_A = 0$; $\hat{\pi}_{g=8} = 0.0105$). The second borrower B enters with grade 10 but as default, because he defaulted somewhere in the third quarter of 2004 indicated with ☠ ($y_A = 1$; $\hat{\pi}_{g=10}$). Borrower C was not found in the rating database at 1st January 2004 as he was rated for the first time just before the beginning of the second quarter 2004. Therefore he is not contained in slice 'Q1/2004'. Borrower D enters with grade 12 as non-default, because the default we observe is past the end of the 12 month period which ends by 31st December 2004. Borrower E is found in the database with a rating grade 5 but he ended the business connection with the bank (indicated by ☹). Therefore it is impossible to observe if he has defaulted or survived within the 12 month period. This observation for borrower E should be included in the slice 'Q1/2004' as a weighted non-default, where the proportion is calculated as the quota (number of months it has been observed)/12. A non-consideration or full consideration may cause biases.

In the same way, the following slices have to be constructed. We show the compositions of the slices as a summary in the left side of Figure 7.

For practical issues, ultimo data files can be used best. So for the slice 'Q1/2004', we use the ultimo data files from December 2003. In Figure 7 we present the slice on a quarterly basis but sample creation can also be done on a monthly basis. This has the advantage that some elements of monitoring are fulfilled and nearly no rating and default is lost. The only exception is when a rating changes within a month. Therefore, the initial rating was not seen in the ultimo data file. The same is true when a rating is completed and the rated borrower gets into default before he has passed his first end of month. We recommend analysing these special cases separately, for example regarding detection of fraud.

When using the introduced method of rolling 12-month-windows, it is of concern that the slices greatly overlap. For a tuned (entries and exits are balanced, dates of rating compilations are evenly distributed all over the year) portfolio of borrowers with long term business relationship, two subsequent slices may overlap by about 11/12. As a consequence, we expect that we get often the same test results for two or more subsequent slices. We will see this in the next section, where we demonstrate our theoretical considerations by applying them to real world rating data.

7. Empirical Results

7.1. Data Description

In this section, we demonstrate the application of our concepts to real rating data. The data used is part of a rating system introduced in the beginning of 2004 for small business clients in Germany.[43] We analysed slices beginning in February 2004 up to January 2005.[44] So for backtesting slice 'Jan2005', we considered the defaults and non-defaults up to the end of December 2005. Here we can see that for backtesting a complete vintage of ratings, in fact a period of two years, is needed.

The rating system follows mainly the architecture sketched in Section 2.2, and is composed of various parallel sub-models for the machine rating module. These sub-models differ according to whether there is a tradesman, freelancer / professional[45] or a micro corporate to be rated. Micro corporates dominate with about 45% of all ratings, followed by tradesman (about 30%) and remaining freelancer and professionals with about 25%.

The basic structure of all sub-models contains approximately a dozen quantitative and qualitative risk drivers as it is usual for this kind of portfolio in banking practice. Within the second module, 'expert guided adjustment', up or down grading of the machine rating can be done. For micro corporates a 'supporter logic' module is available.

In our empirical analysis, we want to examine the slices 'Feb2004' to 'Jan2005' and in detail the comprehensive slice 'Jan2005'. Altogether, more than 26,000 different ratings can be analysed in the slices 'Feb2004' to 'Jan2005'. Whereas slice 'Feb2004', consists of little more than a hundred ratings because of the recent launch of the rating system, the numbers in the slices increase steadily up to more than 24,000 in 'Jan2005'.

Note that with our concept of rolling 12-months-windows, the slices overlap by a high degree. For example 'Jan2005' and 'Dec2004' have 88% observations in common, slices 'Jun2004' and 'Jul2004' about 75%.

---

[43] In order to avoid disclosure of sensitive business information, the data base was restricted to a (representative) sub-sample.

[44] For the construction of e.g. the slice 'Feb2004' we used the ultimo data store of 31st January 2004.

[45] like architects, doctors, or lawyers

7.2. The First Glance: Forecast vs. Realised Default Rates

When talking about the quality of a rating system, we get a first impression by looking at forecast default rates and realised default rates. Figure 8 shows that re-alised default rates vary between 2% and 2.5%, whereas the forecast PD underestimates the realised default rate slightly for almost all slices.

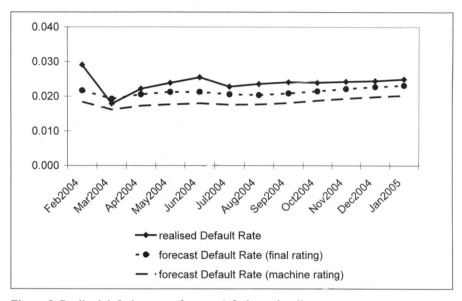

Figure 8. Realised default rate vs. forecast default rate by slice

Furthermore, it can be seen that on average, the final rating is more conservative than the machine rating. This means that the 'expert guided adjustments' and 'supporter logic' on average lead to a downgrade of borrowers. This might be an interesting result, because in banking practice the opposite is often assumed. The line of thought is, rating analysts or loan managers are primarily interested in selling loans which is easier - because of bank internal competence guidelines or simply by questions regarding the credit terms - if the machine rating is upgraded by the expert. The "accurate rating" is often assumed to be of subordinate importance for the loan manager. Here we have an example, which disproves this hypothesis. We will see whether this difference of machine rating and final rating regarding the quality of forecasts is significant or not in Section 7.4.

7.3. Results of the Hypothesis Tests for all Slices

As we are interested in whether the deviation of the final rating from the default rates is significant, we focus on the SPGH and the HSLS test. Table 6 shows the results.

For $\rho = 0.01$, the SPGH rejects in no slice the null hypothesis of "being calibrated", the HSLS rejects in two slices tightly. For the very conservative approach with $\rho = 0.00$, in some slices the null hypothesis has to be rejected for SPGH and HSLS. The simultaneous binomial tests (results are not shown here explicitly), shows that even for $\rho = 0.00$, the null hypothesis in no slice could be rejected, indicating a good quality of the rating system, too. Note the different test decisions of the consulted tests SPGH and HSLS for some slices.

Table 6. Test decisions by slice, final rating, 1 Mio runs, $\alpha = 0.05$

slice	ρ	SPGH				HSLS		
		lower bound	upper bound	Test statistic	Decision	upper bound	Test statistic	Decision
Feb2004		-1.5063	2.2255	0.2075	No rej.	25.3473	5.7982	No rej.
Mar2004		-1.8380	2.0736	-0.3214	No rej.	27.7315	6.1607	No rej.
Apr2004		-1.8948	2.0137	0.2490	No rej.	21.5598	6.8883	No rej.
May2004		-1.9512	1.9780	0.9859	No rej.	21.3653	10.8339	No rej.
Jun2004		-1.9549	1.9697	2.0617	Rej.	20.8402	17.1008	No rej.
Jul2004	0.00	-1.9544	1.9697	1.3236	No rej.	20.6058	33.3231	Rej
Aug2004		-1.9549	1.9673	2.0724	Rej	20.3097	67.6734	Rej
Sep2004		-1.9626	1.9675	2.4033	Rej	20.3765	78.3339	Rej
Oct2004		-1.9570	1.9691	2.1408	Rej	20.5659	68.2907	Rej
Nov2004		-1.9575	1.9604	1.6973	No rej.	20.6235	70.2873	Rej
Dec2004		-1.9592	1.9629	1.0893	No rej.	20.6672	78.3400	Rej
Jan2005		-1.9569	1.9620	0.9927	No rej.	20.9511	96.3306	Rej
Feb2004		-1.5063	2.3911	0.2075	No rej.	26.5294	5.7982	No rej.
Mar2004		-2.2839	2.9406	-0.3214	No rej.	30.5962	6.1607	No rej.
Apr2004		-3.1715	4.0670	0.2490	No rej.	29.4874	6.8883	No rej.
May2004		-3.9862	5.1376	0.9859	No rej.	35.4975	10.8339	No rej.
Jun2004		-4.7208	6.1255	2.0617	No rej.	43.0297	17.1008	No rej.
Jul2004	0.01	-5.5315	7.2272	1.3236	No rej.	53.6896	33.3231	No rej.
Aug2004		-6.2755	8.2214	2.0724	No rej.	65.1878	67.6734	Rej
Sep2004		-6.9194	9.0275	2.4033	No rej.	76.8287	78.3339	Rej
Oct2004		-7.5017	9.7802	2.1408	No rej.	90.2356	68.2907	No rej.
Nov2004		-8.0797	10.5260	1.6973	No rej.	103.8628	70.2873	No rej.
Dec2004		-8.6682	11.2619	1.0893	No rej.	119.0537	78.3400	No rej.
Jan2005		-9.1811	11.9508	0.9927	No rej.	130.8062	96.3306	No rej.

From Table 6, we can also see how well the approximation of the SPGH to the standard normal under H_0, works as the number of ratings in the slices increases for $\rho = 0.00$. The same is true for the HSLS, when we take into account that only 10 of 14 grades have a large number of observations[46] $\chi^2(0.95, 10) = 20.48$. Sec-

---

[46] Ratings Grades 1 to 3 of the master scale are intended mainly for sovereigns, international large corporates and financial institutions with excellent creditworthiness and could only in exceptional cases be achieved by small business clients. The worst rating grade is assigned to a very low number of borrowers in the data base, what is comprehensible because the rated portfolio mainly consists of initial ratings, so potential borrowers with a low creditworthiness are not accepted by the bank at all and therefore do not get into the rating database.

ondly, we might find it impressive how broad the non-rejection area is when taking correlation into account, even when used for a very low asset correlation of $\rho = 0.01$. Notice that the non-rejection areas for $\rho = 0.01$ of SPGH, HSLS and Sim Bin, get even broader when the number of ratings increases, although the relative distribution of the borrowers over the grades only changes negligibly. The same phenomenon was observed in the simulation study A, Table 2.

7.4. Detailed Analysis of Slice 'Jan2005'

Now we turn to a more detailed analysis of slice 'Jan2005', as we can observe up to now that the rating system passes our quality checks well. The distribution, not shown here explicitly, of the observations over the rating grades, is roughly bell-shaped, for example about 900 observations in grade 4, up to 4,500 in grade 8 and 1,000 in grade 12.

We can see in Figure 9 that for three rating grades, the realised default rate is in the rejection area for the binomial test. Hereby we assumed $\rho = 0.01$. The realised default rate increases in the rating grades as is assumed and therefore confirms our previous impression of the rating system we obtained from the SPGH and HSLS.

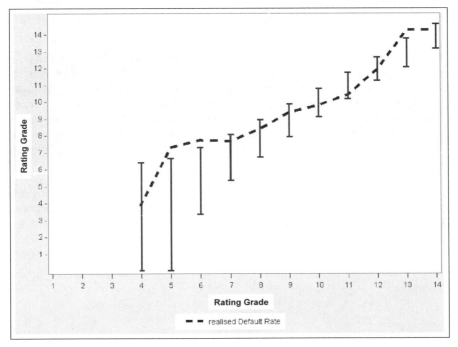

Figure 9. Realised default rates and exact binomial test by grades, slice 'Jan2005', 1 million runs, $\rho = 0.01$, $\alpha = 0.05$

Next we analysed the power of our tests. As could be seen from Table 7, the high number of ratings leads to a high power of all tests in all analysed circumstances. When assuming no correlation, the power is > 0.9999 for each of the three tests. When assuming $\rho = 0.01$ we get, e.g. for the SPGH in Mode 3, a power of 0.7548. This means that the SPGH - when in fact all borrowers should have got a rating one grade worse - would have detected this with a probability of about 76%.

Table 7. Analysis of Power, final rating, slice 'Jan2005', 1 million runs, $\alpha = 0.05$

ρ	SPGH	HSLS	Sim Bin
	Mode 1: $q = 0.5$		
0.00	> 0.9999	> 0.9999	> 0.9999
0.01	0.7894	> 0.9999	> 0.9999
	Mode 2: all borrowers graded up by $s = 1$		
0.00	> 0.9999	> 0.9999	> 0.9999
0.01	0.6798	0.4888	0.5549
	Mode 3: all borrowers graded down by $s = 1$		
0.00	> 0.9999	> 0.9999	> 0.9999
0.01	0.7548	0.8201	0.8227

To get a complete picture of the quality of the rating system and the regarded portfolio, we look at its discriminatory power.[47] Figure 10 displays the ROC-Curves for the machine rating and the final rating. For both rating modules, no discrepancies could be observed from the ROCs. We see that the ROC-Curve of final rating is always atop of the ROC-Curve of the machine rating, indicating an increase in discriminatory power when human expert assessment is brought into account. The AUROC of the final rating is therefore a bit higher (0.7450), than those of the machine rating (0.7258).

As could be seen from Table 8, the AUROC and MSE of the machine rating and final rating differ significantly. For comparing the MSE, we used the Redelmeier test described in detail in Section 4.4.[48]

---

[47] For a definition of the measures ROC-Curve and AUROC and their statistical properties, we refer to Chapter XII.

[48] As it was a prerequisite that the machine rating should pass a test on calibration we conducted the SPGH and the HSLS. We find that we could not reject the null hypothesis of being calibrated with $\rho = 0.01$, but we have to reject the null hypothesis with $\rho = 0.00$.

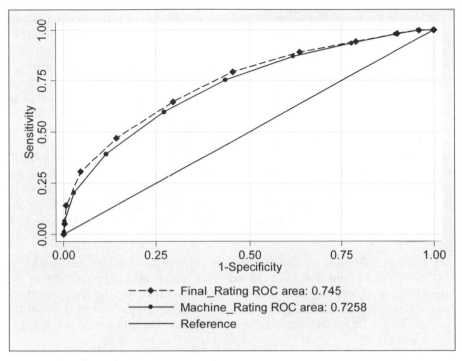

Figure 10. ROC-Curve for final rating and machine rating, slice 'Jan2005'

Table 8. Machine Rating vs. Final Rating

	MSE	AUROC	H_0	p-value
Machine Rating	0.0230	0.7258	$MSE_{mach.rating} = MSE_{fin.rating}$	< 0.0001
Final Rating	0.0226	0.7450	$AUROC_{mach.rating} = AUROC_{fin.rating}$	< 0.0001

To draw an overall result, the rating system passes our quality checks very well. With the high number of ratings in the analysed portfolio, we would have been able to detect potential shortcomings, but we did not find any. As the system was introduced two years ago, this was the first backtest that was performed, and the more highly this good result is to be regarded.

8. Conclusion

In this chapter we dealt with validation of rating systems, constructed to forecast a 1-year probability of default. Hereby, we focused on statistical tests and their application for bank internal purposes, especially in the Basel II periphery. We built up a simulation based framework to take account of dependencies in defaults (asset correlation), which additionally has the potential to appraise the type II error, i.e. the non-detection of a bad rating system, for optional scenarios. Hereby, the well known exact and approximated binomial test and the Hosmer-Lemeshow-χ^2 test are used, but we also introduced the less popular Spiegelhalter test and an approach called simultaneous binomial test, which allow the testing of a complete rating system and not just each grade separately. As it is important for banks to compare the quality of modules of their rating system, we also refer to the Redelmeier test. As for any applied statistical method, building test samples is an important issue. We designed the concept of "the rolling 12-months-window" to fulfil the Basel II and bank's internal risk management requirements as well as using the bank's IT-environment (rating database) effectively and is in harmony with our definition of what a rating should reflect, namely the bank's most accurate assessment of the 1-year-PD of a borrower. All concepts are demonstrated with a very up-to-date, real-life bank internal rating data set in detail.

We focus mainly on statistical concepts for rating validation (backtesting) but it has to be emphasised that for a comprehensive and adequate validation in the spirit of Basel II, much more is required. To name a few, these include adherence of defined bank internal rating processes, accurate and meaningful use of ratings in the bank's management systems and correct implementation in the IT-environment.

References

Balthazar L (2004), PD estimates for Basel II, Risk, April, pp. 84-85.

Basel Committee on Banking Supervision (BCBS) (2005a), Basel II: International Convergence of Capital Measurement and Capital Standards: a Revised Framework – Updated November 2005. http://www.bis.org/publ/bcbs118.pdf

Basel Committee on Banking Supervision (BCBS) (2005b), Studies on the Validation of Internal Rating Systems – revised version May 2005, Working Paper No. 14. http://www.bis.org/publ/bcbs_wp14.pdf

Brier G (1950), Verification of Forecasts expressed in Terms of Probability, Monthly Weather Review, Vol. 78, No. 1, pp. 1-3.

DeGroot M, Fienberg S (1983), The Comparison and Evaluation of Forecasters, The Statistician, Vol. 32, pp. 12-22.

Finger C (2001), The One-Factor CreditMetrics Model in The New Basle Capital Accord, RiskMetrics Journal, Vol. 2(1), pp. 9-18.

Hamerle A, Liebig T, Rösch D (2003), Benchmarking Asset Correlation, Risk, November, pp. 77-81.

Hosmer D, Lemeshow S, Klar J (1988), Goodness-of-Fit Testing for Multiple Logistic Regression Analysis when the estimated Probabilities are small, Biometrical Journal, Vol. 30, pp. 911-924.

Murphy A, Daan H (1985), Forecast Evaluation, in: Murphy A, Katz R (eds.), Prob-ability, Statistics, and Decision Making in the Atmospheric Sciences, Westview Press, Boulder, pp. 379-438.

Redelmeier DA, Bloch DA, Hickman DH (1991), Assessing Predictive Accuracy: How to compare Brier Score, Journal of Clinical Epidemiology, Vol. 44, No. 11, pp. 1141-1146.

Scheule H, Rauhmeier R (2005), Rating Properties and their Implication on Basel II-Capital, Risk, March, pp.78-81.

Sobehart JR, Keenan SC (2001), Measuring Default Accurately, Risk, pp. S31-S33.

Sobehart JR, Keenan SC, Stein RM (2000), Benchmarking Quantitative Default Risk Models: A Validation Methodology, Moody's Investors Service.

Somers R (1962), A New Asymmetric Measure of Association for Ordinal Variables, American Sociological Review, 27, pp. 799 -811.

Spiegelhalter D (1986), Probabilistic Prediction in Patient Management and Clinical Trails, Statistics in Medicine, Vol. 5, pp. 421-433.

Appendix A

We show that the SPGH test statistic Z_S is equal to the Z_{bin} test statistic of the approximated binomial test in case where there is only one single PD. This is when all obligors are rated in the same rating grade g. We start with (19) and substitute $\hat{\pi}_i = \hat{\pi}_g$ respectively $\pi_i = \pi_g$ because we argue under H_0:

$$
Z_S = \frac{\dfrac{1}{N_g}\sum_{i=1}^{N_g}(y_i - \pi_g)^2 - \dfrac{1}{N_g}\sum_{i=1}^{N_g}\pi_g \cdot (1-\pi_g)}{\sqrt{\dfrac{1}{N_g^2}\sum_{i=1}^{N_g}(1-2\pi_g)^2 \cdot \pi_g \cdot (1-\pi_g)}} =
$$

$$
= \frac{\sum_{i=1}^{N_g} y^2 - 2\cdot\pi_g\cdot\sum_{i=1}^{N_g} y + N_g \cdot \pi_g^2 - \sum_{i=1}^{N_g}\pi_g \cdot (1-\pi_g)}{\sqrt{N_g \cdot (1-2\pi_g)^2 \cdot \pi_g \cdot (1-\pi_g)}} =
$$

$$
= \frac{\sum_{i=1}^{N_g} y - 2\cdot\pi_g\cdot\sum_{i=1}^{N_g} y + N_g \cdot \pi_g^2 - \sum_{i=1}^{N_g}\pi_g \cdot (1-\pi_g)}{\sqrt{N_g \cdot (1-2\pi_g)^2 \cdot \pi_g \cdot (1-\pi_g)}} =
$$

$$
= \frac{\sum_{i=1}^{N_g} y - 2\cdot\pi_g\cdot\sum_{i=1}^{N_g} y + 2\cdot N_g \cdot \pi_g^2 - N_g \cdot \pi_g}{\sqrt{N_g \cdot (1-2\pi_g)^2 \cdot \pi_g \cdot (1-\pi_g)}} =
$$

$$
= \frac{(1-2\pi_g)\cdot\sum_{i=1}^{N_g} y - (1-2\pi_g)\cdot N_g \cdot \pi_g}{\sqrt{N_g \cdot (1-2\pi_g)^2 \cdot \pi_g \cdot (1-\pi_g)}} = \frac{\sum_{i=1}^{N_g} y - N\cdot\pi_g}{\sqrt{N_g \cdot \pi_g \cdot (1-\pi_g)}} =
$$

$$
= \frac{N_g \cdot \bar{y} - N\cdot\pi_g}{\sqrt{N_g \cdot \pi_g \cdot (1-\pi_g)}}
$$

and get (14).

Appendix B

We want to derive the test statistic Z_R of the Redelmeier test as it is shown in (22) according to Redelmeier et al (1991). We start with the MSE from module 1 as

$$MSE_{m1} = \frac{1}{N} \sum_{i=1}^{N} \left(y_i - \hat{\pi}_{i,m1}\right)^2 = \frac{1}{N} \sum_{i=1}^{N} \left(y_i - 2 \cdot y_i \cdot \hat{\pi}_{i,m1} + \hat{\pi}_{i,m1}^2\right) \qquad (24)$$

Because of the randomness of the defaults the MSE will differ from its expected value

$$E\left(MSE_{m1}\right) = \frac{1}{N} \sum_{i=1}^{N} \left(\pi_i - \hat{\pi}_{i,m1}\right)^2 = \frac{1}{N} \sum_{i=1}^{N} \left(\pi_i - 2 \cdot \pi_i \cdot \hat{\pi}_{i,m1} + \hat{\pi}_{i,m1}^2\right) \qquad (25)$$

The difference of the realized and the expected MSE for module 1 is

$$d_{m1} = E\left(MSE_{m1}\right) - MSE_{m1} = \frac{1}{N} \sum_{i=1}^{N} \left(y_i - 2 \cdot y_i \cdot \hat{\pi}_{i,m1} - \pi_i + 2 \cdot \pi_i \cdot \hat{\pi}_{i,m1}\right) \qquad (26)$$

The same consideration has to be done for module 2:

$$d_{m2} = E\left(MSE_{m2}\right) - MSE_{m2} = \frac{1}{N} \sum_{i=1}^{N} \left(y_i - 2 \cdot y_i \cdot \hat{\pi}_{i,m2} - \pi_i + 2 \cdot \pi_i \cdot \hat{\pi}_{i,m2}\right) \qquad (27)$$

To determine whether two sets of judgments are equally realistic we compare the difference between d_{m1} and d_{m2}:

$$d_{m1} - d_{m2} = \frac{2}{N} \sum_{i=1}^{N} \left(\hat{\pi}_{i,m1} - \hat{\pi}_{i,m2}\right) \cdot \left(\pi_i - y_i\right) \qquad (28)$$

As it can be seen from (28) the true but unknown PD π_i is still required and has therefore be assessed. A choice might be to set all π_i equal to the average of the corresponding judgments ($\hat{\pi}_{i,m1}, \hat{\pi}_{i,m2}$) (consensus forecast).[49] This seems to be a reasonable choice since we presumed that each module itself has satisfied the null hypothesis of being compatible with the data. Using the consensus forecast

$$\pi_i = 0.5 \cdot \left(\hat{\pi}_{i,m1} + \hat{\pi}_{i,m2}\right) \qquad (29)$$

we get

---

[49] Other approaches are possible, e.g. one may get the "true" π_i's from an external source.

$$d_{m1} - d_{m2} =$$

$$= \frac{2}{N} \sum_{i=1}^{N} (\hat{\pi}_{i,m1} - \hat{\pi}_{i,m2}) \cdot (0.5 \cdot \hat{\pi}_{i,m1} - 0.5 \cdot \hat{\pi}_{i,m2} - y_i) =$$

$$= \frac{1}{N} \sum_{i=1}^{N} \hat{\pi}_{i,m1}^2 - \hat{\pi}_{i,m2}^2 - 2 \cdot y_i \cdot (\hat{\pi}_{i,m1} - \hat{\pi}_{i,m2}) =$$

$$= \frac{1}{N} \sum_{i=1}^{N} \left[(y_i - 2 \cdot y_i \hat{\pi}_{i,m1} + \hat{\pi}_{i,m1}^2) - (y_i - 2 \cdot y_i \cdot \hat{\pi}_{i,m2} + \hat{\pi}_{i,m2}^2) \right] = \qquad (30)$$

$$= \frac{1}{N} \sum_{i=1}^{N} (y_i - \hat{\pi}_{i,m1})^2 - \frac{1}{N} \sum_{i=1}^{N} (y_i - \hat{\pi}_{i,m2})^2 =$$

$$= MSE_{m1} - MSE_{m2}$$

It is interesting that in the case we use the consensus forecast for substituting π_i the term $d_{m1} - d_{m2}$ is simply the difference of the two realized MSEs.

In the next step we calculate the variance using the fact that the expected value of $d_{m1} - d_{m2}$ is zero under the null hypothesis, see (23).

$$Var(d_{m1} - d_{m2}) = Var\left(\frac{2}{N} \sum_{i=1}^{N} (\hat{\pi}_{i,m1} - \hat{\pi}_{i,m2}) \cdot (\pi_i - y_i) \right) =$$

$$= \frac{4}{N^2} \sum_{i=1}^{N} (\hat{\pi}_{i,m1} - \hat{\pi}_{i,m2})^2 \cdot \pi_i \cdot (1 - \pi_i) \qquad (31)$$

Finally we get the test statistic

$$Z_R = \frac{d_{m1} - d_{m2}}{\sqrt{Var(d_{m1} - d_{m2})}} =$$

$$= \frac{\sum_{i=1}^{N} \left[(\hat{\pi}_{i,m1}^2 - \hat{\pi}_{i,m2}^2) - 2(\hat{\pi}_{i,m1} - \hat{\pi}_{i,m2}) \cdot y_i \right]}{\left[\sum_{i=1}^{N} \left[(\hat{\pi}_{i,m1} - \hat{\pi}_{i,m2})^2 (\hat{\pi}_{i,m1} + \hat{\pi}_{i,m2})(2 - \hat{\pi}_{i,m1} - \hat{\pi}_{i,m2}) \right] \right]^{0,5}} \qquad (32)$$

XV. Development of Stress Tests for Credit Portfolios

Volker Matthias Gundlach

KfW Bankengruppe[1]

1. Introduction

Advanced portfolio models combined with naive reliance on statistics in credit risk estimations run the danger of underestimating latent risks and neglecting the peril arising from very rare, but not unrealistic risk constellations. The latter might be caused by abnormal economic conditions or dramatic events for the portfolio of a single credit institute or a complete market. This includes events of a political or economic nature. To limit the impact of such sudden incidents, the study of fictional perturbations and shock testing the robustness/vulnerability of risk characteristics is required. This procedure is known as stress testing. It allows the review and actualisation of risk strategies, risk capacities and capital allocation. Thus it can play an important role in risk controlling and management in a credit institute.

This view is shared by the banking supervision, in particular by the Basel Committee on Banking Supervision of the Bank for International Settlements (BIS). Consequently, stress testing for credit risk plays a role in the regulatory requirements of the Revised Framework on the International Convergence of Capital Measurements and Capital Standards (Basel II). Nevertheless, it has not reached the standards of stress testing for market risk estimations, which has been common practice for several years (see Breuer and Krenn, 1999).

In the following, we describe the purpose and signification of stress testing for credit risk evaluations. Then we recall the regulatory requirements, in particular of the Basel II framework. We describe how stress tests work and present some well-established forms of stress tests, a classification for them and suggestions how to deal with them. We also include examples for illustration. To conclude, we offer a concept for an evolutionary way towards a stress testing procedure. This is done in view of the applicability of the procedure in banks.

---

[1] The material and opinions presented and expressed in this article are those of the author and do not necessarily reflect views of KfW Bankengruppe or methods applied by the bank.

2. The Purpose of Stress Testing

Stress testing means (regular) expeditions into an unknown, but important territory: the land of unexpected loss. As the latter is of immense relevance for financial institutions, there is growing interest in this topic. Moreover, there are various reasons for conducting stress testing due to the explicit or implicit relation between unexpected loss and economic capital or regulatory capital, respectively. Crucial for the understanding of and the approach towards stress testing, is the definition of unexpected loss. Though it is clear that this quantity should be covered by economic capital, there is no general agreement as to how to define unexpected loss.

It is quite common to regard the difference between expected loss and the value-at-risk (VaR) of a given confidence level, or the expected shortfall exceeding the VaR, as unexpected loss. One of the problems with this approach is that such an unexpected loss might not only be unexpected, but also quite unrealistic, as its definition is purely of a statistical nature. Therefore, it is sensible to use stress tests to underscore which losses amongst the unexpected are plausible or to use the outcome of stress tests, instead of unexpected loss to determine economic capital.

Though the idea of using stress tests for estimating economic capital seems quite straight forward, it is only rarely realized, as it requires reliable occurrence probabilities for the stress events. With these, one could use the expected loss under stress as an economic capital requirement. Nevertheless, stress tests are mainly used to challenge the regulatory and economic capital requirements determined by unexpected loss calculations. This can be done as a simple test for the adequacy, but also to derive a capital buffer for extreme losses exceeding the unexpected losses, and to define the risk appetite of a bank. For new credit products like credit derivatives used for hedging against extreme losses it might be of particular importance to conduct stress tests on the evaluation and capital requirements.

Using stress tests to evaluate capital requirements has the additional advantage of allowing the combination of different kind of risks; in particular market risk, credit and liquidity risk, but also operational risk and other risks such as reputational risk. Because time horizons for market and credit risk transactions are different, and it is common for banks to use different confidence levels for the calculation of VaRs for credit and market risk (mainly due to the different time horizons), joint considerations of market and credit risk are difficult and seldom used. Realistic stress scenarios influencing various kinds of risk therefore could lead to extreme losses, which could be of enormous importance for controlling risk and should be reflected in the capital requirements.

In any case, there can be strong correlations between the developments of market, liquidity and credit risk which could result in extreme losses and should not be neglected. Consequently, investigations into events causing simultaneous increases in market and credit risk are more than reasonable. An overview over several types of risk relevant for stress testing can be found in Blaschke et al. (2001).

The quantitative outcome of stress testing can be used in several places for portfolio and risk management:

- risk buffers can be determined and/or tested against extreme losses
- the risk capacity of a financial institution can be determined and/or tested against extreme losses
- limits for sub-portfolios can be fixed to avoid given amounts of extreme losses
- risk policy, risk tolerance and risk appetite can be tested by visualising the risk/return under abnormal market conditions.

Such approaches focusing on quantitative results might be of particular interest for sub-portfolios (like some country-portfolios), where the historic volatility of the respective loans is low, but drastic changes in risk relevant parameters cannot be excluded.

Stress tests should not only be reduced to their purely quantitative features. They can and should also play a major role in the portfolio management of a bank, as they offer the possibility of testing the structure and robustness of a portfolio against perturbations and shocks. In particular they can represent a worthwhile tool to:

- identify potential risks and locate the weak spots of a portfolio
- study effects of new intricate credit products
- guide discussion on unfavourable developments like crises and abnormal market conditions, which cannot be excluded
- help monitor important sub-portfolios exhibiting large exposures or extreme vulnerability to changes in the market
- derive some need for action to reduce the risk of extreme losses and hence economic capital, and mitigate the vulnerability to important risk relevant effects
- test the portfolio diversification by introducing additional (implicit) correlations
- question the bank's attitude towards risk

3. Regulatory Requirements

As we have seen in the previous section, the benefits of using stress tests are manifold for the controlling and portfolio management. Tribute to this fact is also paid by the Basel II Revised Framework (see BIS, 2004). Here stress testing appears in Pillar 1 (about the minimum capital requirements) and Pillar 2 (about the supervisory review process) for banks using the IRB approach. The target of the requirements is improved risk management.

The requirements in the Basel II Revised Framework are not precise. They can be summarized as:[2]

- *Task*: Every IRB bank has to conduct sound, significant and meaningful stress testing to assess the capital adequacy in a reasonably conservative way. In particular, major credit risk concentrations have to undergo periodic stress tests. Furthermore, stress tests should be integrated in the internal capital adequacy process, in particular, risk management strategies to respond to the outcome of stress testing.
- *Intention*: Banks shall ensure that they dispose of enough capital to meet the regulatory capital requirements even in the case of stress.
- *Requirements*: Banks should identify possible events and future changes in economic conditions, which could have disadvantageous effects on their credit exposure. Moreover, the ability of the bank to withstand these unfavourable impairments has to be assessed.
- *Design*: A quantification of the impact on the parameters probability of default (PD), loss given default (LGD) and exposure at default (EAD) is required. Rating migrations should also be taken into account.

Special notes on how to implement these requirements include:

- The use of scenarios like:
  - economic or industry downturn
  - market-risk events
  - liquidity shortage
  is recommended.
- Recession scenarios should be considered, worst-case scenarios are not required
- Banks should use their own data for estimating rating migrations and integrate the insight of rating migrations in external ratings
- Banks should build their stress testing also on the study of the impact of smaller deterioration in the credit environment.

Though the requirements for stress testing are mainly contained in Pillar 1 of Basel II, the method is a fundamental part of Pillar 2, since it is an important way of assessing capital adequacy. This explains the lack of extensive regulations for stress testing in that document as Pillar 2 acknowledges the ability to judge risk and use the right means for this procedure. As another consequence, not only regulatory capital should be the focus of stress tests, but also economic capital as the counterpart of the portfolio risk as seen by the bank.

Not only the BIS (see CGFS, 2000, 2001, and 2005) promotes stress testing, but also some central banks and regulators[3] have taken care of this topic (e.g.,

---

[2]   The exact statements can be found in §§ 434-437, § 765, § 775 and § 777 of BIS (2004).

[3]   Regulators are also interested in contagion, i.e. the transmission of shocks in the financial system. This topic is not part of this contribution.

Deutsche Bundesbank (2003, 2004), Fender et al., 2001), in particular regarding the stability of financial systems. They have published statements which can be regarded as supplements to the Basel II Revised Framework. These publications give a better impression of the regulatory goals and basic conditions for stress testing, which can be summarized as:

- Stress tests should consider extreme deviations from normal developments and hence should invoke unrealistic, but still plausible situations, i.e. situations with low probability of occurrence
- Stress tests should also consider constellations which might occur in future and which have not yet been observed
- Financial institutions should also use stress testing to become aware of their risk profile and to challenge their business plans, target portfolios, risk politics, etc.
- Stress testing should not only be addressed to check the capital adequacy, but also used to determine and question limits for awarding credit
- Stress testing should not be treated only as an amendment to the VaR-evaluations for credit portfolios, but as a complimentary method, which contrasts the purely statistical approach of VaR-methods by including causally determined considerations for unexpected losses. In particular, it can be used to specify extreme losses in a qualitative and quantitative way.

4. Risk Parameters for Stress Testing

The central point of the procedure of stress testing – also seen in Basel II – is the change in risk parameters. For regulatory capital, these parameters are given by the probability of default (PD), loss given default (LGD) and exposure at default (EAD). In this connection, a superior role is played by the variations of PD, as LGD and EAD are lasting quantities which – due to their definition – already are conditioned to disadvantageous situations, namely the default of the obligor. The possibilities of stress effects are hence restricted, especially for EAD. The latter might be worsened by a few exogenous factors such as the exchange rate, but they should also be partly considered in the usual EAD. The exogenous factors affecting the EAD might only be of interest if they also have an impact on the other risk parameters and hence could lead to an accumulation of risky influence.

The possible variances for the LGD depend heavily on the procedure used to determine this quantity. Thus, deviations which might arise from the estimation methods, should be determined, as well as parts of the process that might depend on economic conditions. As the determination of the LGD is conditioned – by definition – to the unfavourable situation of a default, it should take into account lasting values for collaterals, and lead to values that can be seen as conservative. Thus, there should not too many factors be left, that could lead to extreme changes for the LGD. Mainly the evaluation of collateral could have some influence which cannot be neglected when stressing the LGD. In particular, it might be possible that factors affecting the value of the collaterals also have an impact on other risk parameters and hence should be taken into account.

The PD is by far the most popular risk parameter which is varied in stress tests. There are two main reasons why variations in the PD of an obligor can occur. On the one hand, the assignment of an obligor to a rating grade might change due to altered inputs for the rating process. On the other hand, the realised default rates of the rating grades itself might change, e.g., because of modified economic conditions and their impact on the performance of the loans. This allows two options for the design of the integration of PDs into stress testing: modifications either of the assignment to rating grades or of the PDs of the rating grades for stress tests.

Altered assignments of rating grades for obligors in stress tests have the advantage that they also allow the inclusion of transitions to non-performing loans. The change of PDs corresponds to a change of rating grade. The possible deviation in the assignment of rating grades can be promoted by the rating procedure. Thus, the possibilities of variances and the sensitivity of the input for the rating process should be investigated in order to get a first estimate for possible deviations. Consequently, as well as the analysis of historic data for rating transitions, expert opinions on the rating methodology should be a part of the design process for the stress test.

The modification of PDs for the rating grades, could have its origin in systematic risk, i.e. in the dependence on risk drivers, one of the main topics in designing stress tests, as will be discussed below. While it is sensible to estimate the volatility of PDs in a first step and use the outcome of this procedure for tests on regulatory capital, the differentiation of the effects of systematic and idiosyncratic risk on PD deviations should be considered in a second step. This will lead to more advanced and realistic stress tests, in particular on economic capital.

An analysis of the transition structure for rating grades might also be used to determine PDs under stress conditions. The advantage of modifying PDs against modifying the assignment of rating grades is a greater variety for the choices of changes; the disadvantage is the absence of a modified assignment to the performing and non-performing portfolio. This has to take place on top of the modification of PDs.

Estimating economic capital PD, LGD and EAD might not be sufficient to design stress tests. In addition, parameters used for displaying portfolio effects, including correlations between the loans or the common dependence on risk drivers are needed.[4] Investigations on historic crises for credit risk show that correlations and risk concentration exhibit huge deviations in these circumstances. In any case,

---

[4] The basis for widely used portfolio models like CreditRisk+ or CreditMetrics, which are used by banks for estimating the VaR, are provided by factor models. The (abstract) factors are used to present systematic risk affecting the loans. In these models it makes sense to stress the strength of the dependence on the factors and the factors themselves.

their variations should be considered in stress tests with portfolio models if possible. Some advanced models for estimating economic capital might even require more information, in particular economic conditions.

Portfolio models such as CreditMetrics not only consider the default of loans, but also the change of value by using migration probabilities. In this case, the migration probabilities should be stressed in the same way as PDs.

Stressing of risk parameters in tests need not take place for the whole portfolio, but only for parts of it. Also, the strength of the parameter modification might depend on sub-portfolios. Such approaches are used to pay tribute to different sensitivities of parts of the portfolio to risk relevant influences or to study the vulnerability of certain (important) sub-portfolios. They can be particularly interesting for investigations on economic capital with the help of portfolio models. In these cases, parameter changes for parts of the portfolio need not have a smaller impact than analogous variations for the whole portfolio due to effects of concentration risk or diversification, respectively.

5. Evaluating Stress Tests

As stress testing should be a part of the internal capital adequacy process, there should be an understanding of how to use the outcome of stress tests for controlling and managing portfolio risk. The starting point for this should be the regulatory and economic capital as output of the underlying stress tests. The first task consists of checking whether the financial institution holds sufficient capital to also cover the requirements in the stress situation. As there should be limits, buffers and policies to guarantee this, the evaluation of stress testing should be also used to review these tools. Since the latter might be applicable to different portfolio levels (e.g. limits for sub-portfolios, countries, obligors), they should be checked in detail.

The concept of stress testing would be incomplete without knowing when action has to be considered as a result of the outcome of tests. It makes sense to introduce indicators and thresholds for suggesting when:

- to inform management about potential critical developments
- to develop guidelines for new business in order to avoid the extension of existing risky constellations
- to reduce risk for the portfolio or sub-portfolios with the help of securitisation and syndication
- to readjust an existing limit management system and the capital buffer for credit risk
- to re-think the risk policy and risk tolerance

Indicators for the call on action could be:

- the increase of risk indicators as expected loss, unexpected loss, expected shortfall over a threshold or by a specified factor
- the increase of capital requirements (regulatory or economic) over a threshold or by a specified factor
- the solvency ratio of capital and capital requirements under a threshold
- a low solvency level for meeting the economic capital requirements under stress
- a specified quantile of the loss distribution for the portfolio under stress conditions does not lie within a specified quantile of the loss distribution for the original portfolio
- expected loss for the portfolio under stress conditions overlaps the standard risk costs (calculated on the basis of expected loss for the duration of the loans) by a specified factor or gets too close to the unexpected loss for the unstressed portfolio
- the risk/return lies above a specified threshold, where risk is measured in terms of unexpected loss

The interpretation of the outcome of stress tests on economic capital can easily lead to misapprehensions, in particular if the capital requirement is estimated on the basis of a VaR for a rather large confidence level. The motivation for the latter approach is the avoidance of insolvency by holding enough capital, except for some very rare events. Stress tests might simulate situations coming quite close to these rare events. Adhering to the large confidence levels for estimating economic capital, offers the possibility of comparing the capital requirements under different conditions, but the resulting VaR or economic capital should not be used to question the solvency. In fact, it should be considered whether to use adapted confidence levels for stress testing or to rethink the appropriateness of high confidence levels. One can see the probability of occurrence or the plausibility of a stress test as a related problem. We refer to a detailed discussion on this topic and an approach to resolution to Breuer and Krenn (2001).

6. Classifying Stress Tests

According to regulatory requirements, a bank should perform stress tests on its regulatory as well as its economic capital. This differentiation of stress tests is not essential and mainly technical, as the input for determining these two forms of capital might be quite different as described in the previous section.

Another technical reason for differentiating stress tests is the division into performing and non-performing loans, as their respective capital requirements follow different rules. For non-performing loans, loss provisions have to be made. Thus one has to consider the following cases for stress tests:

- A performing loan gets downgraded but remains a performing loan – the estimation of economic capital involves updated risk parameters

- A performing loan gets downgraded and becomes a non-performing loan – provisions have to be estimated involving the net exposures calculated with the LGD
- A non-performing loan deteriorates – the provisions have to be increased on the basis of a declined LGD

As already discussed in the previous section, defaults can be included in stress tests via a worsened assignment to rating grades. If stress tests focus on PDs rather than rating grades, then stress rates for the transition of performing to non-performing loans are required for the same purpose. Ideally, they depend on ratings, branches, economic states, etc. and are applied to the portfolio after stressing the PDs. Moreover, the methodology of a bank to determine the volume of the provision for a defaulted credit should be considered. A typical approach is to equate the loss amount given the default (i.e. the product of LGD with the exposure) with the provision.

Typical ways to categorize stress tests can be taken over from market risk. They are well documented in the literature (CGFS (2005), Deutsche Bundesbank, 2003 and 2004). The most important way to classify stress tests is via the methodology. One can distinguish stress tests with respect to techniques in statistically and model based methods, and with respect to conceptual design in sensitivity analysis and scenario analysis. While the latter is based on modelling economic variances, sensitivity analysis is statistically founded. The common basis for all these specifications is the elementary requirement for stress tests to perturb the risk parameters. These can be the basic risk parameters (EAD, LGD, PD), of the loans as already mentioned for the tests on the regulatory capital. However, these can also be parameters used in a portfolio model like asset correlations or dependencies on systematic risk drivers.

The easiest way to perform stress tests is a direct modification of the risk parameters and belongs to the class of sensitivity analysis. The goal is to study the impact of major changes in the parameters on the portfolio values. For this method, one or more risk parameters are increased (simultaneously) and the evaluations are made for this new constellation. The increase of parameters should depend on statistical analysis or/and expert opinion. As these stress tests are not linked to any event or context and are executed for all loans of a (sub-) portfolio, without respect to individual properties, we refer to them as flat or uniform stress tests. Most popular are the flat stress tests for PDs, where the increase of the default rates can be derived from transition rates between the rating grades. An advantage of these tests is the possibility of performing them simultaneously at different financial institutions and aggregating these results to check the financial stability of a system. This is done by several central banks. Such tests are suited to checking the space and buffer for capital requirements, but it does not mean any help for portfolio and risk management.

Model based methods for stress testing incorporate observable risk drivers, in particular, macroeconomic variables for representing the changes of risk parameters.

In the following, we will refer to these risk drivers as risk factors. The respective methods rely on the existence of a model – mainly based on econometrical methods – that explains the variations of the risk parameters by changes of such risk factors. One can distinguish univariate stress tests, which are defined by the use of a single, isolated risk factor, and multivariate stress tests, where several factors are changed simultaneously. These tests can be seen as a refinement of those previously described: stressing the risk factors leads to modified risk parameters which are finally used for the evaluation of the capital requirements. Note that risk factors can have quite different effects on risk parameters throughout a portfolio. Changes in the risk factors can lead to upgrades as well as downgrades of risk parameters. For example, an increase in price of resources such as oil or energy can have a negative impact on PDs in the automobile or any other industry consuming lots of energy, but it could have a positive impact on the PDs in the country trading these resources.

By using univariate stress tests, banks can study specific and especially relevant impacts on their portfolios. This has the benefit of isolating the influence of an important observable quantity. Consequently, it can be used to identify weak spots in the portfolio structure. Thus, univariate stress tests represent another kind of sensitivity analysis, now in terms of risk factors instead of risk parameters. They have the disadvantage of possibly leading to an underestimation of risk by neglecting potential effects resulting from possible correlations of risk factors.

This shortcoming is abolished by using multivariate stress tests. The price is the reliance on additional statistical analysis, assumptions or the establishment of another model describing the correlation of the risk factors involved. This is done in a framework known as scenario analysis, where hypothetical, historical and statistically determined scenarios are distinguished. It results in the determination of stress values for the risk factors which are used to evaluate stress values for the risk parameters.

With respect to the design of scenarios, we can discriminate approaches driven by the portfolio (bottom-up approaches) and driven by events (top-down approaches). Bottom-up approaches tend to use the results of sensitivity analysis to identify sensitive dependence on risk factors as starting points. As a consequence, those scenarios are chosen which involve risk factors having the largest impact. For example, for a bank focusing on real estate, GDP, employment rate, inflation rate, spending capacity in the countries, it is acting in, will be of more relevance than the oil price, exchange rates, etc. Thus, it will look for scenarios involving the relevant risk factors. Top-down approaches start with a chosen scenario, e.g., the terror attack in New York on September 11, 2001, and require the analysis of the impact of this scenario on the portfolio. The task in this situation is to identify those tests which cause the most dramatic and relevant changes.

Historical scenarios are typical examples of top-down approaches. They refer to extreme constellations of the risk factors which were observed in the past and in the majority of the cases can be related to historical events and crises. They are transferred to the current situation and portfolio. This can be seen as a disadvantage of this approach, as the transferred values may no longer be realistic. Another drawback is that generally, it is not possible to specify the probability of the scenario occurring.

Also, statistically determined scenarios might depend on historical data. They are based on the (joint) statistical distribution of risk factors. In this approach, scenarios might be specified by quantiles of such distributions. Whilst it might be very difficult to produce suitable distributions in particular, joint distributions, the advantage is that it is possible to evaluate the probability of the scenario occurring as this is given by the complement of the confidence level used for the quantile. The existence of such probabilities of occurrence allows the calculation of expected extreme losses which can be used for the estimation of economic capital. The crucial point of this approach is the generation of a suitable risk factor distribution. Only if the latter is chosen compatible with the state of economy, (hence does not rely too heavily on historic data), can useful conclusions for the management of the portfolio be derived.

Finally, there are hypothetical scenarios which focus on possible rare events that might have an important impact on the portfolio, but have not been observed yet in the form they are considered. The crucial point is the presentation of the consequences of the event on the risk factors. For the estimation of this expert opinion, it is necessary to accompany the macro-economic modelling of the dependence of the risk parameters on risk factors. If macroeconomic parameters are not part of the input for determining the risk parameters which are stressed, there are three steps required for macro stress tests. Firstly, it is necessary to model the dependence of the risk parameters on the risk factors. Secondly, it is necessary to choose values for the risk factors which are representative for stress events. Since it is intended to reproduce correlations and causal interrelations between risk factors and stress events, intricate (macro-economic), methods of estimation and validation are needed. A disadvantage of hypothetical scenarios might be the need to specify the probability of occurrence of such hypothetical scenarios. On the other hand, there is the major advantage of having forward-looking scenarios which do not necessarily reflect historical events. Thus, hypothetical scenarios present interesting adjuncts to VaR-based analysis of portfolio risk and are a worthwhile tool for portfolio management.

The use of risk factors as in the multivariate scenario analysis has the additional advantage of allowing common stress tests for credit, market and liquidity risk. Here, it is necessary to consider factors that influence several forms of risk or scenarios that involve risk factors for them.

7. Conducting Stress Tests

In the following section we will discuss how the stress tests we have just introduced in the previous section, can be and are, applied in financial institutions. We
try to provide details how to determine and conduct stress tests, focussing mainly
on the performing part of credit portfolios.

7.1. Uniform Stress Tests

The most popular stress tests in banks are uniform stress tests, in particular for the
PDs. The intention is to use increased PDs for the calculation of economic or
regulatory capital. In the easiest case, there is a flat increase rate for all PDs[5] of
obligors or/and countries, but in general, the change might depend on rating
grades, branches, countries, regions, etc. We suggest several ways to derive the
stress PDs:

1. Analyse the default data with respect to the dependence on rating grades,
   branches, countries, regions, etc. This data could originate from the bank's own
   portfolio or from rating agencies. Determine the deviations of the default rates
   from the PD. Another way to derive such variations might arise from the analysis of spreads for respective credit derivatives. The stress PD then can be determined from the PD by adding the standard deviation, a quantile or other
   relevant characteristic of the deviation distribution. It might seem to be a good
   idea to use the quantile to determine also a probability of the stress occurring,
   but one should question the quality and the relevance of the distribution before
   using this approach.
2. Use migration rates (referring to the bank's own portfolio or coming from rating agencies), to determine transitions between rating grades. These transitions
   might depend on branches, countries, etc. In an intermediate step, stressed migration matrices can be generated by omitting rating upgrades, by conditioning
   on economic downturns (Bangia et al. 2002), by uniformly increasing the
   downgrade rates at the expense of uniformly decreasing the upgrade rates or on
   the basis of a time series analysis. Next, one can derive for every original rating
   grade, a stressed rating grade by evaluating quantiles or any other characteristics for the transition probabilities. Consequently, it is possible to build the
   stress test on the rating grades. Now, the stress test consists of replacing the
   original rating grade by the stressed rating grade. Alternatively, one can replace
   the original PD by the PD of the stressed rating grade. A different approach
   uses the stressed migration rates. Depending on their derivation, they possibly

---

[5] Such stress tests are often used by central banks to test the stability of the respective financial systems. In the studies in Deutsche Bundesbank (2003) PDs are increased by
30% and 60%, respectively. These changes approximately correspond to downgrades of
Standard and Poor's' ratings by one or two grades, respectively. The latter is seen as conservative in that paper. Banks should analyse their default data to come up with their own
rates of increase, which we expect to be in the worst case larger than 60%.

have to be calibrated to become transition probabilities. Then they can be used to calculate an expected PD for every rating grade, which can play the role of a stressed PD.

The decision as to which option should be chosen for determining the stress PD should depend on the data, which is available for statistical analysis. Also, expert opinions could be a part of the process to generate the stress PDs. In particular, it makes sense to study the deviations that can be caused by the rating process due to sensitive dependence on input parameters. This could lead to an additional add-on when generating the stress PDs.

The preference for stressed PDs or stressed rating grades should depend on the possibilities of realising the stress tests. Regarding the portfolio model, the dependence of a PD on a branch or country in a rating grade could – for example – represent a problem. A criterion in favour of stressed rating grades is the inclusion of defaults. Such a stressing might lead to assignments of loans to grades belonging to the non-performing portfolio. These can be treated respectively, i.e. instead of the capital requirements, provisions can be calculated. In the case that PDs are stressed, instead of rating grades, one should first consider the stressing of the PDs in the portfolio and then the stressing of transition rates to the non-performing part of the portfolio. In this context, Monte Carlo simulations can be used to estimate capital requirements for the performing, and provisions for the non-performing part of the portfolio.

Transition rates to the non-performing portfolio, usually corresponding to default rates, can be stressed in the same form and with the same methods as the PDs. The same holds for migration rates between rating grades which are used in some portfolio models.

Flat stress tests for LGDs could also be based on statistical analysis, in this case for loss data. The approach to determine and study deviations in loss rates is analogous to the one for default rates. Expert opinion could play a bigger role. An example of an interesting stress test could be provided by a significant fall in real estate prices in some markets.

Uniform stressing of EAD is often not relevant. Deviations of this quantity mainly depend on individual properties of the loans. Variations of exchange rates can be seen as the most important influence on the deviations of EAD from the expected values. It is commendable to investigate this effect separately.

For uniform stressing of parameters used in portfolio models, it seems to be the best to rely on expert opinions, as it is very difficult to detect and statistically verify, the effect of these parameters on the deviations from expected or predicted values of defaults and losses.

While it is already rather intrinsic to determine suitable parameter values for the uniform tests involving single parameters, it even becomes more difficult to do this for several parameters at the same time. Experience derived from historic observations and expert opinion seems to be indispensable in this situation.

7.2. Sensitivity Analysis for Risk Factors

This kind of stress testing is very popular for market risk, where risk factors can easily be identified, but it can also be seen as basic for scenario analysis. This is due to the crucial task of recognising suitable risk factors and introducing a valid macroeconomic model for the dependence of risk parameters on the risk factors representing the state of the business cycle. Of course, there are obvious candidates for risk factors like interest rates, inflation rates, stock market indices, credit spreads, exchange rates, annual growth in GDP, oil price, etc. (Kalirai and Scheicher, 2002). Others might depend on the portfolio of the financial institute and should be evident for good risk managers. Using time series for the risk factors on relevant markets, as well as for the deviations of risk parameters and standard methods of statistical analysis like discriminant analysis, one should try to develop a macroeconomic model and determine those factors suitable to describe the evolution of risk parameters. Typically, the impact of stress on the risk parameters or directly on credit loss characteristics is modelled using linear regression. One of the problems involves determining the extent to which the risk factors must be restricted, whilst allowing a feasible model.

Discovering which risk factors have the biggest impact on the portfolio risk in terms of the VaR or whatever is used for the evaluation of unexpected losses, is the target and the benefit of sensitivity analysis. Stressing is analogous to the uniform stress test on risk parameters. Stress values for a single risk factor are fixed on the basis of statistical analysis or expert opinion. The consequences for the risk parameters are calculated with the help of the macroeconomic model and the modified values for the risk parameters are finally used for evaluating capital requirements. Risk factors, which have an impact on several risk parameters and which also play a role for stress testing market risk, might be of particular interest.

Sensitivity analysis could also be used to verify the uniform stress testing by checking whether the range of parameter changes due to sensitivity analysis is also covered by the flat stress tests. Moreover, it can be seen as a way to pre-select scenarios: only those historical or hypothetical scenarios which involve risk factors showing some essential effects in the sensitivity analysis are worth considering.

7.3. Scenario Analysis

Having specified the relevant risk factors, one can launch historic scenarios, statistical selection of scenarios and hypothetical scenarios. These different methods should partly be seen as complementing each other. They can also be used for specifying, supporting and accentuating the other.

7.3.1. Historical Scenarios

Historical scenarios are easy to implement, as one only has to transfer the values of risk factors corresponding to a historic event to the current situation. In most cases, it does not make sense to copy the value of the risk factors, but to determine the change of value (either in absolute or in relative form) which is accompanied by the insertion of the event and assume it also applies to the actual evaluation.

The following events are most popular for historical scenarios:

- Oil crisis 1973/74
- Stock market crash (Black Monday 1987, global bond price crash 1994, Asia 1998)
- Terrorist attacks (New York 9/11 2001, Madrid 2004) or wars (Gulf war 1990/91, Iraq war 2003)
- Currency crisis (Asian 1997, European Exchange Rate Mechanism crisis 1992, Mexican Peso crisis 1994)
- Emerging market crisis
- Failure of LTCM[6] and/or Russian default (1998)

Though the implications of historical scenario analysis for risk management might be restricted due its backward looking approach, there are good reasons to use it. First of all, there are interesting historic scenarios which certainly would not have been considered, as they happened by accident, i.e. the probability of occurrence would have been seen too low to look at them. Examples of this case are provided by the coincidence of the failure of LTCM and the Russian default or the 1994 global bond price crash. It can be assumed that both events would rarely have contributed to the VaR at the time of their occurrence, due to the extremely low probability of joint occurrence for the single incidents.[7]

There is also much to learn about stress testing and scenario analysis from working with historic scenarios. On the one hand, the latter can be used to check the validity of the uniform stress tests and sensitivity analysis; on the other hand, they can be very helpful in designing hypothetical scenarios. Thus, the analysis of his-

---

[6] The hedge fund Long-Term Capital Management (LTCM) with huge, but well diversified risk positions was affected in 1998 by a market-wide uprising of risk boosted by the Russia crisis. This led to large losses of equity value. Only a joint cooperation of several US-investment banks under the guidance of the Federal Reserve could avoid the complete default of the fund and a systemic crisis in the world's financial system.

[7] The movements of government bond yields in the US, Europe and Japan are usually seen as uncorrelated. Hence their joint upward movement in 1994 can be seen as an extremely unlikely event.

torical scenarios offers the unique possibility of learning about the joint occurrence of major changes to different risk factors and the interaction of several types of risks, e.g., the impact of credit risk events on liquidity risk. For these reasons, we regard historical scenario analysis as a worthwhile part of establishing a stress testing framework, but not necessarily as an essential part of managing and controlling risk.

7.3.2. Statistically Determined Scenarios

A special role is played by the analysis of scenarios which are chosen on the basis of risk factor distributions. These are not directly related to the other types of scenario analysis. Central to this approach is the use of (joint) risk factor distributions. While it should not be too difficult for isolated common risk to generate such distributions on the basis of historic data, a situation involving several factors can be far more intricate. Nevertheless, distributions generated from historic data might not be sufficient. It would be much better to use distributions conditioned to the situation applying at the time of stress testing. This could represent a real problem.

We would like to point out that only in the case of a reliable factor distribution, should this approach be used. If expected losses conditioned to a quantile are evaluated in order to interpret them as unexpected losses and treat them as economical capital requirement, then the risk factor distribution should also be conditioned to the given (economic) situation.

7.3.3. Hypothetical Scenarios

Hypothetical scenario analysis is the most advanced means of stress testing in risk management. It should combine experience in analysing risk relevant events with expert opinion on the portfolio, as well as the economic conditions and statistical competency. The implementation of hypothetical scenario analysis is analogous to the one for historic scenarios. The only difference is provided by the choice of values for the risk factors. This can be based on or derived from historical data, but expert opinion might also be used to fix relevant values.

The choice of scenarios should reflect the focus of the portfolio for which the stress test is conducted and should have the most vulnerable parts of it as the target. Common scenarios (together with risk factors involved) are provided by the following:

- Significant rise in oil price (increased oil price, reduced annual growth in GDP to describe weakened economic growth, indices describing increased consumer prices, etc.)

- Major increase of interest rates (indices describing the volatility of financial markets, increased spreads, reduced annual growth in GDP to describe weakened economic growth, volatility of exchange rates, consumer indices, etc.)
- Drop in global demand (reduced annual growth in GDP, stock market indices, consumer indices, etc.)
- Emerging market crisis (reduced annual growth in GDP to describe weakened economic growth, widened sovereign credit spreads, decline in stock prices, etc.)

Hypothetical scenarios have the additional advantage that they can take into account recent developments, events, news and prospects. Note that scenarios involving market parameters like interest rates are well suited for combinations with stress tests on market and liquidity risk.

8. Examples

In the following we will present the outcome of some stress tests on a virtual portfolio to illustrate the possible phenomena, the range of applications and advantages corresponding to the tests. The portfolio consists of 10,000 loans and exhibits a volume of 159 billion EUR. The loans are normally distributed over 18 rating grades (PDs between 0.03% and 20% and a mean of 0.6%) and LGDs (ranging from 5% to 50% with a mean of 24%). Moreover, they are gamma-distributed with respect to exposure size (ranging from 2,000 EUR to 100 million EUR with mean 1 million EUR).

To determine economic capital, we employ the well known portfolio model CreditRisk$^+$ (Gundlach and Lehrbass, 2004). We use it here as a six-factor-model, this means that we incorporate six (abstract) factors corresponding to so-called sectors (real estate, transport, energy, resources, airplanes, manufacturing) which represent systematic risk drivers. For our version of CreditRisk$^+$, each obligor j is assigned exactly to one sector $k = k(j)$. This is done according to a weight w_j, $0 \leq w_j \leq 1$. For each sector k there is a corresponding random risk factor S_k, which is used to modify the PD p_j to ρ_j via

$$\rho_j = p_j \cdot w_j \cdot S_{k(j)}. \tag{1}$$

The random factors S_k have mean 1 and are gamma-distributed with one parameter σ_k corresponding to the variance of the distribution. Correlations in CreditRisk$^+$ are thus introduced via the S_k, i.e. in our CreditRisk$^+$-version, only correlations between obligors from the same sector are sustained. The strength of the correlations depends on the weights w_j and the variation σ_k. These parameters can both be modified in stress tests, though it seems more natural to increase the σ_k.

The loans in the portfolio are randomly distributed over the six sectors, representing systematic risk, and thirteen countries, which play a role in some of the scenarios. The dependence of the loans on respective systematic risk factors varies between 25% and 75% and is randomly distributed in each sector. The sectorial variation parameters σ_k's are calculated from the volatilities of the PDs according to some suggestion from the original version of CreditRisk$^+$ and range between 1.8 and 2.6.

In the stress tests we only take account of the dependence of the risk parameter PD, on risk factors β_i. When modelling this interrelation, we used a simple linear regression to predict the changes of rating agencies' default rates for the sector and country division of the portfolio and transferred this dependence to the PDs p_j used in our model

$$p_i = \sum_i x_{ji}\beta_i + u_j \, . \tag{2}$$

Here the u_j's represent residual variables and the indices refer to a classification of PDs according to sectors and countries. Due to the small amount of data and the crude portfolio division, we ended with a rather simple model for the PDs with respect to their assignment to sectors and countries involving only an oil price index, the S&P 500-Index, the EURIBOR interest rate, the EUR/USD exchange rate and the GDP of the USA and EU.

We performed several stress tests on the virtual portfolio. The evaluation of these tests takes place in terms of expected loss, regulatory and economic capital. For the latter, we calculate the unexpected loss as the difference between VaR for a confidence level of 99.99% and expected loss. We focus on the outcome for the whole portfolio, but also report on interesting phenomena for sub-portfolios. The calculations of regulatory capital are based on the Basel II IRBA approach for corporates, while the estimations of VaR are done with CreditRisk$^+$. Loss provisions are also considered in some tests. In the case that the assignment of obligors to rating grades is stressed, non-performing loans and hence candidates for loan provisions are implicitly given. In other cases, they are determined for each rating grade according to a stressed PD. The volume of the respective portfolio is reduced respectively.

We have considered the following stress tests, including uniform stress tests, sensitivity analysis, and historical and hypothetical scenario analysis:
1. flat increase of all PDs by a rate of 50%, a) with and b) without loan loss provisions
2. flat increase of all PDs by a rate of 100% a) with and b) without loss provisions
3. uniform upgrade of all rating grades by one
4. flat increase of all LGDs by 5%
5. flat increase of all PDs by a rate of 50% and all LGDs by 5%
6. flat increase of all sectorial variances σ_k by a rate of 50%
7. flat increase of all LGDs by 10% for real estates in UK and USA (burst of real estate bubble)

8. drop of stock market index (S&P500-Index) by 25%
9. rise of oil price by 40%
10. September 11 (drop of oil price by 25%, of S&P-Index by 5.5%, EURIBOR by 25%)
11. recession USA (drop of S&P-Index by 10%, GDP of USA by 5%, GDP of EU by 2%, increase of EUR/USD-exchange rate by 20%)

The outcome is summarised in the following table where all listed values are in Mill. EUR:

Table 1. Outcome of stress testing on a virtual portfolio

No.	Stress Test	Regulatory Capital	Economic Capital	Expected Loss	Loss Provision	Sectorial Increase of Economic Capital
0	None (Basis portfolio)	3,041	1,650	235	0	
1 a)	PD *150%	3,715	2,458	353	0	
1 b)	PD *150% with provisions	3,631	2,255	320	332	
2 a)	PD *200%	4,238	3,267	470	0	
2 b)	PD *200% with provisions	4,151	2,996	427	332	
3	Rating class + 1	3,451	1,911	273	376	
4	LGD + 5%	3,676	1,985	283	0	
5	LGD + 5%, PD *150%	4,490	3,935	567	0	
6	Systematic factor *150%	3,041	3,041	235	0	
7	Real estate bubble	3,106	1,686	240	0	32% for real estates, 45% for UK and USA
8	Stock price decline	3,591	2,368	329	0	58% for USA, Western Europe, Japan
9	Rise of oil price	3,430	2,057	300	0	65% for transport and airplanes
10	Terror Attack New York September 11	3,897	2,622	399	0	77% for USA, Western Europe, Japan
11	Recession USA	3,688	2,307	351	0	68% for USA and South America, 57% for airplanes

The inclusion of loss provisions does not seem to play a major role in the overall outcome of stress testing, as the sum of the provisions and the economic capital is rather small. Nevertheless, the discrimination of economic capital and provisions (in particular with the comparison of the latter with expected loss), is quite interesting. Also, the distinction between stressing PDs and stressing the assignment to rating grades has a rather limited impact on the result of the stress testing. Furthermore, it is not a surprise that stress testing has a larger impact on economic capital than on regulatory capital.

The significant diversity of impact on the sectors and countries by the scenario analysis underscores the importance of this kind of stress testing for detecting weak spots in the portfolio and for portfolio management. As the portfolio used here is rather well diversified, the effects would be larger in a real portfolio. Also, the simultaneous stressing of several risk parameters has major effects. This is underlined by the joint increase of PDs and LGDs. Also, the role of parameters describing systematic risk cannot be overestimated, as is indicated by the test given by the increase of systematic risk factors. Some of the scenarios lack the exhibition effects one would expect (like a major deterioration of airplane industry in the historic scenario concerning the terrorist attacks of September 11), which could not be indicated by the linear regression, but which could be produced in the design of the stress test using expert opinion.

9. Conclusion

Stress testing is a management tool for estimating the impact on a portfolio of a specific event, an economic constellation or a drastic change in risk relevant input parameters, which are exceptional, even abnormal, but plausible and can cause large losses. It can be seen as an amendment as well as a complement to VaR-based evaluations of risk. It allows the combinations of statistical analysis and expert opinions for generating relevant and useful predictions on the limits for unexpected losses.

Stress testing should not only be seen as a risk management method – though it can be used in various ways, but also as an means towards analysing risk and risk relevant constellations. In particular, it should lead to a higher awareness and sensitivity towards risk. This requires a better knowledge of risk drivers, portfolio structure and the development of risk concentrations. It cannot be achieved in a standard way. Instead experience, research and sustained investigations are required. In particular it makes sense to use an evolutionary approach to overcome the complexity of requirements for stress testing.

We would like to make the following suggestion as an evolutionary way towards a reasonable and feasible framework of stress testing. The basis of stress tests is provided by rich data for defaults, rating transitions and losses. The starting point for the development of stress tests should be an analysis of the volatilities of these rates and estimations for bounds on deviations for them. The statistical analysis should be accompanied by investigations of the reasons for the deviations. It should be studied which fraction of the deviations arise from the methodology of the rating processes and which from changes in the economic, political, etc. environment. Expert opinion should be used to estimate bounds for the deviations arising from the methodology. Statistical analysis should lead to an identification and quantification of the exogenous risk factors having the main impact on the risk parameters needed to determine capital requirements. The combination of these two procedures should enable the establishment of uniform stress testing.

The analysis of default and loss data with respect to estimating deviations from the risk parameters should be followed by statistical analysis of the dependence of these deviations on risk factors and an identification of the most relevant factors. For the latter, first considerations of historic events which are known to have a large impact on portfolio risk should also be taken into account. These investigations should culminate in a macroeconomic model for the dependence of risk parameters on risk factors. With this model sensitivity, analysis for risk factors can be performed. The outcome of these stress tests can be used to check whether the uniform stress tests involve sufficient variations of risk parameters to cover the results of univariate stress tests. As a consequence, the uniform stress tests might have to be readjusted. Moreover, the sensitivity analysis should also be used to check whether the chosen risk factors are contributing to drastic changes in the portfolio. If this not the case, they should be neglected for further stress tests.

The involvement of relevant risk factors should also be a good criterion for picking historical and hypothetical scenarios. It makes sense to consider historical scenarios first in order to benefit from the experience with historical data. This experience should also include the consideration of the interplay of different kinds of risks like market, credit, operational, liquidity risk, etc. The design of hypothetical scenario analysis should be seen as the highlight and culmination point of the stress testing framework.

Scenario analysis based on statistical analysis is a method which is not connected too closely with the others. Nevertheless, a lot of preliminary work has to be done to generate reliable tests of this kind. The main problem is the generation of probability distributions for the risk factors, in particular joint distributions and distributions conditioned on actual (economic) situations.

The evolutionary approach towards a feasible framework for stress testing can be summarized by the chart in Figure 2.

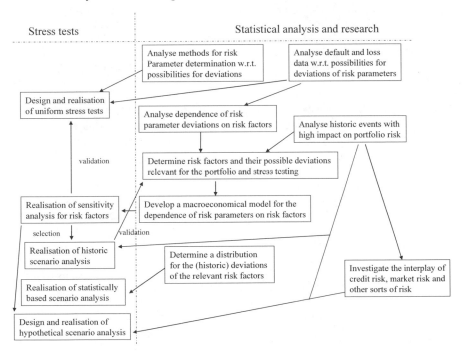

Figure 1. Development of a stress testing framework

Having established a stress testing framework, we recommend

- regular uniform stress tests for regulatory and economic capital in order to provide a possibility for evaluating the changes made to the portfolio in terms of possible extreme losses
- hypothetical scenario analysis suitable to the actual portfolio structure and the conditions provided by the economy, politics, nature, etc.

The latter should partly be combined with stress tests on market and liquidity risk. Also, effects on reputational and other risks should not be neglected. Furthermore, one should have in mind that a crisis might have a longer horizon than one year, the typical period for evaluations of risk, even in the common stress scenarios.

References

Bangia A, Diebold F, Schuermann T (2002), Ratings Migration and the Business Cycle, With Application to Credit Portfolio Stress Testing, Journal of Banking and Finance, Vol. 26 (2-3), (March 2002), pp. 445-474.

Basel Committee on Banking Supervision (2004), International Convergence of Capital Measurement and Capital Standards, Bank for International Settlements.

Blaschke W, Jones M, Majnoni G (2001), Stress Testing of Financial Systems: An Overview of Issues, Methodologies, and FSAP Experiences, IMF Working Paper.

Breuer T, Krenn G (1999), Stress Testing Guidelines on Market Risk, Oesterreichische Nationalbank, Vol. 5.

Breuer T, Krenn G (2001), What is a Plausible Stress Scenario, in Kuncheva L. et al. (eds.): Computational Intelligence: Methods and Applications, ICSC Academic Press, 215-221.

CGFS – Committee on the Global financial System (2000), Stress Testing by Large Financial Institutions: Current Practice and Aggregation Issues, Bank for International Settlements.

CGFS – Committee on the Global Financial System (2001), A Survey of Stress Tests and Current Practice at Major Financial Institutions, Bank for International Settlements.

CGFS – Committee on the Global Financial System (2005), Stress Testing at Major Financial Institutions: Survey Results and Practice, Bank for International Settlements.

Deutsche Bundesbank (2003), Das deutsche Bankensystem im Stresstest. Monatsbericht Dezember.

Deutsche Bundesbank (2004), Stresstests bei deutschen Banken – Methoden und Ergebnisse. Monatsbericht Oktober.

Fender I, Gibson G, Mosser P (2001), An International Survey of Stress Tests, Federal Reserve Bank of New York, Current Issues in Economics and Finance, Vol. 7(10), 1-6.

Gundlach M, Lehrbass F (eds.) (2004), CreditRisk$^+$ in the Banking Industry, Springer Berlin Heidelberg New York.

Kalirai H, Scheicher M (2002), Macroeconomic Stress Testing: Preliminary Evidence for Austria. Oesterreichische Nationalbank, Financial Stability Report 3, 58-74.

Contributors

Stefan Blochwitz is Head of Section in the Department of Banking Supervision of Deutsche Bundesbank's Central Office in Frankfurt am Main. He is in charge of implementing Basel's internal ratings based approach (IRBA) in Germany from a supervisory perspective and is a member of the AIG-subgroup on validation issues. His responsibilities include setting up the supervision of credit risk models as well as research activities in credit risk measurement and management.

Bernd Engelmann is a founder and a managing director of Quanteam AG, a derivatives technology and consulting boutique in Frankfurt that focuses on the development of tailor-made front-office and risk management solutions for the financial industry. Prior to that, Bernd worked in the research department of the Deutsche Bundesbank where his focus was on the construction and validation of statistical rating models. He has published several articles in this field. Bernd holds a diploma in mathematics and a Ph.D. in finance from the University of Vienna.

Ulrich Erlenmaier works for KfW Bankengruppe's risk control and management unit in Frankfurt am Main. He is responsible for the development and validation of rating systems. Previously he worked for Aareal Bank in Wiesbaden (Germany), where he supervised a project for the development and implementation of new Basel II compatible rating systems. Ulrich holds a diploma in mathematics and a Ph.D. in economics from the University of Heidelberg.

Walter Gruber holds a Ph.D. in business mathematics and is managing partner of 1 PLUS i GmbH. He started his professional career at an investment bank in the Treasury division and ALCO Management. Following that, Walter worked as team leader, banking supervision, on the board of management of Deutsche Bundesbank in the areas of research and the principal issues of internal risk models and standard procedures. He also represented the Bundesbank on various international boards (Basel, IOSCO). Following this he was managing director of a consulting firm where he worked as consultant and trainer in banking supervision, risk management and product assessment procedures. Walter has published several papers, in banking supervision, market and credit risk models and derivative finance products. He has also had several standard works published in these fields.

Volker Matthias Gundlach is senior project manager for KfW Bankengruppe's risk and portfolio management unit in Frankfurt am Main. He is responsible for the development and realisation of stress tests. Previously he worked for Aareal Bank in Wiesbaden (Germany), where he developed a credit portfolio model, set up a credit risk reporting and evaluation for MBS. Matthias holds a diploma in mathematics from the University of Würzburg (Germany), an MSc and a PhD in mathematics from the University of Warwick (UK) and a 'Habilitation' in mathematics from the University Bremen (Germany). He edited two books for Springer Verlag on stochastic dynamics and the portfolio model CreditRisk$^+$. His other research activities include work on ergodic theory, stochastic dynamical systems and mathematical biology.

Alfred Hamerle is Professor of Statistics at the Faculty of Business, Economics and Information Systems, University of Regensburg, Germany. Prior to his present position, he was Professor of Statistics at the University of Konstanz and Professor of Statistics and Econometrics at the University of Tübingen. His primary areas of research include statistical and econometric methods in finance, credit risk modelling and Basel II, and multivariate statistics. Alfred has published eight books and more than eighty articles in scientific journals.

Evelyn Hayden holds a Ph.D. in finance from the University of Vienna, where she worked as an assistant professor for several years. At the same time she participated in banking-industry projects as a freelance consultant. Currently Evelyn works at the Austrian National Bank in the Banking Analysis and Inspections Division. Her research interests are in the area of risk measurement and management with focus on the development and validation of statistical rating models and the estimation of default probabilities.

Stefan Hohl is a Senior Financial Sector Specialist at the Financial Stability Institute (FSI) of the Bank for International Settlements (BIS). He is primarily responsible for the dissemination of information on sound practices for effective banking supervision, covering a broad range of topics. Before joining the FSI, Stefan was a Senior Economist (Supervision) in the BIS Representative Office for Asia and the Pacific in Hong Kong. This followed his work for the Deutsche Bundesbank, Frankfurt, in the department for Banking Supervision, being responsible for the Deutsche Bundesbank's market risk models examination and validation team. He is an Adjunct Professor at City University of Hong Kong and a qualified mathematician.

Michael Knapp is academic adviser at the Chair of Statistics, Faculty of Business, at the University of Regensburg. After his business studies and various internships, Michael wrote his doctorate on 'Point-in-Time Credit Portfolio Models'. The main emphasis of his research activities is the development of credit portfolio models, the PD / LGD modelling and concepts for credit portfolio controlling.

Marcus R. W. Martin heads the professional group for risk models and rating systems at the banking examination department I of Deutsche Bundesbank's Regional Office in Frankfurt. He is examiner in charge and senior examiner for conducting audits for internal market risk models as well as for internal ratings based approaches (IRBA) and advanced measurement approaches (AMA).

Gregorio Moral is lead expert for Validation of Credit Risk Models in the Treasury and Risk Management Models Division (TRM) of the Banco de España (BE).

He has contributed to the development of the validation scheme adopted by the BE for Basel II. Currently, he represents the BE on several international validation groups. His present work involves on-site visits to some of the largest banking institutions in Spain, the examination of the models used by these institutions to manage credit risk, and the review of the implementation of Basel II. He develops review procedures, publishes on validation issues and contributes to seminars on validation approaches. He has been working in the TRM Division, focusing on credit risk models since 2001. In his previous supervisory experience, he worked as an examiner reviewing a range of banking institutions. His research interests include applied topics in credit risk, especially the estimation and validation of risk parameters. He holds a degree in mathematics from the Universidad Complutense de Madrid.

Ronny Parchert holds a degree in business administration (BA) and is a managing partner of 1 PLUS i GmbH. He is specialised in Basel II and credit risk management. He commenced his career working for a saving bank as a credit risk analyst in the loan department and as risk manager for the ALM-positions. Following this, Ronny worked as consultant and trainer in banking supervision, risk management and risk measurement. Ronny has had several papers published, particularly concerning banking supervision, as well as market and credit risk management.

Christian Peter works as a senior analyst for the risk controlling and management department of KfW Bankengruppe in Frankfurt am Main, Germany. Among other things he has been involved in the development of a rating and pricing tool for specialized lending transactions and has supervised projects on collateral valuation as well as EAD and LGD modelling. Christian holds a diploma in business engineering and a Ph.D. from the Faculty of Economics and Business Engineering of the University of Karlsruhe (TH), Germany.

Katja Pluto works at the banking and financial supervision department of Deutsche Bundesbank. She is responsible for international regulation of bank internal risk measurement methods, and represents Deutsche Bundesbank in various Basel Committee and European Working Groups on the issue. Before joining the Deutsche Bundesbank, Katja had worked at the credit risk management department of Dresdner Bank.

Daniel Porath has developed and validated scoring models for various banks when he was a senior analyst at the INFORMA consulting company. Afterwards, he entered the bank supervision department of the Deutsche Bundesbank where he developed a hazard model for the risk-monitoring of German credit cooperatives and savings banks. He was also involved in the supervisory assessment of the banks' risk management methods and in the on-site inspections of banks. Since 2005 he is Professor for Quantitative Methods at the University of Applied Sciences at Mainz. His research is focused on empirical studies about rating methods and the German banking market.

Robert Rauhmeier has been a member of the Group Risk Architecture, Risk Instruments at Dresdner Bank in Frankfurt am Main since 2005. He works on the development, enhancement and validation of the groupwide rating models of Dresdner Bank. Prior to that, he worked for KfW-Bankengruppe in the risk controlling and management department for two years. In that role he supervised the project 'Conception and Implementation of a Backtesting Environment' and covered various rating and validation projects. Robert studied economics and holds a Ph.D. from the University of Regensburg. His thesis involved an analysis of the 'Validation and Performance measuring of Bank Internal Rating Systems'.

Daniel Rösch is currently Assistant Professor ("Privatdozent") at the Department of Statistics at the University of Regensburg, Germany. He received his Ph.D. in business administration for a study on asset pricing models. His research areas include modelling and estimation of credit risk, internal models for credit scoring and portfolio credit risk, and development and implementation of banking supervisory guidelines. He also works as a consultant in these fields for leading financial institutions. Daniel has published numerous articles on these topics in international journals.

Harald Scheule is a senior lecturer in finance at The University of Melbourne. Prior to taking up this position in 2005, he worked as a consultant for banks, insurance and other financial service companies in various countries. Harald completed his Ph.D. at the University of Regensburg, Germany. He wrote his thesis on 'Forecasting Credit Portfolio Risk' in collaboration with the Deutsche Bundesbank.

Dirk Tasche is a risk analyst in the banking and financial supervision department of Deutsche Bundesbank, Frankfurt am Main. Prior to joining Bundesbank, he worked in the credit risk management of Bayerische HypoVereinsbank and as a researcher at universities in Germany and Switzerland. Dirk has published several papers on measurement of financial risk and capital allocation.

Carsten S. Wehn is a market risk specialist at DekaBank where he is responsible for the methodology and development of the internal market risk model. Before joining the DekaBank, he was senior examiner and examiner in charge at the Deutsche Bundesbank, where he conducted audits for internal market risk models at commercial banks. Carsten studied applied mathematics in Siegen, Germany, and Nantes, France, and he holds a Ph.D. in mathematics from the University of Siegen.

Nicole Wildenauer is a research assistant and Ph.D. candidate at the Chair of Statistics at the University of Regensburg, Germany. She is a graduate of the University of Regensburg with a degree in Business Administration, specialising in Finance and Statistics. Her research interests include the estimation and prediction of central risk parameters including probability of default and loss given default in the realm of Basel II. Her Ph.D. thesis is titled "Loss Given Default Modelling in the Banking Sector".

Index